LAWYER

A BRIEF 5,000 YEAR HISTORY

R. Blain Andrus

AMERICAN BAR ASSOCIATION
Defending Liberty
Pursuing Justice

LAWYER

A BRIEF 5,000 YEAR HISTORY

Cover design by ABA Publishing.

Printed in the United States of America.

13 12 11 10 09 5 4 3 2 1

Library of Congress Cataloging-in-Publication Data

Andrus, R. Blain.
   Lawyer : a brief 5,000 year history / by R. Blain Andrus.—1st ed.
      p. cm.
   Includes bibliographical references and index.
   ISBN 978-1-60442-598-7
   1. Lawyers—Humor. 2. Law—Humor. 3. Law—History. I. Title.

K183.A53 2009
340.09—dc22

                                                                          2009030825

Discounts are available for books ordered in bulk. Special consideration is given to state bars, CLE programs, and other bar-related organizations. Inquire at Book Publishing, ABA Publishing, American Bar Association, 321 North Clark Street, Chicago, Illinois 60654-7598.

www.ababooks.org

To my family: Maxine, Alicia, Richard, Robert, and Carly.

CONTENTS

VII

THE DEVELOPMENT OF ANCIENT LAW: OLD BONES, OLD LAWYERS   59

VIII

CIVILIZATION, COSMOLOGY, AND THE DIVINE ADVOCATE   73

PART III
ANCIENT GREECE   83

XXVI

XXVII

XXVIII

The Great Lawyer Possesses Deep and Extensive Knowledge Based on Personal Experience and Learning.

The Great Lawyer Has a Refined Sense of Justice—Even in These Cynical Times.

The Great Lawyer Embraces Meaningful Evaluation of His or Her Abilities and Faults. Evaluation Is Actively Sought through Peers, Clients, and Introspection.

ACKNOWLEDGMENTS

ONE DAY WHILE RUNNING through the streets of Reno, Nevada, a question popped into my head: Who was the first lawyer? A few days later I started looking around for a book or article that answered this simple question. I found a tremendous amount of scholarly material on American lawyers, English barristers, Roman orators, Greek rhetoricians—but nothing that reached all the way back to "the beginning." And the more research I did the more I realized that the real question was not just who was the first lawyer, but also how did this silver-tongued devil connect, if at all, with the modern-day lawyer? In other words, the issue was one of evolution. Consequently, it occurred to me that what I needed to do was to step away from the legal academics and start digging around in writings of those scholars dealing with the dawn of civilization. I was fortunate enough to eventually discover the Assyriologist, Professor Martha T. Roth, and her book *Law Collections from Mesopotamia and Asia Minor*. After reading through this book I knew that I had found, from a secular point of view, "the beginning." But what about Genesis? This question started me thinking, from a religious point of view, about the possibility of insights into the history of lawyers that might be found in the Bible. It was these secular and religious threads, and the lack of any existing material providing a fully woven narrative, that convinced me to start putting pen to paper (literally—since, without any curmudgonly pride, I do not know how to type). My reams of yellow legal paper eventually turned into the book you are holding, but not without help.

I am grateful to Erin Nevius, Executive Editor for the American Bar Association, for believing in this project; Neal Cox and the design team for their work on the cover, giving it an inviting visual feel that stands in contrast to the typical starkness of many "technical" books; Emile Pfaff and Annie Beck of Lachina Publishing for all their hard work; and, most important, my legal assistant, Lisa Hoppe, for wadding through the mounds of handwritten yellow pages and producing a typed manuscript that could be read without the aid of an oracle.

PROLOGUE

T‍HIS BOOK IS ABOUT THE LOOK, sound, and smell of lawyers. I know it is not a pleasant thought, but the deification, vilification, and pure fascination with lawyers cannot be denied—particularly in the United States. Just consider the number of books, movies and TV shows that revolve around lawyers. I remember, for example, when *L.A. Law* was on the air, it was reported that law school applications rose dramatically. Why? Because it was one of the first TV shows to reveal that some lawyers make lots of money and have sex—sometimes even with clients. Prior to this series, people only saw lawyers in the image of the hard working Perry Mason driving around in his generic car, always at the office and being assisted by the ever-vigilant and virginal Della Street. We believed that Ms. Street's only involvement with Perry's rising penal practice was professional. It was all so sanitized! *L.A. Law* made us grow up and consider the possibility that even the angelic Della might have been tangled up in Perry's briefs.

The Top 25 Lawyer Movies

In 2008, the *ABA Journal* asked twelve prominent lawyers who teach film or are connected to the film industry to choose what they regarded as the best movies ever made about lawyers and the law. The *Journal* collated the nominees and produced the following 25 top picks (in order):

1. *To Kill A Mockingbird* (1962)
2. *12 Angry Men* (1957)
3. *My Cousin Vinny* (1992)

Together these 25 law films garnered 31 Oscar wins and 85 nominations. So if one simply watches all of these films, can he or she skip reading this book? In the words of my youngest daughter: "No way dude!" But even though this book will give the reader a much better idea of law and lawyers than the 25 films, there is no doubt that the films will provide hours of great entertainment.

Our task, however, is not procreation but creation, specifically of that entire class of people called lawyers. But do not despair: This book is dripping with blood and guts—and sex. The reason is not because I want to shamelessly pander to your prurient interests, but because we will be talking about lawyers. And while it is not lawyers per se that fascinate us, we often believe that they have the inside scoop on who murdered whom and who, figuratively and literally, is screwing whom.

This book, however, is not just an external account of lawyers. It tries to put you inside their heads. A very scary place! (I ought to know.) But it seems to me that law is, as the Beatles said about love, "here, there, and everywhere." People are therefore often confronted with legal situations—frequently without having acquired much knowledge or experience about the law, the legal system, or lawyers, and sometimes with having acquired too much "knowledge" and "experience" courtesy of Hollywood. In my experience, either case can lead to feelings of helplessness, unrealistic expectations, and sometimes just plain nausea. So what quicker and cheaper way to get at least a glimpse inside the law, both for its instrumental and intrinsic value, than to attempt to get inside the collective mind of its most hated and celebrated mouthpiece: the lawyer?

I have made a diligent effort to search the dark corners of history in order to find the remains of *Homo erectus legalus*—the first lawyer. I admit, however, that the bones of this primal, silver-tongued devil have eluded me. Nor is this book a full body-cavity search of lawyers. A rubber-gloved inspection of that magnitude would, in my opinion, be an extremely valuable contribution to society in general and the legal profession in particular, but it is a project that is far beyond the scope of this modest effort. We are not, in other words, heading for a cabaret of full nudity but one that merely boasts a tasteful, old-time striptease: glimpses and shadows. Nevertheless, if you make it through the mix of broad sweeps and fine detail that lies ahead, I believe you will come away with a good sense of the primal ooze that gave rise to the first lawyer and the religious, cultural, philosophical, economic, and political forces that have preserved "him" from extinction—at least so far.

OPENING STATEMENT

OF NO SURPRISE TO THE MANY PEOPLE who pay attention to this sort of thing, there has been a modern-day explosion in the number of lawyers—particularly in the United States of America. Setting aside the weird science of parallel universes, the current number of lawyers, just in America, is about 890,000 and rising. This same type of incredible growth has also occurred with regard to the size of the legal service industry in general. Between 1977 and 1989, revenues devoted to legal services in the United States were reported to have increased approximately 480 percent, to a total of $73 billion. Yes, billion! This means that legal services grew almost twice as fast as the gross national product (which grew by about 370 percent during the same period, to a total of $250 billion). And in the late 1990s, and on into the twenty-first century, it has been reported that corporations alone spend about $100 billion a year on outside law firms. Yes, billion! This tremendous growth in legal services has spawned a new criticism of lawyers. In fact, the former president of the United States, George W. Bush, not only criticized lawyers but made them part of his second-term agenda—along with other "stuff" like the war in Iraq, terrorism, social security, the budget deficit, and immigration. He made it clear in a December 20, 2004, speech: The first thing we do is starve the lawyers! In other words, we cut off the damage awards that are killing American businesses.

Lawyer Proliferation

There are roughly 890,000 lawyers in America right now, and that number keeps going up (at least until running into the—hopefully temporary—2009 "recession"). For sake of comparison, in 1960 there were about 213,000 lawyers in the United States. And in the year 2000, China, with a population of more than ten times that of the United States, had some where around 150,000 lawyers.

So who or what is behind this explosion? One might be quick to respond: lawyers! But to conclude that there are increasing legal services because there are more lawyers who are increasing legal services that are increasing the number of lawyers is a bit circular. Some deeper reasons start to surface when one focuses on two principal areas of legal practice: corporate, and personal client/ small business. From the corporate perspective, the explosion in lawyers and legal services appears to be driven by such factors as the following:

1. An ever-increasing international competitive environment (an example of what has been called "intergroup tournaments"). Worldwide flows of direct investment from one country into another have climbed, for example, from a mere $30 billion a year in the early 1980s to $800 billion in 1999. And sales recorded by the foreign affiliates of multinational companies rose from $2.4 trillion in 1982 to $13.6 trillion in 1999. In other words, "we" (select the county of your choice) might be able to blame the foreigners on the current horde of lawyers.

2. Transformations in institutional mechanisms involving:
   (a) Governmental regulation of business ("conformity enforcers");
   (b) Expansion of corporate liability; that is, the willingness of victims to sue ("resource shifting");
   (c) A rise in the financial conception of the corporation and the tendency of corporations to diversify ("diversity generation"); and
   (d) The deregulation of corporate finance and corporate transactions (i.e., more money, of varying size, shape, color, and tangibility, circulating in more complex ways—securitization, credit default swaps, commercial mortgage-backed securities, asset-backed securities . . .).

As economic exchange moves from domestic manufacturing to global financial transactions, the business people create an ever-increasing demand for corporate (read: Big Business) lawyers—not unlike what happened with the world-wide expansion of the ancient Roman Empire (discussed in Part IV). The reason for this "externality" is that there are simply more deals to put together and they are increasingly complex—that is, the environment contains the perfect conditions for the use of adrenaline junkies as messengers of trustworthiness, bobbing and weaving among regulators, diversity generators, litigious consumers, and intergroup tournaments. What this means is that the expense of lawyers can help in signaling a party's discount rate. Additionally, if a deal nose-dives, there is more of a chance for legal conflict due to the lack of long-standing relationships (or the growth of future relationships), thereby lowering concerns about opportunistic behavior that previously motivated businesses to attempt to work out their differences. So if Big XYZ Company sues Bigger ABC Company, it is not personal (in contrast to the "personalization" of economic relations in primitive societies), particularly since nobody knows anyone anyway. It is also the case that when parties are not familiar with each other, they are more likely to misjudge the opponent's expectations, preferences, and likely course of action. Such unfamiliarity can lead to a lack of trust, which, in turn, increases the risk that the parties will lose out on a mutually profitable settlement (the goal of a non-zero-sum game).

☒ · ☒

From Free to Fee

In early America, the *Laws and Liberties* of 1648 omitted the stipulation contained in Section 26 of the *Body of Liberties* of 1641 that a lawyer may not receive remuneration for his services. Hence by 1648 (at least *sub silentio*) the paid attorney was recognized—though certainly not welcomed.

☒ · ☒

Turning to the personal client/small business perspective, the explosion in lawyers and legal services appears to be driven by such factors as the following:

1. The lifting of restrictions on lawyer advertising and prohibitions on bar association regulation of lawyers' fees—letting competition drive the market;
2. An apparent public awareness, often "enhanced" by lawyers, of possible legal problems and the perception that the situation calls for a lawyer. I have heard it said, for example, that even the Hell's Angels are willing to drag out legal counsel when their trade name is allegedly being infringed;

3. The increasing participation of women in the work force, generating additional legal needs in such areas as employment, occupational safety, taxes, estate planning, and property;

4. A rise in the average age of the population (time has dragged more and more people kicking and screaming into the two age groups that historically produce the highest level of legal demand: 35–44 and 45–54); and

5. A rise in education levels, resulting in higher income and the need (and to the delight of most lawyers, the ability to pay) for legal services. As noted by two economists, "in the 1890s the richest 10 percent of the [United States] population worked fewer hours than the poorest 10 percent. Today, the reverse is true. The idle rich have become the working rich!"

One should not, however, believe for a second that concerns regarding the number and activities of lawyers are of recent vintage—or unique to former President George W. Bush. The English Ordinance of 1292, for example, focused specifically on a growing desire to limit the number of attorneys. The reason for this was the perceived connection between too many lawyers and excessive litigation! Sound familiar? The public outcry was that excessive amounts of lawyers lead to excessive amounts of litigation because lawyers create a demand for their services or produce litigation through their misconduct and incompetence.

In Connecticut, an act of 1730 provided that in order "that said mischief [meaning the number of attorneys, especially those who were unscrupulous and incompetent] may be prevented, and only proper persons be allowed to plead at the bar . . . and that the fees of attorneys may be stated and known; and for the better regulating all pleadings at the bar that there shall be allowed in the Colony eleven attorneys, and no more. . . ." Period.

And in ancient Greece we hear of an unreasonable readiness to sue, of improperly severe sentences, of . . . but we will deal with their concerns down the road.

Based on an overall approach that is loosely grounded in the tradition of analytic history (and a healthy dose of *Sitz im Leben*), the deep question we will be exploring is whether lawyers have been and continue to be a social good or are simply an uncomfortable fact of the human condition.

BIBLICAL TIMES

IN TRACKING DOWN THE ORIGIN of lawyers, we will start from the beginning. The problem is: Which beginning is *the* beginning? The one set out in the Bible? Or the one being pieced together in modern times by scientific research? I have decided to start with Genesis. It is in the poetic prologue of this biblical book that God brings order out of chaos—and what better place to start looking for lawyers than in a swirling mass of chaos.

It is certainly arguable that Genesis' account of human growth and development does not ring true to those schooled in the principles of biological and social evolution. Indeed, the Bible freely mixes devolution with evolution. Religious and moral insights are not generally presented as a process of slow and painful development but as concepts that sometimes seem to exist without traceable antecedents: BANG! However, despite such scientific weaknesses, there is no doubt that Bible stories have significantly influenced moral history, particularly as an underpinning for certain notions of law and justice—and hence influenced the origin and development of lawyers. It has been observed, for example, that most of the substantive and procedural rules that are decreed in the later law books of the Torah or Pentateuch (the first five books of the Bible) flow from the stories contained in Genesis. This is because these rules are often a reaction to the perceived injustices contained in those earlier narratives—as Professor Alan Dershowitz has argued, they are rights coming from wrongs.

Wrongs Making Rights

But how exactly do rights come from wrongs? It might be that our concept of rights starts with a nonmetaphoric core that we experience as infants: (1) something, such as a toy, belongs to us (possession); (2) we vigorously react against undue constraints on our bodily movements; and (3) we react against the infliction of pain. Consequently, abstract rights in our adulthood are built on metaphorical versions of these early embodied experiences. If we take these childhood experiences and apply them to slavery, we can see why slavery is wrong—even if it is permitted by law, as in America's pre–Civil War South. Slaves did not have the right to own things; their bodily movements were constrained; and pain, psychological and physical, was inflicted. A similar type of analysis can be performed on many stories contained in Genesis in order to arrive at rights from wrongs.

We will discover that the psyche of a typical, modern-day lawyer is a jumble of Judeo-Christian and pagan traditions—with a healthy dose of Islam. Biblical stories such as Adam and Eve, Cain and Able, Solomon, and Susanna and the Elders compete, in lawyers' hearts and unconscious memories, with the ancient Egyptian sacrifices to the sun god Ra, the special liturgy of the ancient Babylonians, and the numerology of Pythagoras. We therefore could just as easily have started our search from the pagan side of things. However, Judeo-Christian morality has ultimately had a much deeper impact on the Western legal tradition (and therefore on lawyers) than paganism.

I also admit that I was particularly intrigued by the notion of Adam and Eve being represented by lawyers—a fascination that, ironically, seems to be pagan in origin (something I must have picked up in law school). The difference between Judeo-Christian and pagan traditions of law is that Judeo-Christian lore depicts God's law as democratic, in the sense of it belonging to all the people (a concept developed in large part by the Jews), while the traditional pagan notion interposes "priests" between mankind and the gods. In light of this historic Judeo-Christian/pagan difference, the use of lawyers by Adam and Eve in their troubles with God smacks of paganism—because, if looked at from a Judeo-Christian viewpoint, why would they need lawyers to represent them if the law truly belonged to them?

The influences of paganism on lawyers comes in many forms; for example, via Mesopotamian, Grecian, and Roman law's procedural and substantive influences on the common law, civil law, and canon law. But the one that I merely note at this point, and that will be discussed in more detail in Part II, relates to paganism's nonexclusivity—the more gods the merrier. This pagan attitude contrasts sharply with the Judeo-Christian and Islamic notion of one God and the worship of only that God—thus we see diversity generators and conformity enforcers leading to intergroup tournaments: Kill the pagans in the name of God; feed the Christians to the lions.

But back to the point. Having decided that we should start our search for the origin of lawyers in the Bible, we will start at the beginning: Genesis. Then we'll work our way through some of the "legal highlights" of biblical times. So let there be light!

THE STATE OF INNOCENCE V. ADAM AND EVE

C OULD A DAM AND E VE HAVE BEEN "SAVED" with the help of a good lawyer? Perhaps. The problem is that Genesis gives no indication that there was anyone around who could represent them. In fact, as will be discussed later, they should probably have had separate counsel. But besides Adam and Eve, it appears that there was only God (the Judge), the State (of Innocence), and a bunch of animals, only one of which we are sure could talk. While the serpent might have been the perfect prototype lawyer, he may have been working for the State. If, however, God had decided, in the interest of justice, to whip up a couple of lawyers (or at least let Satan do the job), how might this legal team have approached the case?

A Serpentine Reputation

It is interesting to note that Hypereides, a democratic politician of ancient Greece who is said to have been as "irregular" in his political alliances as in his extravagant lifestyle, claimed that all lawyers are like snakes—some are adders who are harmful to men, while others take on the role of the adder-eating brown snake. Hypereides, interestingly, was, in addition to being a politician, a rhetor and apparently hoped that his audiences would see him as the brown snake swallowing his viperous opponent. (The Greek rhetores are discussed in Part III.)

Both Adam's lawyer (Vinnie) and Eve's lawyer (Sal) might have taken the aggressive approach and, right out of the box, called God to the stand. Why? In order to grill "Him" on questions of psychological and philosophical free will. Who better than God, the creator of the two defendants and therefore the ultimate expert witness, to testify about whether or not they were under some type of "irresistible impulse" with regard to eating the seductive but forbidden fruit? That is: Is will ever radically free? Proof of irresistible impulse could mean no criminal culpability—or at least, a sentence of less than life outside the Garden.

Vinnie and Sal, by calling God to testify (oddly, at the same trial in which "He" is the judge), would have been representing their clients zealously (without being labeled as zealots), a requirement that is generally built into a modern-day lawyer's code of ethics. The nasty truth, which I will reveal to you in strictest confidence, is that lawyers are expected to be aggressive in advocating their client's case: argumentative when necessary, skeptical of the other side's claims, and inquisitorial in their quest for information. And if Adam and Eve had been acquitted or given a light sentence (perhaps based on the notion of "a sort of sin" versus actual sin), the two lawyers would certainly deserve to have been paid handsomely—or at least sent a nice basket of fruit.

Price of the Win

Success by Vinnie and Sal might have resulted in the prevention of life as we know it. The reason for this is that God's love for mankind can be seen as overweening and therefore destructive of our creative energy. Consequently, in order to progress, the old—the endless and never-changing Garden of Eden—had to be destroyed. If this is true, progress is then truly a bargain with the Devil. Nevertheless, some of the defenses to be discussed might have been used by Vinnie and Sal to defend against the charge of transgression and yet not have condemned Adam and Eve to eternal stagnation.

The point, in more practical terms, is that lawyers often have to (or at least should) consider their legal strategy in light of what remedy "best" fits the situation. Simply focusing on "winning" may result in destruction of the client's world.

Another tactic: Vinnie and Sal might have argued that God's commandment to "multiply and replenish the earth" was, itself, ambiguous. Was it directed at Adam and Eve as autonomous individuals, or at their DNA? The words, taken in their context, could easily be interpreted as a command to reproduce, pointed not at their clients but at their respective genes. That is to say, the *Logos* became information and the information became life and death—or at least sex. The effectuation of this command, however, took a bite of forbidden fruit. God the creator could compel DNA to reproduce but also respected human autonomy: free will over the selfish gene. Hence, the need for seductive and accessible forbidden fruit. (The accessibility of the forbidden fruit seems to indicate that God considered the net cost of the offense to be less than the cost of attempting to prevent it from occurring.)

Both Vinnie and Sal, instead of mucking around in the messy debate of free will versus moral determinism—divine omniscience, preconscious mind, let alone grilling God as a "hostile" witness—might also have considered attacking the commandment used to condemn Adam and Eve. That is, they might have focused on the subject matter and not the subject. It is arguable that "Do not eat of the tree of knowledge of good and evil" conflicts with the first commandment given by God, "Multiply and replenish the earth." While the tension is not obvious on the face of the two commandments, the facts appear to be that Adam and Eve were not able to procreate until they bit into the fruit. Consider the following evidence:

1. There is no indication in Genesis that Adam and Eve had any children while in the Garden of Eden—even though they were naked, in a romantic garden, for seemingly a long period of time, and neither of them appears to have been gay;
2. Only by eating some or all of the fruit would their eyes be opened, and they would become as the gods, knowing good and evil; and
3. After eating of the fruit, their eyes were opened and they realized not that they were gods, but that they were naked—and wandering around, a bit embarrassed, in a romantic garden.

The effectiveness of this defense, based on a frontal assault on the commandments, ultimately rests on the answer to the following questions: Could Adam and Eve multiply and replenish the earth without first biting into the fruit of good and evil, and did God, the Lawgiver, know the answer to this question at the time the two commandments were given?

The use of arguably conflicting legal commands as a defense strategy is not limited to Garden-variety cases. Take, for example, the 1942 exclusion order affecting nearly 120,000 Japanese residents of the western United States, 79,000 of whom were American citizens. One of those caught up in this World War II executive order was Fred Korematsu—born in Oakland, California, where he graduated from high school. Fred decided to disregard President Roosevelt's evacuation order (requiring those of Japanese descent to be kept indefinitely in internment camps) so that he could remain behind with the Caucasian woman whom he planned to marry. He was eventually arrested by the FBI.

His case went up to the United States Supreme Court. And although the Court upheld the constitutionality of the evacuation order, three of the justices dissented. One of them thought along the same lines as Vinnie and Sal. Justice Owen Josephus Roberts considered Korematsu's conviction unconstitutional on the technical grounds that he was confronted with two conflicting military orders at the time of his arrest: one was the evacuation order and the other was a wartime order requiring him to remain in the zone in which he resided— *Catch-22*. And just like Adam and Eve, Fred couldn't do both.

A somewhat related approach for Vinnie and Sal might have been to point out the "distinction" between rules and principles. (This is a distinction of continuing legal importance that is recognized in, among other legal systems, classical canon law—as well as twenty-first century financial matters: What were the rules or principals behind the federal government rescuing Bear Stearns but letting Lehman Brothers collapse?) The first rule, "Multiply and replenish the earth," appears to be amply supported by principles related to biological urges (sex), family (continuation of genes), and personal growth (information). But what about the rule "Do not eat of the tree of knowledge of good and evil"? Setting aside the question of whether the rule's motivating context is "literally" about sexing up with a bite or two or oversexing by overindulging, what is the rule's supporting principle? Vinnie and Sal might have been able to argue that if the underlying principle for this second rule relates to sex (or the unknowledge thereof), then, as pointed out above, it conflicts with the first rule. And if its underlying principle relates to knowledge, discernment, and wisdom, then it (arguably) also conflicts with the principles supporting the first rule. Therefore, in order to make sense of the whole, Adam and Eve, as rational human beings created by a rational God, had to eliminate the tension by integrating rule and principle: Eat fruit first, then make babies.

A Question of Copyright

One possible answer to the question of the principles behind "Do not eat of the tree of knowledge of good and evil" is copyright. Perhaps "Don't touch the fruit" is grounded in a type of divine ("common") law copyright that protected the information contained in the forbidden fruit—a "right of first publication." Typically protected by this type of copyright is the art or craftsmanship of the author, and not facts or ideas. So the legal (copyright) question is: Is sex art or fact? Or a bit of both?

There is also an additional underlying argument in favor of the "fruit and babies" selection. Sal and Vinnie might have argued that their clients' particular integration of the conflicting rule and principle was efficient and therefore the legally correct choice. According to our economically inclined advocates, their clients followed the commandment that had the greatest potential for maximizing human satisfaction (a social good) and therefore resulted in more of everything: goods, services, wealth, and especially information, instead of endlessly wandering around in a garden. In a sense, destruction (by Adam and Eve) was the counterpart of creation (by God).

As stated by Joel Mokyr in *The Gifts of Athena,* with regard to the rise of Western economies:

> [W]hat, exactly, was the role of useful knowledge? It is simply incorrect that all modern economic growth is due to technological change. Economies can grow as a result of continuous reallocation of resources or the establishment of law and order and concomitant commercialization. They can grow because people become more conscientious and cooperative, more thrifty, diligent, and prudent, and more trusting of one another. Some scholars . . . have pointed to culture as the primary cause of the rise of the West: traditions of honesty, hard work, frugality, and education for one's offspring are transmitted from generation to generation and can differ a great deal among different societies. Hard work, trust, and frugality can indeed help an economy do better; but if the useful knowledge base does not expand, such laudable efforts will run into diminishing returns. Only an increase in useful knowledge [leading (arguably) to innovation] can permanently remove the ceiling on prosperity growth.

So, first a bite of fruit and then make babies.

In pursuing this economically based defense, Vinnie and Sal might have focused on "information"—a key aspect of the theory of rational action. It certainly appears that the forbidden fruit contained messages. And with a bite or two (or the whole forbidden thing?), these messages flowed to Eve and then to Adam. "Acquiring Ideas Is Eating" is typically only metaphorical ("That idea is tough to swallow"; or remember what the dormouse said: "Feed your head"), but in this case it was literal. Furthermore, the fruit's forbiddenness indicates that the messages were juicy ones and not just strings of arbitrary bits. Thus as an informational source, the fruit was in a relatively high state of entropy—meaning that ambiguity, unpredictability, and uncertainty were high (as is generally the case with sex). But once Eve, in a lower state of informational entropy, received the messages, she (according to Sal) became aware of its potential for answering questions and therefore wanted Adam, as her "help meet," to take a bite. Adam, trusting (according to Vinnie) the woman given to him by God, did so. In the context of Vinnie and Sal's potential defense, the point is that at a fundamental level, maximizing human satisfaction by increasing the size of the pie (of any flavor) is about information. And the entropy of a message source is equivalent to the amount of information it can send in any given message. The forbidden fruit appears to have been full of it—a Googleplex. As a result, Adam and Eve's actions of fruit destruction as an intermediate step in value creation merited not condemnation, according to Vinnie and Sal, but commendation.

Perhaps yet another way of looking at this situation, at least from a lawyer's perspective, is to see it as a conflict between legal positivism and natural law—a conflict within the context of legal philosophy of historic and continuing importance. In brief, positivism treats law essentially as a body of rules laid down ("posited") and enforced by whatever or whoever is the legitimately constituted law-making authority. This authority has been called the "discourse of the master," that master being a dictator, legislative body, a god, et al. Its theoretical core is what one scholar calls "the separability thesis"—the notion that the legal is conceptually distinguishable from the larger realm of the nonlegal.

In contrast, natural law tends to treat "good" law as the embodiment of rules and principles containing a moral component that have been derived through the use of reason. Thus it might be, as pointed out above, that the first rule, "Multiply and replenish the earth," is supported by principles derived from biological urges, family (tied to, among other things, physical survival), and personal growth—the "oughts." In contrast, the rule "Do not eat of the tree of knowledge of good and evil" is simply supported by lawmaking authority— "Don't touch the fruit because I said so." Consequently, Vinnie and Sal might have argued that their clients actually broke no commandment but simply made a choice, foisted upon them, among legal positivism, natural law, and possibly an uneasy Lutheran-type mixture of the two.

Along somewhat the same lines, the two lawyers could also have argued that their clients broke no commandment but simply played out the tragedy in which they were cast. Drawing on the same concepts later explicated by the mad, misogynistic philosopher Friedrich Nietzsche, they might have pressed the point that tragedy ("goat song") is not the struggle between good and evil: for if good triumphs, it is expected, and if evil prevails it is merely sad.

Instead, tragedy is a battle between two forces, both of which have a claim on the good—arguably the dramatic power behind Clint Eastwood's Academy Award–winning movie *Million Dollar Baby.*

Following this line of thought, Vinnie and Sal would have first pointed out that both commandments are good since they came from an omniscient and loving God (sucking up to the judge—almost always a good thing). Next they would have stressed that the two commandments set up opposing forces in which only one of them could prevail—either "Don't touch the forbidden fruit" because I, God, said so or "Multiply and replenish the earth" because I, God, said so. And finally they would have concluded that with a bite of the "apple" it was not crime or sin that was born, but human tragedy.

In fact, Adam and Eve's "downfall" was the birth not only of tragedy, but also of law itself. Our percipient pleaders might have gone on to point out to the High Court that the very segregation between "good fruit" and "bad fruit" makes law possible. The reason for this is that the law (frequently using a witch's brew of rules and facts) defines categorically the limits of the permissible, or, as in this case, the impermissible. Consequently, their respective clients committed no crime but were in fact "set up" to give birth to law.

As an important aside, the concept of legal categories (especially categorizing and recategorizing methods) is still very much a part of what makes law the law. The United States Supreme Court, for example, determined that a lower federal court had gone too far in its efforts to desegregate the public schools of Kansas City, Missouri School District. The decision in that case turned on categorizing the lower court's orders as a forbidden "interdistrict remedy." That is, the Court first used prior case law to identify good fruit ("intradistrict remedies" used for dealing with segregation) from bad fruit ("interdistrict remedies" used for dealing with segregation) and then, through a number of other categorizing moves, determined that the lower court had taken a bite of bad fruit.

Perhaps this Garden of Eden case, not unlike the Missouri school district case, has racial overtones. Both Vinnie and Sal might have considered whether or not this is a "Jewish God" out to get two Christians or a "Christian God" out to get two Jews or an "Islamic God" out to get two "infidels" and so on and so forth.

On Categorization

As stated by Richard A. Posner in *The Problematics of Moral and Legal Theory:* "Lay people think that the law is something written down in a book. Lawyers learn, in their very first year of law school, that the law is an inference from often ambiguous and even conflicting cases." And one way to rationalize this "mess" is to categorize. Keep in mind, however, that legal categorization is largely a parasitic activity—it's a motivated activity that feeds off of nonlegal categories (which themselves are often fuzzy, radial, and subject to stereotyping). The concepts of time, space, substance, and causality, for example, are largely metaphorically created categories—all of which have, in one way or another, been used (and perhaps abused) by various legal categories. The same can be said for philosophical categories, religious categories, moral categories, economic categories, and so on. As a result, it is often important for a lawyer to consider not just a concept's existing legal category but also the category that that category is feeding off of—in other words, to consider the meaning of the concept within the context of the host category.

Obviously, categorization is a complex issue—particularly given the fact that virtually nothing is a "good thing" categorically, even food. Recent empirical evidence from cognitive science paints an emerging picture of categorization as an imaginative and dynamic process that is flexible in application and elastic in scope. Consequently, many descriptive categories are normatively infused (e.g., bad fruit versus good fruit) rather than value-neutral.

⚘ · ⚘

We want to believe that justice is blind, but history teaches us that sometimes her blindfold is actually a mask. The reason for this all too frequent mix of justice and treachery is that legal systems are the continuing creation of human beings with various motivations and interests—motivations and interests that range from settling disputes to exacerbating them, from using the law as an instrument of social justice to employing it as a weapon of oppression. For example, during the first enclosure movement in England from about 1490 to about 1570, the lawyers (hired by the upper classes) frequently used the law as a means by which to beat some of the peasantry about the head and shoulders.

There was a growing market for agricultural products during the late fifteenth and early sixteenth centuries. This demand for such things as wool (a big money maker for young Shakespeare's father) and meat was fueled by an absence of entropy, a decline in warfare and a resulting population growth, urban reorganization, and post-1520 inflation due to Continental wars and the importation of precious metals into Europe from the Americas. Under these conditions a number of the rising landed gentry were pissed off about collecting rents at the low, "medieval" levels being paid by the copyholders, peasants whose families had been long freed from serfdom and who had received a copy of the charter of freedom "indefinitely" setting the rent for "their" land. These rental rates had been agreed upon decades earlier, when economic conditions were different and the "owners" (technically, holders of a dominant freehold) were ecstatic just to get any return on their vacant lands. The objective therefore was to find a way to terminate these various arrangements, kick the peasantry off the land, and enclose it, planting nice English hedges for fencing. And it was the lawyer's job to assist his client in meeting these objectives. After all, transfers of wealth are transfers of freedom—a good thing, right?

Armed with the law, many lawyers were up to the task. Copyholds were challenged in the English courts as fraudulent, and long-term leases were claimed either to have run out or to be void for some technical reason; lawyers, in other words, mucked around in the law, searching for "loopholes" to justify the client's ends. (The Western legal tradition is not the same as the Western moral tradition—for example, the rich looking out for the poor—and perhaps a good reason to believe that justice does not give an adequate account of law.) Additionally, a standard tactic was for the lawyer to advise his client to simply run the peasant families off the land and plant hedges as soon as possible. If the grubby villagers should invade the ever so attractive fencing, the advocate would file a bill of complaint in the Star Chamber for riot. The peasants would then be hauled before the court and get their ears cropped. Slick!

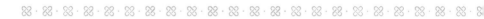

The Star Chamber, Shining Example of Justice

The Court of Star Chamber was known as such because of the stars painted on the ceiling of the chamber in Westminster Palace where the court convened. In addition to being used as a political weapon, the court was also eventually used to enforce unpopular political and ecclesiastical policies. It was a prerogative court that operated without a jury and followed non–common law procedures until its elimination in 1641.

Back to the Garden. Eve appears to have had a defense that was not available to Adam. Genesis says that God first told Adam about not eating from the tree of knowledge of good and evil before Eve was plucked from Adam's ribs. Her lawyer, Sal, might have argued that his client lacked notice of the commandment—and Notice Is Information. It appears that the commandment was oral, and Sal, of course, would have left no stone unturned in order to establish the lack of a writing. And if one did exist, he might have argued that Eve could not read—after all, she was a mere "child." Sal, however, appears to have a problem: Eve tells the serpent that she and Adam are not to eat of the fruit (or even touch it), disclosing that she knows all about the divine commandment. On the other hand, Sal might have been able to properly "prepare" his client about her recollections regarding the commandment.

It might also have been possible for Sal to have argued on behalf of Eve that, as a woman, she used a reasoning process that was different from that used by Adam. Instead of the typical masculine response of looking for the correct answer based upon a hierarchy of values, Sal might have argued that Eve approached the dilemma created by the two commandments by attempting to reconcile their inherent tension. More specifically, he might have first framed the situation not as a two-party transaction (Adam/Eve ⟷ God) but as a multiparty transaction, and then argued that his client saw the potentiality of the world as composed of a network of relationships (i.e., God, Adam, Eve, and the "fruit" of Adam and Eve) rather than as people standing alone. If the real world is a world bigger than the Garden, it needs to be held together through interdependence and cooperation—which, in Eve's view, would be enhanced by an increase in knowledge, discernment, and wisdom—rather than through a system of rules that would tend to separate humans from each other (and from God).

It is instructive to observe that this technique of reframing a situation in order to view it differently (and hopefully with more depth) is not limited to lawyers. Take, for example, nuclear decay. For decades scientists have measured the rate at which the nuclei of radioactive atoms break apart or decay, known as the half-life. In order, however, to provide a deeper insight into the quantum world, some scientists have recast the physical process of nuclear decay into the language of quantum information. Viewed in this way, the spontaneous splitting of an atomic nucleus—its half-life—can be seen as an act of information transfer. A given nucleus starts out in a pure, unbroken state (like pre–forbidden fruit-eating Adam and Eve) and evolves into a superposition of decayed and undecayed state (like Adam and Eve immediately post–forbidden fruit): both "A" and "not-A" simultaneously, a scientific poke in the eye of rationalism. Then something happens. "Something" measures the state of the atom, thus gathering information about the nucleus. And in doing so, this something transfers information about the nucleus' state into the surrounding environment. This information transfer deciphers the superposition—the simultaneous broken and unbroken state—and the nucleus "chooses" whether to be in a pure decayed state or a pure undecayed state. With regard to the atom, that something is Nature; in the case of Adam and Eve, that something is God.

The biblical story of the unrepresented Eve tells us that upon God gathering information about the forbidden-fruit-eating Adam and Eve, the "choice" was decay—based on the breach of a divine commandment. But Sal's reframing of the physical process of eating the fruit into a multiparty informational transaction constitutes an argument for Eve having chosen, despite the forbidden decoherence, a pure undecayed state that must legally be respected given the inherent tension created by the two commandments.

Rather that trying to prove "irresistible impulse," both Vinnie and Sal could have attempted to prove a complete lack of criminal intent on the part of their respective clients. They might have first elicited testimony from God that Adam and Eve were unable to separate perception (of the enticing fruit) from action (eating it) and therefore did not truly know the difference between right and wrong. The two lawyers could then have argued that their respective clients should not, in all fairness, be punished for doing an act for which there was an absolute lack of criminal intent. No *mens rea.*

A Guilty Mind

In 1507 CE, the Bamberg Capital Court Statute (Bambergensis) established the general principle that criminal responsibility was to be limited to prohibited acts committed either intentionally or, in some cases, negligently. There was no criminal responsibility under the Bambergensis without proof of culpability (in German, *Schuld*), in the sense of *mens rea*: "a guilty mind."

And in a June 2006 case involving the killing of a police officer by a defendant claiming affliction of a mental disease at the time of the shooting, the U.S. Supreme Court, among many complex issues of mind and crime, addressed the issue of *mens rea*. The Court stated that evidence tending to show that a defendant suffers from a mental disease and lacks capacity to form *mens rea* is relevant to rebut evidence that he or she did in fact form the required *mens rea* at the time the crime was committed. (It is interesting to note that the Court appears to have simply assumed that free will exists— thereby rejecting determinism.)

But what about animals? The serpent, for example. Scholars of animal trials are not unanimous about whether medieval jurists generally thought animals were capable of forming the necessary *mens rea* to commit a proper crime. In several documented instances, however, actual malice, and thus the necessary criminal intent, was proven to exist in animal defendants. If you think this is all nonsense, wait until Part V when we find out what it is like to try a rat.

Similarly, Adam also appears to have a defense that's unavailable to Eve: the notion of mind versus act, which was hinted at in one of the prior defense strategies. The mind versus act approach, however, appears to have a slight wrinkle when it comes to Eve. It was Eve who ate from the tree of knowledge of good and evil first. This means that while she arguably did not have the requisite intent at the time she took a bite, she did encourage Adam to eat after (presumably) gaining such knowledge. Her lawyer, however, might have been able to put on scientific evidence that the enlightening effects of the fruit were not instantaneous (i.e., she was still of innocent mind when she gave the fruit to Adam) and, in any case, pushing contraband, mind-expanding fruit was not a specifically prohibited act.

Something that might have jumped out at you in the defenses suggested so far is that they all sound like they are being made by lawyers: free will versus irresistible impulse; rules versus principles; positivism versus natural law; critical race theory; due process; cultural feminism; act versus intent; efficiency and wealth maximization. What about a simple argument for application of a type of "correctability ruling"—"God, could you please give these poor kids a break?"

Moses essentially used this approach in arguing with God to spare the Jews following the golden calf episode. After breaking the commandment against idolatry, God threatened to wipe out "His people." But instead of agreeing with the logic of law, Moses, according to various scholars, argued (among other things) that all vows are made to be broken when fulfillment of the vow leads to an unjust result. A rigid obedience to harsh rules is itself a kind of slavery—the very thing from which God had just freed the Jews.

It is also the case, as stated by one legal scholar, that "[s]elf-abasement, implied by the phrase '*beg for mercy*,' is critical: it is another costly action that can serve as a signal to all concerned that the offender switches allegiance from the deviant subcommunity [in this case the serpent and his evil master] to the dominant community [of God]." However, the begging in this case might lose some of its force if done by Vinnie and Sal rather than by the clients.

The point is that lawyers advocating on behalf of a client often speak in a specialized voice—what one scholar has called the "discourse of the hysteric." This voice, if not properly handled, along with dress, manner, and support staff, can serve as a signal that removes the lawyer from the concerns of ordinary people. In fact, when lawyers want to shift into hypermode, they can start speaking in a "scholarly voice." This "discourse of the university" (for example, legal positivism versus natural law theory) can have the effect of sucking out any lingering emotion from a situation and putting the discussion beyond the language, understanding, and concern of most human beings—including judges.

And what about the serpent? This low-lying, deviant reptile was a beast of the field, and was it not God, on the fifth day, who created the beasts? I should think that both Vinnie and Sal, top graduates of the Garden of Eden School of Law, would have smelled entrapment. Genesis seems to indicate that Eve was not predisposed to commit the crime; it was only after the serpent (arguably an agent of the State) enticed this upright girl that she took a bite of the fruit—and then, looking like Carmen Miranda, enticed Adam. Or so Sal, on Eve's behalf, would claim. And Vinnie, on Adam's behalf, would appear to have a type of "fruit of the poisonous tree" defense: If Eve was entrapped, then so was Adam. (It is interesting, or perhaps just disturbing, to note that only lawyers could take a fruit of knowledge and turn it into a poisonous fruit.)

Now for the primary reason for planting two lawyers in the Garden: the finger-pointing defense. The Genesis story tells us that after Adam and Eve ate of the fruit, they knew they were naked; they sewed fig leaves together, and when they heard God's voice, they both hid—so far so good. But under that one brutal question from God: "Has thou eaten of the tree, whereof I commanded thee that thou shouldest not eat?"—Adam cracks.

Garden-Variety Malpractice

> If Vinnie or Sal were to have accepted both Adam and Eve as clients, they would have run into potential conflicts of interest and consequently, the specter of malpractice. In order to attempt to avoid such problems, either of them could have employed (as do modern-day lawyers) the following approach suggested by a legal malpractice carrier: "If you [Vinnie, Sal] intend to engage in a joint or multiple client representation [of Adam and Eve], give full disclosure to [both potential] clients regarding potential and reasonably foreseeable conflicts of interest and their ramifications. Discuss the effect of both potential and actual conflicts upon your representation of [the] clients. Advise [them] that there is no confidentiality between them on matters concerning the joint representation. Advise [them] to seek the advice of independent counsel on the issue of whether joint representation is appropriate. Obtain the written consent [assuming the childlike Adam and Eve can write] of each of [them] after full disclosure and before continuing the representation."

Vinnie might have instructed Adam not to say anything on the grounds that his answer could be incriminating. However, having answered prior to engagement of counsel, he confessed to the "crime" but then attempted to mitigate his involvement by pointing the dirty end of the stick at his codefendant, Eve: She made me do it! Vinnie might have been able to make something of this point and gotten Adam a lighter sentence than Eve.

Again, what about the serpent? He was not even subject to the command-ment. In fact, there is no indication that this "snake in the grass" could even reach the fruit, or bite into it, or swallow it whole—remember, Acquiring Ideas Is Eating. Unlike Adam and Eve, the serpent is not summoned, informed of his crime, or even questioned. Furthermore, he tells the truth: that their eyes will be opened after a bite of fruit. Despite such facts, this poor, harmless Gar-den snake is cursed by God above all cattle, and above every beast of the field. Where is the justice? Where was his lawyer!

ADAM AND EVE JOIN THE CANON, COMMON, AND CIVIL LAW

Moving from the fanciful to the practical, medieval canonist lawyers did make use of the story of Adam and Eve—and the serpent. In this biblical story, the canonists (discussed in more detail in Part V) saw the pattern for the *ordo iuris*: the elements of procedural and substantive rules wrapped up in the medium of the divine. God's command not to eat from the tree, despite the fact that the punishment seems a bit post hoc, contained the important concept that a per-son should not be punished for an action unless that action has been prohib-ited and sufficiently defined (*nulla poena sine lege*). God's command thus served as a model for human law—an activity of some importance to lawyers.

Concept versus Action

It has been argued by some scholars that "law" is not truly a concept (which may be why, as discussed later, the ancient Mesopotamians, Greeks, and Hebrews did not have a word for the abstract concept of "law") but, instead, a professional activity bounded and shaped by such things as custom, tra-dition, and community values, norms, and feelings: Lawyers "do" law. First, they think through a legal problem and grope their way to a solution. Sec-ondly, they present in oral and/or written form the solution to the client, the public, the other side, a judge, jury, and others. "Law" was likely a concept in many ancient societies, as it is a concept in modern societies—it's just that some scholars looking for the word have missed the conceptual metaphor.

The English common-law lawyers made similar use of the story of Adam and Eve. For example, the lawyer-dialogist in John Ferne's *Blazon of Gentrie* (1586) saw the foundation of human law in Eden. God, through the discourse of the master, gave law to Adam and Eve, tried them for eating the forbidden fruit, and heard Adam's "feeble defense." "Thus," according to the lawyer-dialogist, "we borrow the form of pleading from Adam. And the antiquity of law, from Paradise, which are both sacred and heavenly." Now you know why practicing law is a slice of heaven.

After eating of the forbidden fruit, God called to Adam: "Where art thou?" The early canonists had no doubt that God knew exactly where Adam was. After all, to them, God was the ultimate police force in the universe. They therefore saw this divine shout not as evidence of some type of Gnostic lack of foreknowledge but as setting the requirement that an accused must have a sufficient summons before he can be punished. Procedural justice must be accorded to all.

Finally, Adam was permitted to answer God. The canonists saw this as requiring that a defendant be given the opportunity to speak in response to a charge. God, calling out to Adam, knew exactly what Adam had done but still gave him the opportunity to reply. The canonists said that this same chance must be given to even an obviously guilty man under the procedures of the *ius commune* (a category of law, developed from a mixture of canon and Roman law, discussed in Part V). It is possible that the guilty might be able to offer up mitigating circumstances that would at least affect the severity of the punishment. Adam tried this approach with his "She made me do it" defense. A defense of "irresistible impulse" (i.e., loss—not lack—of free will), as suggested earlier, might have been more successful.

One of the most common forms of legal reasoning, and not just in modern times, is reasoning by analogy—a kissing cousin of casuistry. This inductive reasoning process, of Sir Francis Bacon fame, traditionally works in four basic steps:

1. Some identified fact pattern A (the sample) has a certain characteristic X, or characteristics X, Y, and Z (the property or properties);
2. Identified fact pattern B (the target) differs from A in some respects (dissimilarities) but shares characteristic X, or characteristics X, Y, and Z;
3. The law treats fact pattern A in a certain way;
4. Because B shares certain characteristics with A (relevant similarities), the law should treat B in the same way—assuming, of course, that within the applicable cultural context and social purpose the relevant similarities are perceived to outweigh the dissimilarities.

In other words, the law should treat "similar" cases in a similar manner. For example, in the Garden of Eden fact pattern, Adam (allegedly) broke a commandment and was summoned by God to answer for this "crime": X (crime), Y (summons), and Z (answer). In medieval London, a pig (allegedly) committed a crime by killing a child: X (crime). Divine law required Adam to be summoned to appear and answer for his (alleged) crime, so the pig, like Adam, since it allegedly committed a crime, should be summoned (Y) to answer (Z), through its lawyer, the charge. Right?

⊠ · ⊠

Proper Reasoning

In order for analogical reasoning to operate properly, the lawyer has to know—or at least be able to sell to a judge—that A (the Garden of Eden case) and B (the London pig case) are relevantly similar and that there are not relevant differences between them. Thus the major challenge facing analogical reasoners, whether involving analogy of cases or analogy of doctrine, is to decide what is and is not relevant. For example, is the fact that Adam committed his crime in the Garden of Eden and the pig committed its crime in London relevantly different? What about the fact that Adam is a man and the pig is, well, a pig?

Keep in mind that there is often a substantial gap between the *soundness* of an analogy and its *persuasiveness*. Furthermore, the process of induction is, at least currently, not translatable into an algorithm—a process that grinds along according to a finite set of rules and then reliably spits out a result. Computer programs are algorithmic, but lawyers (and humans in general) are, deep down, inductively rational pattern-recognizers.

⊠ · ⊠

LEGAL REASONING

In thinking about legal reasoning, it is important to be aware of the "scandal of induction." One scientist, in an oh-so-gentle fashion, has put it this way: "No scientific reasoning, and indeed no successful reasoning of any kind, has ever fitted the inductivist description." Ouch! A primary reason for this position is the claim that it is impossible to extrapolate observations unless one has already placed them within an explanatory framework. Observation, however meticulous, does not in and of itself ensure truth. What repeated observation does, setting aside the argument that Bayesian inference can provide an objective method of induction, is to refine an opinion.

Let's put this argument on induction in sharp focus. Assume there is a very smart pig routing around at old McDonald's farm just south of Reno, Nevada. His name is Big Pig. And Big Pig notices that McDonald, for the past two years, has fed him every day. He predicts, based on this observation, that

McDonald will continue to feed him every day. From an inductivist's point of view, Big Pig has "extrapolated" his observations into a hypothesis (a form of analogy known as inductive generalization arrived at by moving from particular propositions to a general proposition), with each day-after-day-after-day feeding adding justification to the hypothesis. So why attempt to escape—it is the Pig Pen of Eden.

Several days after coming up with the hypothesis, Big Pig finds himself sharing the pen with a new pig purchased by McDonald. Her name is Little Pig. Big Pig and Little Pig get to oinking about life on the farm. Big Pig tells Little Pig about his hypothesis (arrived at inductively)—which he has named the "benevolent–pig owner hypothesis." Little Pig is intrigued with this hypothesis and, in fact, notices that every time McDonald feeds Big Pig, she also gets fed. And what's more, her trough is always filled with the same assortment of tasty food that McDonald gives Big Pig. So Little Pig, who before being sold to McDonald had followed her former owner to law school, applies these observations to the benevolent–pig owner hypothesis. In doing so, Little Pig concludes that her situation (the target case) is analogous to Big Pig's situation (the source case) and the benevolent–pig owner hypothesis must therefore apply to her (moving from particular to particular—the form of analogy known as reasoning by example).

All seems right with the world until one beautiful spring day, when Little Pig notices that Big Pig has an apple in his mouth and is roasting over a pit. A cruel reminder that interpretation does not always equal observation. Instantly, Little Pig dredges up what she had learned in law school and starts distinguishing her situation from Big Pig's—after all, she is smaller, is a different breed of pig than Big Pig (subordinate level of categorization), has different markings, has a different name. . . . In the end, however, the answer to whether or not Little Pig will end up as a "hamicide" statistic may not rest in analogical reasoning per se but in the "problem" of induction.

Another form of legal reasoning, a deductive process identified by Aristotle and frequently employed by civil-law lawyers, is the use (and misuse) of the syllogism, the historic workhorse of logic. Perhaps the most famous syllogism of all time is "All men are mortal; Socrates is a man; therefore Socrates is mortal." The truth of this argument seems compelling. After all, who could argue with the conclusion—Socrates downed a dose of hemlock and died!

The reason for its compelling nature, however, is that the conclusion (Socrates is mortal) is already contained in the major premise—the definition of "man." In other words, the first premise ("All men are mortal") says that there is a group of "things" (a category) defined as "men," all of which are "mortal" (a general proposition). The minor premise (in this case, a particular proposition) says that Socrates ("a man") falls within the category defined as "men"—therefore Socrates must be mortal. Thus, through the rationalist notion of "container logic," the concepts of "men," "mortal," and "Socrates" have all been connected (i.e., A is in B, and C is in A, so C is in B)—snug as nested Russian dolls.

The use of Adam and Eve in syllogistic reasoning was employed by medieval scholars and, in a somewhat updated version, proceeded along the following lines: Adam and Eve broke one of God's commandments by eating the forbidden fruit and were punished; Bob, Ted, Carol, and Alice broke one of God's commandments by engaging in unnatural sexual acts—therefore Bob, Ted, Carol, and Alice must be punished. In terms of the syllogism: A (commandment breakers) is within B (punishment), C (Bob, Ted, Carol, and Alice) is within A (commandment breakers), so C (Bob, Ted, Carol, and Alice) is within B (punishment).

However, the soundness of this syllogism (versus its validity) lies in the truth or falsity of its premises: Is there a God? Did He, She, It punish Adam and Eve for breaking a commandment? Has God given a commandment against unnatural sexual acts? If, however, you assume, as they did in the Middle Ages, that the answers to these questions is clearly yes, yes, and yes, then the syllogism's conclusion of punishment for Bob, Ted, Carol, and Alice is compelling. The syllogism is valid; its premises are true, and therefore the argument is sound. Off with their heads!

It seems clear that the common-law lawyers, like the civil and canon law lawyers, extracted from the Adam and Eve case rules and principles to account for particular divine judgments. These rules and principles, grounded in certain basic moral sentiments, were then applied, using analogical and syllogistic reasoning, to new cases in which there had not yet been a judgment. The result was to find within the growing body of judgments certain fixed points in the law that could be used by lawyers to argue, again by analogy or syllogism, a client's case. They created conformity enforcers and set them adrift in a sea of potential diversity generators.

It is important to appreciate that the roots of analogical and syllogistic reasoning, used and abused extensively by modern-day lawyers separately and in combination with other forms of reasoning, stretch back to a point in time long before the Middle Ages. The ancient Mesopotamians frequently put forward a hypothesis (protasis) and then, by a judgment based on the elements of that hypothesis, reached a conclusion (apodosis) that they found in the hypothesis—a type of "casuistic-lite" embodied in conditional or hypothetical propositions. For example, from the laws of King Hammurabi: "If a woman is not discreet but a gadabout, thus neglecting her house and discrediting her husband: [then] they shall throw this woman in the water." This type of "if . . . then" (protasis/apodosis) reasoning was not confined to law. In fact it appears that it was the framework for much of Mesopotamian rational discourse. In the context, for example, of diagnostic medicine it was said, "If a man who is feverish has a burning abdomen, so that at the same time he feels neither pleasure nor dislike for food and drink, and also his body is yellow: [then] this man has a venereal disease." By taking the elements of the hypothesis (fever, burning abdomen, no appetite, and a yellow skin color) and utilizing simultaneity of cause and effect combined with a particular principle, the doctor reaches the conclusion (venereal disease).

On the one hand, this conditional scheme of hypothesis and conclusion appears to be a type of analogical reasoning. On the other, it appears to be syllogistic in nature. The fact is that it smacks of both.

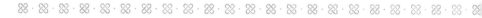

Analogies in the East

Analogic reasoning is not limited to the Western legal tradition. According to the Islamic jurist al-Shafi'i (767–820 CE), "God [Allah] has not permitted any person since the Prophet's [Muhammad's] time to give an opinion except on the strength of established legal knowledge," and "legal knowledge after the Prophet's death includes the Qur'an [the recorded revelations of God to the Prophet Muhammad], Sunna [recollections of the words and deeds of Prophet Muhammad and his companions], consensus, narrative, and analogy based on these texts."

Other Islamic jurists cite the case where the Prophet Muhammad allows a daughter to go on pilgrimage in the place of her ailing father. The Prophet argues: "If your father has a debt and you pay it for him, do you think that it will suffice?" These texts suggest, according to certain scholars, that Muhammad utilized analogy (a common form of human reasoning) to answer a question and accorded others the same privilege.

From the analogic point of view, the protasis is stripped down. In the example from the laws of King Hammurabi regarding the "gadabout" we are not told the name, age, physical condition, mental state, or domestic situation of the women to be thrown in the water—only that she was "not discreet," "neglected her house," and "discredited her husband." What we are told, however, are the socially important elements—those relevant facts that give the rule its moral juice. By suppressing all the contingent and insignificant elements (at least as determined by the discourse of the master), it is easier to see that a new case (the "target case") is analogous to one decided previously by King Hammurabi (the "source case"). It also highlights the problem of induction. And from the syllogistic point of view, the "if . . . then" statement can be used to form part of a mixed hypothetical syllogism. For example: If a woman has not been discreet, has neglected her house, and has discredited her husband, then she is to be punished. This particular woman now before the court has not been discreet, has neglected her house, and has discredited her husband; therefore, she is to be punished—throw her into the river. This form of logical reasoning, both thousands of years ago and in the twenty-first century CE, is extremely prevalent in the law, constituting one of the most basic and common forms of legal reasoning.

But whether used analogically or syllogistically, the most shocking thing is the frequent similarity between conditional schemes of hypothesis and conclusion and the way in which rumors are created. Certain scholars have pointed out that stories are turned into rumors through leveling, sharpening, and assimilating. In the first step, a story is leveled—meaning that all kinds of details that are essential for understanding the story's true meaning are left out. A similar process takes place when the protasis is stripped of various elements. Next the story is sharpened—the remaining details are made more specific. In the conditional scheme, the socially important elements are brought out—that is, sharpened. And finally, in the case of rumors, after leveling and sharpening, the story is changed so that it makes more sense to those spreading the rumor. Similarly, this process of assimilation often takes place in analogic and syllogistic legal reasoning in order to make sure that the conclusion being propounded makes cultural sense. In other words, modern-day lawyers, not unlike the ancient Mesopotamians (and many tabloid newspapers and magazines), often level, sharpen, and assimilate the "facts" of their cases in order to trim off the ontological fat and make them more appealing to the judge or jury. And after this trimming process takes place, the legal narrative may have the same relationship to the actual events that a rumor has to the true story. But in the legal context (assuming the lawyer is successful and has not lapsed into pure crap) it is more than a rumor—it is the law!

Now on to murder.

II

THE FIRST MURDER CASE— THE STATE V. CAIN:

A Tale of the Trail of Blood from the Land of Nod to Brentwood, California

ADAM AND EVE AND EVEN THE NASTY OLD SERPENT could have used a good lawyer. But God, the Lawgiver and Adjudicator, apparently did not consider it necessary to make counsel available, and post-Garden-party society had not yet evolved (or devolved) to the point where a lawyer or two might have sprung into existence. This lack of counsel, at least arguably, led to a guilty verdict in one of the first recorded murder cases: *The State (of the Lone and Dreary World) v. Cain.*

The "facts" of the case are set out in Genesis. We know that Cain and Abel were brothers, sons of the unrepresented Adam and Eve (apparently the fruit worked), and that both believed in God. At a certain point in time, each of them made a divine offering. Cain, the firstborn and a farmer by trade, offered the fruit of the ground.

25

Abel was a Nevada-style rancher and therefore offered the firstlings of his flock. God, for some unstated reason, was in the mood for meat and not fruit. With the rejection of his offering, "Cain was very wroth, and his countenance fell." And since it would take the likes of Nietzsche's madman to do in God, Cain turned against his brother. God could see the signs of anger in Cain's face and counseled with him. But the session was unsuccessful "and it came to pass, when . . . [Cain and Abel] were in the field, that Cain rose up against Abel his brother, and slew him."

The principle witness to the crime is Abel's blood, crying out to God. Because Abel was last seen with Cain, Cain is hauled in for questioning. No assistance of counsel is provided. And under the attack of the Grand Inquisitor's "examination," Cain makes a big mistake. God asks: "Where is Abel thy brother?" Cain responds with the immortal words: "I know not. Am I my brother's keeper?" While the retort has a certain literary quality to it, an innocent man might not have been so flippant. In addition, this is the accused's complete defense. And God brushes it aside with His next pointed question: "What has thou done? The voice of thy brother's blood crieth unto me from the ground. . . ." Abel's blood crying out might appear to be solid evidence. The problem, of course, is that Cain, like his "condemned" parents, was not represented by legal counsel.

An Interesting Legal Precedent

> The literal translation of this passage is, "The voice of thy brother's *bloods* crieth unto me from the ground. . . ." This indicates that it was not only Abel's blood that cried out, but also the blood of his never-to-be born descendants. These days, defendants aren't usually charged with murdering their victim's unconceived progeny.

Consider, for example, the modern-day case of *People v. Simpson,* in which, after cross-examination, the blood of the victims went from a cry to a whimper.

In brief, the prosecutor, Marcia Clark, after reviewing most of the evidence against O.J. Simpson, an African-American sports legend, was eager to file charges against him for the murder of his Caucasian, blonde, beautiful ex-wife, Nicole Brown Simpson, and her friend Ronald L. Goldman. She, however, decided to delay filing the racially (and sexually) charged case until various blood tests were performed and reviewed.

Dennis Fung of the serology unit of the Scientific Investigation Division at the Los Angeles Police Department (LAPD) had collected evidence including a bloody glove, a bloodstained sock, and various samples from a trail of blood that seemed to lead from the murder scene directly to Simpson's upper-class home in Brentwood, California. The department also had a blood sample from Simpson.

Fung handed over all this evidence to Collin Yamauchi, the LAPD criminalist who was to perform the testing. In addition, Yamauchi was given reference blood samples from Nicole Brown Simpson and Ronald Goldman obtained during their autopsies.

Generally, for an initial test, Yamauchi would have used conventional ABO blood typing to categorize the blood samples. This testing separates blood types into six basic categories. Due, however, to the high-profile nature of the case, Yamauchi's boss asked him to use DNA. Yamauchi therefore conducted restriction fragment length polymorphism (RFLP) on some of the collected blood drops and polymerase chain reaction (PCR) analyses on others, the choice of test depending on the size of the drops. The RFLP and PCR tests conducted by the LAPD lab were also done by a private lab in Maryland called Orchid Cellmark, and by the California Department of Justice lab. All tests yielded the same results.

The DNA of the blood-group drops on the pathway of the crime scene matched Simpson's, a characteristic shared by fewer than one person in 170 million. Blood found on a sock in Simpson's bedroom could have come from only one person in 6.8 billion, and Nicole Brown Simpson was one of those persons. And the bloody glove found at Simpson's home was consistent with a mixture of his and the two victims' blood. But none of this points to probability of guilt if, as Simpson's lawyers claimed, the cops had conspired to frame their client: *in malam partem* (the evil part of the office).

In her opening statement to the jury, Clark provided a preview of the tale of blood—a tale in which Nicole's and Ron's blood would not just cry out, but scream. In addition to the drops on the pathway at Nicole's condo, the bloodstained sock, and the bloody glove, Clark highlighted two facts:

1. Each of the bloody, size-twelve shoe prints leaving the murder scene matched Simpson's blood type; and
2. The bloodstain on the center console of Simpson's Ford Bronco was consistent with a mixture of Simpson's and Ronald Goldman's blood.

Johnnie Cochran, one of the leads of Simpson's massive defense team, rose and made his opening statement to the jury. Cochran, among other things, disparaged the work of the LAPD employees who had collected and analyzed the evidence. He claimed that the DNA tests the jury would hear about during the trial would prove that blood found underneath Nicole's fingernails was inconsistent with her own, Goldman's, or Simpson's.

It was not Cochran, however, but another of Simpson's lawyers, New York hotshot Barry Scheck, that ultimately reduced the cry of Nicole Brown Simpson's and Ronald Goldman's blood to a whimper. Scheck's efforts had little to do with establishing that someone other than Simpson had murdered Ron and Nicole, and everything to do with undermining the integrity and competence of the LAPD. Scheck told the jury that the LAPD's work could not be trusted, and therefore the forensic evidence against his client amounted to nothing. In pursuing this task, Scheck's maneuvering epitomized the nihilistic function of a typical defense lawyer.

The most remarkable thing was that Scheck actually accomplished his assigned goal. By the end of the case, he had a plausible scientific basis for arguing away every piece of physical evidence against Simpson. To be sure, many of these explanations were fanciful, and, in part, contradictory, positing a police department that was both totally inept and brilliantly sinister. Scheck's arguments were based on a conspiracy so large that, analyzed objectively, it seemed a practical impossibility. But Scheck's passion and skill made his theories real for the jury. And for that reason, it has been argued that he, more than any other person on the defense team, was responsible for the verdict.

Keep in mind the use of passion in Scheck's defense of Simpson (the discourse of the hysteric—"take *your* rationalism and shove it!"). Juries are told over and over to base their decision only on the law as applied to the facts of the case before them. However, contrary to Aristotle's description of law as "reason without passion," it is impossible to remove emotion from the decision-making process. And every good practicing lawyer, deep down in his or her gut, knows this to be true.

A defense lawyer's story that is merely a deconstruction of the prosecution's story supplies no meaning itself. (In fact, this is one of the criticisms of critical legal studies.) And without meaning there is, at least for humans, no order or control, and judgment becomes impossible or at least, with regard to the defense lawyer's client up on charges, highly problematic.

There is, however, an approach for building meaning and emotion into a defense. The defense lawyer might tell a nonlinear story to the jury that uses popular cultural images and symbols, but still wraps itself around a coherent, rational meaning. The advocate might, for example, first deconstruct the linear history of the crime as told by the prosecution—keeping in mind, however, that each juror carries around in his or her head an idealized cognitive model for the concept of "story." The advocate can then provide jurors with a meaningful escape from the uncertainty that the deconstruction has created. This proffered exit, which maybe more literary than "legal" (assuming there is a difference), will guide the jury into a drama of compelling significance. The lawyer, playing upon the deep cultural myth of the archetypal hero, calls upon the jury to solve—with the lawyer's assistance, not unlike the host of the popular children's program *Blue's Clues*—the riddle of the evidence. In other words, the lawyer can lead the jurors away from focusing upon what happened before the trial and encourage them to become the heroes of the courtroom drama.

In the context of the Simpson trial, it appears that Barry Scheck played the role of the skeptical postmodernist and deconstructed the prosecution's story without proffering any meaning: "All the forensic evidence against my client amounts to nothing. It's all crap!" But the dream team did not leave its defense in the hands of a nihilist—there is, after all, tremendous discomfort in nothingness, and judgment becomes highly difficult. Cochran's role was to play the affirmative postmodernist: He made it clear that the challenge for the jurors was the same one faced by the mythic quest hero. Each juror found himself or herself in this position, according to Cochran, because this was an extraordinary drama about justice—not one simply about the prosecution's historical narrative of what happened in the past. The real action is inside this courtroom. The drama, Cochran says, forces you into a heroic struggle against "genocidal racism." And this racism has been seen on the face and heard in the voice of the prosecution's star witness, Mark Fuhrman—a Los Angeles police officer with hateful views toward African Americans and mixed-race couples. It is not necessary to look back at the poor victims, although we pray for their souls and their families, but only at Fuhrman—a man of corruption; a symbol of abusive power. It is this jury's quest to do justice—and not just for O.J. but for the whole nation. (Heroic stuff!)

Rather than using the *now* as a means to attempt to remedy past injustices, there is the possibility that the Simpson not guilty verdict was based, at least in part, on preventing future harm. It has been noted that whether Simpson was guilty or not, it is possible that a guilty verdict could have led to rioting in the streets: This was, after all, just a few years after the Rodney King riots. If this possibility was consciously or unconsciously considered by the jurors, then perhaps Simpson's acquittal may have prevented death, injury, and destruction—and therefore may have been the "best" decision, or at least a choice of the lesser evil.

This interpretation of the verdict is arguably grounded in utilitarianism—the philosophy of Jeremy Bentham, a lawyer, at least by training, born into a family of lawyers. Bentham saw morality not as an end in itself but as a means for making the world a better place. Consequently, as one scholar has opined, it was clearly "better" (economically? morally?) to opt for acquittal and no fatalities (assuming Simpson does not re-offend) than to convict Simpson and face death and injuries in the streets. Is it possible that the dream team skillfully suggested this "higher morality" to the jury?

Rationality of Self-Interest

Jeremy Bentham (1748–1832) was born in London and studied at Oxford before qualifying for the Bar. His father hoped that Jeremy would become the Lord Chancellor of England, but his son never actually practiced law, complaining that the "Demon of Chicane" was rife in the legal system. He therefore chose to concentrate on legal theory rather than on its practice. His writings have spread wide and deep in the areas of political, economic, and legal thought.

Bentham's utilitarianism assumes a view in which rationality is taken as *the* defining characteristic of human nature. Therefore it is natural for humans to use their reason to maximize their perceived self-interest. Based on these factors, utilitarianism propounds a utopian moral system in which each individual has the maximum freedom to pursue his or her own self-interest consistent with others having the same freedom. And the combined legacy of utilitarianism and social Darwinism is the firmly held view of human rationality as the maximization of self-interest.

Could Cain, with good legal counsel (and loads of cash—or at least his dead brother's cattle as a retainer), have silenced the blood of Abel? Possibly. In any case, his lawyer would certainly have advised Cain against uttering the immortal but arguably incriminating words, "Am I my brother's keeper?" He would have encouraged his client, at the expense of great literature, to show the proper concern, and instead of being banished to the land of Nod on the east of Eden, Cain might have ended up in the sunshine of Brentwood, California—or at least Simpson's asset-protection-friendly state of Florida. (Although as of the date of this writing, O.J. Simpson is, based on other criminal charges, residing in the Lovelock, Nevada Correctional Center.)

III

THE JUDGMENT OF SOLOMON

OR, HOW TO SPLIT

THE BABY

Moving from the biblical beginning of mankind to about the tenth century BCE, the famous decision of Solomon involved a judge, two prostitutes, and no lawyers. Both of the prostitutes lived in the same house and gave birth at about the same time. The plaintiff claimed that the defendant's child died in the night because the defendant "overlaid it," that is, rolled over on the child and suffocated him. Upon discovering the dead child, the defendant, according to the allegations, got up and took the plaintiff's child and gave her the dead one. The plaintiff then awoke in the morning to nurse her child and discovered it was dead. She took one look at the child and realized it was not hers.

The defendant denied the allegations: "Nay, for my son is the living one and thy son is the dead."

Anyone familiar with Solomon's decision in this kidnapping case might quickly respond that the truth was discovered and justice done—all without lawyers! Furthermore, it has been observed that Solomon's wisdom equates with justice not because he followed the rules but because he came up with exactly the right solution for the case: one that forced the moment to its crisis and evoked the love and compassion of the plaintiff. The problem with this view of the case (from a secular perspective) is that it is not, at least arguably, just the end result of a legal dispute that matters. Frequently, it is the method used to get there that is, in the long run, most important for society. And lawyers often aid or hinder in a society's employment of a "proper" methodology. Consider, for example, the prosecution's decision not to ask for the death penalty in the *Simpson* case previously discussed.

❈ · ❈

Means to an End

Many of the classical canon lawyers understood that the means of deciding a case was more important than the end achieved based on the New Testament. They noted that St. Paul had said that a person, in order to be excommunicated, had to be "denominated" (*nominatur*) a sinner. Denomination of the sinner was not just the simple fact of guilt, but that there had been a *finding* of guilt. This meant that there had to have been some type of judicial process.

❈ · ❈

It has been argued that Marcia Clark's decision not to ask for the death penalty was not based on justice or morality but on "pure politics"—or, phrased in legalese, "the discourse of the state." By her own admission she considered the crime a "particularly heinous" one—it was, after all, a double murder. The concern, however, was that if the prosecuting team asked for the death penalty, the cognitive dissonance between Simpson as football hero and Simpson as brutal double murderer would be so great that they might not get a conviction. In a death penalty case, each juror must be willing, in principle, to vote for death. And Clark, a prosecutor with a depth of experience prior to the *Simpson* case, knew that a death-certified jury may turn out to be "a panel of tough talkers who, when push comes to verdict, can't bring themselves to convict. Why? Because it has only just dawned on them that their actions may result in a person's death."

If you are morally opposed to the death penalty, you undoubtedly agree with the state's decision not to ask for it. Nevertheless, there is ample room to criticize Clark's reasoning. The prosecution's next case, for example, might not be against a beloved celebrity but against the founder of a notorious gang, or a poor, unknown African American—a "No-J." And based on Clark's reasoning in the *Simpson* case, driven by a concern of jury nullification, how do you think the discourse between politics and justice will play out? The connection between the rule of law and full enforcement of the law is, in fact, revealed in disputes about the acceptability of this very type of prosecutorial discretion.

It has been argued that because the modern-day state, in contrast to the individual or family, is responsible for distributing the burdens of punishment for criminal activity (specifically including the death penalty), it is extremely important that the state not discriminate in selecting some people and not others to suffer for their crimes or to suffer different punishments for the same crime—principles embedded in the rule of law. Immanuel Kant (1724–1804), a leading philosopher of retribution punishment, stressed, for example, the imperative of maintaining equality among offenders—a type of "Moral Accounting" in which society's books need to always be in balance. He was so firm in this requirement for the "Family of Man" that he regarded any deviation as an aspect of the principle that "if justice goes, there is no longer any value in mankind living on earth."

Looking back at the "crimes" of Adam and Eve and Cain, one might raise the question as to why Cain walked from the murder rap (although not into the sunshine of Brentwood, California, or the asset protection of Florida) and became the builder of a city—despite the fact that his punishment was to be a wanderer—and Adam and Eve were punished. It would seem that Cain, based on his parents having eaten from the tree of knowledge of good and evil, knew the difference between right and wrong whether through genetics or family-mediated learning processes—nature, nurture, or a bit of both. So he knew it was wrong to kill his brother, dispose of the body, and then lie to God, even though God had not yet outlawed murder. Adam and Eve, in contrast, did not know right from wrong before eating from the tree, committed a victimless crime, and, while attempting to sidestep blame, did ultimately admit their transgressions. Where's the justice? Where were the lawyers?

Back to Solomon and his prostitutes. It can be argued that, in this case, both the plaintiff and defendant as well as the court could have benefited from good legal counsel. The defendant's lawyer would certainly have probed into how the plaintiff knew that the defendant's child had been "overlaid." Her testimony included the fact that she was asleep at the time of the child's death. There is also no evidence that the plaintiff had any medical training. She is therefore offering an opinion on a matter about which she is not qualified to opine: the cause of the child's death.

The plaintiff's attorney might have examined the defendant regarding the child; for example, birthmark—yes or no; if yes—size, shape, color, and location. It is also possible that the child might have had other distinguishing features known only to the mother.

And what about a maternity test? OK, no DNA probe, since this case arose over 3,000 years ago. Still, one or both of the lawyers would likely have objected to Solomon's command: "Fetch me a sword." This is arguably a slight breach of judicial discretion, even in Nevada. It may be that "Law Is Violence," but hopefully not outright baby killing. In fact, Rabbi Judah ha-Nasi, a master of the law and editor of the Mishnah—the first major redaction of Jewish oral traditions—agrees: "If I had been present when he said 'Fetch me a sword,' I would have put a rope around his neck, for if God had not been merciful and prompted the mother to give up her child rather than see it die, he would surely have been killed by him."

⊗ · ⊗

Due Process

Interestingly, this same fetch-me-a-sword approach to a problem was employed by Alexander the Great. According to legend, when Alexander captured Gordium, the capital of Phrygia, he encountered a famous chariot, tied to a pole with a knot (the "Gordian knot") of amazing complexity. The promise associated with the knot was that he who could untie it would conquer all of Asia. So Alexander, using raw power to circumvent the rules of the game, took his sword and cut the knot clean through. The question raised is whether this approach constitutes boldness or anti-intellectualism. Similarly, the question raised in Solomon's case is whether his was a bold approach to a legal problem or simply antijudicial—in other words, outside the rules of the game.

⊗ · ⊗

So, while the truth in Solomon's case was discovered and "moral justice" served, lawyers could have made some interesting arguments had they been involved. Was the proper methodology followed? Can you really effectively judge with a sword? Lawyers would undoubtedly have made this a much longer and more complex Bible story.

IV

DANIEL, "PUBLIC DEFENDER,"

AND THE ART OF
CROSS-EXAMINATION

ONE OF THE EARLIEST EXAMPLES of the important art of cross-examination—what American jurist John Henry Wigmore, an expert in the law of evidence, has called "the greatest legal engine ever invented for the discovery of truth"—comes from the tale of Susanna and the Elders. This story, contained in the Greek versions of the Book of Daniel, tells us that in Babylon around the second century BCE, a man named Joakim was married to Susanna. She was extremely beautiful and God fearing. Joakim was wealthy and his home was used as the local courthouse. Adjoining his home was a lovely garden in which, after court, Susanna liked to take walks. Every day the two "ancients" appointed as judges would watch Susanna as she strolled among the greenery. Neither judge, however, confessed to the other the depths of his lust for Susanna—until one particular day. On that day they both decided they had had enough and wanted to find the perfect moment for a Near-Eastern *ménage à trois*.

Their chance finally came. Susanna was walking with only two maids and decided that since it was so hot she would cool off by taking a bath. The two elders sensed the moment was right and hid. Susanna asked her maids to go and get some oil and washing balls, and to make sure the garden doors were shut. Once the maids left, the two old boys seized the moment and, with all their vigor, ran to Susanna: "Behold the garden doors are shut, that no man can see us, and we are in love with thee; therefore consent unto us, and lie with us. If thou will not, we will bear witness against thee, that a young man was with thee; and therefore thou didst send away thy maids from thee."

Susanna took one look at the lusty old men and decided to take her chances with the made-up young lover. She started screaming, then everyone started screaming. The servants heard the cries and rushed to the garden.

The next day the locals assembled at Joakim's house for a trial. The testimony of the judges was heard: "As we walked in the garden alone, this woman [Susanna] came in with two maids, and shut the garden doors, and sent the maids away. Then a young man, who there was hid, came unto her, and lay with her. Then we that stood in a corner of the garden, seeing this wickedness, ran unto them. And when we saw them together, the man we could not hold: for he was stronger than we, opened the door and leaped out. But having taken this woman, we asked who the young man was, but she would not tell us: these things do we testify."

The assembly, acting as judge and jury, believed the judges and condemned Susanna to death. Susanna did not testify, but she did cry out to God: "O everlasting God, that knowest the secrets, and knowest all things, before they be: Thou knowest that they have borne false witness against me, and, behold, I must die; whereas I never did such things as these men have maliciously invented against me." Thus, we hear the female voice in this legal drama only as a private, religious plea.

The Lord was listening. But He did not send a flood, or an earthquake, or a voice from the sky. He sent a lawyer—of sorts.

The advocate's name is Daniel and from the back of the crowd he cries out: "I am clear from the blood of this woman." This pitched voice of the hysteric is a great attention getter—mainly because the people have absolutely no idea what he is talking about, as is often the case with lawyers. So he waxes eloquent: "Are ye such fools, ye sons of Israel, that without examination or knowledge of the truth, ye have condemned a daughter of Israel? Return again to the place of judgment: for they have born false witness against her." What Daniel is telling them (the all-male court) is that his private investigator (God) has, at the last minute, rushed in with evidence favorable to his client and through the art of cross-examination, the truth will be revealed—and balance in Susanna's life will be restored. So Daniel says to the crowd: "Put these two aside one far from the other and I will examine them." Brilliant! His strategy is to have the "People's Court" separate the old farts so that he can examine them individually, neither of them knowing what the other has said. In this way he can bring out inconsistencies in their testimonies and thereby reveal his client's innocence. This is a technique that is frequently used, and sometimes aggressively so, by lawyers in modern-day trials. It is the reason we love Perry Mason.

Daniel calls his first witness. He asks one question—ever so politely: "Now then, if thou hast seen her, tell us under what tree sawest them companying together?" The answer: "Under the mastic tree." The next witness is called. Daniel also asks him just one question: "Now therefore tell me under what tree didst thou seest them companying together?" The court falls quiet. The answer comes: "Under a holm tree."

The assembly is stunned—there is a moment of silence, and then cries go out, "Let's get 'em"!

In fairness it should be pointed out that the result might have been different if the old boys had been represented by competent counsel, perhaps Vinnie or Sal. With proper "witness preparation"—not coaching, mind you—the two antagonists might have gotten their story straight.

Examining and "Preparing" Witnesses

It is noted that the type of question Daniel asked falls within the category of "WH questions"—why, where, when, which, who, what, and how. Lawyers are typically taught not to ask such open-ended questions on cross-examination, given that the most valuable purpose of cross is generally to let the lawyer "testify." Therefore Daniel, according to notions of good trial practice, should have asked a tag question, particularly with regard to the second judge: "Now therefore it was a [—] tree under which thou sawest them companying, was it not? " Or better yet: "It was a [—] tree"—question mark. But it must be remembered that, with regard to trees and sex, Daniel had God on his side.

In the United States, ethical rules for lawyers mandate that they not counsel or assist a witness to testify falsely. Nor may they knowingly use perjured testimony or false evidence in a legal proceeding.

With regard to the story of "Susanna and the Elders," it is interesting to note that for centuries Roman and canonical law generally provided for the right of a criminal defendant to see all witnesses presented against him and to hear those witnesses testify in open court, as Susanna had. In the twelfth century CE, this procedure changed.

It gradually became the practice in both secular and ecclesiastical courts for the judge to examine each witness in secret, out of the accused's presence. Other than the judge and the witness, only the notary, who wrote down the testimony, was in attendance. The accused could submit written questions to the judge, but the judge was not required to ask them. And the help or harm of what the witnesses had said came out when the transcribed testimony was read aloud in open court by the notary.

You Would Never Lie on the Stand, Would You?

Charges of unethically coaching a witness and suborning (to induce to commit) perjury are extremely difficult to prove. The line between legitimate witness preparation and unethical coaching is fuzzy. Consider, for example, whether former U.S. President Bill Clinton, a lawyer by education and training, tried to mold the recollections of his secretary in a sexual harassment case filed against him while he was president. According to various sources, Clinton, after his deposition had been taken, talked to his secretary about his meeting with a certain female White House intern, asking "questions" such as, "We were never alone, right?"

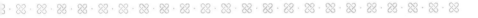

The exact time and place of this procedural change, as well as the reasons for its development, are open to speculation. It appears to have started in Bologna, Italy, near the end of the twelfth century CE and gradually spread to courts in other parts of western Europe. It also appears, somewhat ironically, that the story of "Susanna and the Elders" served as the justification for this new procedure.

It is clearly the case that the apocryphal story does not justify the blanket exclusion of the accused from witness examination. Its point has to do with the separation of witnesses from one another—not from the defendant—and belief in the principle that the examination of witnesses by the adverse party or her advocate is the best means of bringing out the truth.

What appears to have happened is that judges in the municipalities of northern Italy, motivated by a desire to keep lawyers from complicating and slowing down trials (imagine that), began to ban parties and their lawyers from hearing witness testimony. The story of "Susanna and the Elders" may simply have been the most convenient authority that the judges could find to justify this new practice. In other words: bad analogical reasoning.

Muzzling Lawyers

In the Islamic legal system (a "natural law" system) called Shari'a, courts are investigative rather than adversarial. This means that the judges, who are

religious scholars, act largely as fact finders. Criminal defendants have no right to representation or to confront their accusers. But judges, as part of their fact-finding mission, review evidence and question witnesses on behalf of the accused. Lawyers have virtually no in-court role in criminal matters because judges believe they will obscure the truth. Shocking! This view of the relationship between lawyers and the truth is not, however, limited to the Middle East. Except in the case of treason, it was not until around 1700 that English lawyers for the defense could speak in court in criminal cases, and it was not until sometime after 1800 that they could cross-examine the prosecution's witnesses.

With the misuse of the story, confrontation of witnesses was diminished but not eliminated. A defendant still had the right to see the witnesses against him when they were brought to court to be sworn—that is, to take an oath before God to tell the truth. The one exception to this rule related to an inquisition involving alleged heresy, a crime so serious (in the Catholic Church's opinion) that the witness's safety would be endangered if the defendant even knew the witness's identity. Consequently, over the course of the thirteenth century it became standard practice not to produce accusing witnesses before a defendant who was up on heresy charges. His only procedural safeguard was that the inquisitor would ask him if he had any "enemies." If any of the named individuals were among the witnesses against him, their testimony, on the basis of bias, might be excluded. (I imagine that defendants frequently confessed to a long list of enemies.)

SUSANNA AND THE ELDERS AS CONTINUING "LEGAL PRECEDENT"

Lest you think that the foregoing issues are limited to the twelfth century, consider the New Deal "economic war" and the twenty-first-century "war on terrorism," with its detention of "enemy combatants."

During the Great Depression of the 1930s, the U.S. Congress enacted the National Industrial Recovery Act (NIRA) of 1933 (which controlled prices and wages in industry) and vested responsibility for carrying out its provisions in the National Recovery Administration (NRA). The NRA, in an effort to organize markets, was charged with formulating "codes of fair competition," interpreting existing codes, and issuing compliance regulations. In carrying out these "progressively" inspired tasks, the NRA was given the authority to hold hearings on negotiated codes, to approve codes, to allow changes in approved codes, and to formulate procedural rules that governed its own activity. And guess who Congress attempted to eliminate from much of this juicy legal work?

The NRA's sweeping discretionary powers were explicitly designed to cut out lawyers. The NIRA's explicit policy, according to one academic, "was to discourage the participation of lawyers in negotiations over codes of fair competition and to insist on the non-legalistic character of the NRA's hearings." Put another way, the NIRA, based on a notion that lawyers might be disruptive, was a "lawyer-unfriendly" administrative mechanism.

On September 11, 2001, the United States was attacked by a new type of enemy: a group of individuals of varying nationalities operating in various countries throughout the world, committed to acts of terrorism against U.S. citizens. The attacks by these Muslim extremists against the twin towers in New York City and the Pentagon in Washington, D.C. resulted in the United States government taking various actions. For our purposes the most relevant response was the government's position that "an American citizen alleged to be an enemy combatant . . . [can] be detained indefinitely without charges or counsel on the government's say-so!"

It appears that the government's concern was that affording access to a lawyer might impede the collection of intelligence. Much like the twelfth-century judges, the government of the early part of the twenty-first century appeared to want to keep lawyers from complicating and slowing down the process. And interestingly enough, the government, like the twelfth-century judges' misuse of "Susanna and the Elders," (arguably) justified its exclusion of lawyers by the misuse of earlier precedent.

The American Bar Association's August 2002 Task Force on Treatment on Enemy Combatants recognized that there was precedent for treating U.S. citizens as enemy combatants, but that any such categorization did not eliminate certain rule of law requirements. In a 1942 case, for example, German soldiers smuggled themselves into the United States, hid their uniforms, and planned acts of sabotage. These individuals were arrested, prosecuted for what were regarded as crimes of war, convicted, and sentenced. The Task Force, however, pointed out that this case may not provide the overall precedential value claimed by the government. In particular, the Task Force argued that the case "does not stand for the proposition that detainees may be held incommunicado and denied access to counsel, since the [German] defendants . . . were able to seek review and they were represented by counsel."

In contrast to this questioning tone, it is interesting to note the American Bar Association's support of the NIRA, as well as other recovery laws of the Great Depression. Clarence Martin, then ABA president, in discussing the growing wave of New Deal legislation, concluded that a state of emergency (an "economic war") justified putting ends before means: "In the absence of court decisions, which are probable, it would be unfair, as well as impolitic, at this moment, to argue or attempt a determination of the constitutional questions involved in, and the legal effort of, this legislation. Eliminating these matters [meaning the possible unconstitutionality of such legislation], as a temporary expedient, should have the support of this association." Additionally, one academic has observed that "[m]any lawyers adopted the emergency rationale that government lawyers used to justify the enactment of the NIRA. The perceived state of emergency and its unavoidable link to the patriotic duties of the profession was another major factor that circumscribed the 'professional' tendency to criticize the law." Apparently, the war on terrorism has not so moved the American Bar Association—or certain lawyers—to "circumscribe the 'professional' tendency to criticize the law." Good!

An important point raised in the twelfth century, the twentieth century, and the twenty-first century is that lawyers, as I warned you right from the start, have the nasty habit of asking questions, pursuing factual and legal matters, and pressing arguments—in other words, complicating things. The elimination of lawyers can indeed lead to a certain kind of institutional efficiency, but then so does summary confiscation of property, as well as arrest and punishment without all that messy stuff called proof. And if you insist on proof, the twelfth century judge's response was: Trust me, I'll get it; and in modern times, the government's response is: Trust us, we'll get it. So who do you trust?

V

JEWISH LAW AND JEWISH LAWYERS:
Torah! Torah! Torah!

In our wide-ranging search for the origin of lawyers, we will discover that the first true "lawyers" were not Jewish (or English, or New Yorkers) but, in very broad terms, Greek and hence, pagan. Nevertheless, the importance of Jewish attitudes, values, and law on the rise of the lawyer class—becoming increasingly Judeo-Christian over the years—cannot be overstated.

Rules and Law

It is said that the biblical Hebrews did not actually have a word for "law" as an abstract concept. The biblical word most often translated as "law," *tora (Torah)*, actually means teaching. Thus, *tora* expresses the morally and socially didactic nature of God's demands. Likewise, a technical term for "law" itself did not exist in Mesopotamia or ancient Greece. One reason for this is that the notion of "law" (in contrast to specific laws) is an abstract concept and ancient knowledge was generally concrete in nature. The arguments regarding the lack of an abstract concept for "law" in certain ancient—as well as some modern—societies could be the result of a failure to locate and understand the applicable conceptual metaphors. Maybe there was no word because there was always a handy set of rules to refer to, and not so much, as in modern times, a body of knowledge open to further thought and interpretation.

It has been observed, for example, that Jewish emphasis on justice led to the creation of a system of criminal trials with a heavy procedural and evidential burden placed upon the prosecution; consider, for example, the tediousness of the televised O.J. Simpson trial. Consequently, an accused, at least historically, could not waive his right against self-incrimination. (In contrast, there are the *Miranda* warnings mumbled in every American cop show: "Everything you say can and will be used against you in a court of law and blah, blah, blah.") Testimony by the accused, in-court or out-of-court, voluntary or coerced, spontaneous or elicited, that tended to incriminate was supposed to be disregarded by the court. In contrast, the medieval (non-Jewish) European handling of "misstatements" was less straightforward. A party who had made an unfortunate statement or admission could deny the statement, but only if he brought forward at least two individuals to swear with him against the united recollections and records of the court. There was also the possibility of bad-mouthing the lawyer.

In some systems of medieval jurisprudence, the use of witnesses could be avoided by insisting on the engagement of a lawyer, whose assertions were not binding on the client. (This is generally not the case in modern-day American jurisprudence, in which *nescit vox missa reverti*—"a word once uttered cannot be recalled.") Consequently, if the lawyer "misspoke," all the client had to do was to point out that his lawyer is a fool or insane, or both. In England, for example, it was not uncommon for medieval litigants to disavow what their serjeant (a professional pleader) had said. As a result, the use of a serjeant, instead of going it alone, allowed a litigant to increase his chances of avoiding the pitfalls lurking in the mass of technical rules. In France, this practice of bad-mouthing the lawyer had a twist: an advocate's assertions were binding on the client—unless contradicted on the spot.

In contrast, the ancient Jewish criminal system, with its exceptionally strict rules of procedure, placed almost insurmountable obstacles in the way of a judiciary out to convict a defendant. "You found him holding the sword, blood dripping, the murdered man writhing," says the Talmud; "if that is all, you saw nothing." This check on deduction and coercive power (i.e., elimination of unfair advantage) is not part of a balancing test but can be seen from a conceptual point of view: Obedience to the law should not flow simply from threats of punishment, but from the love of God and only secondarily from fear of divine punishment. In addition, the Jews, unlike the pagan polytheists, did not see good gods as responsible for good things and evil ones as responsible for bad things. In Judaism, there is only one God, full of divine justice. Therefore man himself is responsible for his acts and he cannot blame them on the gods—except perhaps metaphorically: "The Devil made me do it." No Original Sin in Judaism!

From Rabbi to Constitution

The Talmudic rule against self-incrimination can be traced into the canonical law as the maxim that "no one [is] required to reveal his own shame." The rule then shows up in the *glossa ordinaria* to the Gregorian *Decretals* and in sixteenth- and seventeenth-century treatises on civil procedure. From rabbinic, canonical, and civil law, the rule seeped into the English common law and into the Fifth Amendment to the United States Constitution.

THE FORMATION OF JEWISH LAW, BIBLE TO TALMUD

In light of the importance of Jewish thought on the modern-day lawyer class, we need to take a quick look at Jewish law. Jewish law is described by the term *halakha* (from the Hebrew for "law," derived from the verb *to go*). This term designates both the system of law—the codes and legal decisions—developed over 3,000 years, and the concept of a single rule of law. The Halakha, said to rest upon the twin principles of God's sovereignty and the sacredness of the person (or more technically, the ethics of the Torah and the prophets), comprises the entire subject matter of Jewish law, including public, private, and ritual.

Jewish biblical law, a cornerstone of Halakha, traditionally consists of the written law and the oral law—both of which were given by God to Moses in the Bible. The five books of Moses are often referred to as the Torah (literally, "teaching"), and in orthodox Jewish discourse the Torah is called the written law because, in traditional accounts, Moses wrote it down at God's request. Each book sets out detailed codes of law (for example, the Covenant Code in Exodus; the Holiness Code in Leviticus; and the Deuteronomic Code in Deuteronomy), specifically including 613 *mitzvoth* (commandments) revealed to Moses on Mount Sinai—not just ten. "Torah" may also refer to the entire contents of the Hebrew Bible, including the five books of Moses (Genesis,

Exodus, Leviticus, Numbers, and Deuteronomy), the Prophets, and the Writings. Finally, the word *Torah,* based on the notion of teaching, often refers to the entire content of divine revelation and, by extension, to all the teaching of the Jewish legal tradition.

The Torah is the written law portion of Jewish biblical law; rabbinic literature is the oral half. Rabbinic literature is frequently referred to as "tannaitic," from *tanna,* an Aramaic word for one who remembers or studies, a repeater. During the period of the Tanna'im (50 BCE–220 CE), professional "rememberers" were chosen to transmit to succeeding generations the oral traditions (the Oral Torah) they had received from preceding generations. Ultimately, however, these scholars, who were active during the early Roman Empire, found it necessary to organize and collate this material and then reduce it to writing, thereby shifting media. This switch in metaphor from Memory Is Writing to Writing Is Memory arose because existing political strife made learning difficult (particularly given the decline in the number of knowledgeable Jews), the volume of material generated over the years was substantial, and the emergence of different schools of interpretation threatened to undermine the uniformity of the material and to impede its effective conveyance. In other words, there was a rise of diversity generators and intergroup tournaments over conformity enforcers, creating a critical instability that lead to the emergence of novelty: a written oral tradition.

In about 200 CE, Rabbi Judah ha-Nasi (c. 135–220 CE), who you will recall was a bit ticked at Solomon's threat to split the baby, finished editing and arranging tannaitic material into a compilation of discussions and statements about Jewish law called the Mishnah, considered to be the first document of rabbinical Judaism and second in importance and sanctity only to the Written Torah. The word *mishnah* stems from the Hebrew root meaning "to repeat," suggesting oral teaching, and is a written compilation of sixty-three tractates (treatises), arranged topically into six main sections and containing all the detailed laws and observances that had developed out of the Torah. The Mishnah provides detailed codes, laws, and regulations that govern agriculture ("Seeds"), the calendar ("Feasts"), family law ("Women"), torts, commercial law, criminal law, the structure of the judiciary ("Damages"), religious rites at the temple and synagogue ("Holiness"), and the maintenance of ritual purity under all circumstances ("Cleanliness"). The scholars of the Mishnaic era are known as Tanna'im.

With regard to the possible impact of the Mishnah on the evolution of lawyers, it is important to note that while this document looks like a code of rules, it is really something else. The text, for example, takes a great deal for granted and consequently requires more elucidation than it supplies—arguably a recognition that meaning is motivated and not static. It also fails to tell the reader how its contents might actually be put into practice—not unlike, to the benefit of lawyers, many modern statutes and cases. That is, the Mishnah correctly implies that context and purpose are essential to meaning—all "apples" are not the same.

What the Mishnah does, instead of merely stating an offense and its punishment, is to cover the main themes of Jewish life in a way that teaches the important point that human life is one of constant study. Thus the Mishnah has given rise to (or at least advanced) a tradition of careful, detailed text-study and interpretation—something carried out by medieval legal scholars and something that is of ever increasing importance to lawyers in our modern age of written constitutions, statutes, and regulations.

The next three centuries, from 200 CE to 500 CE, were dominated by the Amora'im (*amora*, Aramaic for "discusser"). These scholars, working away in the academies of Jewish communities in Mesopotamia and Palestine, debated and reconciled the rulings of the Tanna'im. Their records comprise the Gemara, commentaries on the Mishnah, and Tosefta (*Tosefta* means "supplement" and is a collection of interpretations of the Judaic laws in the Mishnah). The Gemara elaborates on the Mishnah, including both omitted material and confusing points. Together the Mishnah, Tosefta, and Gemara compose the Talmud, written in a mix of Hebrew and Aramaic. There are, in fact, two Talmuds. The first, edited in the Palestinian academies, is referred to as the Jerusalem or Palestinian Talmud (c. 425 CE). The second, more comprehensive version (6,000 large pages), was completed about a century or two later at the academies of Babylonia, and is therefore referred to as the Babylonian Talmud. This version, for various reasons, has long been of primary importance. The Talmud(s), somewhat like the minutes of a millennium-plus religious study session, interprets the laws and regulates all aspects of daily living and interaction.

It has been emphasized by a number of Jewish scholars that study of the Talmud is very difficult. This is due to both the material and its form: the mode of arguing and reasoning, wide-ranging associations, curt and allusive formulation, broad scope, and the intermingling of themes and concepts. All of this leads, in the jargon of contemporary scholarship, to an entire complicating complex of philological-historical-phenomenological problems. (Wow, this sounds a lot like law school—despite the traditional assumption that legal reasoning must be linear.)

POST-TALMUD JEWISH LEGAL SCHOLARSHIP

The final piece of significant material produced in the Talmudic period is referred to as midrash. This work, produced between 400 and 1200 CE, is, in one context, a line-by-line interpretation of the Hebrew Bible. There are two main types of midrash: *midrashei halakha,* which are legal exegeses of biblical passages, and *midrashei aggadah,* traditionally defined as interpretations of everything in tannaitic and amoraic literature that is not Halakha—this includes biblical narratives, parables, legends, homilies, and allegories.

Even though not strictly "legal" interpretations, *midrashei aggadah* have been used to highlight the importance of narrative and interpretation in modern-day legal practice. Steven L. Winter in *A Clearing in the Forest—Law, Life, and Mind,* for example, has demonstrated how the midrash of Abraham and the smashing of his father's idols can be read, not unlike many stories of legal import, in two different ways, both of which conform to the story's text. It's an acknowledgment that what's being done is an interpretation of an interpretive work. Each of the competing interpretations, he points out, is constructed relative to the different cognitive models used to organize the story's meaning. The traditional interpretation is created by viewing the midrash from within a paradigm of faith in the One True God. A revisionist interpretation could be created by reading the same story through the lens of a modern, Freudian paradigm—that this midrash is about rivalry between father and son.

Judaism also has a tradition of codification. The earliest attempts at creating Jewish codes date from the centuries following the completion of the Talmud. From the give and take of legal debate, the authors of the various codes extracted normative rulings and attempted to present them in a nice, neat package. A major achievement in codification is the *Mishneh Torah* (Repetition of the Law) of Rabbi Moshe ben Maimon (1135–1204 CE). This work was followed by the comprehensive and authoritative code called the *Shulhan Arukh* ("The Prepared Table") by Rabbi Joseph Caro (1488–1575 CE), which provides instruction on such things as eating, sleeping, praying, bathing, and sex. Jewish codes are not, however, codes in the Continental, civil law sense—Jewish works do not supersede preexisting law nor do they purport to be the exclusive source of law. A Jewish code of law is said to resemble a restatement of the law; in other words, it contains the author's view of the law, arranged systematically, stated concisely, and aiming for completeness.

⊗ · ⊗

King Codifiers

Rabbi Moshe ben Maimon, or Maimonides, also known as the RaMBaM, was a noted twelfth-century commentator, codifier, philosopher, and physician who lived in Spain, Morocco, and Egypt. His key work, the fourteen-volume *Mishneh Torah,* occupies a central position in the overall development of rabbinic literature. And in broad generalization, this work became a prism through which reflection and analysis of virtually all subsequent study of the Talmud had to (and in some circles, still has to) pass.

Rabbi Joseph Caro was a sixteenth-century codifier and mystic who lived in Turkey and Israel. In putting together the *Shulhan Arukh*, Rabbi Caro frequently relied on court decisions. Hundreds of decisions by Rabbi Isaac ben Sheshet Perfet (known as Ribash, 1326–1408 CE), for example, were incorporated into the code. Ribash was chief rabbi of Algiers and head of its rabbinical court. In fact, with regard to the O.J. Simpson case previously discussed, one of his *responsa* contains the first known explicit reference, at least with regard to Halakha, to the hermeneutic rule: "the lesser evil."

PROFITS AND PREJUDICE

As is evident from the foregoing overview, there is a strong emphasis in Judaism on the Law (or, at least, on the laws). This emphasis, accompanied by an aptitude for debate, has undoubtedly helped prepare many Jewish people, over the centuries, to become very able lawyers. Somewhat ironically, however, discrimination against Jews serving as lawyers (as well as judges and law professors) was prevalent both before and after the period when Jewish people were finally allowed to become citizens of various European countries. Austria, for example, barred Jews from obtaining state-paid posts in its judiciary. Jews in eastern Europe were even more restricted in their opportunities within the law. Nevertheless, they were, despite such obstacles—or perhaps because of such obstacles—a strong force within many European legal circles prior to the time of Hitler's political rise. Notable among Jewish lawyers of the day were Joseph von Sonnenfels (1732–1817), a legal reformer under the Hapsburg Empress Maria Teresa (1717–1780), and Hans Kelsen (1881–1973), the great legal philosopher who, until fleeing the Nazis, taught in Vienna and drafted the Constitution of the post–World War I Austrian Republic.

At the time of Hitler's rise, Jews were gradually excluded from the practice of law. Their elimination from the legal profession within the area of Hitler's influence even extended to such "questionable characters" as the non-Jewish lawyer who continued to consult a Jewish physician, to whose treatment the lawyer owed her life. And in 1938 the remaining Jewish lawyers were reclassified as "Jewish legal advisers." It was then shouted by some, "The German guardian of the law for the German! The Jewish adviser for the Jew! Once again German lawyers can take pride in the title of attorney!"

Americans are not, however, in any position to take an attitude of moral superiority. It was not that long ago that the doors of most New York law firms were closed to Jewish lawyers. On Wall Street, firms practicing corporate, patent, and maritime law were filled exclusively with white Christian males. Jewish lawyers, considered to be outside this "goodness-of-example," were essentially confined to areas of law that "white-shoe" firms had no desire to handle: real estate, negligence law, hostile takeovers, and the nasty business of litigation. True gentlemen settled disputes in the conference room—and not in court.

It was after World War I that a rise in predominantly Jewish corporate and financial clientele made possible the growth of Jewish law firms. And if Jewish lawyers could make money from Jewish businessmen—welcome to the brotherhood. Remember, for example, even those nice Jewish boys Meyer Lansky and Bugsy Siegel joined forces in the 1930s with that nice Italian boy Lucky Luciano (an example of the fact that elimination of an arbitrary barrier [i.e. ethnicity] can assist in taking advantage of positive network externalities). Where business leads, lawyers (and mobsters) follow, prejudices and all.

There was still, however, deeply ingrained social and professional anti-Semitism at work in society's less money-oriented sectors. In 1922, for example, the Yale University Board of Admissions (ruling over a nonprofit institution) was very concerned about "the Jewish problem." There was also strong opposition to the appointment of Felix Frankfurter (1882–1965), one of President Roosevelt's trusted and influential advisers, to the United States Supreme Court, despite the fact that his appointment was meant to replace the "Jewish seat" held by Justice Benjamin Cardozo, who had died in 1938. The cost of discrimination in the Ivy League and Supreme Court was arguably much less than it was for law firms missing out on billable hours. The truth is that money is largely race, religion, and sex neutral. And, as the Roman Emperor Vespasian taught his son Titus, money has no odor—even when collected as a tax on urine.

The law, from the time of Moses, has been a magnet for Jews who desire to improve society. Once emancipated in France, England, and Germany after WWII, Jews found the legal profession an attractive avenue for earning money and achieving social justice in Europe, and, after years of emigration, in America. Louis Marshall, a famous trial lawyer, believed that respect for law is "one of the abiding virtues of the Jewish People." Like the ancient prophets, Marshall zealously pursued justice and did so within the framework of an appreciation of Jewish law and its heritage.

A true "Jewish lawyer" is one who, steeped in the knowledge of Jewish law, respects and applies Jewish traditions. He or she manifests the holiness of being Jewish in daily life and is an educated, committed Jew by virtue of that knowledge and practice of Halakha.

VI

THE SADDUCEES, THE PHARISEES,

AND THOSE NEW TESTAMENT LAWYERS

EVEN A CASUAL READER OF THE BIBLE might be quick to point out that even if there were no "real" lawyers mentioned in the Old Testament, there were certainly lawyers at the time of Jesus—and, in fact, he had nothing good to say about them. With regard to the existence or nonexistence of lawyers in the New Testament, we need to start with the Sadducees and Pharisees.

The title "Sadducee" (Hebrew: *Zedukim*) was derived from the name Zadok, the High Priest in the days of King David, circa 1000 BCE. The Sadducees were active in public life and dominated temple worship. After struggling to maintain group identity, the Sadducaic movement eventually disintegrated. The most generally accepted explanation for its demise revolves around the destruction of the Second Temple, the rebuilt Temple in Jerusalem, in 70 CE by the Romans. Because the Sadducees were headquartered in the temple, they were no longer, according to this theory, able to function after its destruction. A somewhat more intriguing theory, grounded in the notion of intergroup tournament, is that the demise was engineered by the Pharisees. The theory goes that the Pharisaic hakhamim (an organized

51

body of rabbinic scholars) plotted to kick out the Sadducees from the Temple sometime around 60 CE, and were eventually successful.

The Pharisee versus Sadducee confrontation was rolled up in the question of who should control the institutions of the Temple, priesthood, and government after the successful Maccabean revolt. The revolt, around 240 years before the destruction of the Temple, was led by a prominent family (the Maccabees) against the Syrian king Antiochus Epiphanes. Many Jews, especially among the upper classes, favored the idea of participating fully in the privileges of Hellenistic society available only to Greek citizens—the Sadducees. Other Jews, perhaps a majority of the population of Jerusalem and the countryside, detested these "Hellenizing Jews" as traitors to God—the Pharisees.

Over the next 200 years, the Pharisaic ideology acted to combat Hellenistic influences prevalent in Palestine—such as shocking displays of public nudity. And following the Maccabean revolt, the Pharisees appear to have become more formally organized—indeed, they seem to have initially held some sway over how things were run. But John Hyrcanus, leader of the powerful Hasmonean family who eventually took over after the revolt, split with the Pharisees over his embrace of Greek culture and the Pharisees were subsequently expelled from membership in the Sanhedrin (the governing religious body) by the Sadducees.

The Pharisees were characterized by scholarship and intellectual pursuits, hence the label "Separate Ones." The Apostle Paul, upon being summoned to the Sanhedrin in 60 CE to answer charges of illegal conduct, stated that he was "a Pharisee, the son of a Pharisee."

The Pharisees, in the complex intergroup tournament of the time, ultimately came out on top—be it from nefarious plotting or the Roman destruction of the Second Temple. And after the demise of the Sadducees, the Pharisees successfully consolidated their support, in effect becoming the Jewish sect. History ruled in their favor and therefore it is their traditions that are preserved in the Talmud.

Back to the question of lawyers' existence or nonexistence in the New Testament: Consider the Book of Luke, Chapter 11. In this chapter of the King James Version of the Bible, Jesus is chastising a variety of people for their hypocrisy. A nearby "lawyer" speaks up and asks: "What about us?" Jesus replies: "Woe unto you also, ye lawyers! For ye lade men with burdens grievous to be borne, and ye yourselves touch not the burdens with one of your fingers. . . . Woe unto you, lawyers! for ye have taken away the key of knowledge: ye entered not in yourselves, and them that were entering in ye hindered."

This sounds bad: the immortal souls of lawyers appear to be in grave danger. In fact, eternally damned. But wait! Setting aside that such alleged attacks by Jesus might be inauthentic (and somewhat un-Christian), the problem is that the word "lawyer" does not mean lawyer in the modern sense. The word in this biblical passage is translated into English from the Greek word *nomikos,* which, although literally meaning "lawyer," is biblically equivalent to "scribe" or "Pharisee." Either of these terms is best understood as referring to the religious leadership of Jesus' day. In other words, the Jewish scribe (generally a Pharisee's agent and assistant) was not really a legal advocate for hire but a scholar and intellectual of Judaism—a "rabbi." Jesus' attack is therefore not technically upon "lawyers" but upon the religious leadership of Jerusalem. Thank heavens!

PART II

PAGAN
TIMES

IT MIGHT COME AS A BIT OF A SHOCK that there appears to be no explicit connection between the law in biblical tradition and the rise of the lawyer class as we know it today. There is a simple explanation for this: In ancient times, "Law" was primarily religious. In other words, it came from God. As a result, "legal issues" called for the wisdom of an astrologer, oracle, priest, prophet, king or judge—not the natterings of a lawyer.

There is, however, the duty, frequently mentioned in the Bible, of the rich to look out for the poor. Scholarship has taken this responsibility to include those persons who were without juridical status; for example, people whose lack of land possession rendered them not fully recognized citizens of the "state." Consequently, they could not carry a complaint against a full citizen before a judge unless they were supported by a full citizen—one who would take it upon himself to protect the underdog's rights. Such persons were not, however, professional legal practitioners. The closest the biblical tradition gets to the idea of a lawyer, which arguably is very close in certain respects, is the scribe. (Modesty prevents me from pointing out that the lawyer class might also be tied to the tradition of prophets, crying out for justice. Thank heaven for apophasis.)

As we turn, however, from the Bible to the pagan tradition, there are several obvious factors that significantly aided in the birth and development of the modern-day lawyer class. The first has to do with the secularization of the law—something that happened in ancient Greece. The second relates to paganism's nonexclusivity.

PAGANS AND THE CASE METHOD

The typical modern-day lawyer receives his or her formal legal training in law school. And one of the principal training techniques, particularly in the United States, involves the case method: the study of law through the medium of written, judicial decisions that have been rendered in actual disputes. This teaching method presents the student with the opportunity to view a dispute by playing the role of the various parties to the litigation. All too frequently, however, the viewpoint is limited to that of the court, with the student's blood-pounding attention focused on attempting to explain and critique the judge's written decision. But it sometimes occurs to the professor to disrobe his or her students and actually force them to consider the litigation from the lawyer's, the client's, and society's perspectives. Each of these tasks, at least in theory, requires the student to face different intellectual and emotional challenges—helping to develop that important, but illusive, lawyering skill known as "practical wisdom."

The case method is intended to strengthen not only the students' ability to reason, but also their powers of sympathetic and empathetic understanding for different viewpoints and, in theory, to suppress their own biases. Most important, however, this method is said to increase students' tolerance for the disorientation that movement between and among different attitudes can cause, by training them (at least in theory) to skillfully move back and forth and up and down a particular moral-political issue or system that is not their own without spewing chunks.

Empathy in Your Toolbox

How does empathy help a lawyer? There are two schools of thought on this question. The first states that empathy, the ability to put yourself in someone else's shoes and feel what that person is feeling, creates that important sense of duty toward others that lawyers need. Also, arguably, the person who understands how two contending parties feel is in a better position to help in compromising their dispute than a person who cannot empathize with the disputants. Thus, psychopaths might not make the best lawyers—except when it comes to billable hours.

The second take on empathy is grounded not in morality, but in utility. The ability to emphasize with a client is a tool, among many others, that helps the lawyer to be a better lawyer—but not necessarily to be a "better" person. Kant, in fact, pushed this point even further. Acting out of empathy is a mode of action that he thought "is without any moral worth." The reason is that empathy is based on feeling and does not follow from any directive of reason.

So perhaps the answer to the question is that a lawyer should use his heart only in conjunction with his head.

So how does the case method relate to paganism? The answer lies in the notion of nonexclusivity (a diversity generator). Unlike exclusive religions, Judaism for example, nonexclusive religions, like paganism, are accepting of other gods—and hence generally tolerant of the religious practices and moral precepts required by such gods (a type of non-zero-sumness). In the context of ancient Greek cults, for example, various inscriptions show people with numerous concurrent allegiances. This attitude of relative openness, in conjunction with the secularization of the law, undoubtedly aided in the creation and development of the lawyer class that "started" in ancient (pagan) Greece and gained steam in ancient (pagan) Rome. And the case method, like paganism in general—the gods often fought with each other and with humans—has the capacity to create an appreciation of the frequent incommensurability of values, or at least the dynamics that give rise to claims of incommensurability. This capacity, however, to see points of view that previously seemed wrong or unfair sometimes comes with a price: the dulling or displacement of earlier convictions.

In the case of paganism, this capacity for an appreciation of other gods and various religious practices undoubtedly contributed to its demise in the face of conformity-enforcing Christianity. But in conjunction with the increasing secularization of the law, the nonexclusive attitude of paganism arguably makes possible that sense of critical (scientific?) detachment from one's personal commitments that is, at least arguably, essential to good lawyering.

The Gods Must Be Crazy

Because the gods were always quarrelling with each other, Zeus, sovereign of the gods, set up a dispute resolution mechanism. If a quarrel arose that might become dangerous, the Olympian gods were brought together for a feast. Styx, a Titan goddess, was also invited. She brought with her a golden ewer (pitcher) filled with the water from the river of Hades. The two deities in conflict would take hold of the ewer and pour some water onto the ground. They then made a libation. While drinking, each would swear under oath that he (or she) was not responsible for the quarrel; that he was in the right. One of the two was bound to be lying, and as soon as the lying god swallowed the sacred water, he fell into a coma. He was certainly not clinically dead, for Greek gods do not die, but he lost everything connected to his nature as a god for a very long time.

VII

THE DEVELOPMENT OF ANCIENT LAW:

OLD BONES, OLD LAWYERS

LAWS SET DOWN IN THE BIBLE take one of two forms: apodictic (absolute, divine prohibitions, such as "Thou shall not kill") and casuistic ("If a man delivers to his neighbor money or goats to keep, and it is stolen out of the man's house, then, if the thief is found, he shall pay double"). Apodictic laws are incontestable duties—thou shalt not—while casuistic laws are conditional—an if/then statement.

This traditional notion of biblical primacy regarding the development of law has, thus far, generally guided our search for the origin of lawyers. As it turns out, however, archaeologists claim to have discovered even older laws, wrapped up in highly sophisticated legal systems, and therefore the possibility exists of unearthing the remains of pre-biblical lawyers. Let's roll up our sleeves and start digging.

LAWS OF UR-NAMMU

In the 1950s and 1960s, archaeologists discovered three tablets of laws apparently from the mouth of King Shulgi, the oldest son of King

Ur-Nammu, founder of the Third Dynasty of Ur (c. 2113–2006 BCE). The city of Ur was located in southern Mesopotamia (present-day Iraq), the ancient country of southwest Asia between the Tigris and Euphrates rivers. These laws are, to date, among the earliest known laws, and if nothing else they are evidence of the antiquity of the human idea that written law can be used for social control. None of Shulgi's tablets, however, are complete. The recovered text first accounts for his divine rise to power as "king of the lands of Sumer and Akkad," and then goes on to highlight his attack on prior abusive taxation policies (there truly is nothing new under the sun), and his establishment of standard weights and measures. On the heels of such reforms follows a policy statement by Shulgi regarding exploitation of the economically weak by the strong: "I did not deliver the orphan over to the rich man; the widow to the mighty man; the man of one shekel to the man of one mina; the man with one lamb to the man with one ox."

Note the use of the first person singular: "I." At this point in time, the law was not conceived of as an object. In other words, it was not a *corpus juris* (a body of law) that saw, heard, and spoke (especially to lawyers), but was the ruler himself. It was the king (not reified law) that maintained a grip, refusing to deliver the weak over to the strong—the Strict Father figure.

At the beginning of an ancient ruler's reign, it was not unusual for him to abolish the debts of the working class, whose precarious socioeconomic conditions made them very dependent upon the rich elite. This type of Nurturant Parent gesture, as you might imagine, bought the new ruler a fair amount of goodwill from the masses—not unlike modern-day mortgage-debt-relief legislation. It did nothing good, however, for the concepts of secure property rights and the sanctity of contract. But these important legal-economic concepts were not all that well developed at this stage in human social development. (Not enough lawyers?)

The speculation is that the laws of Ur-Nammu (at least as preserved in writing) were records of decisions by, or under the authority of, the king in actual cases. This scholarly guess is based upon their somewhat miscellaneous subject-matter organization—a type of common law (versus civil law) codification approach. Further support for this notion can be found in the fact that the land of Sumer provides us, outside of a biblical context, with the first recorded case law precedent—a murder trial. This evil deed was committed around 1850 BCE by three men: a barber, a gardener, and someone whose occupation is unknown (but seemingly not a lawyer). These men killed a temple priest by the name of Lu-Inanna. The killers, for some strange reason, then informed the victim's wife, Nin-dada, that they had murdered Lu-Inanna and told her to keep her mouth shut. She agreed.

Despite the wife holding her silence, the crime was eventually discovered and brought to the attention of the king, who was residing in the post-Ur capital of Isin. King Ur-Ninurta turned the matter over to the Assembly at Nippur, the religious center of Sumer, for trial.

Nine men in the Assembly took on the role of prosecution. They argued that not only should the three killers be executed, but also the wife. Their theory, with regard to Nin-dada, appears to have been that in a situation involving murder, silence is not golden. The prosecutors argued, from a modern-day point of view, that the wife should be considered an accessory after the fact.

On behalf of the wife, two men in the Assembly pointed out that she had taken no part in the murder itself. The rule regarding murder is conceptually a unique path—and her defenders, in effect, argued that she was never on it. In other words, on the path she was traveling, there were no dead bodies.

The Elders then addressed the Assembly: "If a wife has no respect for her husband's life, it may be because she's already slept with another man. That other man may murder her husband knowing she would never tell. Why else would she keep silent? More than anyone else she's the one who caused her husband's death, and she bears the most guilt!" The devastating "logic" of this reasoned argument convinced the Assembly.

Having resolved the issue on the basis of socially persuasive concepts of sex, silence, and murder, Nanna-sig (occupation unknown), Ku-Enlila (the barber), Enlilennam (the gardener), and Nin-dada (the wife) were all sentenced to death.

Two partial copies of this case have been dug up. The fact that this case was written down at least twice has led scholars to conclude that the decision of the Nippur Assembly regarding the "silent wife" was considered, within the legal circles of Sumer, to be an important precedent. There are, in fact, more than 300 known court records (*ditillas*: completed lawsuits) detailing legal procedures and social and economic organization from the days of Sumer. And this practice of lawyers buzzing around precedents is, all these thousands of years later, still with us. Under the common law (defined here briefly as a body of prior cases) current decisions are, at least in theory, generally required to follow prior decisions but may, through a mixture of reasoning and mystery, be distinguished from such precedents. The lawyers trained in this system do not, however, often think of, or even have access to, the reality of the cases they are relying on or distinguishing, but pay attention only to the printed version of what is said to have occurred. As a result, it is generally forgotten that the printed opinion is merely a representation of reality—often created to fit certain image-schemas and conceptual metaphors through leveling, sharpening, and assimilation—that becomes the law's reified reality.

The invention of writing, undoubtedly a key element in the evolution of the lawyer class, most likely occurred near the end of the fourth millennium BCE—a gift from the gods under the patronage of Enki, God of Wisdom. It has been observed that this important development was prompted by the rather mundane need in Mesopotamia to record and administer the economic operations of large institutional households such as royal courts and temples. These households owned and managed arable land, the primary source of wealth at the time. The resulting control over agricultural production gave rise to administrative documents, drawn up by scribes in the service of such households, aimed at keeping track of daily, monthly, and annual operations. These scribes developed and passed down their own administrative terminology, as well as the particular forms of record tablets.

In addition to accounting-type documents, student scribes received training at the *edubba* ("House of Tablets") in the preparation of legal documents. These documents played an important role in recognizing and defining forms of ownership of arable land and systems of land tenure (the extremely significant legal concept of "real property"). And it was the scribe, generally employed by a government or temple representative and following the legal formularies he (and some shes) learned in school, who prepared documents involving such things as purchase agreements, leases, and pledges—the extremely significant legal concept of "contract." A scribe during the Third Dynasty of Ur might have been called on—not unlike a modern-day transactional lawyer—to prepare a purchase and sales contract. This type of document contained the object of the transaction with its physical and legal description, its price, the buyer's and seller's names, and the operative verbs for buying and for taking the object into possession. The document, not unlike any good and expensive modern-day legal document, sometimes continued on with a number of additional clauses recording the payment of the price, the completion of the deed, the symbolic act of having, for example, the slave (the "object" of the sale) pass over a pestle, and the delivery of the object. The document might also contain no-contest, eviction, and delinquency clauses, all confirmed by an oath. A guarantee and royal approval, from an official of the palace, might even be included. The document required the name of the witnesses in whose presence the deed was concluded, and frequently mentioned the location of the transaction and the date when the document was written.

Law, Accounting, and Decapitation

It is interesting to consider this seemingly integrated "accounting" and "legal" training received by student scribes in the context of the modern-day scandals of big business: Enron, WorldCom, Adelphia, Tyco, Bernard Madoff, and on and on and on. As a result of such fraudulent financial and legal activities certain academics have proposed a "radical" corrective action: Teach lawyers more accounting and teach financial business students more law—a return to the beginning. However, don't get too excited about the overall effectiveness of this fix. As one legal scholar has pointed out, the problem is not really the lack of knowledge about technical accounting and legal rules but a corporate and legal culture that has, at times, lost all sense of right and wrong. My specu- lation is that most of the ancient scribes acquired a deep sense of right and wrong after watching a wrongdoer's head rolling around on the ground.

❈ · ❈

On a more abstract level, the invention of writing (as we saw with the Jews and their move from the purely oral into the written, and as we will see with many other cultures and civilizations) provided law with a new space. Through inscription, that which was spoken and heard could also become that which was seen. This additional space for law had, and continues to have, important consequences for the distribution of social power. As discussed above, involve- ment with the written law, created by the "government," became increasingly the task of those with specialized training: the scribes. And in modern times, the law has become even more impenetrable for many people: a vast and time- less universe of paper, statutes, precedent, and archives, which in the twenty- first century continues to push further and further into cyberspace. It has there- fore become, at least for the foreseeable future, the province of those specialized finders and interpreters of legal texts: the lawyers.

As can be seen by the laws of Ur-Nammu, the Lu-Inanna murder case, and the wide-ranging use of scribes, Sumer was a competitive, materialistic land that had laws and an institutional structure for their enforcement—a glim- mer of the rule of law. In fact, it has been argued that Sumer (along with other Mesopotamian civilizations) had a significant influence on many aspects, spe- cifically including laws and legal institutions, of ancient Greece and Rome. Nevertheless, there is no mention, per se, of lawyers in Ur-Nammu's piece of the Fertile Crescent—but, of course, this was a "primitive" society.

Laws of Lipit-Ishtar

The laws of Lipit-Ishtar followed those of Ur-Nammu, around 1934–1924 BCE. They were written in Sumerian, by then a dead language. This ruler, Lipit-Ishtar, hailed from Isin—a city that rose to power in southern Mesopotamia after the fall of the Third Dynasty of Ur, the same Ur founded by King Ur-Nammu. The gods brought Lipit-Ishtar, fifth ruler of the First Dynasty of Isin (the first being Ishbi-Erra, Lipit-Ishtar's apparent great-great-grandfather), to power in order to establish justice and to bring well-being to the people of Sumer and Akkad—the earthly implementation of divine authority and protectiveness.

(As a quick—but important—aside: It is generally no longer believed that political decisions are handed down, directly or indirectly, from on high by omniscient beings who cannot err—to the extreme disappointment, I am sure, of King Lipit-Ishtar and the gods.)

The surviving evidence of the laws of Lipit-Ishtar, excavated from the city of Nippur, consists of a prologue (not unlike, in concept, the opening of the U.S. Declaration of Independence and the preamble to the U.S. Constitution) and an epilogue jointly acting as bookends for almost fifty provisions, about twenty of which are virtually complete and intelligible clauses—and almost all of which end up being echoed in the code of Hammurabi (discussed on page 65). The laws, focused predominantly on protecting an owner's right to property, cover a range of matters, including ownership of land, bailment, renting, runaway slaves (not unlike, in substance, the antebellum slave codes of the American South), inheritance, betrothal and marriage, and injury to hired animals—nothing, however, about lawyers. Obviously, this was still a very primitive society.

Laws of Eshnunna

Eshnunna was an Old Babylonian kingdom lying within the Diyala River valley and extending as far south as the Tigris. During excavations conducted between 1945 and 1949 near Baghdad, two almost duplicate tablets containing the laws from Eshnunna (c. 1770 BCE) were discovered. And a third witness to the collection, a student exercise tablet containing extracts, was excavated in the early 1980s. Like King Shulgi and Lipit-Ishtar, a god (here, Tishpak) assigned the right of authority and delegated the duty of protectiveness to the king—thereby establishing his legitimacy. The laws in this case are, however, often unattributed, but were possibly promulgated by (or sometime around the reign of) a ruler named Dadusha of Eshnunna (c. 1805–1780 BCE). Substantial parts of the tablets contain laws that are similar in substance to those famous laws of Hammurabi, but are about a century older.

The text of the laws of Eshnunna, written in Akkadian, indicate that a number of the laws developed out of an economic focus, not unlike the economic motivation found in the prologue of the laws of Ur-Nammu. For example, once an original economic rule (e.g., the hire of a harvester costs X amount of barley) spawned questions regarding that rule, it was only natural, in an attempt to rationally address such questions, to add decisions of further socioeconomic importance. For instance, a harvester's assistant (plough-keep?) costs one-half the amount of barley as the harvester.

The concerns of the time, not unlike those of King Shulgi, King Lipit-Ishtar, and some of today's rulers, included property rights, marriage rights and the rights of parents over unmarried females, and the protection of persons categorized as free citizens. Accordingly, the laws dealt primarily with theft and related crimes, marriage, divorce, sexual offenses, assault, bodily injury, death from neglect, contracts, rights over slaves, and the sale of property. But, unlike the laws of Shulgi and Lipit-Ishtar, they are introduced in a number of ways, including Johnnie Cochran's famous casuistic "If . . . then" statement, relative formations, and apodictic statements. "If the boatman is negligent and causes the boat to sink, [then] he shall restore as much as he caused to sink" (casuistic form). "A man who lends against its corresponding commodity (?) shall collect at the threshing floor" (relative form). "The son of a man who has not yet received his inheritance share or a slave will not be advanced credit" (apodictic form).

The collection is not highly systematized and therefore appears to have been developed on an ad hoc basis. And guess who's not mentioned?

LAWS OF HAMMURABI

In December 1901, French archaeological teams working in Susa, the ancient Elamite capital located in what is now southwest Iran, discovered a large piece of diorite stela. A month later, the entire black stone monument, seven and a half feet tall, was uncovered. The stela, topped by an imposing scene of the sun god Shamash (God of Justice), contains the law "code" compiled near the end of the forty-three-year reign of the Babylonian King Hammurabi (1792–1750 BCE), the sixth king in the First Dynasty of Babylon. The laws of Hammurabi, based on authority ultimately arising from the bearded, triple-horn-helmeted sun god, are the most famous code outside of the Bible. They were inscribed in Akkadian—the Semitic language of ancient Mesopotamia—and over all they sought to satisfy individual aspirations, while, at the same time, attempting to channel them, and to thereby preserve a strong state.

Laws About Rented Oxen

The laws of Ur-Nammu, Lipit-Ishtar, and Eshnunna are the most significant, but not the only, law collections predating the code of Hammurabi. Other collections, which are much less extensive or complete, include the law code of Bilalama; the Laws of X (c. 2050–1800 BCE), origin unknown, but perhaps belonging to Ur-Nammu's laws; Laws About Rented Oxen (c. 1800 BCE); Sumerian Laws Exercise Tablet (c. 1800 BCE); and Sumerian Laws Handbook of

Forms (c. 1700 BCE), a Sumerian compendium of contracts and contractual clauses, legal provisions comparable to those found in the law collections, as well as isolated phrases. There are several other minor law collections dating from before 1600 BCE.

✿ · ✿

The stela appears to have been taken to the Persian city of Susa as a treasure of war in the twelfth century BCE by Shutruk-Nahhunte I, a Middle Elamite ruler, or by his son and successor Kutir-Nahhunte. This was 600 years after it had been first erected, probably in the temple of the Babylonian city of Sippar, by the Amorite ruler Hammurabi. There is evidence for the existence of at least two other stelae erected by Hammurabi in other locations under his control, including Babylon and probably Nippur, the city of the "silent wife" case. This appears to have been the king's attempt to spread the word. These other stelae were also eventually taken by conquering armies.

It has been observed that even though they were written earlier than the biblical laws given to Moses, parts of the subject matter of the nearly 300 law provisions of Hammurabi deal with the same subject matter as the Mosaic laws. For example, both Hammurabi and Moses (speaking for God?) legislated for the case of a person reduced to slavery for debt. And both embraced the equivalency rule: According to the Bible it is "an eye for any eye," and under Hammurabi's code it follows casuistically that "[if] a man destroys the eye of another man, [then] they shall destroy his eye." So in both cases the balance schema is an eye and nothing more: If you take my eye, I may take yours—but not your life. Such similarities, however, appear not to be the result of the biblical laws being simply copied from those of Hammurabi, but reflect that both sets of laws had to address similar social and political problems prevalent in the ancient Near East (not unlike how modern developed countries, in this age of globalization, must deal with similar issues such as air traffic control, international phone calls, the Internet, and tax problems). In other words: "Proximity Is Similarity." It is interesting to note, however, that all of the laws of Hammurabi are in the casuistic form (e.g., "If a man has kidnapped the son of a free man, [then] he shall be put to death"). This, of course, is not true of biblical laws, which contain both casuistic and apodictic-styled laws. In the case of Adam and Eve, for example, it was not a conditional "If you eat of the tree of knowledge of good and evil, then. . . ." It was "Don't touch the fruit," period.

A primary reason for the use of hypothetical propositions is that the Babylonians, like other Mesopotamians, arguably did not believe in abstractions. Scholarship has observed that their way of analyzing nature did not start with axioms, revealed and demonstrated according to laws that were deduced and articulated, but instead was based on the accumulation of concrete cases. This approach to nature bleeds into the law code of Hammurabi, as well as the codes of other Mesopotamian leaders. Furthermore, Hammurabi's code, unlike the Bible's frequent integration of narrative and law, simply presents a collection of rules (not unlike many modern-day statutes), without specific historical explanation or moral justification.

The Hammurabic laws were displayed in a public place where people could read them or have the laws read to them. This fact is made clear in the prologue, which, like the U.S. Constitution, sets out the overall spiritual and moral justification for the text (but not for each specific law) that follows: "Let the wronged man who has a cause go before my statue [in the twenty-second year of his reign, Hammurabi commissioned and had publicly displayed a statue of himself] called 'King of Justice' and then have the inscription on my monument read and hear my precious words, that my monument may make clear his cause to him, let him see the law which applies to him, and let his heart be set at ease." What Hammurabi is saying is: Read the law (or have it read to you by a scribe), figure out if you have a case and if so, seek justice. This advice is still applicable. Instead, however, of a slab of black rock with about 300 law provisions, the aggrieved, literate person can go to his or her local law library and sift through thousands of statutes, regulations, and cases—or, thank heavens, hire a lawyer.

It appears that Hammurabi's laws (a term used here rather loosely) as well as Ur-Nammu's, Lipit-Ishtar's, and the laws of Eshnunna were not legislation and certainly not a code in the modern sense. This conclusion is supported by the fact that in the thousands of court records that have been recovered, the "laws" are never quoted. Apparently, they were really royal decisions rendered in either actual or hypothetical cases as examples of what a sound decision, based on principles derived from custom or traditional social norms, should be in order to satisfy justice. This possibility can be seen in the epilogue, which begins by summing up the preceding law provisions: "These are the just decisions which Hammurabi, the able king, has established and hereby he has directed the land along the course of truth and of life." There is strong evidence that the rulings, although not quoted, continued to play a part in court decisions centuries after they were promulgated, much like the lingering effect of the Bible, Roman law, and canon law on the common and civil law.

It is also important to keep in mind that Hammurabi's laws, along with Ur-Nammu's, Lipit-Ishtar's, the laws of Eshnunna, and those of all other groups, were developed within the context of a largely oral culture. Consequently, there was a general distrust of the written word. With regard to legal events and practices, this distrust can be appreciated by considering the fact that stone, blocks of wood, papyrus, parchment, or pieces of paper attempt to frame legal reality—text attempting to rule context. Additionally, by deperson-alizing human experience, the written text seeks to control its environment—it tries to seal off the text from life and change. It is no wonder that the judges of Hammurabi chose not to see the king's words as law frozen in a big, black rock, but merely as divine guidance on how to go about making correct decisions.

Over the centuries there has been almost a complete reversal in most soci-eties of text over oral. People, at least in the United States, generally recognize the ways in which textualization (e.g., writings, video, and tape) acts as a cen-tral organizing principle of modern legal-rational society. According to certain academics, people, when surveyed, generally acknowledge and defer to the authority of the textual over the oral. The greater authority of the written word over the spoken derives from the fact that a text can be preserved, retrieved, inspected, and, contrary to Socrates, interrogated. Text therefore converts pass-ing sound bites and events into permanent, timeless artifacts. And these arti-facts, according to this reified view of "the Law," are unbiased, reliable, and undeniable—but not, of course, to Vinnie or Sal.

By the way, the Hammurabic code specifically mentions judges—but nothing about lawyers.

HITTITE LAW

The Hittites, who are mentioned in the Bible as inhabiting Canaan prior to the Israelite invasion (the famous Bath-sheba, for example, was the wife of Uriah the Hittite), built a powerful empire in Asia Minor that lasted from c. 2000 until 1200 BCE. In fact, Hammurabi's dynasty ended just a century and a half after his death, when the city of Babylon was captured and looted by the Hit-tite army. Many of their myths appear to have been similar to those of Meso-potamia, and included a strong folkloric element. Consequently, the gods and goddesses, not unlike the Greeks, feuded among themselves.

Excavators at the site of the ancient Hittite capital of Hattusas (in what is today Turkey) have found clay tablets inscribed with laws. The script used by this warrior society was hieroglyphic and their language was the Indo-European Hittite language of Anatolia. The format of the collection, all in casuistic form, indicates that the tablets were prepared by and for the use of jurists (i.e., legal scholars).

The clay tablets were inscribed at about the same time as the Hittites sacked Babylon (1595 BCE), and are primarily copies of laws compiled between circa 1650 and 1500 BCE. They represent not only a collection but also a revision of more ancient Hittite law, or perhaps more technically a collection of cases that served as precedents. The discovered tablets contain about 200 law clauses that cover various aspects of Hittite life, including land tenure (i.e., ownership/use), black magic, and permitted and forbidden forms of sexual relations.

Hittite laws clearly indicate the use of judges—in fact, the king himself was a judge. For example: §188, "If a man sins with a sheep, it is a criminal abomination and he should be killed. You shall bring him to the king's court. The king may kill him or the king may let him live." There is, however, no mention of a lawyer—for the man or the sheep. This gross oversight was remedied during the Middle Ages when both man and animal caught in flagrante delicto were frequently provided with a lawyer. Clearly an advance in legal thinking.

The Animals Did It

Human–animal contact has played more than a passing role in the rise of the lawyer class. Besides providing lawyers with clients, such contact—occasionally of the carnal kind—has lead to the development of human diseases of animal origins. As pointed out by certain scholars, the major killers of humanity throughout recent history (e.g., smallpox, flu, plague, and measles) are infectious diseases that evolved from diseases of animals. Because diseases have been the biggest killers of people, they have also helped shape world history.

The once mighty kingdom of the Hittites crumbled around 1200 BCE when invaders penetrated its borders and cut off its supply lines of raw materials. The capital city of Hattusas was burned to the ground and never reinhabited. But smaller Neo-Hittite principalities, like the one encountered by the Israelites in the land of Canaan, survived for another 500 years before falling to the armies of the Neo-Assyrian kingdom. And most tragically, at least for purposes of our quest, this fall appears to have occurred prior to the development of a lawyer class.

ASSYRIAN LAW

Until the middle of the fourteenth century BCE, the city of Assur, located on the west bank of the Tigris river, was the capital city of a small territorial state. Starting, however, with King Ashur-uballit I (c. 1365–1330 BCE), this insignificant state started to grow and eventually became one of the major Near Eastern powers: Assyria. The dominant role of the Assyrian empire lasted until the reign of Tiglath-Pileser I (r. 1115–1077 BCE).

Aramaic "scroll scribes" eventually made their way to Mesopotamia and became an integral part of Assyrian administration. In so doing, they competed with the "tablet scribes" of the much less practical but older cuneiform script. The result of this intergroup tournament was, for a time, an administration based on two languages—or more technically, two scripts.

This administrative rumble over who was in the better position to write the law smacks of a particular conflict that arose in the United States during the Great Depression of the 1930s. The strong incentive of various elite lawyers to resist various New Deal measures was fueled not just by their individual obligations to Big Business clients but also by their collective interest in stopping the growing tendency of the state's legislative and administrative apparatuses to usurp law-producing and law-controlling functions. Within President Roosevelt's administration and the legal realists of academia was the view that much of the primary responsibility for producing and developing law should be shifted to the more efficient legislators, legal planners, and administrative commissions and away from the old, stodgy practicing bar and courts. And not unlike the threatened tablet scribes, the corporate lawyers fought back. Hence, the United States, not unlike ancient Assyria, has two "scripts": written court cases, and legislative/administrative statutes and regulations (which, in the end, has simply created more legal space).

Excavation in Assyria's ancient capital has yielded a large number of cuneiform tablets. Among these writings are two groups of laws. Their form and context show that unlike those of Hammurabi and other earlier rulers, they were not royal decisions arrived at in actual or hypothetical cases. Instead they were like the Hittite laws: a compilation by jurists of traditional legal practice. In fact some of the discovered tablets show that Assyrian laws were being obeyed even after the collapse of the Assyrian Empire. Can't you almost smell it!

EGYPTIAN LAW

Based on recovered records, ancient Egypt appears to have had a rather effective legal system.

The ancient history of this part of Africa can be cut up into three large dynastic chunks: the Old Kingdom (2635–2155 BCE), the Middle Kingdom (2060–1700 BCE), and the New Kingdom (1554–1080 BCE). After the last Kingdom, the history of Egypt was marked by invasions from outsiders, and it eventually became part of the Persian Empire, which, in turn, became part of Alexander the Great's conquests. This Macedonian dominance began in 332 BCE and started the so-called Ptolemaic period—named for Alexander's general Ptolemaeus, who became King Ptolemy I after Alexander's death. The period ended, nearly 300 years later, with the death of the romantic and ruthless Cleopatra (69–30 BCE), the seventh Ptolemy.

Conventional thought has, for the most part, been along the lines that the ancient Egyptians did not contribute much to the growth of jurisprudence. Detailed scholarship, however, has discovered and analyzed numerous legal documents littered among the earliest extant hieratic papyri. Throughout Egypt's three dynastic periods there are case records, and a "code" of laws is mentioned as early as the Middle Kingdom—in addition to *The Teaching for Merikare* (a text stressing, among other things, the ability to speak well and persuasively—in other words, the importance of rhetoric).

The truth is that a rich and detailed range of primary legal sources exist that display an articulated practice of both public and private law. Consequently, rather than speak of primitive Egyptian law and sophisticated Greek and Roman law, some scholars are now beginning to look at things the other way around. It may be that Egyptian law and practice (along with other eastern Mediterranean legal systems) influenced both the Greeks and the Romans and not vice versa, at least initially.

As for lawyers, scholarship on ancient Egypt has found no evidence of professional lawyers pleading for clients. Nevertheless, there is some indication of legal representation. Specialized scribes, not unlike those found in Mesopotamia, were most likely available to act on behalf of litigants and criminal defendants. This speculation is based in large part on the fact that the scribes that produced the scrolls containing *The Book of the Dead* were like lawyers who represented their clients by means of a written brief before the ultimate judge, the god Osiris. That is, while a deceased person was expected to personally argue his case in order to attempt to ensure favor in the hereafter, *The Book of the Dead* functioned like a boilerplate brief for the deceased to present to Osiris, Chief Justice of the Supreme Court of the Universe. This brief was intended to fight against the jackal-headed Anubis, playing the devil's advocate, and to hopefully persuade Osiris and his fellow judges to permit the deceased to enter the Netherworld. It is assumed that this same blend of professionalism and self-help was available to live litigants and criminal defendants.

The bottom line of this quick romp from Ur-Nammu of Ur to ancient Egypt is that there is little evidence of hired advocacy in preclassical courts, no lawyer class (at least of the in-court type) per se. A basic procedure everywhere was for the court to examine any relevant documents and then to hear statements by the accuser, the accused, and any witnesses. In Mesopotamia and Egypt (and most likely everywhere else) all witnesses had to take an oath to the gods—a point that leads us to investigate the role cosmology has played in the creation of lawyers.

VIII

CIVILIZATION, COSMOLOGY, AND THE DIVINE ADVOCATE

Before delving into the civilization that appears to be most responsible for the rise of the lawyer class, it will be helpful to step back to the beginning—again. This trek through time, unlike our sweep through the Bible, will primarily be from a pagan (or at least a non-Judeo-Christian-Muslim) point of view. The purpose, however, will be the same: to identify the important bits and pieces that have made lawyers both seen and heard.

It has been observed that cultural activity and a sense of shared purpose have always bound people together and given them power as a society. Wherever preindustrial civilizations have appeared, ceremonial places like temples have acted as an important seat of power, authority, and identity (conformity enforcers)—a function now seemingly served by the modern-day shopping mall. Such ceremonial places were generally tied to the notion of sacred space, and a site frequently became sacred because it was associated with a profound experience. Consider, for example, the Written Torah and Oral Torah given by God on Mount Sinai or the god Baal's place on Mount Zaphon: Importance Is Big. And participation in rituals associated with sacred space enhanced group identity, coordinated the actions of individual members of the group, and prepared the group for cooperative action—such as fighting against the terrifying powers of chaos and death.

COSMOLOGY

A key question that has led humans to construct ceremonial places—originally altars and temples, and currently universities and observatories—involves cosmology. Every civilization and culture that we know of has asked the following question: What is the structure of the universe? Only a handful of societies, however, have paid close attention to the appearance of the heavens in answering this question; the human drive to explain the universe as a whole is much older and more primitive than the urge to make systematic observations of the heavens. Holism over reductionism.

Consider, for example, one of the principal forms of Egyptian cosmology. To the Egyptians the earth seemed like an elongated platter. This serving ware's long dimension paralleled the Nile River; its flat bottom was the alluvial basin to which ancient Egyptian civilization was restricted, and its curved and rippled rim was the mountains surrounding the earth. Above the platter-shaped earth was air (a god), supporting an inverted platter-dome, which was the sky. The terrestrial platter was supported by water (another god), and the water rested on a third platter that bound the universe symmetrically from below. Grafting a platter or two onto the target domain of the world and universe helped to make conceptual sense of the infinite and intangible. The earth, to the Egyptians, looked like an elongated platter bound by water, and the sky did, and still does, look dome-shaped—just go outside and look.

Even though primitive humans paid a great deal of attention to the shape of the space around them, they did not completely ignore the filler. Indeed, some of our ancestors developed a deep reverence for the radiance of the stars, the undisputed gods of the night sky. They also noticed the meander of the planets (the "wanderers"), and the flash of shooting stars. And during the day, there was, of course, the light and warmth of the sun: an undisputed god.

For the ancient Egyptian, the sun was Ra, the principal god. He had two boats: one for his daily journey through the air and a second one for his nightly trip through the water. The stars were painted or studded in the vault of the heavens. They moved, as minor gods, and in some versions of Egyptian cosmology they were reborn each night. Occasionally more detailed observations were made of the heavens. The circumpolar stars (those that never dip below the horizon), for example, were recognized as "those that know no weariness or destruction." Based on this eternal vigilance, the northern heavens became the area where there is no death—the region of eternal afterlife.

Fragments of cosmologies similar to the Egyptian cosmology exist in all those ancient civilizations, such as India and Babylonia, of which we have records. The Chaldeans (Chaldea being a region of ancient Babylonia) appear to have been the first civilization to extend the metaphor of a spherical heaven to include the lower world. These Neo-Babylonians saw the sky revolve around the polar axis, and the planets cross in front of the backdrop of stars. Their astronomers/astrologers assigned a sphere to each of the seven planetary bodies that existed within the sphere of the fixed stars, like the layers of an onion. Each sphere revolved at its own rate determined by its distance from the center. This astronomical view also postulated seven spheres below the earth representing the seven regions of the underworld through which the soul passed at death before rebirth into the upper realm.

In many areas of Mesopotamia, it was not just the sky, planets, and stars that commanded attention. The gods, fortunately for the development of lawyers, wrote their messages to mankind everywhere. As a result, all areas of nature required close attention: the birth of animals and humans and their form when leaving the womb; the configuration of the land, of rivers and cities; the appearance and the behavior of plants and animals; the disposition of the human body and the behavior of men, alone or in groups; the content of dreams; and the examination of the reaction of animals at the moment of their sacrificial slaughter and the appearance of their entrails afterwards. In a wild and dangerous universe, everything out of the ordinary had to be considered as a message from the gods.

A Horse Walks into a Bar . . .

> The gods will warn you if the next year or so will yield poor crops: If a horse attempts to mount a cow (arguably an unusual occurrence), then there will be a decline of the land. The reason for this Mesopotamian divination in typical casuistic, if/then form, had to do with the observed sterility of a horse–cow romance. Thus the apodosis clearly follows from the protasis. Right?

The divine astrologers and oracles, with their knowledge of the heavens and earth, were the keepers of their respective society's cosmology, mysticism, and calendar. These intermediaries between the gods and mankind eventually spun off the priest class. And it is to the astrologers, oracles, and priests that we now turn for another key insight into the rise of the lawyer class.

ASTROLOGERS, ORACLES, PRIESTS, AND PATTERNS

It quickly became obvious to humans that life was fragile and overshadowed by mortality. Additionally, the thin veneer between mankind and raw nature, called civilization, could be wiped out at any moment. If, however, men and women imitated the actions of the gods, they might share to some degree the gods' greater power and effectiveness. Consider, for example, the biblical concept of resting on the Sabbath.

This same notion of participating with the gods—a more priestly than astrological or divinational activity—is evident in the New Year Festival of the ancient Babylonians. Celebrated in the holy city of Babylon during the month of Nisan (March–April, the first of the Mesopotamian year), the festival enthroned the king and established his reign for another year. It was a reenactment of the god's struggle against the forces of destruction. In order, however, to keep chaos at bay and renew the workings of nature and social hierarchy, the special liturgy had to be repeated year after year—and not just anywhere.

The specially designated place was the *ziggurat,* a temple-driven structure where humans could spiritually and physically get closer to the gods. The laws and rituals performed at this temple were binding upon everybody—including the gods, as the notion grew that the divine could be induced to exchange service to mankind for sacrifice. A moral scheme of reciprocation: I scratch your back so that you scratch mine (*do ut des*). The Judeo-Christian concept that more than self-interested exchange relations are possible between humans and the supernatural was, at this point in time, a long way off.

It is important to appreciate that prior to performing certain rituals, the will of the gods had to be determined—a consequence of the fact that we humans are apparently the only animals that reason about unobservable forces. This meant that their encrypted messages, scattered throughout nature, had to be located, read (decoded), and understood in order to have any hope of convincing the gods to be merciful. Unfortunately, the message sometimes called for a beating human heart or beheaded maidens to be buried with a dead ruler. If a priest proclaimed that only a heart or a headless maiden would convince the gods, then boys and girls had to die—*Apocalypto.*

But why? Why did mankind come to believe in such messages? And, more importantly, why did we feel the need to respond?

One answer to both questions is that all around us are things, millions and millions and millions of things, in a state of constant change: growth and decay, being and becoming, friendly and fearsome—chaos, in its more modern meaning. Our most fundamental sense of well-being, according to certain academics, crucially depends on our having the ability to exert control over the complex external and internal environment in which we find ourselves. And one way to do this is to find patterns (one of the primary attractions of mathematics). The real reality of such nonmathematical patterns often does not really matter. What matters, in order to increase chances of survival and hopes of human flourishing, is to "detect" patterns (particularly those that end up with you becoming food) and to behave as though they are real: a false positive over a false negative. This, it has been said, is one way of describing instinctual behavior. And instinct works through biology to control, direct, and codify the behavior of all animals—except "fully" evolved mankind.

However, just because we left many (most? all?) instincts in the Darwinian dust does not mean we also lost our favorite survival technique: seeing patterns. What appears to have happened is that instead of being dominated by instinct, we became faced with choice. (Remember Adam and Eve?) And with the loss of supplied security, we started imposing our fears, desires, and hopes on the things around us—turning many of them, through reification (the creation of objects out of processes), into causal agents that determine the affairs of the world—or more specifically, the affairs of our particular social circle. In fact, we made many of these casual agents powerful gods and imbued them with an emotional character that, although more divine and therefore more inscrutable, was not completely unlike our own. In this way we turned millions and millions and millions of chaotic things into manageable abstract patterns, and the abstract patterns into concrete things called gods. And the thoughts of these gods, scattered throughout nature, had to be located, read, understood, and acted upon in order to survive. Presto! The cure to our plethoraphobia and an important ingredient in the remarkably stable patterns that have characterized social groups since their inception.

This point deserves emphasis. There seems to be little doubt that such things as patterns, as well as shapes and symmetries, underlie nature and art. These things can be subjected to scientific and mathematical analysis. In fact, humans can often grasp them at an intuitive level, such as with music. But what is revealed? It is one thing to discover, appreciate, and even understand the framework of the science and mathematics on which art and science rest, and quite another to say that that framework contains a hidden message of social or moral value. For example, think of all the theories of patterns that arose around the September 11, 2001 attacks on the World Trade Center and the Pentagon. September 11 is numerically written 9/11, the telephone code for emergencies; the flight number of the first plane to hit the towers was 11; and "New York City," "Afghanistan," and "the Pentagon" all have 11 letters. This certainly must be some type of code, right?

The human technique of seeing patterns in all sensory areas—visual, spatial, auditory, tactile, and motor—has been embraced by lawyers on their rise to prominence. Lawyers, in different times and places, have looked for order or patterns to the decisions of judges. As a result they reason and argue that such decisions have some underlying, if unstated, rule, principle, or policy that supports them. And so if this message can be identified, it will assist the lawyer in arguing to a court that the general propositions contained in the opinions ought to be extended to their client's specific case—selecting, of course, only those opinions that are helpful and ignoring (or marginalizing) those that are not.

In addition to patterns, symbolism, throughout history, has given mankind a way of expressing multiple meanings. There is usually an outer meaning for the masses and a hidden, inner one for initiates. (If you don't believe me, just consider how lawyers talk.) The concern of the oligopolistic insiders has always been that with regard to spiritual symbols related to divine messages, the true principles might be discovered and abused by those interested in the pursuit of power (e.g., to control the symbols, specifically including those involved in writing, is to control the gods). For this reason, Egyptian religion, hieroglyphics, and architecture, for example, incorporated a symbolic language.

PYTHAGORAS TO ROME

The Pythagoreans, instead of architecture or words, found their pipeline to the gods in numerology and geometry. And this tie between the gods and mathematics has played a surprisingly important role in the history of lawyers.

Pythagoras, leader of the Pythagoreans, was born on the Greek island of Samos around 580 BCE. He was the son of a successful gem engraver, but did not feel particularly at ease on his small Aegean island. One reason for this may have been that like many introverts, young Pythagoras was a bookworm in a city where, at the time, high-minded intellectuals were an oddity. As a result, coupled with growing military ambitions by the local government, he left on what became a thirty-seven-year journey—traveling throughout Gaul, Egypt, Babylon, and possibly India. Especially in Babylon, Pythagoras came in contact with mathematicians and likely became aware of their studies of numbers. He was also exposed in his extensive travels to the religious and philosophical ideas of the East.

The Famous Theorem

The Pythagorean Theorem—in a right-angled triangle the square of the hypotenuse is equal to the sum of the squares on the other two sides, $a^2 + b^2 = c^2$—is one of the more famous and recognizable math formulas. While traditionally credited to Pythagoras, a Babylonian clay tablet has been found that lists integer pairs corresponding to at least one Pythagorean triad or "triple" (3, 4, 5). This suggests that the general theorem may well have been known long before Pythagoras, who likely learned of it while on his international journey.

Pythagoras settled in Croton (located in the Italian "boot") around 530 BCE. It was in this Magna Graecian colony that the long-haired Pythagoras, then in his fifties, founded a society dedicated to the study of numbers. His 300 or so followers (the Pythagoreans) are believed to have developed a substantial body of mathematical knowledge—in secrecy. They worshipped numbers and believed them to have divine properties. This belief in the power of numbers continued to be pursued in the Middle Ages, surfacing in mystical systems such as those found within the Brotherhood of the Rose Cross (the Rosicrucians) and the Jewish Kabbalah. For example, certain Rosicrucians were hot on the trail of "biblical numbers" such as 666, the lawyer's, er, devil's number.

Similarly, in ancient Rome priests influenced the development of oral forms and were experts in the set written words that had to be adhered to in matters of prayer and ceremony, as well as litigation. Additionally, like other ancient systems, the Romans developed ways in which people could manifest their intentions by actions. The use of acts to initiate litigation made it into the law and accounts for the ritual touching with the hand (*mancipatio*), with the rod (*vindicatio*), and acts performed with coin and scales (*aes et libram*).

No matter what particular method a group used, the true meanings of the sacred symbols were understood only by that group's "priesthood" and carefully hidden from the uninitiated. Certain schools of artists and architects were trained by the priests to understand and communicate the symbolic through their work. Sacred monuments such as megaliths, altars, statues, and the like became associated with particular gods or goddesses, or the natural or supernatural powers they represented. These monuments were frequently aligned with the stars or planets. The sun, moon, planets, and stars were believed to be associated with particular gods and goddesses. To evoke these gods or goddesses, one had to create manifestations of the cycle or numbers associated with the related heavenly body.

These pagan priests and priestesses benefited from convincing clients, particularly the ruling class, of their ability to locate, read, and interpret divine messages and, most importantly, to effectively respond through words, symbols and actions to the particular gods or goddesses. Thus through the priests' secret and sacred knowledge, the gods and goddesses could be called upon (controlled?), often using spiritual symbols and acts, to help in time of need: famine, pestilence, drought, sickness, war, and so on. This same technique of selling services involving control over the mysterious forces of life, death, and prosperity has been used by two of society's most successful contemporary professions: medicine and law.

Exceptions Prove the Rule

In contrast to paganism, with its priests and priestesses acting as conduits to the gods, consider rabbinic Judaism. Jewish law is said to be democratic in the sense that it belongs to all of the people (or at least from an "evolutionary" perspective, an ever-expanding definition of "the people"), a principle reflected in the Talmudic position that each individual can approach God and pray without intercession. It has also been observed that the cultic aspects of traditional Judaism—temple, sacrifice, and priesthood—were visible only in Jerusalem and only before the destruction of the Second Temple in 70 CE by the Romans. What the rest of the world saw was the synagogue in which Jews studied, discussed old texts, and encouraged one another to follow certain moral principles.

In the Catholic Church, however, increased hierarchy within the clergy during the Middle Ages created a separation between clergy and laity. The priest was separated from his parishioners by his rule of celibacy, by his distinctive dress (based on remnants of the imperial Roman toga), and by his use of Latin, a language only the educated could understand, in Church rituals. The effect of this separation on actual religious practice is illustrated by the difference between the medieval celebration of the Eucharist—the sacrament commemorating the Last Supper—and the Last Supper itself. What had once been a communal meal became a ceremony that the priest performed and the parishioners watched, physically separated from the priest by a heavy railing: a situation not unlike the "bar" separating the judge from the lawyer and his client.

In the case of medical science, it has been argued that what doctors sell is the illusion of omnipotence: the illusion that through consulting with the doctor, the patient gains control over his or her body. The truth is that even though medical science has made substantial progress since the days of leeches and bleedings, it is still helpless in the face of many of mankind's ailments. Doctors, however, do not generally throw up their hands and confess ignorance when faced with the symptoms a patient has just described. Instead they put on a look of indifference, as if no such problem exits.

And in the case of the legal profession, what lawyers sell is the illusion that through consulting a lawyer, the client can gain control over his or her social or economic circumstances. In other words, the client is provided with the illusion of control over those same forces that have made the client consult a lawyer. Think about it—it's truly brilliant.

So how is paganism related to the lawyers of today? The answer to this question lies primarily in the recognition that much of the history of humanity derives from our efforts to identify patterns and meaning in the relative chaos of existence (including the stock market). And as a part of this struggle some realized that if they controlled the discovery and interpretation of patterns and their meaning and could convince others that therefore only they knew how to please the gods, they could garner power. The protolawyers were key participants in this game.

Now on to the civilization that appears to be most responsible for the rise of the lawyer class: the Greeks.

PART III

ANCIENT GREECE

IN PART II IT WAS OBSERVED that there is little evidence of hired legal advocacy in preclassical times. Why? The answer, whether within the biblical or pagan tradition, appears to be, at least in part, that law was considered to be divinely sanctioned and revealed. Consequently, there was no need for the role of a hired legal gun—the correct answer to any "legal problem" could be obtained simply by asking someone who had the divine stamp of approval, generally a king like Solomon or perhaps an astrologer, oracle, or priest. This stamp of approval endowed the person with the power to tap into the ultimate source of Law: the metadivine "transcendent primordial force." So what changed? The answer lies, in large part, with the rise of Greek science.

Astrologers, and eventually the priest class, were, among other things, the keepers of the calendar—an extremely important religious and agricultural item that formalized perceived connections among natural events and divine will. If a society did not know exactly when to celebrate a particular festival, what assurance was there that the rains would come? How would you know exactly when to plant or to harvest? Precision is critical if you plan to exploit the regularities that have seemingly been detected in nature. And the various calendared festivals, in turn, served to express a sense of community among worshipers in a shared experience of pleasure and festivity.

In the Fertile Crescent of the Middle East, the Babylonians, building on the work of the Sumerians, developed an extremely sophisticated calendar system by simply counting regular occurrences of the phases and placement of the moon, planets, and stars. This very rational effort, in turn, put Babylonian mathematics on a solid foundation. But it was the Greeks who gave birth to science: not because they were better at calculation than the Babylonians but because, early on, they were not as tradition-bound. The early Greeks, at least after the end of their Dark Age (1100–800 BCE), were frequent movers and as a result developed no particular respect for the gods of the various places they visited and settled. If you lived all of your life in Heliopolis, the city of the sun, you might naturally develop a strong devotion to Ra and his magic boats. In contrast, if you were a newcomer or only visited a particular city occasionally, you might hold a picture of the universe in which the gods of that city are left out, or at least play a less prominent role. You might even start to question why it is that there are so many different gods, some performing the same tasks. After all, how could the universe be created by the god of this city and also by the god of that city? And why does the god of that city require punishment for a particular act and the god of this city does not? The result might be thoughts that dig deeper and wider into the political, social, and natural environment around you, including the nature of the universe. This is what happened to the Greeks, or at least to some of them.

In areas like the western coastal fringe of Asia Minor (present-day Turkey, just across the Aegean Sea from the Greek mainland), in the region called Ionia, there was the gradual development of new modes of thought involving universal concepts and absolute formulations. From the Ionian city of Miletus, for example, came the first man of science, Thales (c. 634–548 BCE). He boldly explored natural phenomena that were previously believed to be acts of the gods.

Said to be history's first absent-minded professor—legend has it that he was once musing on Persian astronomy with such intensity that he fell into a ditch while looking at the stars—Thales wrestled with the ancient problem of whether or not there is one primordial thing that underlies all the constant changes taking place around us, as well as inside us. In other words, is there one thing that underlies all change, over all time, in all places? Thales said yes—and decided, using the concept of reductionism, that that thing is water. Scholars are not exactly sure what he meant by this: Everything consists of water in some sense, or merely that it originally came from water? But in saying that "all is water," he performed a significant mental feat: the proposition that a single physical versus spiritual entity or element is the foundation for all the different things in the world, the first Theory of Everything. In fact, he even provided some empirical evidence for his theory by dying of dehydration in the Olympic festival meadow.

This feat (theorizing, not dying) accomplished at least two important things: (1) it did not look to animistic explanations for what happens in the world—"I have no idea why X happened and therefore I assume that 'God' or the gods did it"; and (2) it shouted out loud the theory that the cosmos is a thing whose workings the human mind can understand.

There is some speculation that Thales' "all is water" theory was derived from Egyptian, Phoenician, and Babylonian creation myths that describe water as the first substance. Aristotle, however, suggested that Thales made his choice because water, particularly in the heat of the ancient Olympic Games, is demonstrably essential to life. But whatever the source of his concept and its exact meaning, the thrust was to put forward an explanation (the first scientific hypothesis ever recorded) as to why the earth seems to be stable (a key aspect of law) within the wider universe.

It seems likely that Ionia, like many frontier societies (including the American Wild West), encouraged hard work and self-sufficiency and in return offered opportunity and prosperity. Additionally, Ionia's geographical location next to the non-Greek civilizations of Anatolia, which were in close contact with the older civilizations of the Near East and Egypt, meant that Ionian thinkers were in a position ideally suited for building on old patterns of thought.

THE RISE OF PHILOSOPHY

In the sixth century BCE, a united Persia conquered Ionia and many people left, founding other cities northward; eventually, there were Milesian settlements all around the Black Sea. This surge of new settlements, however, was just one of many to come. Between 750 and 550 BCE hundreds of settlements were founded by Greek city-states throughout the Aegean and later throughout the Mediterranean, from the eastern coast of Spain to the shores of the Black Sea in the northeast and to the north coast of Africa. Each of these city-states would go on to contribute, in commerce, industry, science, philosophy, literature, and art, to what is today considered to be the culture of ancient Greece.

It was in this milieu of city-states that Pythagoras, discussed in Part II, developed his idea that mathematics is connected with nature: The Essence of Being Is Numbers—not Water. And from this notion, he established a school of philosophy, one that had very strict rules aimed at purifying the body with abstinence and self-control, and cleansing the mind with science and music. The idea of order, thought to be a part of numbers and their relationship to the universe, in turn placed these philosophers at the top of the list to advise on city regulations. The philosopher Solon, for example, drew up new laws and a revised constitutional structure for Athens, the expanding capital of Attica. He decided which areas were to constitute wards, what voting there should be in each ward, and how to arrange the different assemblies—in other words, how to rationally order the "state."

The rise of the philosopher, along with collecting, coordinating, and reducing various holy customs to writing, tended to secularize the law and marginalize the priest class. It was increasingly the philosopher and not the astrologer or priest who advised the ruler or government of a particular city, a practice that culminated in Plato's notion of a philosopher-king.

MATH AND THE LAW

There is a rather intriguing theory as to how the Greeks developed (or perhaps more accurately, as it was based upon Babylonian and Egyptian foundations, advanced) the idea of mathematical proof—a concept that is the single greatest attribute of mathematics and one that has surprisingly played a significant part in the continuing debate of what law is and how to teach it to law students. The terminology of a proof and the way it is put forward and proved, is, according to this theory, much like a case at law. The mathematician, like some lawyers, works with certain agreed statements (axioms), and then goes on to build other premises from them, eventually reaching a conclusion. Thus, the mathematician (hopefully) comes up with an elegant proof for his theorem—and the lawyer (hopefully) "proves" her case.

The fascinating aspect of this theory regarding the idea of proof (creating a kind of chicken-and-egg scenario between math and law) is that Christopher Columbus Langdell, dean of the Harvard Law School from 1870 to 1895, developed his concept of legal science around abstract geometrical models. In order to understand a given branch of legal doctrine in a scientific fashion, one must begin, according to Langdell, by identifying the elementary principles (axioms) on which that field of law is based. These elementary principles are to be discovered by surveying the case law in the area (i.e., the common law). Once the axioms have been identified through inductive generalization, it is then up to the legal scholars to work out, in an analytically rigorous fashion, the subordinated principles entailed by them. Langdell believed that once the basic axioms and subordinate principles have been put into propositional form and the relations of entailment among them clarified, they will form a well-ordered system of rules—a geometry of law—that offers the best possible description of that particular branch of law.

Science by Any Other Name

Contemporary Anglo-American usage seems to hold that the only "true" sciences are the natural sciences such as physics and chemistry. Therefore, "legal science," or a "science of law" is, from this point of view, simply loose talk. On the other hand, many other languages—German, for example—have retained the older, broader meaning of "science" as a coherent, systematic body of knowledge, combining particular facts with general principles (*Wissenschaft*). This meaning is applicable to not only the exact natural sciences, but also to the less exact social and other humane sciences—including the "science of law" (*Rechtswissenschaft*).

In terms of practical application, it has been said that a "scientific system" is one in which small groups of people cohere around an idea, then use the powers of rhetoric and politics to establish that idea's dominance in their field and to crush rival ideas and those who propound them—a definition that does seem to apply to the science of law. As we will see, the common-law lawyers fought against the civil-law lawyers; the barristers fought for superiority over the serjeants-at-law; and the university system fought against the apprenticeship system—all examples of intergroup tournaments.

This concept of structured law was certainly not unique to Langdell, or to the United States. Friedrich Karl von Savigny in Germany, for example, also asserted that it is essential for a society to identify the fundamental axioms on which law is based. In his case the raw data in which to search for such axioms was not common-law decisions but the Roman law as it had been absorbed into the German *Volksgeist* ("the spirit of the nation"). Savigny saw law as embodying something of the spirit of the people (tradition?) and not merely the structure of its social order. However, Roman law was massive, gappy, and inconsistent—at least in its preserved form. Therefore, in order to distinguish the useful from the useless, Savigny advocated the use of certain guiding principles contained in Kantian legal theory. And not surprisingly (since Savigny was a professor of law at the University of Berlin), all this work on extracting and organizing elementary and subordinate principles was to be accomplished by university professors—who, according to Savigny, occupied a "priestly office."

As we head into a discussion of ancient Greece and its impact on the lawyer class, keep in mind the weakening of irrational, magical, and religious superstitions in the face of science. The increasing rigors of science helped secularize the law and enhance the reputation of philosophers at the expense of the priest class. And modern-day lawyers generally find a more comfortable kinship with the philosophers than the priests.

THE GREEKS

For the early Greeks, as was the case with other ancient civilizations such as the Sumerians, Babylonians, Assyrians, Egyptians, and, most certainly, the Jews, law appears to have been "received" as sacred custom, divinely sanctioned and revealed. It was therefore initially part of theology, and the old Greek laws of property were mingled with liturgical regulations in the temple codes. And almost as old as the religiously spawned laws were the god-inspired decisions and directives of tribal kings. This latent dualism between the religious and the secular not only created certain philosophical tensions in Greek thought, but it also boiled to the surface in the Middle Ages and led to an important bit of verbal pushing and shoving between the common-law lawyers and the civil-law lawyers.

What's in a Word?

Because laws were typically inscribed on wood or stone in order to prevent surreptitious alteration, a classical Greek would probably have thought of law as a physical object—whether the law came from the gods or it had been proposed and enacted by humans. The words in Homeric Greek that come closest to "law," *dikē* (custom or justice) and *themis* (what is decent or proper as established by custom, tradition, or precedent) mean, essentially, custom. By the days of Draco and Solon, the word generally used for law appears to have been *thesmos* (a rule laid down or imposed by authority, whether by a king or other type of lawmaker). And by the fourth century BCE, *nomos* (custom, way of life) was the normal word for

a statute: putting into fixed and eventually written form a preexisting custom—a law published in writing and validated by a political process.

ATHENS

Following the early phase of largely unorganized divine and kingly pronouncements primarily based on custom, Greek legal history entered a phase of collection and coordination by such lawgivers as Zaleucus, Solon, Charondas,
and Draco—as in "Draconian," having nothing to do with Count Dracula . . .
except for blood. During Draco's political career, an economic depression had
raised the level of discontent and forced many bankrupt farmers into Athens
to look for work. At the time, overall power was held by a group of aristocrats
(*eupatridai:* "well-fathered") who, like most aristocrats, wanted to maintain
their power and wealth. One of their own, a former Olympic champion named
Cylon, attempted to establish himself as the sole ruler c. 632 BCE. His coup
was short-lived, apparently squashed by the concerted efforts of other nobles
and their peasant followers. The victorious elite then commissioned Draco,
around 620 BCE, to assemble a code of laws aimed at controlling the masses.
His code (or perhaps more accurately his "compilations"), inscribed on four-
faced wooden blocks called *axones,* made death the penalty for almost every
offense—arguably an aggressive incentive for toeing the line. It is for this reason that the Greek biographer, historian, and philosopher Plutarch, in a biog-
raphy of Draco, noted that "[t]hose that were convicted of idleness were to die,
and those that stole a cabbage or an apple [Adam and Eve?] were to suffer even
as villains that committed sacrilege or murder. . . . Draco's laws were written
not with ink but blood."

The main thrust of Draco's laws, however, was well intended: to outlaw the traditional right of a family to avenge the murder of a loved one. By
increasing the expected punishment, Draco thought enforcement cost would
be reduced—everyone would be too afraid to even attempt anything criminal. It didn't work. After living under this harsh regime for more than twenty-
five years with no apparent advances in social calm, everyone agreed that the
merchant and philosopher Solon (c. 638–558 BCE) should revisit the laws. It
appears that he had been well trained to take on this important political-legal
task; Thales, one of the chief inventors of secular philosophy, had been a mentor of his.

In order to try to overcome existing political and legal problems, Solon,
elected as *archon eponymous* (chief magistrate) and also granted extraordinary

powers to reform the state, rewrote—or at least wrote down—many of the laws and established or revamped political institutions. The result of his constitutional tinkering turned out to be, through perhaps not intentionally, the starting point for a democracy that was eventually composed of such institutions as a popular Assembly, to which all adult male citizens were admitted, and a Council that prepared agendas, oversaw routine administrative duties, and carried out certain judicial functions. This Assembly–Council relationship operated much like the later town-meeting governments of colonial New England. The Assembly, like the colonial citizenry, constituted the legislators and the day-to-day responsibilities were vested in managers. In the case, however, of colonial America, the managers were elected, while the Council was chosen by drawing lots (in order to cut down on only the wealthy serving as members).

With regard to the rise of legal practice, Solon ruled that any male citizen could bring charges on a wide variety of offenses against wrongdoers on behalf of a victim. He thus created the right, in fact the responsibility, for individuals to act as prosecutors in cases designated as public. His reforms also provided for a right of appeal to the *Heliaea,* a subpart of the Assembly that sat as a lawcourt, by a person who believed that a magistrate had rendered an unjust decision. If a person was unable to defend himself, a third party could seek justice on the accused's behalf.

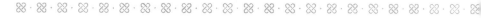

Common and Canon Appeals

The common law had no system of appeal until the nineteenth century, nor did Islamic law historically have a system of appeal (though both legal systems had certain remedies for bad verdicts). Canon law's appeal system, however, with a hierarchy from archdeacon to bishop to archbishop to pope, dates back to the twelfth century.

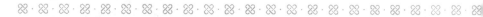

An important transmutation in "the law" started to take place when men such as Draco and Solon assembled their new "codes": evidence of Marshall McLuhan's point that the medium is the message. The sacred usages, generally preserved in oral form, became man-made, written laws—at the time, a heretical notion to many people. This moved the law away from being composed purely of social norms to a collection of standard statutes, but also freed it, at least somewhat, from religion. And this creeping secularization meant that the intentions and actions of the individual—instead of the gods—became more important: Family liability was replaced by individual responsibility, and Orestesian revenge, with its negative-sum-game effect and time drag on more wealth-creating activities, slowly gave way to statutory punishment by the state. These changes all helped provide room for the political and economic expansion of lawyers.

SPARTA

Athens led this increasing secularization of the law; Sparta believed otherwise. Here was a Greek city-state that appears to have developed in very much the same fashion as many others—until around the early sixth century BCE. It was after this time period that an extraordinary change of course and character came over Sparta, what complexity theorists call a "bifurcation point."

The story goes that Lycurgus was a divinely inspired lawgiver who reformed Sparta and gave it a new code or constitution. Unlike Solon, who insisted that he had been ruled by earthly good sense, Lycurgus claimed that he received his edicts directly from the Delphic Apollo, god of law. A close bond between Sparta and Apollo's earthly messenger, the oracle at Delphi, eventually led to the widespread feeling that the oracle was always against Athens and its form of democracy. Thucydides, for example, wrote at the start of the Peloponnesian War that the oracle proclaimed that she would take Sparta's side. (The gods were known to choose sides: In the legendary Trojan War, for instance, Apollo favored the Trojans while Athena helped the Greeks.) And Sparta's five chief magistrates (the *ephors*) were constantly visiting the holy precinct in order to obtain the latest advice on how to administer their state.

The importance, at least for us, of Lycurgus (who may or may not have actually existed), the *ephors,* and the ancient and continuous tie to the oracle is that the law in Sparta remained firmly encased in religious beliefs. This fact provided a significant basis for Sparta's rigorous social structure, with its lack of drunk and disorderly Dionysus, and its allegiance to a legal system focused on the basic issues of freedom, justice, and luxury. Tragically, however, there was no room for the probing and prodding of lawyers.

CODIFYING THE LAW AND CREATING LEGAL PROCESS

Following a period of turmoil caused by a group of oligarchically minded elites and the eventual restoration of democracy in 410 BCE, the Athenians decided it was time to draw up a list of all the existing laws—and not just those of Solon and Draco. It was time to reaffirm that laws, in order to be *laws,* must be public and published. A significant role in this undertaking was assigned to

Nicomachus, appointed head of a board of *anagrapheis* ("inscribers"). It took him and his fellow commissioners six years to gather and codify all the various fragments. And upon completion the assembled laws were inscribed on the walls of the *Stoa Basileios* in the *Agora*—constituting the fullest law "code" ever published by a Greek city. More important for our purposes, this appears to be the start of pleaders in the Athenian law courts actually reading out what they believed to be the relevant law—or at least, as is still the case, the part they liked.

❈ · ❈

Bending the Law, BCE-Style

In 399 BCE (the year of Socrates' famous trial), Nicomachus was apparently accused of refusing to render an account of his office. During the trial it was claimed that he inserted or erased laws in return for payment, supplied parties to suits with opposing laws, refused to hand over laws when brought before a *dikastērion* (jury-court), and sometimes made up a law or two.

❈ · ❈

The laws gathered by Nicomachus and his group were given a hallowed, "constitutional" status—partly by associating most of them with the revered Solon and Draco. The Assembly, after review by the Council, continued to issue decrees, typically beginning with the phrase "It was resolved by the Council and the Assembly of the People that . . . ," on current policy issues. Such decrees did not, however, carry the same status as inscribed laws: In modern-day terms, think regulation versus statute; statute versus constitutional provision. Furthermore, starting after 399 BCE, any proposed law, in contrast to a mere decree, had to be first framed and approved by a group of lawmakers. This committee was established as a check on the power of the Assembly and was chosen by lot from a pool of 6,000 citizens enrolled each year as dicasts (*dikastai*)—essentially a jury pool. The committee's main function was to hear arguments for and against any proposed legislative change. It also conducted, based on requests by the Assembly, investigations of invalid, duplicate, or inconsistent laws. Out of this constitutional structure of individuals—the Assembly, the Council, magistrates, and committee—policy decisions were made and the laws of Athens were cut and recut into stone, and later written on papyrus.

The proposer of a new law or decree was suppose to ensure that it did not fly in the face of existing laws or decrees either in form or content. If a conflict was discovered, the proposer could be prosecuted through a procedure known as "illegal proposal"; if found guilty, he was generally slapped with a fine and his law eradicated. If convicted three times of this same offense, a proposer was then subject to disfranchisement, losing such civil rights as holding any public office or being a juror, speaking in a law-court, or visiting a temple. With the death of ostracism, disenfranchisement became an increasingly popular form of shaming. And after 403 BCE, when formal distinction was made between decrees and laws, a person could be prosecuted for making an "inexpedient" law. Prosecutions for illegal decrees and illegal laws became a popular method of attack against prominent politicians. Imagine the modern-day political possibilities!

It appears that the basis for such attacks rested on the Greek notion of moderation—*meden agan,* nothing in excess. Words were seen as operating within an "economy of meaning," which could only be preserved through a speaker's self-restraint. Excessive words and lawmaking, just like excessive eating, drinking, sexing, and spending, flew in the face of the ideal of a balanced life and therefore constituted a form of dissipation.

Take, for example, Callistratus of Aphidna, considered to be a decadent politician and therefore spoken of in Greek comedy as a butthole, blabbering on and farting out law after law: Bad Is Stinky. (Remind you of any politician you know?) Words and laws in this context were seen merely as a means to pay for a politician's appetite for pleasure and were therefore produced in proportion to that appetite and shared in its excess. This excess, in turn, was seen as having a negative effect on the city-state.

While the Athenians tended to conceive of their system as legislative law, common law did play a part in their jurisprudence. This type of law was a blend of common sense, common morality, and common understanding—all without the records or the professional memory of a guild of lawyers or judges that often facilitate a society's explicit reference to past legal practices.

It has been observed that the courts of Athens were, not unlike many modern courts, generally backlogged. The reason was that despite a rather efficient legal process, Athenians loved to litigate. It was high drama, a bloodless goat-song. And in order to help accommodate this raft of litigation, by the end of the fifth century BCE cases were generally processed through preliminary hearings before "magistrates." It was the case, for example, that "[i]f an alien shall live as husband with an Athenian women by any plot or machination whatsoever, [then] he shall be indicted before the Thesmothetae [a magistrate] by any person who possesses the right." The speculation is that the parties, following filing of a complaint and service of summons, argued before the appropriate magistrate or magistrates and determined each other's position (a process known in modern-day litigation as "discovery"). Most likely the magistrate(s) had a duty, as well as the chance, to try to talk a party with a weak case into dropping the matter or accepting some type of settlement. However, as soon as the magistrate was satisfied that the problem was a legitimate legal dispute, that it would not settle, and that it was one in which he did not have the power to pronounce a final verdict, he arranged to have it transferred to the appropriate court.

❄ · ❄

A History of Settling

Due to the time and expense of litigation and the general inclination to avoid futile battles, most legal systems have contained screening devices to ensure that cases at the center of decisional determinacy will not enter the formal adjudicative process. This is also often the case if small dollar amounts are involved. In Athens, the Forty, a board of circuit judges active in the fourth century BCE, were entitled to settle private cases on their own authority—but only if the amount in dispute was less than ten drachmas, a type of small claims court. Most other cases had to be referred to arbitration.

This same push for settling cases also existed, historically, in Islamic law. There is a report of a judge in Rabat who boasted that in six years he had rendered only six judgments but had resolved hundreds of matters by arbitrating settlements.

❄ · ❄

After 400 BCE there also existed public arbitrators who were chosen by lot from a roster of citizens who were at least fifty-nine years old—the age of discharge from all military obligations. The parties to a private dispute made their arguments and submitted evidence to one of these arbitrators (chosen at the last minute in order to prevent bribery), who was paid a small fee by the prosecutor. The arbitration, like most court proceedings, was held in a public place, where anyone could watch and listen. If the arbitrator was not able to facilitate a compromise (in modern times called mediation), he rendered his judgment. Promptly thereafter, the arbitrator reported his decision to the magistrate that had assigned him the case. Either party, given the compulsory nature of the arbitration, could then appeal the solemnized judgment to the courts.

A plea was entered for those cases accepted for trial, the witnesses for each party made their depositions and swore to them, and statements were then presented to the court in written form. The writings, which had been prepared by the party the witness was supporting, were sealed in an earthenware pot, and at a later date they were read out loud in court by the clerk—the witness then simply confirmed that the statement was correct. It was against the law to introduce new evidence, and unlike Daniel's brilliant attack on the two old judges (Chapter IV), there was generally no cross-examination of witnesses. Litigants typically addressed the jury directly, and the jury, by majority vote, decided the case by a type of secret ballot cast immediately after hearing what the parties and their witnesses had to say. There was apparently no formal period for jury deliberation—most likely due to the large jury sizes (e.g., 501).

Especially relevant for our purposes is the fact that there were no public prosecutors (i.e., no Marcia Clarks—particularly of the working-mother variety) assigned to handle most offenses. Society simply relied upon private citizens to accuse and prosecute anyone thought to be guilty of a public offense— an adversary system Writ Large. A citizen might decide to prosecute out of family or civic duty, or for public attention with an eye toward creating or enhancing a political career. (Something almost unheard of in our enlightened times—right? Surely New York Attorney General Rudy Giuliani's prosecution of junk bond dealer Michael Milken had nothing to do with headline hunting—or his eventual election as mayor of New York City.) It was also the case that in the event of a conviction, the prosecutor might be entitled to a portion of the defendant's fine or confiscated property, arguably a redistributive, rent-seeking activity—bounty hunting. For example, "[I]f anyone gives away an alien woman in marriage to an Athenian man, as if she were related to him [i.e., a citizen], let him be disfranchised, and let his property be forfeited to the state, and let a third part of it belong to the successful prosecutor." Frivolous prosecution was discouraged (but not always as to the more well-heeled) by a law requiring the prosecutor to pay a fine, and possibly suffer disfranchisement, if his case won less than one-fifth of the jury vote or the case was abandoned after starting it. This rule, however, applied only to public cases.

PUBLIC AND PRIVATE CASES

Greek law distinguished between private cases and public cases. Where a public offense was involved—that is, one seen as affecting the community as a whole— anyone who wished to, not just the aggrieved party, was entitled to prosecute. In order to kick-start the discourse of the state, however, the volunteer prosecutor generally had to be a qualified citizen and no case could be brought by anyone who was disfranchised—that is, socially dead. The public offenses that could be pursued by private prosecutors included such things as treason, desertion from the army, and embezzlement of public funds. These types of offenses are easily seen as "polluting" the entire community—not unlike pollution and modern-day citizen suits under various environmental laws. But there were also offenses against individuals that fell within the public category, generally either because the victim was incapable of taking legal action for himself or because the offending behavior was regarded as so serious that it was offensive even to those who did not suffer by it personally, such as maltreatment of an orphan. It therefore appears that not all litigation was redistributive but, in fact, included the creation of nonmarketed social goods: in other words, making society a better place in which to live.

A Cornucopia of Procedure

In addition to procedures categorized as "ordinary," public and private, there were also "extraordinary procedures" that did not follow the normal procedure of summons, indictment, preliminary hearing, trial, and verdict. These procedures (closer to public than private) included *apagōgē*, "delivery," by which any citizen might haul a certain type of offender before the authorities; *ephēgēsis*, in which an accuser could lead a magistrate to where the defendant was and tell the magistrate to arrest him; *endeixis*, "indication," by which any citizen might point out an offender to the authorities; *apographē*, submitting a list of property that the prosecutor alleged the defendant retained; *phasis*, in which a prosecutor would receive half the amount that the defendant was condemned to pay; *eisangelia*, "denunciation" of major offenses against the state, offenses committed by officials, offenses committed by arbitrators, and maltreatment of parents, orphans, and heirs; *dokimasia*, a scrutiny proceeding for checking that a man was not disqualified to be a citizen or to hold an office or to speak in the *Ekklēsia*; and *euthynai*, an investigation that a man had performed the duties of an office rightly.

Where the offense was considered to be a private matter, only the person who alleged that he suffered a wrong could (or at least should) be the prosecutor. A principle reason for this can be found in economics. As pointed out, with regard to modern tort law, one reason is that the victim is the person most likely to know that the tort—or in the case of ancient Greece, where tort and crime were not generally distinguished, the offense—occurred, hence the one that is in the best position to report it if given a suitable incentive to do so. A second reason is that the victim is likely to be an important witness, so giving him the right to the fine eliminates transactions that would otherwise be required between him and the prosecutor. A third reason is that the victim has an additional incentive to prosecute: Prosecuting this offense may deter future offenses against him, an important reason in highly competitive ancient Greece.

While public prosecutors, as indicated earlier, generally did not exist, there were certain cases in which the prosecutor of a case did act in an official capacity. A magistrate, for example, might have observed an offense coming within his area of responsibility, such as a general who prosecuted a deserter, or a market controller who prosecuted someone for disorderly conduct in the *Agora*—not unlike the modern-day U.S. Attorney General's office going after Enron executives for their misconduct in the financial markets. If, however, the offense dictated a penalty greater than the magistrate or official could impose under his own authority, he had to transfer the case to the proper court and then act as prosecutor himself. Finally, there were those who had virtually no other function but to act in a representative capacity. One such group was composed of ten advocates (*synēgoroi*) who, assisting ten auditors (*logistai*), presented cases against any ex-magistrate being prosecuted on a financial charge at his *euthynai*, an examination of an official regarding his conduct while in office—a type of Crown Prosecution Service.

The bottom line is that while most public cases were brought by volunteers (like private attorneys general), it can not be said that publicly appointed prosecutors and legal advisors (lawyers?) did not exist in Athens—and perhaps in other Greek city-states.

En Française

Why is it "attorney general" and not "general attorney"? The reason is the French! French adjectives normally follow the noun that they modify—hence, court martial, malice aforethought, notary public, solicitor general, and so on.

The roles of attorney general and solicitor general stem from the theory of law that the English king or queen was always present in the courts—the judges being merely deputies to administer justice. The monarch could not only appear by attorney but also plead by attorney. This attorney was, however, no ordinary attorney, but one who looked after the interests of the king or queen in court. This attorney had superior standing—especially when, later, the monarch came to appoint an attorney as a representative in all courts. And with the rise of solicitors (along with a touch of French), you end up with both "solicitor general" and "attorney general."

It should not be assumed that this primarily private prosecutorial system existed because city-states such as classical Athens had not advanced far enough to develop an appropriate state institution. States such as Athens (and even early modern England) relied upon citizens to initiate and pursue various prosecutions due to an underlying conviction that made them reluctant, unlike many modern societies, to relinquish this important power. In the case of England, legal scholars have pointed out that the citizens preferred the acknowledged imperfections of their system to what they perceived as the tyranny of the Continental, a centralized control of the administration of justice. Athenians also considered the popular courts as a bulwark that protected their particular brand of democracy and gave meaning to social values. They also craved the competition involved in litigation.

POLITICS AND PROSE

This close relationship between the law-courts and the political system arguably led to a important expertise among many of the Greek "lawyers" that is lacking among most modern-day lawyers: the ability to credibly balance between liberties and security.

It has been pointed out that the legal profession (particularly in the United States) often has a lot to say, and with a fair amount of creditability, about such things as the legal doctrines that protect civil liberties, the administration of those doctrines, the values that civil liberties promote, and the cost of cutting back on such liberties. On the other hand, most lawyers, despite the age-old assumption of omnicompetence, cannot responsibly make recommendations concerning the appropriate scope of such liberties in the face of war and international terrorism. The reason for this is that legal professionals, unless they have transformed themselves into politicians, have no expertise with regard to national security. It's generally not a class taught in law school—at least—not yet.

But in ancient Greece, each law-court appearance was a chance for an orator to enhance his political image. In cases of public importance he could therefore argue, with credibility, important trade-offs between liberty issues before the court and security issues swirling around the Assembly. It was as if an American Civil Liberties Union lawyer was also a member of the National Security Council.

It should be clear by now that each party in an Athenian trial acted as his own lawyer, at least in most cases. A significant exception involved homicide, as the dead person was generally not available. The prosecutor in such cases was a relative of the deceased. There is, however, a certain amount of scholarly debate as to whether or not the prosecution of the murderer could be conducted by a nonrelative. An exception to the general rule also existed with regard to women. Consider the case of Athens's most successful mistress, Aspasia.

Aspasia was taken as Pericles' live-in lover after he divorced his wife (in order, of course, to take Aspasia as his live-in lover). Aspasia was, by all accounts, an extraordinary woman—among other accomplishments, she opened a school in which she taught the arts of discourse and basic philosophy. Even Socrates jested, according to Plato, that both he and Pericles had learned the art of rhetoric from her. Because of her considerable intellect, coupled with the fact that she was originally from Miletus, and therefore technically an outsider, she was frequently accused of exerting undue influence over Pericles. And eventually she was pursued in the courts under the common and wide-ranging procedure of "impiety" (*asebeias*)—a public case. However, because she was a woman, Aspasia could not represent herself in this high-stakes prosecution. Pericles therefore stepped in to handle the defense, weeping copiously at the trial and, fortunately for his living arrangements, coming out victorious.

Despite the basic social norm of honor in self-help, as the complexity of legal procedures grew (undoubtedly related to a rise in socioeconomic complexity) and litigants detected in jurors a sensitivity toward eloquence, the practice of engaging a speechwriter (*logographos*) as added insurance against a loss crept in. The writer, who was generally versed in the law, was engaged to prepare a speech that the client could give in court, employing words, phrases, and sentiments that were consistent with his client's character and in keeping with mass attitudes. This careful mix of the legal and extralegal created, hopefully, a competitive advantage by engaging in what is now called "unbundled legal service," a ghost-lawyer drafting pleadings without appearing for the client in court, or coaching or advising on strategy behind the scenes.

Speechwriting for others was usually done in secret since it was considered to be in bad form (i.e., not within the rules of the game) for litigants to have someone else speak on their behalf. In fact, to speak in court for a fee, as a modern-day lawyer does, not only was disreputable but was a prosecutable offense. One of the key reasons for this "unenlightened" view was that pursuing revenge and victory against one's enemies was considered not only noble but also pleasurable—based on the "fact" that humans, by nature, desire to feel superior. From this psychological principle came the notion that combativeness and disputations must also be pleasant, since, like war, sports, and gambling, they offer the opportunity for victory. For those skilled in such activity, litigation provided a competitive setting where one sought out the pleasure of winning. And in those circumstances where a person did appear on behalf of a litigant (many times acting as a supporting speaker, *synēgoros*), it was almost always an interested friend whose appearance was assumed to imply a personal belief in the litigant's character and cause. An example of this type of advocacy occurred in the 489 BCE prosecution of Miltiades the Younger before the *Heliaea*.

After the Greek victory over Persia at the battle of Marathon (490 BCE), Miltiades promised the Athenians that he would make them rich if they put him in charge of seventy ships. His request was granted and he sailed off to attack Paros, a Persian ally and a very wealthy island. The siege, however, failed. Upon Miltiades' return to Athens he was prosecuted by Xanthippus, Pericles' father, for the offense of making a false promise. Miltiades had been severely injured on Paros and was too weak to make a speech. Instead he laid on a couch while his friends spoke in his defense—not unlike, by the way, what occured during the wounded John Brown's 1859 trial in Virginia for conspiring with slaves and other abolitionists to commit sedition, murder, and treason.

The use of *synēgoroi* existed not only in such extreme cases as Miltiades but also where the litigant was young and inexperienced or not fluent in Greek. In such cases a supporting speaker might take up the full laboring oar of the in-court presentation or at least any unexpired time on a litigant's water clock. In all, however, only thirteen of the hundred or so surviving forensic speeches were delivered by such speakers. The reason for this is that to effectively admit (unlike the secret use of a *logographos*) that you were not capable of defending your own interests was to admit that you did not fully posses the capacity of a citizen.

Athens and the First Antilobbyists

The expectancy of personal belief in a particular cause existed in politics as well as law. The Athenians expected an individual politician to state his own opinion on any given subject in open debate with other individuals of differing opinions. The suggestion that a politician was actively supported by a powerful special interest group was often used as an argument against his credibility.

From the combinatorial effect of orator, speechwriter, and supporting speaker eventually came the LAWYER! His full-blooded emergence, at least in the Greco-Roman world, is documented in such remarks as those of Diogenes Laertius, a biographer (CE 200s), that a "Bias, Wise Man of Priene" was an eloquent pleader of causes, who always reserved his talents for the just side (which is always the case with lawyers—right?). Some of these lawyers were attached to the courts as "interpreters," since many of the jurors had no more legal knowledge than did the parties to the case.

And supporting the thesis of a fifth to fourth century BCE beginning of the lawyer class is the fact that the earliest examples of "lawyer" bashing appear to have come from this time period. One of Plato's fictional dialogues records that Socrates and Gorgias (a Sicilian rhetorician, c. 487–376 BCE) debated the nature of rhetoric. Socrates at one point observes that "the rhetorician [loosely, "lawyer"] need not know the whole truth about [the arts]; he only has to discover some way of persuading the ignorant that he has more knowledge than those who know [the arts]." Later in the dialogue he argues that just as cooking makes a mockery of medicine in that it deceives people into feeling good without actually healing them, rhetoric makes a mockery of justice. In other words, Plato, through Socrates, appears to be saying that methods of legal reasoning obscure moral truth. Shocking!

Then, in Plato's *Theaetetus,* Socrates delivers a critique of "lawyering" that remains arguably as apt now as it was 2,400 years ago:

> The lawyer is always in a hurry; there is [the clock] driving him on, and not allowing him to expiate at will; and there is his adversary standing over him, enforcing his rights—he is a servant, and is disputing about a fellow-servant before his master, who is seated, and has the cause in his hands.
>
> The consequence has been, that he has become keen and shrewd; he has learned how to flatter his master in word and indulge him in deed; but his soul is small and unrighteous. His slavish condition has deprived him of growth and uprightness and independence . . . he has been driven into crooked ways; from the first he has practiced deception and retaliation, and has become stunted and warped . . . and is now, as he thinks, a master in wisdom.

Needless to say, neither Socrates nor Plato are up for induction into the lawyer hall of fame anytime soon.

In fairness, however, to both Socrates—at least as a character in Plato's dialogues—and Plato, legal training does have a tendency to turn (or at least try to turn) the student's brain to moral mush—but not necessarily in a bad way. The training, arguably, can work to strengthen the student's powers of sympathetic understanding for different viewpoints. Such sympathy and perhaps even empathy can then lead him or her to an appreciation of the sometimes incommensurability of values (pro-life versus pro-choice; the death penalty; wilderness versus development; etc.). But it can also teach him how to level, sharpen, and assimilate law and facts to the point of crap.

In contrast to the lawyer, the priest and the philosopher tend to advocate set points of view. Plato, for example, propounded a theory of ideas that sought to elevate "nature" from the sphere of contingent facts to the realm of immutable archetypes or forms. In other words, Plato was a believer in divine and absolute Truth—not necessarily a good thing in the rough and tumble world of modern-day legal practice.

X

A BIT OF RHETORIC ON RHETORIC

R<small>HETORIC IS A DISCIPLINE</small> that is tightly woven into the rise of the lawyer class. Its formalization in ancient Greece began with the Sophists, the earliest of whom were older contemporaries of Socrates, alive circa the fifth century BCE. The Sophists (from *sophizesthai,* "making a profession of being inventive and clever"—see the connection with rhetoric?) were the founders of formal education and popularizes of knowledge in the ancient Greek and Greco-Roman world.

Silver Tongues

It has been observed that rhetoric, in its most pejorative sense of bluffing and posturing, has also played a key role in other professions. Medicine, for example, was a prestigious and profitable profession long before the advent of scientific advances in medical treatment: "Apply two leeches and call me in the morning."

As life in and around the Greek city-states of the fifth and fourth century BCE became increasingly complex, due in large part to growth in philosophical thinking and the proliferation of opinions about social and political order that followed, the need for better-trained leaders became evident. This need was "exploited" by professional itinerant educators—walking universities called Sophists. They took on the task of discerning what constituted good opinions through argumentative assessments of prevailing wisdom—in other words, the discourse of the university. In order to attract business, the Sophists needed to be visible. It therefore became customary for them to teach in a public place, such as an *agora* or public gymnasium (of which Athens, at the time, had three).

These teachers, contrary to the then prevailing notion that virtue had to be inherited, claimed that they could teach people important skills. And since leadership in a city-state, such as the Assembly or Council, depended primarily on a person's ability to speak eloquently and persuasively, the Sophists developed, among other things, the art of political and forensic oratory. They were not, however, deeply democratic or magnanimous. In fact they had little interest in educating the lower classes (mostly composed of the landless), but preferred training leaders from the powerful middle class and the elite of society—at, of course, a significant fee. Their central claim was that a certain minimal "nature" (*physis*) was necessary for education, but that anyone possessing this god-given nature could be taught any form of virtue, especially the ability to speak effectively. In carrying out their mission, the Sophists offered both group tutorials and private lessons with no fixed curriculum—they simply made use of grammar, dialectics, and rhetoric as needed. In so doing, the Sophists laid the foundation for the curriculum of a liberal arts education.

The End of Well-Rounded Lawyers?

Some modern-day legal scholars have argued that the traditional view of lawyers possessing broad and deep knowledge not only of law but also of the liberal arts appears to be on the decline, at least in America. And with this decline of the "all-rounded gentleman" (along with a historic aversion to math and science) has come a decline in the public's respect for the law as a learned profession. One cause for this sad state of affairs could be the popular media's coverage of the law. This pop view frequently portrays legal practice not as an intellectual endeavor but as simply the deals lawyers put together and, most importantly, the money they generate in legal fees (what might be called the "used-car dealer's approach" to the practice of law). With regard to trial coverage, one observer has noted that legal journalism has become more like sports and political reporting: blow-by-blow sound bites that pass for analysis. Additionally, a number of law professors have observed that many of today's students enter law school with a shockingly low level of cultural knowledge. This ignorance can make it difficult for the student to understand the contexts in which certain legal doctrines have developed.

※ · ※

Although frequently treated as part of the Greek philosophic tradition, the Sophists were not philosophers in any strict or professional sense, nor were they interested in moral education per se. They were much too pragmatic. Nevertheless, they were inevitably caught up in the conflicting philosophical currents of the time, and tended to adopt a skeptical attitude on fundamental questions. The Sophists sometimes even advanced views that challenged the entire political, religious, and social traditions of the Greek city-states. By disseminating radical views on the origin of law and order, political society, and religion, they helped fuel the great intellectual crisis of the late fifth and early fourth centuries BCE: a desperate search for lasting certainties, ideals, and laws amid the vagaries of change. Some of the Sophists taught the heretical notion that the laws of the state did not have a divine origin but were purely relative, and that true law is based on the premise that "might is right." It is this gloss on the field of political theory, religion, and ethics that underlies much of the sharp criticism of the Sophists by Socrates and Plato. In particular, Plato carried the conviction that true political stability does not come from coercive domination but instead from the inner conviction of the citizens—a conviction that centers around knowledge of "The Good." And for this knowledge to succeed, citizens, in contrast to the teachings of the Sophists, must be educated to believe that they cannot make (or at least cannot easily make) fundamental social changes, since what is Good is "sacred," "just," and "eternal." Respect for a philosopher-king's explication of The Good, in order to create political stability, must be so deeply etched in the minds of the masses (*hoi polloi*) that it never occurs to them that The Good might simply be the result of choices that they or their predecessors have made and is, therefore, fallible and open to change.

THE BEGINNINGS OF RHETORIC

As a term describing the discipline taught by the Sophists, "rhetoric" (*rhētorikē*) appears to have started with Plato's reports in his dialogues *Gorgias* and *Phaedrus*.

This discipline, started in the fifth and fourth centuries BCE, continued as long as some part of the Roman Empire survived. It was at the core of education in the humanities and liberal arts: "Friends, Romans, countrymen, lend me your ears. . . ." Marcus Tullius Cicero (106–43 BCE) and Marcus Fabius

Quintilianus (c. 35–100 CE) both wrote works on rhetoric in Latin that became textbooks for more than a millennium. These books and commentaries were also produced in Greek, and education in rhetoric, at least in the eastern remains of the Roman Empire, continued up to the fall of Constantinople to the Turks in 1453 CE. A law student, for example, would have been immersed in grammatical and rhetorical training before he even turned to the study of the law itself.

However, with the barbarian sack of Rome in 410 CE and the decline of the Empire, the teaching of rhetoric in the West went into steep decline. But starting in the eleventh century at the University of Bologna, there was, particularly with the rediscovery of the Byzantine Emperor Justinian's *Digest*, a revival of Roman law and consequently a renewed interest in rhetoric. This revival largely paralleled the development of the law of the Catholic Church—known as the canon law.

During the three scholastic centuries when the revival of law as a field of study developed, the basic liberal arts education started by the Greeks was in place and provided a convenient forum for rhetorical training. This seven-course meal consisted of the *trivium* of linguistic arts (grammar, rhetoric, and logic or dialectics) and the *quadrivium* of mathematic arts (arithmetic, geometry, astronomy, and music)—all the disciplines considered to be essential for shaping a boy into a gentleman, a *homo liber*.

However, despite this revival of Roman law, primary focus was still given to the Catholic Church's canonical texts, at least initially. Lawmakers at the time tried to use various interpretive means in order to harmonize conflicts between canonical texts and the newly discovered Roman law, as well as trying to apply the law to their own contemporary circumstances. In other words, they attempted to create a contemporary law, of written and rhetorical consistency, for the Holy Roman Empire.

In essence, rhetoric is intended to increase a person's ability to develop, in any given situation (not just legal ones), accounts and arguments that are plausible and persuasive. The student of rhetoric strives to increase this ability through insights into the elements and nature of such accounts and arguments, as well as through practice. It has been said that the Greeks and Romans held the practical use of words in much higher regard than modern society because they were much closer to the oral customs of prehistoric village life in which, like Mark Antony's speech over the body of Julius Caesar, the fate of an entire society rested on one man's words. Additionally, from an economic point of view, the art of rhetoric is often highly developed in primitive and early cultures due to the high costs of information caused by lack of written records, telecommunications, roads, means of rapid travel, and so on. Such costs, given the difficulty in verifying the truth of a speaker's words, makes character extremely important. And the use of rhetorical techniques bolsters the speaker's character (or at least how it is perceived) and thereby makes his utterances plausible and persuasive—a point that particularly applies to lawyers and witnesses within the confines of a courtroom.

Rhetoric does not merely dress up preexisting truths. Instead, it has been argued that rhetoric, in its broadest sense, is the central art by which community, culture, and self are established, maintained, and transformed. Aristotle, for example, asserted that the capacity for discourse (*logos*) separates human beings from animals. Specifically, *logos* permits humans to distinguish between good and bad, right and wrong. It is this common capacity that in turn makes human associations possible, since these associations rest upon shared moral perceptions. And the art of rhetoric is based on the capacity of individuals to discover and manipulate the shared moral conceptions of their community. That is, the human capacity for discourse and shared moral perception is what makes persuasion possible—an important notion in the world of lawyers.

Certain modern-day scholars, in fact, argue that all arguments, at least in the context of law, are rhetorical in nature. And how persuasive an argument is depends on the availability of common elements to which the jury can relate that are relevant to the advocate's case, and on her advocacy skills in creating or filling forensic space. The degree of skill involved, however, is not the product of how closely the advocate can associate the content of her argument with "the way things are," but depends on how successfully she, in spinning the chosen narrative, utilizes the rhetorical conventions of the community. In other words, "skill" is a matter of how closely the advocate argues in accordance with the techniques of persuasion that the community considers effective: the argument's logic, language, arrangement, appeal to authority, passion, purpose, poetry, and general lack of perceived crap. The advocate's success in persuasion is, in turn, a product of both skill and the availability of relevant community assumptions, frequently residing deep in the collective cognitive unconscious, that favor her case.

RHETORIC AND THE LAW

Obviously, the prime occasion to practice the discipline of rhetoric has historically occurred during public speaking. For instance, the debate of policy questions in legislative assemblies are occasions for great bouts of rhetoric. Similarly, there is judicial rhetoric. This type of court-talk is generally characterized by its inquiry into particular past facts—"Isn't it true that on January 1 you, Ms. Eve, were seen cavorting about with a snake of questionable reputation?"—and the attempt to achieve justice in a particular case.

But isn't justice simply the result of the law applied in some mysterious way to the facts? If so, what is all this rhetoric about the application of rhetoric to the law and to lawyers?

Indeed, the law rests on authority (the state) and is supported by public force (the police). At this basic level, it might appear that law has little or nothing to do with the strategic studies of discourse that make up rhetoric. But law is constituted in words. Furthermore, if a law is authoritative, it is always controversial (e.g., the death penalty, abortion, the teaching of evolution, school prayer, same-sex marriages, stem cell research, the use of genetic records, patents on human gene sequences). It is at this level of discourse that the profession of law and the discipline of rhetoric have an erotic connection.

Lawyers and rhetoricians are both hated and loved because of their verbal skills—consider lawyer-President Obama. It can be argued that both lawyers and rhetoricians learn how to best use "the truth" because they are best at being clear. This is because both learn how ambiguous, uncertain, and dependent on context all communication is; how difficult it is to describe facts and their consequences, legal or otherwise; and how much narration is governed by viewpoint. In fact, both lawyers and rhetoricians learn that the key to persuasion is to be clear by creating "the truth"—by being virtual-reality generators. By both creating and imparting "the truth" about a matter to his audience, a lawyer or rhetorician can employ the subtle differences that can make or break an argument. And at its most basic level, an argument is the attempt to persuade an audience; in a legal context, this means use of the law's and the judicial system's coercive power in a way that benefits the lawyer's client, which in turn generally benefits the lawyer.

Impressive rhetoric calls for one to know both the audience and his or her own strengths and weaknesses. As the Irish-American historian Thomas Cahill has explained, "For Cicero [a Roman lawyer/orator], 'to speak from the heart' would be the rashest foolishness; one must always speak from calculation: What do I want to see happen here? What are the desires of my audience? How can I motivate them to do my will? How shall I disguise my weakest arguments?"

❦ · ❦

To Speak the Truth

In the context of a trial, it has been said, jurors often base their decision, at least in part, on their own interests and knowledge, not on the substantive matter at issue. Based on this premise, the most important piece of knowledge for successful persuasion is knowledge of one's audience. For the trial lawyer this generally takes place during jury selection (called "voir dire," from the Old French, meaning "to speak the truth," referring to the oath to speak truthfully when examined). It is during this stage of the trial that the lawyer gets to talk with the potential jurors. Such talk is not just the words said but includes the tone and manner of what is said. For an interesting example of the importance of jury selection, see the movie *The Devil's Advocate*.

To help in obtaining answers to such Ciceronian questions, many trial lawyers, once they take on a case in a new city, go on a semiotic treasure hunt: They switch on the radio talk shows, read the local newspapers, and watch the local TV news. Through these media sources, the lawyer hopes to discover such things as what's likely to be on potential jurors' minds, the tenor of local sentiment on particular issues, and the feelings, words, and images people in the community use to make sense of others and events around them. This information assists him in maximizing the effectiveness of his communication by utilizing the familiar signs and patterns in which relevant meanings are formed and conveyed. The lawyer, in working to effectively advocate his client's case, tries to gain control over reality—and the reality that counts most is the one the judge and jury carry around in their heads.

An interesting and important example of the law as rhetoric and rhetoric as law involved a Philadelphia lawyer named Andrew Hamilton. The *New York Weekly Journal* was America's first pre-Revolutionary journal of political criticism. When William Cosby, the newly appointed royal governor of New York, removed Lewis Morris from his position as the province's chief justice, Morris and some of his wealthy supporters established the *Journal*. They then hired John Peter Zenger, a German immigrant who was scratching out a living printing religious tracts, as the editor in order to insulate themselves from criminal charges should any article contained in the publication be deemed too incendiary.

The *Journal*, which first appeared in March 1733, was a unique type of colonial paper that devoted its coverage to local politics and aimed most of its criticism at—surprise, surprise—Governor Cosby and his supporters, including, just to make it truly personal, Cosby's wife. It published unsigned complaints involving a number of legitimate political criticisms, at least measured by today's standards. In the eighteenth century, however, the criticisms allegedly qualified under English common law as seditious libel (defamation in published writing), a criminal act. Despite Zenger's apparent guilt, three separate grand juries refused to indict. New York's Attorney General then filed an information (an indictment based upon an individual's oath versus a grand jury's oath) charging Zenger with libel. This action was widely condemned by the general population.

In 1735 Zenger was arrested, charged with "presenting and publishing several seditious libels . . . influencing [the people's] Minds with Contempt of His Majesty's Governor," and imprisoned for eight months prior to standing trial. The youthful James DeLancey, Morris's successor as chief justice, set bail at the extraordinary sum of 400 pounds sterling. Zenger's lawyers, on the eve of the trial, moved to have DeLancey disqualified. They argued that because the Chief Justice held his office "during pleasure of the Crown," he lacked the independence required by English law to act as the trial judge. DeLancey was slightly offended by this move and not only denied the request but disbarred the lawyers. He was fair-minded enough, however, to provide Zenger with a lawyer. And so he appointed John Chambers—a supporter of Governor Cosby.

Following Chambers's opening statement, a man rose dramatically from his chair in the City Hall courtroom and announced that he would act as Zenger's lawyer. The man was sixty-year old Andrew Hamilton of Philadelphia, widely regarded as the foremost trial lawyer in the colonies.

Now for the part on law and rhetoric and vice versa. Hamilton conceded Zenger's publication of material critical of Cosby but claimed that truth is a defense to libel—sounds like a good, solid, legal defense. The problem is that under the existing law, which focused only on the cost side of free speech, the argument was unsound. The well-established rule was the greater the truth, the greater the libel. That was the law. So to Hamilton's claim, Chief Justice DeLancey responded: "A libel is not to be justified; for it is nevertheless a libel that it is true." Or as the poet William Blake stated it in the *Auguries of Innocence:* "A truth that's told with bad intent beats all the lies you can invent."

Hamilton next maintained that the issue of libel was not for DeLancey to decide, but belonged to the jury. The Chief Justice also disputed this point. However, under strenuous argumentation by Hamilton, DeLancey finally acquiesced to counsel's position, at least somewhat. He told the jurors that truth is not a defense to libel, but permitted them to return a general verdict, meaning simply "guilty" or "not guilty"—without distinguishing between issues of law and issues of fact. The decision, seemingly grounded not in narrow logic but in social reasoning, was "not guilty"—which brought great cheers from the spectators in the courtroom. Based on Hamilton's rhetoric, the law on libel publicly embraced the fundamental concept that only a jury ("the voice of the people") should possess the ultimate authority to limit political criticism.

THE FIRST LEGAL RHETORICIANS

Possibly the first theorist of legal rhetoric was Corax of Syracuse, who wrote and taught around 465 BCE. His views on the subject were initially formulated in the context of a specific legal problem that surfaced in Syracuse, a Greek colony on the island of Sicily. The problem arose because a democratic government had overthrown a dictatorship. The courts, as a result of this change in government, were faced with disputes over property: Who was the rightful owner—the owner before the dictatorship or the owner given the property by the dictatorship? These legal disputes increased the need for training in legal rhetoric (i.e., advocacy).

As previously discussed, ancient Greek trials in the popular courts consisted primarily of a speech by the plaintiff or the prosecutor and a speech by the defendant. There were no professional judges. Trials lasted a day in the case of public actions and no more than a few hours in the case of private actions, with the speeches limited by the use of a water clock. There was, technically, no appeals process. In this institutional context, legal oratory skill was therefore an essential part of the life of a Greek citizen (or at least those of the upper classes). Teachers of rhetoric, such as Corax and his student Tisias, who brought Corax's teaching to Athens, offered instruction in the art of legal advocacy—at Ivy League prices.

Corax and Tisias trained their students to argue from a probability point of view. A plaintiff suing for assault might argue that because he feared his attacker, he would not have attacked first. The alleged attacker might then argue that the plaintiff was more likely to strike first because he would want the advantage of the first blow. Greeks preferred this type of circumstantial reasoning because they distrusted direct evidence in both "criminal" and "civil" trials. Their concern, given the prevalence of agonistic values in Greek society, was that direct evidence could be faked or bribed—and apparently often was. But a sound "logical" argument could not.

⊗ · ⊗

Ancient Perjury

A man who gave false or illegal evidence in ancient Greece was subject to prosecution for false witness, and the man who put him up to it could also be prosecuted. Any such charge, however, was difficult to prove. The canon lawyers of the Middle Ages attempted to deal with this same problem by use of oaths. The oath of witnesses included promises that they would speak truthfully—and, contrary to the agonistic values of the ancient Greeks, for both sides. The oath also required that the witness would add no falsehood to the truth (i.e., not just the truth and the whole truth, but also nothing but the truth), and that the testimony was not motivated by fear, bribery, love, or hate.

⊗ · ⊗

The Sophists, in general, held a worldview close to that of pragmatism; they saw the world as incomplete, ambiguous, and uncertain. Nevertheless, it was a world that could be interpreted and understood through language. The important point was to deal with concrete argumentation and decision making in the areas of law and politics. Thus, the world of the Sophists, despite its uncertainties, was a practical one—one of particular cases. This aspect of sophistry, in contrast to certain of its excesses and vices, was prominent in the work of Isocrates (436–338 BCE).

Born into a rich family, Isocrates studied with both Sophists and Socrates. The Peloponnesian War, however, destroyed his family's fortune and forced him to seek a living as a writer and teacher. Ironically, he was afraid to speak in public and therefore began his career as a speechwriter. He also loathed the specialization of the theoretical sciences, which he thought to be of no practical value, and sought to fashion opinion through rhetoric. Consequently, Isocrates, as he turned from speechwriting to teaching (opening his own school of rhetoric around 392 BCE), flogged this art as the core of a Greek citizen's education. His notion of rhetoric included a study of the liberal arts: philosophy, science, mathematics, literature, history, and communication (not a bad mix even for a modern-day lawyer). In his work *Against the Sophists,* Isocrates advocated the pursuit of practical wisdom, for which he felt moral character was essential. Such character, however, could not really be taught, but the study of speech and politics could help encourage and train moral consciousness. It is this idea of the good, or moral, orator that became a key aspect of later Roman rhetoricians.

A similar theme regarding the importance of character (*aretē*), although approached from a nonpagan point of view, resurfaced in the seventeenth century with the idea of a calling. This Protestant idea, particularly in its Calvinist version, has deeply influenced the practice of law.

The original Protestant notion of a calling was grounded in the imperative of humans helping to complete the work of God's creation through their own labor. In this teleological context, all work was seen as a means by which salvation might be achieved, a type of "Work Reward" program. But as the religious underpinnings of this notion of "calling" gave way, the concept that an activity is capable of conferring meaning on the whole of a person's life needed to be redefined. Rather than measuring work, in general, by its relationship to God's creation, some feature of the work itself had to be identified that could be seen as providing a path to salvation; not just a "Work Reward" program, but more like a meritocracy. Not every kind of work, however, contains the breadth of human values needed to provide such internal justification: administering to the spiritual needs of humankind (i.e., a "priest") would seem to qualify; digging ditches appears to be more problematic.

The distinction between work involving issues of human values and work that is more routine led, in the nineteenth century, to the idea of a profession. While the question of which jobs count as professions remains controversial, a critical element of a group's claim to such status centers around whether or not the work of its members contains a sufficiently broad range of human values to have a transformative effect on its members' personalities. That is, does the work extend beyond reward by an employer or a mere exchange of value and actually promote the development of a distinctive professional character? *Aretē?*

A compelling argument has been made that law is rich enough in human values to sustain an internal justification for constituting a profession. And the introduction to this world of values, at least as used and abused in the context of the law, begins with the lawyer's initial legal training. As previously discussed, the student, particularly through the teacher's use of the case method, is brought face-to-face with different intellectual and emotional challenges. Such challenges are in turn intended, at least in theory, to help reshape the student's (moral?) character—not unlike Isocrates' notion that study (in his case, of rhetoric) can help train moral consciousness and eventually lead to the acquisition of practical wisdom.

The transformative notion of a profession reached its extreme, modern-day conclusion in the writings of a late nineteenth-century lawyer and social theorist, Max Weber (1864–1920). For Weber the predicament of modern man is "disenchantment of the world"—the collapse of a teleological worldview that had, as noted earlier, permitted individuals to see their lives as serving God's purposes. And in Weber's opinion there is no exit. The appropriate response, however, is not nihilism but vocation. This means that one must first acknowledge the modern predicament resulting from rationalism, individualism, and bureaucratic law, and then, in spite of it, embrace one's chosen profession as a vocation. That is, one must treat one's secular existence as if it were a religious calling ("God's call"). The lawyer must become a secular "priest" full of utter devotion to the law—which means seeing the law as more than just a tool. Life, however, as a modern professional, according to Weber, can never be truly redeeming, but only transforming enough that it offers the devotee a glimpse of what it is like to lead a meaningful life.

ARISTOTLE

Aristotle, a philosopher and scientist (384–322 BCE) whom you undoubtedly have heard of in other contexts, adopted the sophistic emphasis on the contingent, the contextual, and the practical elements of rhetoric in his treatise *Rhetoric*. Interestingly, Aristotle adopted this emphasis despite the fact that he had been a student of Plato, the absolutist. He highlighted the point that philosophy (which included science), like sports and drama, was competitive.

As part of his theories on political community and the rule of law, Aristotle sought to systemize rhetoric. He first contrasted demonstrative reasoning, which aims at scientific certainty, with practical reasoning, which he called dialectical ("conversation" or "dialogue") reasoning. He then pointed out that dialectical reasoning proceeds by question and answer down to finer and finer detail, whereas rhetoric involves continuous exposition—long-windedness. Furthermore, in dialectics, only reasoned arguments are allowed, but in rhetoric the personality of the speaker and his character (*aretè*), as well as the individual and collective emotions of the audience, contribute to persuasion.

Proving an Objective Worth

Modern-day philosophy, in the opinion of many scholars, is an example of dialectical reasoning; reasoned proof is arguably the point of modern philosophy. One scholar has noted that the link between philosophy and all other fields of study (including law) can only be explained if philosophy is able to provide certain benefits or services that are otherwise not available through any other means—meaning science. So, arguably, in order to demonstrate their worth, philosophers must create reasoned proofs (or at least attempt to do so).

A prime example of this point, in fact, occurred during Aristotle's lifetime: the case of Demosthenes' crown. In 336 BCE, the orator Ctesiphon proposed a decree that the people of Athens should confer a gold crown on his friend Demosthenes in honor of his merit and virtue and "because he continues saying and doing what is best for the people." Specifically, Demosthenes had opposed Philip, king of Macedonia. A long-time rival of Demosthenes by the name of Aeschines, who had defended Philip's call for the unification of Greece, was outraged and attempted to stop the decree from being passed by bringing a "prosecution for illegalities" (*graphē paranomōn*) against Ctesiphon.

Aeschines' speech was *Against Ctesiphon;* Demosthenes, acting as an advocating witness (a *synēgoros*) for Ctesiphon, prepared and gave *On the Crown.* Ctesiphon was acquitted. Demosthenes' speech became such a classic of rhetoric that Cicero wrote a prologue to it and translated it into Latin, to be memorized by Roman schoolboys. And Queen Elizabeth I of England, the daughter of King Henry VIII and a master of the spoken word, extensively studied Demosthenes. The defeated Aeschines, however, chose to go into exile, never to return to Athens; not because he couldn't pay the fine of 1,000 drachmas, but because the humiliation of losing in court killed his political future. Though several of Aeschines' arguments appear to have been legally sound, he was no match for the persuasive rhetoric of Demosthenes.

Despite the differences, however, between pure dialectical reasoning and rhetoric, Aristotle finally decided that rhetoric belonged to the realm of the dialectical (thus fusing cases and exposition) and not the demonstrative or some other form of reasoning. Nevertheless, he viewed legal questions from a problem-oriented perspective rather than one involving deductive logic.

Dialectical reasoning is not a single form of reasoning, but one that brings together related mental operations. This is why, in large part, both theology and canon law eventually embraced the dialectical method during the Middle Ages as the primary means of organizing and furthering knowledge. It is a method that starts with common sense and then subjects this starting point to a process of critical examination in which practical reasoning and logic play a large part. Similar to demonstrative reasoning—basically the scientific method—dialectical reasoning takes into account available data and experience, forms hypotheses, tests them against concrete particulars, weighs competing hypotheses, and stands ready to repeat the process in the light of new data, experience, or insight. However, unlike demonstrative reasoning, the dialectic method of reasoning starts with premises that are doubtful or in dispute or are simply socially accepted and often unexamined, and ends by determining which of the various opposing positions is supported by stronger evidence and more convincing reasons. It never ends, however, with certainty. This is why dialectical reasoning, and law, will not yield the satisfaction of a mathematical proof.

Having shoved rhetoric into the category of dialectical reasoning, Aristotle next identified three types of rhetoric: deliberative, judicial, and epideictic, all three of which Cicero later picked up on in his discussion of the orator. Deliberative rhetoric is political discourse in which a listener is asked to evaluate a proposed future action (e.g., "This law should be passed because . . ."). Speeches of this type, in ancient Athens, included those delivered in the Assembly and the Council when such bodies were acting in their legislative capacity. And in the twenty-first century the linguist George Lakoff in *Whose Freedom? The Battle over America's Most Important Idea* has opined that "[President George W.] Bush's second inaugural address was a work of rhetorical [political] art. More than half of the time, the use of 'freedom,' 'free,' and 'liberty' was in a context neutral enough to fit the simple, uncontested sense—of either the progressive or conservative senses. The words could mean whatever one wanted them to mean, depending on one's political leanings. Many of Bush's phrases could have been said by a Democrat with the opposite policies."

Judicial rhetoric, on the other hand, is forensic discourse in which the listener is asked to judge a past action (e.g., "Ladies and gentlemen of the jury, the evidence will show that the defendant Cain, on April 1, willfully and with malice of forethought, murdered his brother"). At the time of Aristotle, this type of rhetoric included speeches prepared for high-profile political trials, generally written and delivered by an expert politician, and also run-of-the-mill trials, sometimes written by a professional speechwriter. Finally, epideictic rhetoric is ceremonial discourse in which the audience is asked to judge the artistic abilities of the speaker. These type of speeches included public funeral orations and speeches (not unlike the Gettysburg Address) prepared by professional rhetoricians as examples of eloquence.

Modern legal thought has picked up on Aristotle's radial classification of rhetoric and frequently treats the "interpretation" of written law as a combined deliberative and judicial process. This means that sometimes emphasis is on the reading of a text that provides the most useful effects in the future, and sometimes the emphasis is on a reading that is the "historically accurate" one in the sense of the drafter's original intent or purpose. For the lawyer advocating his or her client's position, this debate opens up both the past and the future as potential avenues for argumentation. Outstanding!

FAITH IN ORAL ARGUMENTS

In the fifth and fourth centuries BCE, the Greeks displayed a certain ambivalence toward legal texts. The reason for this was that while the equality of citizens depended, at least in part, on the existence of written laws, they recognized that such an embodiment of statutes and decrees, standing alone, could become an instrument of tyranny. (Consider the United States of America's Internal Revenue Code.) The Greeks felt that it was possible—as we saw with the Sumerian's, Akkadian's, and Babylonian's general distrust of the written word—that a written law could obscure its author's pure thoughts and introduce a new authority to supplant the citizen's collective voice. In several of Plato's dialogues, for example, Socrates criticized writing, saying that written words are dead; they can only repeat exactly what they say, unable to answer back and explain what they mean. Based on such concerns, inscribed statues and decrees in democratic Athens were to be presented in the form of spoken discourse and to include a reference to the living voice of the lawmakers.

Rhetoric and Process

It has been argued that the importance of the jury system is not based on whether the verdict in each particular case comports with the factual truth of what really happened, but rather lies in the process of listening to the lawyers' arguments, of jurors talking among themselves, of debating, of questioning, of agreeing, of being swayed one way and then the other—all forms of rhetoric. Without this process, there would be only tyranny: tyranny of the law and tyranny of the facts. Law and facts, the argument goes, do not tell us much about ourselves. We only really learn from each other.

In contrast, consider the *Aktenversendung* previously used in Germany. The *Aktenversendung* (literally, "the sending of the file") was a procedure by which courts, when faced with a difficult application of the law, were supposed to send the entire file of the case to a law faculty. The law professors would study and discuss the case and hand down a judgment (primarily based on Roman law) that was binding on the court. This procedure, which lasted in Germany until 1878, had an enormous influence on German law. It reflected and embodied an emphasis on written instead of oral procedure, on secrecy instead of transparency of proceedings, and on separation of issues of fact from issues of law.

Concern over the written word is also present in modern-day society. The United States trial system, in particular, relies on oral presentation much as ancient Greece did. Lawyers tell their client's story through a highly regulated conversational style (OK, an extremely weird conversational style) with witnesses—the reason for much of the "Just answer the question," "I object, Your Honor," and "May counsel approach the bench?" Jurors are frequently swayed as much by the unusual rhythm and tone of this lawyer-witness/lawyer-judge discourse as by the "facts" that are presented. Their judgment of a witness's credibility can be swayed by the witness's demeanor (is he sweating?) and his appeal in answering questions. Like the Greeks, the U.S. legal system generally believes that there is truth in oral conversation—particularly if you are Johnnie Cochran performing the law in hip-hop cadence: "If it doesn't fit, you must acquit."

Aristotle drew a line between written law (*idios nomos*) and unwritten law that seems to be generally agreed upon—a "common law" or ethos. And having established this basic distinction, Aristotle went on to discuss the topics on which to base an argument about the meaning of legal texts. He recognized that arguments about the definition or interpretation of the terms of a text are often crucial to judicial outcomes. For example, a person accused of spousal abuse might admit to having "engaged in a physical response" or "misbehaved" but not to having committed a "violent assault."

William Blackstone, the famous eighteenth-century English lawyer and educator, stated that the incapacity of a bastard is "that he cannot be heir to anyone, neither can he have heirs by or of his own body; for being *nullius filius* ["son of no one"], he is therefore of kin to nobody, and has no ancestor from whom any inheritable blood can be derived." It has been pointed out that this statement regarding the incapacity of a bastard is just a fancy way of saying that a bastard cannot be an heir or have heirs because the law does not permit it: Simply put, society doesn't like bastards. However, the way in which the statement is constructed makes it seem like a sound argument rather than a conclusion reached from a socially motivated framing concept structured by a cultural prejudice. Clever!

Aristotle also suggested techniques for arguing for an interpretation of a text that is beyond its "plain meaning." In essence, what he advocated was that the potential tyranny of a legal text can be overcome by making it more equitable and flexible through the use of rhetoric—a sentiment at the heart of the debate over whether law is art or science. Such fairness could be achieved, according to Aristotle, through constructing arguments about a text by looking to different sources of interpretation. This insight has generally been adopted, with relish, by many modern-day lawyers, judges, and certainly law professors. Issues of whether a statute is clear and what techniques should be used to get at an unclear statute's "true" meaning continue to be areas of hot debate among lawyers.

The Greek writings on rhetoric of the fifth and fourth centuries BCE had, as indicated earlier, a significant impact on later Roman legal culture. A child from a prosperous family located in the Latin portions of the empire would ideally learn to speak both Latin and Greek—initially from his nurse, who was often Greek. Later, a family slave might shuttle the child back and fourth from school where he would learn to read and write and then to apply himself to the study of Greek and Latin literature: Homer, Hesiod, and Virgil. Students who continued on would study music, astronomy, and geometry. The ultimate goal of all this formal training was to achieve skill in rhetoric. It was this skill that made possible a public career—in order to be influential in courts or civic assemblies, the student needed to acquire fluency in speaking.

As previously noted, the value placed on persuasion after the fall of Rome began anew in twelfth- and thirteenth-century western Europe as university students demonstrated their learning through oral arguments. At Oxford and

Paris, students, high on the arts and sciences developed in ancient Greece and Rome, studied Aristotelian logic—all with the aim of becoming "sophisters" who could take part in public disputations. On receiving their bachelor's degree, students displayed their newly acquired skills by holding open disputes.

The form of rhetoric taught and practiced during this medieval period emphasized appeal to reason in contrast to attempted persuasion by appeal to emotion. The focus was therefore on methods of proof, and the concept of a hypothesis was refined by the rhetoricians in order to supplement traditional Aristotelian dialectics. Proof of a hypothesis was understood to require the presentation of evidence, which in turn implied the notion of probable truth. The existence of probabilities (e.g., a particular fact being more likely than not, Corax's notion of "the most probable") led the rhetoricians to emphasize presumptions and their use in logic. The use of hypotheses also spawned rules that attempted to avoid distortion and error in the presentation and evaluation of evidence.

The similarities between this revamped form of rhetoric and the law did not go unnoticed. A twelfth-century treatise, for example, states that "both rhetoric and law have a common procedure." The author, Cardinal Agostino Valier, goes on to make it clear that rhetoric's concept of hypothesis is associated with the legal concept of a case. This popular treatise, *Rhetorica Ecclesiastica,* also states that to find the truth of a disputed matter four persons are necessary: a judge, a witness, an accuser, and a defender. (What about lawyers?)

In the fifteenth and sixteenth centuries, the humanist reformers of the Renaissance grabbed on even tighter to the rhetorical traditions of the Greeks and Romans. With the transfer of priceless documents from the East to the West, the best minds of western Europe began a scrupulous reappraisal of scholasticism, an attempt to fuse pagan learning and Christianity—which, for two centuries, had been devolving into an artificial type of dialectic. The return to classical sources taught the humanists that one of the principal goals of education was the pursuit of eloquence. They were, however, distrustful of abstract speculation and of purely technical or theoretical concerns and therefore adopted a Ciceronian ideal of the orator as a heroic figure. The mission of this hero was to use his learning, experience, and talent for persuasion to guide others toward useful and worthwhile goals—like Christianity.

In winding up this section on rhetoric, it is again emphasized that rhetoric does not apply in the same way to all disciplines. There is, at least arguably, a discipline-specific rhetoric of law—in contrast to the rhetoric of politics—and this specific application of rhetoric to the law helps shape how lawyers advocate and how judges write opinions. In other words, how law is done. It is generally assumed in modern-day academic circles that law is, at its heart, the practice of rhetoric (in contrast to the words of gods), and that this particular type of rhetoric is the rhetoric of historical foundations and logical conclusions. And of particular interest is the notion that this type of rhetoric relies, above all else, upon the denial that it is rhetoric that is taking place. The reason for such denial can be seen by comparing the rhetoric of law with the rhetoric of literature.

There are fundamental differences between legal scholars and literary critics, though on the surface both disciplines appear to be quite similar. Both the legal scholar and the literary critic engage in a process of interpretation—an effort, often in excruciating detail, to discover the meaning of a preexisting text. In the case of a legal scholar the text is generally a case, constitutional provision, statute, or administrative regulation. And for the literary critic, the text is generally a novel, short story, or poem. Despite, however, the similarity of starting with a preexisting text and similarities in methods of critique, the law, unlike literary criticism, involves the use of political power: "Property" is created, transferred, and destroyed; relationships are altered; people are executed. Law carries a sword—and if it doesn't have one handy, it can always, like Solomon, demand one. It has also been argued that there is a basic difference in the purpose of the two academic fields. Literary criticism adopts an essentially nonprescriptive stance: The critic does not attempt to tell the author how to create more realistic characters or construct a better plot. The legal scholar is not nearly so shy. He often has no hesitation in telling judges how to create a better text by "proper" interpretation of prior cases, "proper" use of social policy, and how to reason through to a "proper" conclusion.

What all this boils down to is that literary critics generally love to love those talented writers deemed worthy of interpretation and evaluation and legal scholars frequently love to pull the wings off of those high and mighty judges who clearly do not have the brainpower to be legal scholars.

In looking to other disciplines, lawyers, law professors, and judges often choose to rely on those disciplines that offer the kinds of "final" answers that the business of deciding requires—disciplines of closure, such as economics, empirical social science, game theory, and analytic philosophy—recognizing (at least in moments of reflection) that the process is often like rounding off an irrational number: Simply find a point to your liking and cut off the information. However, as any scientist will tell you, rounding off at three decimal places instead of ten can result in a completely different picture. In contrast, those involved in literature generally look to disciplines of openness: cultural anthropology, psychoanalysis, and continental philosophies.

While there are differences between law and literature, it should not be assumed that there has not been crossbreeding between these two disciplines.

Legal scholarship involving eighteenth- and nineteenth-century America points to various groups that had a keen interest in the relationship between law and literature and the assumed role of Roman and civil law in this relationship. For these group members, law and literature were not distinct subjects. They believed that the law was a type of literature, that both law and literature served practical purposes, and therefore should be studied together. The members of these groups saw little difference in the study of a great book and the study of a legal system. As a result, these lawyers and jurists wrote legal arguments, opinions, and treatises in what has been called the "Grand Style" and the continuing value of these writings lies as much in their literary quality as in the coherence and elegance of their legal arguments. There are also contemporary legal theorists who see law-in-literature and law-as-literature. While there are a number of variations on law and literature scholarship, practitioners of the movement generally believe that the basic human dimension of law can be discovered from the study of the great works of literature, as so much great literature has examined conflicts without black-and-white solutions. The movement appears to be aimed at bringing out the human element (arguably) missing in traditional law. In other words, rounding off at ten decimal places instead of three.

ANCIENT ROME

BY THE TIME GREECE became part of the expanse of Rome, the idea of "lawyer" had been significantly, and organically, advanced. His role in relationship to law and society had generally been distinguished from that of the astrologer, oracle, and priest, as well as from that of the philosopher. The law was no longer strictly religious in nature and therefore a direct, divine connection was not always essential. The differences between philosophy and the practice of law also started to surface.

The dividing line, however, between philosophy and legal practice was not, in ancient Greece or Rome (or in modern times), always crystal clear. As discussed, the discipline of rhetoric constituted a continuing tie between the two disciplines. The rhetorical art of accounts and arguments that are plausible and persuasive undoubtedly stems from the idea of a proof that is based on axioms and subordinate principles. And proof lies at the heart of the Greek (as well as Arab) mathematical/philosophical tradition: the search for Truth with a capital "T," proof that a hypothesis is correct. Aristotle, however, pointed out that demonstrative reasoning that aims at scientific certainty is not the same as dialectical reasoning. Furthermore, in strict dialectics only logical argument is allowed, whereas in rhetoric the personality of the speaker and the emotions of the audience also contribute to persuasion. Nevertheless, Aristotle concluded that dialectical reasoning has room for rhetoric. And with the development of rhetoric, the lawyer class developed a voice to go with the increasing intellectual rigor of studying law. And this voice, at its dramatic best, became louder and clearer in the Roman Empire.

Simplicity or Billable Hours?

It is important to keep in mind that the increasing difficulty of studying and practicing law was largely the result of the law being written down. Whereas the effectiveness of an oral command depended upon its simplicity, writing facilitated the dissemination of more complex commands. And lawyers love complex commands—more billable hours.

XI

ROMAN LAW

Roman law certainly predates the famous *Twelve Tables.* Little, however, is known about this early stage of development, and therefore books discussing the law of ancient Rome routinely begin around 450 BCE—the time of the *Tables,* the *Lex Duodecim Tabularum.* Nevertheless, if the *Tables* were simply a compilation of various prevailing rules, which appears to be the case, the rules themselves must have come first, most likely in the form of pronouncements made by kings, based on custom and religious practice, or perhaps picked up, to some extent, from Mesopotamia. In fact, several of the rules have been attributed to Romulus (son of Mars), the legendary founder of Rome (753 BCE), and Numa Pompilius (715–673 BCE), Romulus's Sabine successor. These early royal laws were, according to some accounts, eventually compiled by Sextus Papirius as the *Ius Papirianum,* most likely from existing priestly compilations of laws, procedures, and related rules. This written set of pontifical laws, if it ever existed, is now lost to time.

When the Romans threw off the rule of kings and began to experiment with republican forms of government, there was a push to write down existing law. This push, starting in 462 BCE, stemmed from social conditions not unlike those that framed the backdrop to Solon's "codification." The rumble was therefore led by a commoner—in this case a plebeian named Gaius Terentilius Harsa. The thrust of this advocate's attack was on the arrogance of patricians (aristocratic families) toward plebeians as displayed in the powers of the ruling magistrates.

After the consuls announced that the codification of laws by the commoners would not happen, the tribunes—the representatives of the plebians—proposed a compromise. If the Senate would not accept

125

something passed by the plebeians, how about a commission of lawmakers drawn from both plebs and patricians? This commission's task would be to firm up laws beneficial to both sides and thereby equalize their liberty. Sounds fair. The senators, just ever so slightly intimidated by the restless masses, were suddenly not opposed to the idea of lawmaking, but insisted that only they could do it. This response was not all that surprising, particularly coming from a group that framed the question of liberty (rhetorically) as: What value does it have in a world where everyone has the same amount? The worn down plebs accepted the fact that reform was up to the elite. And soon thereafter (c. 451 BCE), the Senate allegedly sent a delegation out into the world to study the laws of other cities, including those of Solon—it seems clear, for example, that the word for "punishment" (*poena*) was derived from the Greek (*poinē*). And shortly after the return of this commission to Rome, the Senate appointed ten officials as the sole magistrates to draft the laws. These ten patricians produced a "code" of ten (probably wooden) tablets which, after revisions, were successfully presented by the Senate to the other main political body—the *comitia centuriata,* "organization of the people in hundreds," a military assembly.

The concept of ten officials as the designated magistrates to draft laws turned out to be very popular and therefore when it was determined that the "code" was incomplete, a second group was elected for the following year. This new board, which included some plebeians, produced two supplementary tablets. Together the tablets, approved in 450 BCE as *lex* (law) by the *comitia centuriata,* became known as the *Twelve Tables* and were set up in the Roman Forum for all to read. The board was quickly made extinct.

Historians generally consider that with the *Twelve Tables* the Republic developed the most important legislative monument conceived by Rome until the compilation ordered by the Emperor Justinian.

Legal scholarship has emphasized the fact that the *Tables* were essentially the product of the aristocratic patricians drafted for the plebeians—or at least a set of laws that could be shared with them. In other words, one that was carefully crafted in order to achieve a Nash equilibrium. Consequently, even though accepted by the plebs, procedures and substantive matters that the patricians regarded as inappropriate for the commoners to have any involvement with appear to have been excluded. Nothing in the *Twelve Tables,* for example, spells out the powers and duties of consuls or other aristocratic officials (unlike modern-day constitutions that distinguish among legislative, executive, and judicial functions)—despite the fact that this was one of the plebs' original goals. In fact, contrary to the Roman historian Livy's claim that the *Tables* contained "the source of all private and public law," public law hardly made an appearance.

Control of the state religion was also a powerful political weapon. For instance, by simply reporting unfavorable omens ("I hear thunder"), augurs could postpone action within the various assemblies or kill the election of a pro-democratic official. Accordingly, the rituals and the priestly offices were the exclusive domain of the patricians—just in case there needed to be any divine fudging. And since they were not willing to share this power with the plebs, divine law, much like public law, did not generally show up in the *Tables*. They were therefore, in addition to being carefully packaged, highly secular.

It is also the case that the important "judicial" task of interpreting the *Tables*, which dealt right from the start with procedure (especially, and not surprisingly, concerning the enforcement of debt obligations), was entrusted to none other than the patrician college of the *pontifices*, the council of priests. The opinion of this college was authoritative, and each year one of its members was chosen for the purpose of interpreting private law and named "pontificate." The pontiffs were priests of the Roman State religion, and in that holy capacity their main function was to help keep a proper relationship between man and the gods—a task that was exclusive to sacred law (*fas*).

A Literal Bridge

"Pontiffs" literally means "bridge makers"—highlighting the importance of their historic responsibility to oversee the maintenance of an actual bridge, the *pons Sublicius* (the Sublician Bridge). The state of this important bridge across the Tiber was a religious as well as civil matter.

In reaching the right answer to various questions involving *fas*, a pontiff could not (at least outwardly) base his position on justice or equity, usefulness or economic efficiency, or advantage to the state. Such considerations might have been appropriate for resolving issues of secular law (*ius*), but not the sacred—which saw itself as divine Truth. And since these considerations were not used by the pontiffs in the realm of sacred law, it has been pointed out that, even though arguably appropriate, they were not used in the realm of the secular. Roman legal reasoning, both in the hands of the pontiffs and later, the jurists, was therefore self-contained. It relied upon its own internal logic and did not generally look to other disciplines for support. In a word, Roman legal reasoning, although perhaps not to the same extent as religion, was highly formalistic. Consequently, it seems unlikely that the arguments used by Roman lawyers were expressly grounded in economic or social realities. This does not mean that they ignored the necessities of life—only that there were no free-ranging Vinnies or Sals. Instead, such devices as playing with the meaning of words (a favorite, as we saw in Part III, of Aristotle) and the ever-popular reasoning by analogy appear to have been used as a means of reaching legal conclusions.

The *Twelve Tables,* rudely destroyed by Brennus and his gang of Gallic invaders in 390 BCE, embodied primitive, and to the extent underpinned by religion, pagan law. Even Gaius's *Institutes,* 600 years later (c. 161 CE), were still pagan in orientation. Nevertheless, later Roman texts were assembled and used by Christianized emperors such as Constantine (r. 306–337 CE). And Justinian I, a devout Christian emperor, is generally considered to have been pivotal in the development of a revised version of Roman law. However, despite Justinian's devotion to Christianity, his *Institutes* (appropriating the name of Gaius's *Institutes*), in contrast to the *Codex* and *Novellae,* made no mention of God nor was it supported by scriptural authority—instead it consisted entirely of the writings of pagan jurists.

JUSTINIAN AND HIS LEGACY

Emperor Justinian (483–565 CE) was one of the most important figures in the survival and spread of Roman law. He was born Petrus Sabbatius in the Illyrian region of the eastern part of the Roman Empire, in what is now Yugoslavia. His family was part of the peasant class and he therefore would most likely have stayed in his hometown of Tauresium had his uncle Justin not risen through the military ranks to become chief of the imperial palace guard in Constantinople ("New Rome"), capital of the Roman Empire. The childless Justin requested that his nephew join him in order to acquire the command experience, learning, and political connections that would make the young Petrus a suitable heir.

He apparently excelled in his military duties and studies, especially theology and law. The Emperor's death in 518 led to the elevation of Justin to head of state. By then the thirty-six-year-old Petrus, who had taken on the additional surname of Justinianus (Justinian) in honor of his uncle, was well prepared to help guide his uncle, if not to reign through him. The new Emperor made his nephew his official coruler. And on April 1, 527, Justinian, upon the death of his uncle, began a long reign over the Empire.

As emperor, Justinian's mission statement provided for retaking the western part of the Empire (overrun by a variety of Goths and Moors) and reorganizing the ancient law of Rome in order to make it more useful in his "modern age." He failed to reconquer the entire western half of the Roman Empire, but after several military campaigns conducted over a twenty-year period, he managed to take back Italy—leaving the peninsula devastated and impoverished.

(A clear violation, by the way, of lawyer-liberator Gandhi's position that one cannot justify destroying a country in order to save it.) And through conquest and intrigue, Justinian also extended the borders of the Empire to the Alps, as well as sweeping in most of North Africa and some of southern Spain.

With regard to updating the ancient law of Rome, the Emperor's *Codex,* along with his *Digest, Intuitiones,* and *Novellae,* collected and codified the entire corpus of Roman law then in force. This remarkable collection, taken from a millennium of Roman legal development (510 BCE to 530 CE), was assembled from the scattered and fragmented literary remains of a Roman Empire that Constantine, due to the lingering pagan influences in Rome, had abandoned over a century earlier. It is important to keep in mind that Christianized Romans such as Constantine and Justinian significantly changed the original materials of classical Roman law (which over the centuries had itself been in flux) in order to, among other things, further Church policies and consolidate the Church's social/political position.

Justinian and his writers also simplified and rationalized Roman law. The rearrangement of the law's form and structure was intended to ease the actual practice of law, rendering it more efficient and inexpensive. And changes to the substantive law, such as streamlining the rules of pleading in lawsuits, likewise favored economic growth.

Roman law, starting around the time of the *Twelve Tables* until the introduction of the *formulae* system, provided that a "plaintiff" had to summon the "defendant" by an oral request (*ius vocate*). It was up to the plaintiff to persuade or force a defendant to appear before a magistrate in order to trigger the first stage of the two-stage trial process. The plaintiff, once he and the defendant were standing before the magistrate, was required to speak the appropriate form of his claim in set words of "magical force." The magistrate, after deciding on the exact question to be tried (*litis contestatio*), appointed a private judge (*iudex privatus*) to hear the matter—unless, however, it was agreed to be arbitrated by a third party (*iudex unus*) whom both parties trusted. The lay judge explored the facts, heard the evidence of witnesses and the parties' arguments, and then rendered his judgment under the authority and instructions handed down by the magistrate. If the judgment was in favor of the plaintiff, it was, assuming a nonsomatic remedy, always in the form of a sum of money. The reason for this was most likely due to the court's transitory nature. Once a particular verdict had been rendered, that court ceased to exist and therefore it could not follow up on an order given to a party to do or not to do something. In other words, the decision lost its teeth once the court disbanded.

After the second century BCE, a plaintiff could bring an action by obtaining a document from a political official that identified the nature of the claim he intended to assert (i.e., a complaint). This document, acquired through petition, evolved into the individual edicts and model forms of action granted by a magistrate known as the *praetor*. Thus, slowly, the older legal actions procedure, with its excessive formality, archaic nature, and limited effectiveness, started to give way to a much broader formulary procedure. The praetor, freed from the limits of the *Twelve Tables* by the *lex Aebutia* (c. 150 BCE), in fact, published a list (on wooden boards displayed in the Forum) of the various actions that he was willing to grant. This list, known as the praetor's edict or simply "the Edict," eventually constituted the basic framework for how the praetor would interpret the law of the Roman people and the legal principles established by magistrates, as well as how he would apply those principles; for example, "I will grant an action if . . ." or "I will allow possession of goods if . . . ." The Edict, the *ius honorarium*, was continually updated, thereby providing Roman law with a flexibility that enabled it to grow—not unlike how many modern-day U.S. lawyers and judges see the common law as an expanding catalog of causes of action based on an expanding set of rights and duties.

Praetors eventually came in two stripes: urban and alien. It appears that the "alien" praetor, established by 242 BCE, had an even more significant influence on Roman law than did the urban type (*praetor urbanus*). While the jurisdiction of the *praetor urbanus* was limited to citizens, the responsibility of the alien praetor (*praetor peregrinus*) extended to strangers in the city and to disputes, often involving substantial sums of money, between citizens and noncitizens. Furthermore, with regard to the ever-increasing expanse of the empire, praetors were sent out as provincial governors armed with the power to issue edicts. In light of Roman respect for reason, both the alien and urban praetors stretched beyond the traditional law of the people and applied a legal philosophy based upon reason—specifically one that represented a rational extension of principles. This kind of law became known as the *ius gentium* (the law of nations).

HADRIAN AND THE PROFESSIONALIZATION OF THE LAW

The reign of Hadrian (117–138 CE), who came not from the elite in Italy but from Spain, was a turning point in the history of Roman law and jurisprudence. The *praetorian* and *aedilician* remedies (the aediles performed such functions as maintaining order in the marketplace) were redacted by the jurist Publius Salvius Julianus in order to create the *Edictum Perpetuum*. Thereafter, the law began to rapidly emerge as imperial law: Changes came through the "constitutions" or ordinances of the emperors. All this had an effect on the traditional division of lawsuits, as described above, of a preparatory stage before the praetor and a trial stage before the private judge; increasing importance was attached to the bureaucratic extraordinary process acting under the authority of the emperor and to the direct imperial involvement in lawsuits, both ending in *decreta* (written decisions).

Ultimately this new form of legal procedure (*cognitio extraordinaria*) eliminated the praetor and the private judge in favor of a legal process that was administered entirely by an imperial official or, on occasion, the emperor himself. So just as the formulary system had replaced the legal action system, the *cognitio* replaced the formulary system. The plaintiff was now required to file a written pleading with the court, and a summons was issued with the court's backing. Regular courts were organized and witnesses were summoned under penalty and interrogated by the judge. With the professionalization of the court system, a nonsomatic remedy following judgment was no longer necessarily limited to money. The judge could order restoration of property or specific performance—"do this" (e.g., multiply and replenish the earth) and "don't do that" (e.g., touch the fruit). He became more godlike.

THE CONTINUING IMPORTANCE OF *IUS CIVILE* AND *IUS HONORARIUM*

So Roman law ultimately developed two distinct bodies of law: the traditional rules for Roman citizens stretching all the way back to the *Twelve Tables,* which became rigid and hard to change (the *ius civile*), and a more flexible set of rules based on ideas of fairness and justice. The second set, the *ius honorarium,* developed largely from the praetor's Edicts. Both sets of law, at least until the imperial takeover by Hadrian, were administered by the praetors.

This notion of *ius civile* and *ius honorarium* continues on in various modern-day legal systems, including those in the United States of America. U.S. lawyers are often called upon to consider both the legal (*ius civile*) and equitable (*ius honorarium*) remedies that might be available to a client's case. (The 2009 housing crisis, for example, involves both the legal questions of freedom and security of contract and the equitable question of a mortgagor's equity of redemption.) An interesting example of the application (or, as it turned out, nonapplication) of law and equity to a particular case occurred in the tobacco Medicaid litigation in Florida.

In the 1990s the State of Florida filed suit against the tobacco industry (excluding, of course, the cigar industry—since Florida is home to the nation's leading producer of premium cigars). The basic thrust of this litigation was to make the evil tobacco industry pay for all of the Medicaid costs incurred by the good state of Florida due to smoking-related illnesses. Under both the *ius civile* and the *ius honorarium* the state, however, faced a problem. On the legal side, the tobacco industry had the defense of "assumption of risk"; that is, the state knew of the dangers of smoking and still opted to participate in the federal Medicaid program. On the equitable side, the industry had the defense of "unclean hands"; roughly $825 million of Florida's pension assets were invested in tobacco stocks and for a number of years the Florida prison system manufactured unfiltered cigarettes and both distributed them to inmates and sold them to local governments. The point is that both the defense of assumption of the risk (on the *ius civile* side) and the defense of unclean hands (on the *ius honorarium* side) are rooted in the historic principle that parties are generally accountable for the consequences of their own conduct. But Florida is a state, and states have the godlike power to legislate—in other words, the power to enact positive law (don't touch the fruit!).

So in 1990 and 1994, the Florida state legislature amended the Florida Medicaid Third-Party Liability Act of 1978. One of the things the amendments did was to sweep away manufacturers' affirmative defenses—meaning, in the case of the tobacco industry, the defenses of assumption of the risk and unclean hands. But is that legal? In a suit challenging the constitutionality of the Act, the Florida Supreme Court, voting 4 to 3 in June 1996, upheld the bulk of the Act, calling it "a rational response to a public need." As one academic has phrased it: The state needed money; the manufacturers had money; so the manufacturers needed to give and the state needed to take. It was an act that was simple, that was effective, and that completely disregarded the rule of law. But the good news is that the lawyers involved on the plaintiff side of the tobacco Medicaid litigation made billions in legal fees—yes, billions!

ROMAN LAW IN THE WEST

Roman law in the West was resurrected around 1080 CE with the discovery of Justinian's legislation in a library in Pisa, in particular the *Digest,* which was a conscious attempt to preserve the best of the golden age of classical Roman law. This convenient discovery, along with the development of another round of scientific jurisprudence, provided a foundation for the earliest of Western Europe's medieval law schools to explore Roman law in detail. At the University of Bologna, the world having just survived the passing of the millennium, these scholars fervently revived the study and teaching of Roman law. They were interpreters and adapters of the ancient text, considered by them to be living law. The typical literary form they employed was the gloss: examples frequently introduced by the words "take the case" or "imagine the case," with explanations written between the lines and in the margins of the text. These scholarly interpreters were dubbed the Glossators.

In the emerging Italian city-states of the eleventh and twelfth centuries (and also in what is now France), it was much more than a body of old laws that the Glossators resurrected. It was the idea of empire that had been rediscovered, as embodied in the maxim that "the unity of the law is founded upon the unity of the empire." Justinian's legislation represented a particular kind of cultural and political order, and with adaptation to existing circumstances, the legislation could serve the propagation of a unifying theme in the fragmented West of the twelfth and thirteenth centuries, much as it had served the ideological needs of Justinian as ruler of the eastern remains of the Roman Empire.

A Healthy Mix of Past and Present

What the Glossators did with Justinian's texts was to essentially avoid the costly process of legal reinvention. In the United States, post-Revolutionary lawyers followed a similar path. Their task involved investing the past with meaning for the present and future and preserving the exceptional version of American republicanism against decay, while at the same time modifying the past in order to accommodate social and economic change. This same type of process is still in place. Modern-day lawyers use legal narratives and the doctrine of precedent as ways of making new law (or simply "updating" the law) while preserving continuity with the past. In all these cases, the authority of an older rule and its procedural and substantive law is applied to a new rule.

The Commentators (or Post-glossators) of the fourteenth and fifteenth centuries were the next group of legal scholars to focus on Justinian's legislation. The Commentators, in challenging the glossatorial school, argued that the techniques of the glosses—summaries (*notabilia*), maxims (*brocardica*), classifications (*distinctiones*), and problems of law (*quaestiones*)—were threatening to obscure the original Justinian texts and the original meaning on which the law rested. The Commentators, somewhat like the modern-day movement to strip away much of the judicial grime and get back to the "original" meaning of the United States Constitution, sought to recover the true text and restore the integrity of the sovereign word. They also took the important step of writing treatises ("commentaries") that combined a more purified Roman law with both the statutory law of the Italian cities and the canon law of the Catholic Church. One of the most famous Commentators was Bartolus de Sassoferrato (c. 1314–1357), a professor at the University of Perugia. The Bartolists, as his students came to be known, attempted to resurrect Justinian's texts and reconcile them to the demands of the real world. Their aim was not to simply explain the meaning of the laws, as the Glossators had done. Instead, they sought to derive from the texts, using a "scientific approach," rules that would carry the authority of the imperial law in a manner that fit with their society.

The legal humanists of the fifteenth and sixteenth centuries challenged the scholastic jurisprudential approach taken by both the Glossators and the Commentators: They questioned the texts themselves. From the humanists' viewpoint, the *Corpus iuris civilis* needed to be replaced by a prior, stronger text—the surviving documents of the unedited Roman law. They were preoccupied, initially using philological methods in combination with juridical analysis, with recovering and transmitting the original text or sources of this law (including the *Twelve Tables*) rather than with simply relying upon its secondhand representation in Justinian's compilation. Consequently, these jurists, who from the fragmented compositions of the *Corpus iuris civilis* orchestrated the rebirth of classical historiography, associated the name of Justinian's chief legal eagle, Tribonian, with corruption, intervention, and the breakdown of the transmission of antique learning in its purer forms. (If you lean to the right, just replace Tribonian's name with Chief Justice Earl Warren. If you lean to the left, replace it with Chief Justice John G. Roberts, Jr. In either case, if you care at all about the U.S. Supreme Court's effect on American society, you might get the legal humanists' point at a more gut level.)

The humanist Lorenzo Valla (1407–1457) argued that in the process of condensing Roman law, Tribonian mutilated the writings of the jurists, and all the signs of changes in the text constituted crimes. Additionally, in order to make the prohibition against citation of the original authorities more effective, Justinian ordered that a number of manuscripts collected by Tribonian be burned, which did not help Tribonian's case with the humanists. Furthermore, Tribonian's sins were, in Valla's eyes, compounded by Glossators such as Accursius and Commentators such as Bartolus, whose respective works were full of barbarous idioms and written in a convoluted style.

Valla and his immediate successors constituted the first stage of the attack on scholastic jurisprudence. But like Barry Scheck's role in the O.J. Simpson case, this stage was largely deconstructive. In order to accomplish the important task of conduit creation, a second stage, similar to Johnnie Cochran's affirmative role, was needed—one that went beyond the philological-historical method of textual criticism and actually provided a path for solving contemporary legal problems.

One of the earliest legal humanists of this second stage, Andrea Alciato (Alciatus, 1492–1550) from Milan, was a professor of civil law at the University of Bourges in France. Alciatus's goal was to combine legal and humanist studies, starting with the reconstruction of Roman political institutions not only from a historical perspective, but also from that of a jurist. And Ulrich Zäsi (Zasius, 1461–1535), who was a clerk of the city council and a professor at the University of Freiburg at Basle in Germany, shared Alciatus's desire to recover the original classical text obscured by centuries of changes in order to get at general legal principles and concepts. Most of the other legal humanists were, however, French, and were frequently followers of Calvin's reformation called Huguenots. They were therefore forced to teach abroad. Prominent among this group, although intellectually in line with the first stage of legal humanism, was Guillaume Budé (Budaeus, 1468–1540), who was interested in the extent of Greek influence on Roman law and in the factors that cause legal change, and Jacques Cujas (Cujacius, 1520–1590). Cujacius specialized in spotting corruptions in classical texts and then balancing a "true" reading of a particular legal conclusion against the *ratio iuris* (the principle behind the rule; for example, what's wrong with eating the fruit?).

In their efforts to recover the legal heritage of ancient Rome, the legal humanists, without intending to do so, actually started the process of undermining the authority of Roman law. This occurred in two ways: First, they were not all in agreement about their purpose in studying the *Corpus iuris civilis*. Were these texts a means for discovering the law of Justinian's time, or should they be viewed as a filter through which the classical law of even earlier times could be identified? And secondly, by emphasizing the relationship between law and society, they challenged the claims of Roman law to universal validity. The more it was related to the circumstances of ancient society, the more the humanists demonstrated the irrelevance of such law as a resource along the path being traveled by contemporary society. The humanist François Hotman stated that a lawyer who appeared before a French court armed with only the Roman rules of property and succession, without taking into account the impact of feudalism on land holdings, would be as well equipped to argue as if he had arrived among the savages of North America.

It appears that many practicing lawyers were impervious to the humanist attack on the *Corpus iuris civilis*—not because they were unaware, but because they found the challenge unhelpful. There were some, however, who saw legal humanism as a serious threat to their way of life. This was especially true in France. The French civil-law lawyers, as a class, formed a strong social and political force that would not tolerate any possible loss of their status without a fight. These practitioners, when faced with the inquiries of a judge, needed to know the contemporary law. And that law was the law that had been worked out in detail over the centuries through a type of grinding evolutionary process: the numerous volumes of bottom-up law extracted and assembled by the Bartolists.

Despite a certain backlash, the humanists significantly influenced the way in which Justinian's law was ultimately regarded. The jurist Hugues Doneau (Donellus, 1527–1591) observed that classical Roman law was elaborated through particular forms of action, and therefore legal debate had actually centered on procedure and not rules of substantive law. Much of the *Corpus iuris civilis* reflected this mixing of substance and procedure. Donellus, teaching at Leyden in Holland, therefore asked himself the important question: What is the relationship between individual rights and the procedural means for enforcing them? He answered this question by demonstrating that individuals enjoy two kinds of rights: the original subjective right and the right to sue. Consequently, Donellus laid the foundations for the modern distinction, employed by lawyers in their day-to-day practices, between substantive law (contract law, tort law, property law, etc.) and civil procedure—the means of getting to court, and staying before the court, in order to enforce a person's rights (by damages, injunction, reforming a contract, etc.).

It is important to recognize that in addition to the first stage ("skeptical") and the second stage ("principled"), there was a third stage that truly rocked Western legal science. This stage—"systematic"—actually went beyond legal humanism, and was led chiefly by Protestant jurists at German universities. They undertook to derive from basic principles and concepts an entire body of law, and not just individual aspects and parts. According to Harold J. Berman in *Law and Revolution, II: The Impact of the Protestant Reformations on the Western Legal Tradition,* the new Protestant school of legal science: "(1) classified and analyzed legal concepts and principles (2) derived from inborn reason and conscience, (3) illustrated them by interrelated legal rules (4) found in a wide variety of legal sources. The new method of analysis and synthesis built on the first two stages of legal humanism—the skeptical and the principled—but went beyond them. It was linked with an effort to bring the entire body of legal rules within a common framework of concepts and principles."

In doing so, however, the jurists of this third stage moved further and further away from Roman law. Both Konrad Lagus, an ardent follower of Martin Luther and Philip Melanchthon, and Nicolas Vigelius, a pupil of Johann Oldendorp, freed themselves entirely from the agenda imposed by the Roman law texts.

At the same time that Roman law was being reborn and debated in Europe, Norman conquerors and Angevin kings made a return to the notion of the English "common law." This return, however, was not exclusionary, and Roman law—specifically including Justinian's rediscovered legislation—reached England in canonical texts, as well as through the contributions of civil-law jurists, lawyers, and writers.

XII

RISE OF THE LAWYER CLASS IN THE ROMAN EMPIRE

It can be hard (but not impossible, as proven by the humanists) to find traces of Greek influence in the *Twelve Tables*. And even later in Roman history, the Romans appear to have been consciously adverse to borrowing law from the Greeks—or from anyone else, at least in theory.

This seeming lack of Greek law stands in stark contrast to the clear influence Greek culture had on other aspects of Roman life, such as art, drama, literature, philosophy, rhetoric, and architecture. This is especially true during the later Republic. It would therefore appear that even though there may be little direct continuity between Greek rules of law and Roman rules of law, there is, through drama, philosophy, and, above all, rhetoric, an unbroken chain linking Greek lawyers to Roman lawyers.

As was the case in ancient Greece, one path to power and wealth in the Roman Empire was through the study of law. And the basics of this potentially lucrative art were taught in many of the major cities of the East and West, frequently in the homes of experts. However, there were institutions geared to providing this type of instruction. The most famous one was in Berytus on the Phoenician coast, which flourished for three centuries. Aside from textiles, for which the entire province was famous, Berytus's reputation increasingly depended upon its school of law. Students from all over the Empire began traveling to the city to receive instruction, and Berytus (modern-day Beirut) greatly influenced Roman legal development—at least until a series of earthquakes, tidal waves, and fires in the mid-sixth century reduced everything to rubble. Courses were conducted in Latin, not Greek.

After a multiyear course of education, law students dispersed into the Roman provinces in search of fame and fortune. The first step in a young lawyer's career often came by appointment to act as an assistant assessor (*apparitore*) to a magistrate. From this position, the lawyer might get the opportunity to someday preside in one of the tribunals before which he had previously pled. There was also the chance, as happened to Cicero, of heading up the government in a province, and, by merit, reputation, or favor, to ascend to ever-higher positions in the state. One success story is that of Publius Alfenus Varus, who allegedly started out life as a cobbler and eventually, through his legal work, rose to the consulship in 39 BCE. And often overlooked is the fact that early in his career Julius Caesar established a reputation as an excellent lawyer, having prosecuted a respected ex-counsel for plundering his province.

This same process of lawyer becoming politician/statesman is evident in the United States of America. Twenty-six of its forty-four presidents have been lawyers, including Adams (both John and his son John Quincy), Jefferson, Lincoln, Garfield, Cleveland, McKinley, F.D.R., Obama, and the ever-so-interesting Nixon. A large percentage of United States senators and members of the House of Representatives have law degrees; from 1790 to 1930, two-thirds of the senators and about half of the members of the House of Representatives were lawyers. Of the eighteen-member cabinet appointed by lawyer-President William Jefferson Clinton in 1993, thirteen were lawyers. And for the first time, the President's wife was a lawyer (a feat repeated by President Obama and his wife, Michelle). This same pattern of lawyer domination, for good or bad, is repeated in many state and local legislatures and bureaucracies.

⟨⟩ · ⟨⟩

Lawyer-on-Lawyer Violence

I am not sure what it means that most of the U.S. presidents who have been assassinated have also been lawyers: Lincoln, Garfield, and McKinley. Lawyer-President Garfield was assassinated by America's only lawyer-Presidential-assassin, Charles Julius Guiteau. So there you have it. In the United States, lawyers kill lawyers: Burr and Hamilton, Guiteau and Garfield.

⟨⟩ · ⟨⟩

In ancient Rome, lawyers, after the fall of the pontiffs' monopoly on legal advice, eventually came in the form of "jurists" and "orators." There is no exact modern-day equivalent for Roman jurists. These legal practitioners advised litigants and judges on points of law, gave legal opinions, and helped draft legal instruments. They generally did not represent private parties before the various courts. This function was filled by orators like Cicero. In the Augustan period starting around 23 BCE, jurists also began formally to teach law and, with their students, to write about it. By the beginning of the second century CE, the emperor was enlisting jurists into imperial service as his counselors and as bureaucrats—a move that ultimately eliminated the jurists, but gave rise to a legal profession more in line with its modern-day version, at least in many civil-law jurisdictions.

Early jurists were generally upper crust. This point is illustrated by the fact that the famous jurists from the mid-third century BCE (the Republican period) were nearly all members of the Senate—the "Who's Who" of the state. In fact, many of the jurists had been consuls. And most important for our purposes, they were deeply involved with the praetors and the Edicts.

One interesting line of thought as to why these jurists were members of the nobility is tied to the lack of regular courts and professional judges, and the fact that until the postclassical period Rome had no fully functioning law schools. The result of these (arguable) defects was to allow the administration of the law to be carried out by powerful private citizens. These Big Men of the upper classes not only had an interest in social order, they were, for all practical purposes, the law. In other words, it was much more a rule of men than a rule of law. And therefore, it was only through such powerful individuals (patrons) that the privately run system of hauling defendants into court could be carried out. For example, it might take a plaintiff appealing to his patron to use his "army" of slaves to even be able to capture a defendant—particularly one who had his own army of slaves. (Remember, there was no police force.)

In Rome, the *Forum Romanum* was the Big Show, the center stage on which the drama of political life was carried out. Politicians and lawyers in their tailored white togas took leading roles, delivering well-rehearsed speeches or indulging in extemporaneous debates. And the Basilica Julia, rebuilt and enlarged by Caesar Augustus, was a key component of the busy Forum. Speakers belted out rhetoric, attempting to attract the attention of spectators. It was here that a panel of jurors usually met in four sections to hear civil lawsuits such as inheritance disputes. For important cases all 180 jurors sat together as a single panel.

One of the outstanding features of Roman law also appears to have increased the importance of engaging a lawyer (orator or jurist). This feature was the high degree of its conceptualization. What this means is that a particular area of substantive law was, in contrast to the Greeks, carefully defined and then tied to a specific cause of action. Imagine A sues B based on sale. If it turns out, as the facts of the case develop, that the contract was not one for sale but for hire, A loses his case. And he cannot turn around and sue B on the basis of hire due to the principle of Roman law that once a certain stage of the action occurs, the plaintiff (A) cannot initiate a new action on the same facts. Consequently, it was extremely important (at least until the praetors relaxed the rules a bit though their use of the *ius honorarium*) for a plaintiff to fit the facts of his case into the right area of law and then, with the right touch of passion, ask the appropriate magistrate for the appropriate remedy. Competent legal advice could, as is still the case in the twenty-first century, greatly assist in that process.

Legal advice might also be of service in simply finding the applicable law. The reason for this is that while Roman law became highly conceptualized, it achieved only a low level of systematization. That is, the ancient Romans repeatedly failed to arrange legal rules and institutions in even a semi-systematic manner. In fact the system, during Rome's long period of world dominance, sometimes verged on chaos.

IMPERIAL LAW AND ITS RECORDS

In addition to the *ius civile,* the *ius honorarium,* and the *ius gentium,* there eventually came into existence imperial law. Imperial influence on the formation and administration of Roman law started with Caesar Augustus. While declining the power of personally enacting public laws for the Roman people, the magistracies that Augustus and his immediate successors held made it possible to direct legal developments in many ways. One such way was through the issuance of responses to officials and private parties concerning questions and petitions (rescripts).

Most of the rescripts were handled, due to their volume, by the central imperial chancellery. Within the chancellery, the office *ab epistulis* handled communications with subordinate agencies and the office *ab libellis* took care of petitions submitted, either in person or through a personal representative, by private subjects. In exceptional cases, the emperor would make the decision himself, generally after deliberation with his council—and clearly without much concern regarding separation between legislative, executive, and judicial functions. And whether it was the work product of a subordinate or of the emperor himself, a record was kept of rescripts and *decreta* (judicial decisions) in the imperial archive, as well as in some of the provincial repositories. In fact, requests and responses were generally posted in public places—a rule of law virtue.

It was part of the work of a lawyer in preparing a case or legal opinion to locate and analyze edicts, instructions, and replies favorable to his client, and to distinguish those that were unfavorable, not unlike the use of precedent by lawyers under Anglo-American law. In fact this legal effort even extended to the decisions of judges. Scholarship, however, has noted that it is unlikely that these judicial decisions were accorded official authority as binding precedents unless rendered by the emperor himself. Instead, they were merely given faithful attention.

It appears that the first book to attempt to make accessible the growing mass of technical material to those not belonging to the "cult" of pontiffs was the *Ius Civile Flavianum* (c. 304 BCE). This work was allegedly produced by one Gnaeus Flavius, a former slave. It was, however, only a bare collection of fixed formulas to be recited in the course of court actions; it did not even pretend to undertake a systematic presentation of the law or a theoretical analysis of its concepts.

The second publication appears to have been much the same as the first. This material, presented in literary form, occurred when Sextus Aelius Paetus Catus, consul in 198 BCE, issued a book later cited by ancient authorities as the *Ius Aelianum*. It simply updated the material contained in the *Ius Civile Flavianum*. And almost a century later, a similar collection of forms for sales transactions, the *Venalium Vendendorum Leges*, was put together by the eminent orator and jurist Manius Manilius.

The first attempt at a true systematic treatment of Roman law was seemingly also made by Sextus Aelius, perhaps the first professional jurist in Roman history, in his book known as *Tripertita* (tripartite presentation of the law). This work, unfortunately lost to time, exerted considerable influence on future writers and is supposed to have contained the text of the *Twelve Tables* and the results of their interpretation by the pontiffs and jurisconsults—all the stuff that gave rise to the *ius civile*—as well as including a collection of forms. This work by "the Sagacious One" marked the transition from the mere case methods of the older jurists to a new scientific approach to the law. And thus, in modern economic terms, it constituted a significant step toward lowering information costs in terms of both search and evaluation.

Traditionally, philosophical interests and methods of handling legal problems had been pursued separately. The first person to combine both appears to have been Quintus Mucius Scaevola (the "Pontifex"). Around 95 BCE Mucius, the most famous jurist of the Republic, took the *ius civile* and, seemingly influenced by Greek methods of classification, arranged it into categories or classes. This work, composed of eighteen books, was known as the *Ius Civile* and consisted not only of interpretations of the *Twelve Tables,* but also of statutes that modified the *Tables* and certain miscellaneous matters that could be tied to them. It started with wills, legacies, and intestate succession, areas of extreme importance to the Romans. Mucius also grouped the methods of acquiring ownership and possession of property together, but the remaining subjects of private law constituted a dog's breakfast. Additionally, given the fact that the *Twelve Tables* were far from a comprehensive codification of Roman law, the *Ius Civile* contained a number of omissions. For example, *stipulatio,* the oldest Roman form of contract, was not even discussed.

About a century and a half after the *Ius Civile* appeared, the hotshot jurist Marcus Massurius Sabinus wrote his famous commentary on the civil law. This work, building on Mucius's scheme, brought together additional topics that were just beginning to be recognized as having a relationship to each other. For instance, Sabinus, unlike Mucius, did not treat theft of property and damage to property as being separate from each other—thus recognizing a category of wrongdoing (delict) that gave the victim a civil action for a penalty against the wrongdoer. (Recall that O.J. Simpson was found not guilty of murder but was successfully sued for Big Money damages in a civil action—the undoubted reason that his lawyers advised him to take up residence in the asset-protection-friendly state of Florida.) Neither Sabinus's work nor the Pontifex's *Ius Civile* has survived. However, the arrangement of Sabinus's work has generally been able to be reconstructed because later jurists wrote extensive commentaries on it.

Both the Pontifex's civil law and Sabinus's work excluded the praetor's Edict—even though there was, in theory, no difference between civil and edictal law. Indeed there was, at the time, only one court system: that of the praetors. And just as there were commentaries, like the *Ius Civile,* on civil law, there were numerous commentaries on the Edict. This separation was, however, unnecessary and added to the law's lack of systematization—thus increasing its informational inefficiencies.

The earliest Roman work to combine civil and edictal law appears to have been Gaius's legal textbook, the *Commentarii Institutionum,* or simply the *Institutes.* This beginner's book written circa 161 CE attempted to present a systematic outline of institutions using a dialectical approach, without much reference to concrete cases. It did not, however, lead other jurists to see the advantages to be had in treating civil and edictal law as an integrated whole. Moreover, and compounding the confusion, the commentaries on the Edict of the great jurists followed the disordered lack of arrangement of the Edict itself.

Why? What was behind this rather pervasive lack of interest in organizing the law? One possible answer is that the Romans simply had little interest in law reform and a jurist did not become famous for undertaking such a task. In contrast, they were interested in legal interpretation. The reason for this, it is said, stretches back to the fact that the college of pontiffs (all patricians) were

originally granted the exclusive right of interpreting the law. This then transformed, at a later date, into prestige being awarded for giving legal opinions—
not for the mundane task of organizing the law.

Finally, with regard to the lawyer class of ancient Rome in general, Edward
Gibbon's observation contained in his six-volume masterpiece, *The History of
the Decline and Fall of the Roman Empire,* is a must:

> In the practice of the bar these men [i.e., the young lawyers] had consid-
> ered reason the instrument of dispute; they interpreted the laws according
> to the dictates of private interest; and the same pernicious habits might still
> adhere to their characters in the public administration of the state. The honor
> of a liberal profession had indeed been vindicated by ancient and modern
> advocates, who have failed the most important stations with pure integrity
> and consummate wisdom; but in the decline of Roman jurisprudence, the
> ordinary promotion of lawyers was pregnant with mischief and disgrace. The
> noble art, which had once been preserved as the sacred inheritance of the
> patricians, had fallen into the hands of freedman and plebeians, who, with
> cunning rather than with skill, exercised a sordid and pernicious trade. Some
> of them procured admittance into families for the purpose of fomenting dif-
> ferences, of encouraging suits, and of preparing a harvest of gain for them-
> selves or their brethren. Others, recluse in their chambers, maintained the
> gravity of legal professions, but furnishing a rich client with sublets to con-
> found the plainest truth, and with arguments to color the most unjustifiable
> pretension. The splendid and poplar class was composed of the advocates,
> who filled the Forum with the sound of their turgid and loquacious rhetoric.
> Careless of fame and or justice, they are described for the most part as igno-
> rant and rapacious guides, who conducted their clients through a maze of
> expense, of delay, and or disappointment; from whence, after a tedious series
> of years, they [the clients] were at length dismissed, when their patience and
> fortune were almost exhausted.

We can all be thankful that society has evolved beyond this grim picture of
justice and blood-sucking lawyers—right?

PART V

MEDIEVAL
TIMES

By the time of Classical Greece the notion and role of a lawyer (versus astrologer, oracle, scribe, priest, or philosopher) had been, in general terms, worked out, and a rudimentary self-consciousness existed. Society, with its ever-increasing complexity, accepted that a good blood sacrifice was not the answer to every problem and that specialized knowledge (as evidenced by ever-finer divisions of labor) was a commodity that could be sold or bartered to those who needed help in handling a legal matter. This notion was carried on, and in fact greatly enhanced, within the Roman Empire; a significant path to position and power within the Empire was through the study of law and rhetoric. Then, suddenly, the lawyers disappeared! Something called the Dark Ages—brought on by the collapse of the Roman Empire, along with a few minor annoyances such as the bubonic plague and the loss of sunlight—significantly diminished the need for lawyers by obscuring large amounts of knowledge for centuries. During this period of rapidly increasing entropy, humankind devolved back to the point, in many places, of planting fields with a stick. Multitudes starved to death. Plague ran rampant. On land, bandits killed anyone who attempted to travel along the old Roman roads carrying desperately needed supplies. At sea, pirates destroyed the former Mediterranean lanes of trade. In fact, some economists have concluded that the growth rate of gross domestic products (the value of all goods and services produced in an economy) per capita in Europe between 500 and 1500 was essentially zero. Is it possible that without lawyers true civilization cannot exist?

The Coinciding Deaths of Lawyers and Money

With regard to the "disappearance" of lawyers, it is important to recognize that with the collapse of the Empire (generally agreed to date from the second sacking of Rome in 476 CE), the classical money economy that had survived for over a thousand years also collapsed. This collapse in the West was so complete that during the long period of the Dark Ages and on into the Middle Ages, coined money played a greatly reduced role in society from what it had played in Greece and Rome at their respective heights. That is, after more than a thousand years of using coins, people retreated into a "moneyless" economy. This fact raises the important question of whether it is just pure coincidence that both money and lawyers disappeared at the same time.

With the onset of the Dark Ages, the lawyer class went unconscious and was largely folded back into the priest class. Starting, however, with the writings of St. Augustine and St. Thomas Aquinas, the role of the philosopher, at least in the context of religious/moral philosophy and specifically including casuistry, was revived in the West. And slowly, with "punctuated equilibria," the development of Christian thought (injected with a healthy dose of Greek philosophy), and, perhaps most important, the rise in wealth and power of the Church, the lawyer class reemerged in the Middle Ages. It is emphasized, however, that this time the priest–philosopher–lawyer sequence did not face the same challenges that existed duting its initial evolutionary process. Nevertheless, their roles in society had, in comparison with classical Greek and Roman times, become significantly more blurred. This point is illustrated by the fact that even in the later part of the Middle Ages and on into the early modern period a number of men, such as Martin Luther and John Calvin, were clergymen, philosophers, and lawyers all rolled into one. And the legal philosophy of a number of lawyers during this period, it has been argued, can only be understood as an integral part of their total philosophy, including their religious philosophy and their philosophy of the natural sciences. Consequently, they were steeped in knowledge not only of law but also of theology and of the physical sciences. Their views on one of these subjects was related to their views of the others.

The medieval blur between religion, philosophy (which included the natural sciences), and law is evident in the rise of the canon law. With the loss of the Greco-Roman legal tradition, the canon law, created by the Catholic Church and various medieval legal scholars, became, for a time, the indigenous law of all the peoples of Christendom. This law, and not Roman law, was considered to be the learned law. And it was the priest class, with its ability to read and write, that studied and developed the canons. But despite this heavy religious influence, "the Law" slowly began to take on a more competitive and secular nature, just as had happened in ancient Greece and Rome—thereby giving rise, as the Dark Ages turned into the Renaissance of the Middle Ages, to royal law, feudal law, urban law, mercantile law, and the *ius commune* (in a more secularized form). And most important, it began to pave the way, through ever-increasing complexity, for the return of lawyers as a class separate from priests and philosophers.

XIII

A SNAPSHOT FROM DARK TO LIGHT

THE DARK AGES, from the fall of Rome in 476 CE to the early years of the Renaissance, were basically dark—or at least dim. In the West, life became gradually barbarized, but not always in a bad way, by the settlement of Germanic peoples within the Empire. And with the slow collapse of Roman administration, as barbarian kingdoms emerged in the fifth and sixth centuries, regionalism developed. This splintering of the Roman Empire ultimately led to territorial "kingships"—the principal medieval form of political rule. Still, within these kingdoms, particularly in such areas as Gaul, Spain, and Italy, elements of Roman civilization persisted on into the seventh century. In the East, the Roman Empire survived but became ever more Greek in outlook.

The survival of Roman culture in the East, however, was still generally downward sloping—just more gradually than in the West. Take the imperial capital of Constantinople. New copper coins continued to be produced and used, and a new glazed tableware was developed during the seventh century to replace the fine-wares of earlier times. But, as archaeologist-historian Bryan Ward-Perkins notes in *The Fall of Rome: And the End of Civilization*, "even Constantinople shrank dramatically in both wealth and population from the booming centre of perhaps half-a-million people of the years around AD 500. Seventh-century Constantinople still stood out as a great city; but this was mainly thanks to buildings from its past, and because the other great cities of the Aegean, like Ephesus [and Corinth and Athens], had declined even more calamitously."

Ward-Perkins goes on to state that "[b]y AD 700 there was only one area of the former Roman world that had not experienced overwhelming economic decline—the provinces of the Levant [the region between modern Turkey to the north and Egypt to the south], and neighboring Egypt, conquered by the Arabs in the 630s and 640s." This observation will influence our speculation, discussed later in Part V, regarding Islam's seeming impact on the common law and its lawyers.

From "We" to "I"

For both the West and the East, it was the seventh century that marked the end of antiquity and the beginning of the Middle Ages. And the central feature of mature medieval social and political life (1100–1500) was the group. This collective attitude—the "we" versus the "I" of modern times—supported a system of dispute resolution in which social groups often appeared as parties through representatives. Furthermore, in England, with the rise of professional pleaders by at least the early thirteenth century, these representatives sometimes engaged a lawyer (a "narrator").

There were a variety of rural and town groups that dominated medieval society. Rural groups included the village—those who were bound by a network of obligations and privileges to the lord of the manor—and the parish, a local ecclesiastical unit though which free and unfree men owed obligations to and enjoyed privileges from the parson and the Church.

Medieval town aggregations, unlike the rural groups, were generally established through the voluntary action of its members. These groups included the merchant guilds and boroughs. They came into existence, in contrast to ancient Mesopotamian guilds, by individuals voluntarily assuming financial and other responsibilities to the king or local lord in return for monopoly privileges. The guild or borough served not only as a means for fixing collective obligations and privileges but also as a type of metabolic network through which most forms of a town's socioeconomic life were carried out.

This collective structural form deeply influenced the shape of social norms. Obligations and privileges attached to the group, and the group then allocated them out among its members. Each member, moreover, was individually liable for all obligations, often enforced by *charivari,* a kind of punishment meted out by neighbors, and was therefore more than willing to accept the internal group dynamics that spread various burdens. But personal rights, too, arose in this somewhat democratic, fully Christian setting. The first tentative articulations of these rights focused, interestingly enough, on the individual. The canonists of the twelfth and thirteenth centuries identified, perhaps in an effort to weaken the power of secular authorities derived through the feudal/manorial ("we-type") system, a variety of rights from social to economic. And during the period from 1150 to 1300, the jurists of the *ius commune* defined the rights of Christians and non-Christians to property, self-defense, marriage, and procedure as being rooted in natural law (*ius naturale*).

Charivari

The cluster of practices often called *charivari* occurred in almost all Western European cultures (and others, including Quebec, New England, and Louisiana) in every historical period up to the twentieth century. According to one academic: "Charivari . . . consisted of gangs of local youths and young adults who would harass people whose behavior violated local family norms. . . . The harassment would typically last a day or a few days; it would involve festive or carnival elements. . . . Sometimes the gang would make noise in front of the offender's home . . . and sometimes it would force the offender to engage in some humiliating public action . . . or enduring members of the gang pelting him with mud and excrement. Authorities generally tolerated this behavior before powerful governments came into existence. . . ."

It is argued that members of a community signal to each other their reliability as cooperative partners. "One signal of reliability," according to a legal scholar, "is participation in (costly) nonlegal punishment of deviants who threaten or appear to threaten the community. The problem of free-riding is partly overcome by everyone's desire to reveal that he or she is a cooperative type."

Groups frequently appeared, as in other incarnations of court proceedings, as parties before manor, borough, ecclesiastical, and royal courts, often with a few members acting as representatives of the group. For example, town-based merchants, according to court records from the year 1268, tried to seize control of the coal being mined from land owned by the bishop of Durham and the prior of Tynemouth. The armed band of town burgesses led by the mayor went to the property, burned down the prior's mills, roughed up the monks, and stole a ship "laden with sea coal." The town merchants pled, through their representatives, the defense that if the monks traded coal without going through the merchants, not only would they lose a share of the profits, but the king's tax on coal could not be collected. The merchants won.

It appears that medieval courts simply assumed that the member representatives could stand in for the group, without ever inquiring into their qualifications for the role. In contrast, in modern-day group and class actions a significant amount of legal energy often goes into analyzing whether or not the "representative" members of a group can stand in for the group. In fact, there is sometimes an issue over deciding which lawyer is going to be counsel for the representative group. In other words: How does one select the top dog out of the pack of hounds that are barking to pull the class-action sled?

But outside of class-action suits, there is a prevailing modern-day ambivalence toward the group versus the individual. It's frequently claimed that this ambivalence flows from the paradigm story of two people in the state of nature where each claim a single piece of property. (In law school and bar exams this property is frequently called "Blackacre.") As stated by one legal academic, "They discuss the problem, reach an impasse, and then turn to a third party, the stranger, to resolve their dispute. Courts are viewed as the institutionalization of this stranger, and adjudicate the process through which the judicial power is exercised." As can be seen, the story focuses on the individual and does not account, as Sal might have argued on behalf of Eve, for social groups—or bureaucratic institutions: The search is for direct, not systemic, causation. "There is no room," according to the legal academic, "in the story for the sociological entities so familiar to contemporary litigation. Social groups, like inmates of a prison or patients in a hospital, have no place in the story. Nor is there recognition of the existence of groups that transcend institutions, like racial minorities or the handicapped groups whose social identity and reality are as secure in our society as the individual in the state of nature. Furthermore, there is no room in the story for the public school system, the prison, the mental hospital, or the housing authority. The world is composed exclusively of individuals."

As the medieval period progressed, there was a slow rise in the status of the individual (the "I") at the expense of the social, economic, and political authority of local groups (the "we"). Towns had been ravaged by plague (the Black Death) and famine. Consequently, the individual worker became a scarce commodity and therefore of increasing value. In England this labor shortage presented a serious problem for large landowners. In the century prior to the 1340s the upper classes had invested heavily in the type of farming that exploited large amounts of land through the use of cheap labor. As a result of the plague there was, however, no longer a blotted rural population and the surviving laborers took advantage of this fact by demanding higher wages. By treating laborers like dirt when competition for their services was limited, the rich failed to create loyalty insurance against a competitive labor market. (A lesson to be remembered during economic downturns.)

The landowners did not take this threat to their livelihood lying down. They did what many wealthy people do—they hired lawyers. Members of the legal class, composed primarily of the sons of the rising gentry, drafted legislation for presentation to the Crown and Parliament fixing wages at the pre–Black Death level and also restricting the physical mobility of laborers searching for better jobs. In other words, the aristocracy used lawyers, like modern-day legislative lobbyists, to push through laws favorable to their financial interests. Shocking!

Along with the hotly resisted but ever-increasing status of the individual came an increase in the independence of towns (and the eventual collapse of the manorial system, the form of economic and social organization that underpinned the military and political relationships known as feudalism). The northern French city of Coucy-le-Château, for example, bought its charter of liberties from the penniless widow of the lord for 140 livres in 1197. And in England, boroughs sought official sanction by obtaining charters of incorporation from the king or Parliament; the citizens of London obtained a borough charter from King Henry I in the twelfth century. Additionally, the growth of a market economy throughout Europe produced ever more specialized and capital-intensive economic units. These units, like towns, cities, and boroughs, sought formal incorporation in order to protect monopoly privileges in broadening geographic markets—all at the expense of feudalism.

Rural communities underwent similar changes. The parish of the Middle Ages became an administrative arm of the monarchy, controlled directly by the king. And with an emerging cash economy—resulting in a clearer understanding of the effects of supply and demand on money—and the ever-increasing value of the individual, workers gained more and more security of land possession/ownership and consequently more and more power with regard to the lord of the manor.

Monks and Man-Centric Rights

William of Ockham, a Franciscan monk who was born in Surrey and educated at Oxford (c. 1280–1349), had a significant influence on the concept of the individual's natural rights. Ockham's ideas arose in connection with a dispute between the Spiritual Franciscans, who maintained that neither Christ nor his apostles owned property, and the Conventuals, who claimed they had. The two sides appealed to the pope for a judgment. The pope, searching the Scriptures, determined that the right to own property predated the Fall of Adam and Eve. Therefore the Church and its orders had the capacity to *own* property—a position opposed by Ockham. Ockham construed the Franciscan's situation regarding property, given their vow of poverty, as one of *use* only. When the pope responded that this use was in fact a right (*ius*), Ockham countered by distinguishing *ius* from *usus*, making the idea of a "right" more subjective (in contrast to the somewhat depersonalized Roman notion expressed by *ius*). This change in emphasis has been said to be the beginning of a trend in which the individual becomes the center of interest for legal thought—striving to describe his legal attributes, the extent of his faculties, and his individual rights.

Groups continued to play an important role in the "early modern period" (1500–1700), but the "corporation"—in England, taking the form of joint-stock companies—became the principal form of group organization. The social norm was no longer unincorporated groups of workers and social reformers but a mix of individualism and communitarianism, along with state-authorized entities.

DOMINANCE OF THE GROUP IN THE FAR EAST

While the West saw the rise of the individual—spearheaded, despite popular belief to the contrary, by Christianity—the dominance of the group continued in the Far East under Confucianism. Confucian doctrines and values, which stress the designation of institutions and relationships that promote harmonious living, were, for example, evident in the legal codes promulgated by the Japanese government in the seventh century. And it was the centralization of governmental power that cultivated national cohesion as a means of guarding against possible invasion. This power focused upon administrative practice, in contrast to judicial and procedural control.

Even with Japan's gradual weakening of the central government by the twelfth century, the ruling military class continued to support the historic emphasis on group identity and conformity with its prescribed social structure. This military-feudal society reached its peak during the years 1603 to 1868, a time during which Japan isolated itself from the rest of the world. Japanese Neo-Confucianism emphasized the duties of inferiors to superiors. Law's purpose was therefore aimed at achieving the government's purposes through individual constraint and the maintenance of strict behavioral codes. Individual rights and conflict (such as through litigation) were inconsistent with the Confucian notion of "harmony"—a notion that was bad for the evolution of a lawyer class in the Empire of the Rising Sun.

Returning to the West, the "modern period" (1700 to present) has continued the shift toward an urban, individualistic, entrepreneurial-capitalistic society. The rural groups of the medieval and early modern periods have been replaced by new groups linked together only by a specific financial or commercial goal—which, of course, has contributed to the rise in litigation and the number of lawyers.

XIV

MUDDLE IN THE MIDDLE AGES:
CANON LAW, CIVIL LAW, ROYAL LAW, URBAN LAW, FEUDAL LAW, MERCANTILE LAW, AND THE IUS COMMUNE

WITH THE DISAPPEARANCE OF THE ROMAN EMPIRE, procedures based on "rational proofs" had, outside of the ecclesiastical courts, fallen by the wayside in much of western Europe. In its place Germanic procedures based on "irrational proofs"—ordeals, oaths, and battle—came into use in order to resolve both civil and criminal cases. There was, however, still a thread of rationality that continued in the ecclesiastical courts and its governing body of law called canon law.

A good example of this rational trial system occurred when Pope Stephen VI, upon his accession in the year 896, accused his predecessor and bitter enemy, Formosus, of sacrilege. The dead pope's body was dug up, dressed in papal robes, and placed on a throne in St. Peter's. A trial was held (the so-called Cadaver Synod) in which rational proof was taken by witness testimony. A deacon was appointed to act as Formosus's defense counsel. Unfortunately, the deacon lost the case, probably due, in large part, to the uncooperative nature of his client. The dead pope was found guilty of perjury, of coveting the papacy, and of having violated the canons forbidding the transfer of a bishop from one diocese to another (he had been Bishop of Porto before being elected Bishop of Rome). Formosus's official acts and ordinations were declared null and void, and the three fingers on his right hand, which he had used to swear oaths and give blessings, were cut off. He was then dragged down the nave and reburied in a common grave. Grave robbers later exhumed the body, and finding nothing of interest, tossed it into the Tiber. Now that's due process!

Canon Law

In general terms, the "canon" (*canones,* from the Greek word *canōn,* a measuring rod) was the ancient esoteric system of measurement common to many civilizations. The reason it was common was that it was derived in a similar way everywhere: the measuring scales came from an integration of planetary and human proportions. The canon therefore provided a mathematical standard that could be applied to music, art, architecture, sculpture, astronomy, government, and other arts and sciences. The Washington Monument, for example, built in 1889 in Washington, D.C., is a white marble obelisk that pays homage to the aesthetic canons (i.e., the standards of beauty) of ancient Egypt. And men around the world, when asked to rate the attractiveness of line drawings of women with varying ratios, chose women with a waist circumference that is about 70 percent of her hips—a canon aspect of the "hourglass" ratio of breast-to-waist-to-hips.

Canon Lawyers and the Cosmos

Mikolaj Kopernik (1473–1543) was a Polish physician and a canon lawyer better known by the Latinized form of his name: Copernicus. It was Copernicus who came to the startling realization that the Earth is not at the center of the universe, but, along with the other planets in our solar system, revolves around the sun. And in the spirit of full disclosure, Copernicus has not been the only lawyer to mess up the cosmos. Edwin Hubble, a lawyer turned astronomer, "revealed" that the universe is not just resting in eternal comfort but is actually expanding. In 1936 Hubble observed that the greater

the distance between a galaxy and the Earth, the faster that galaxy is moving away from us. (And the greater the distance between galaxies, the faster
they are moving.)

❈ · ❈

Plato believed that the canon had been developed by the Egyptians and
that it was a primary reason why their civilization had flourished for thousands
of years. And the Greek philosopher Epicurus (341–270 BCE) had a rule that
nothing should be accepted as true unless it was either attested to or not con-
tested by observational evidence. This rule belonged to the "canonic," which
was Epicurus's name for epistemology—the theory of knowledge dealing with
what we know, how we know it, and how reliable our knowledge is. In the
hands of the Catholic Church, a "canon" became, in essence, a measurement of
right and wrong thought and conduct—explicated over the centuries with the
help of canon lawyers.

Customary criminal procedure of the Church, in the developing canon
law, frequently corresponded to Roman secular laws. For example, canon law
came to incorporate the language of Justinian's legislation that guaranteed a
criminal defendant the right to encounter opposing witnesses in court. It also
governed a wide array of civil matters, including contracts involving oaths or
pledges of faith as well as most aspects of marriage and family life and of church
polity and property. In legal talk, canon law had a claim to exclusive personal
jurisdiction over the Church and clergy and asserted subject-matter jurisdiction over a variety of substantive law areas.

The canon law, using the dialectical method and "created" from the medium
of the divine by various scholars, became the indigenous law of all the peoples of
Western Christendom from the twelfth century. Between 1150 and the time of
the Protestant Reformation in 1520, canon law governed the law of marriage,
divorce, wills, and all cases in which the clergy were litigants. It also influenced,
among other things, the rights of the poor, the jurisprudence of the oath, property rights, criminal procedure, and the rights of ecclesiastical magistrates to exercise secular jurisdiction. This law, and not Roman law, was therefore considered
to be the *ius commune,* the learned law. It drew extensively on Romanist learning
carried on in the monasteries and universities, as well as on new developments
in philosophy and theology, but it was not taken directly from the Theodosian
Code, the Justinianic *Corpus iuris civilis,* Greek philosophy, or the Bible.

With specific regard to England, there is no doubt that the early medieval church courts were institutions of the *ius commune.* Their practice was
controlled by trained canonists who started appearing in English ecclesiastical

courts in the twelfth century, some of whom may have known as little about the common law as some of their counterparts in the common-law courts knew about the *ius commune*. However, legal historians agree that some common-law lawyers may have previously been canon lawyers and that early on, many English lawyers probably practiced in both the ecclesiastical and common-law courts. Consequently, there was considerable common-law influence on the practice of the Church courts and vice versa.

THE DECRETUM AND THE DECRETALS

The *Decretum Gratiani* was the first comprehensive and systematic legal treatise in western European history and was central to the development of classical canon law. It was composed in Bologna, Italy, around 1140, just about the same time as the rise of the newly discovered Roman law, and appears to have come from the private initiative of one man, Gratian (c. 1095–1150). This Camaldolese monk and legal scholar's collection—formed from the canons of Church councils, excerpts of popes, statutes of dioceses and religious orders, dicta of reputable ecclesiastical writers, and extracts from Roman law—became the centerpiece for emerging ecclesiastical jurisprudence, the classical canon law. Its nearly 4,000 chapters took into account all earlier canonical collections, which were frequently highly particular in content, and made lavish use of textual reconciliation methodology. Consequently, Gratian's work was recognized as the definitive textbook on the canon law, and, as a practical matter, also nearly attained the status of law itself.

The full title of this important work is *Concordantia Discordantium Canonum* (*Concordance of Discordant Canons*). The musical metaphor reflects a commitment to the medieval Glossators' main project: to reconcile differences among legal rules enunciated by diverse authorities and to frame reasoned conclusions, through interpretive techniques, that resolve such inconsistencies. A harmony of the Heavens.

The basic text of Gratian's *Concordantia* was eventually housed in two large volumes, referred to as the *Corpus iuris canonici* (a metaphorical "body"). The first volume was the *Decretum*. The second was a collection of papal decretals (papal letters imitating the form of Roman imperial *decreta*) and decisions from contemporary cases. Most of the decretals were written after the *Decretum* and assembled by the canon lawyer Raymond of Peñafort at the direction of Pope Gregory IX in 1234. This second volume is known as the *Decretals*. The material in the *Decretum* and *Decretals* was eventually organized by subject matter with the intent to cover all the areas where the medieval Church exercised jurisdiction over clergy and laity.

Connected with the *Corpus iuris canonici* were the writings of the canonists—contemporary schools called Decretists and Decretalists on the law of the Church. Most of these men (no women) were academics. And like the Glossators and Commentators on the civil law, they played a significant role in shaping the canon law into a system of living law.

Gratian's *Decretum* begins by stating that the human race is ruled by two things: natural law and customary usages. Natural law (*ius naturale*), according to Gratian, consists of what is contained in the Law and the Gospel. The subsequent text in the *Decretum* goes on to support Gratian's statement about the Bible's legal importance, frequently citing scriptural passages.

The central importance of the Bible to these early medieval scholars raises the question: How did they regard the Bible? Gratian's opening statement in the *Decretum* indicates that he associated the Scriptures with natural law: a changeless source of law written on the hearts of humankind by God. This perspective, which, for obvious reasons, is different from the one argued by Vinnie and Sal, was also evident in the writings of the canonists who followed Gratian. They regarded, and cited, the Bible primarily as a way of showing what natural law, along with conscience and circumstances, required of the Church's legal system. The Bible therefore provided a (but not *the*) measuring stick—canon—for evaluating legislation and in rendering guidance for positive law of all sorts. In fact, for the canonist, the science of law was not merely a way of meeting societal needs but was part of the unfolding of God's plan for humankind, a plan that was set out in the Scriptures. This is the primary reason why canonist lawyers and judges saw no incongruity between biblical narratives and legal conclusions (more evidence of our historic priest–lawyer connection). It is also why they continued to cite the Bible and to draw legal conclusions from it even after the canon law became established as an independent subject of study in various European universities.

Though some early Middle Ages canonical collections employed direct use of the Scriptures—for example, a seventh-century collection called *Collectio Hibernensis* contained at least 500 biblical passages, each used as a law—the Decretists and Decretalists did not simply take passages directly from the Bible and treat them as a canon or as a statute. Instead, as indicated in our discussion on Adam and Eve, they drew legal principles from them in order to distinguish law from religion.

As an example of this process, consider the marriage of Joseph and Mary, the earthly parents of Jesus. In deciding what made their union a marriage (since according to Catholic teaching, it was one of perpetual chastity—hence, the "Virgin Mary"), Gratian identified marital affection. Marital affection was what Joseph came with to Mary—and not the traditional method of consummating marriage. Applying this concept to the world of the twelfth century, Gratian made *maritalis affectio* an important part of the Church's teachings. Thus marriages entered into "without dowry or priestly blessing" were valid as long as they were based on affection. And keying off from the concept of *maritalis affectio,* the medieval canon lawyers embraced the importance of unfettered consent—a concept that has significant applications in such modern-day areas as contract law and constitutional law.

One might jump to the conclusion that this entire discussion about the relationship between the Bible and law is only of historic interest. But one would be wrong. In the twenty-first century a former Chief Justice of the Supreme Court of Alabama, among others, has argued for a close connection between God's law (meaning primarily, in the judge's opinion, the Ten Commandments) and secular law. "In the first sentence of the Declaration of Independence," according to Justice Roy Moore, "our forefathers justified the colonies' existence as a new nation under the laws of God. Jefferson and other delegates to the Continental Congress did not invent this connection between God's law and the state. They adapted it from an understanding of their biblical history and in part from one of the best-known and important legal treatises of their time—the *Commentaries and the Laws of England* by Sir William Blackstone."

If the judge means a direct connection between the Bible and secular law, this hardly appears to be the case. Even the canon law has not generally contained this type of connection. The canonists, as noted above, drew only legal principles from the Scriptures—and even then the connection was filtered through the writings of church fathers, papal letters, and pagan Roman law. The historic common law is even more removed in its "connection" to Scripture—perhaps due to the notion that unlike the canon law's primary goal of reconciliation between sinner and God, the common law is focused on such things as efficiency and social control. Furthermore, whatever connection there is has clearly not been limited to the Ten Commandments but has ranged across the breadth of the Bible.

Canon-law lawyers, like later civil-law lawyers, were taught to revere "legislative" text over judicial decisions (an adjudicative versus advocacy model of legal education). Consequently, canonist history is primarily a study of texts, their authors and commentators, and the relationships among them. Specific cases were of interest to the canonists only as showing how texts were used in dealing with real problems. In contrast, English common-law lawyers worked largely from cases decided by the royal courts. Texts were assumed to reflect the jurisprudence of the courts.

Before being admitted to practice before a court, canon-law lawyers (advocates and proctors) were required to swear an oath to faithfully fulfill their duties. Advocates swore to serve their clients to the best of their ability and to avoid all unprofessional conduct—including needlessly delaying litigation and acting in cases they knew to be without merit. And in 1274, at the Second Council of Lyons, it was agreed that both advocates and proctors should be required, based upon a similar provision in Roman law, to renew their respective oaths annually.

The overall effectiveness of such formal oaths is one of scholarly debate. What is clear, however, is that they were not regarded as simple formalities but could actually be used as a source of disciplinary action. In other words, they were meant to govern lawyer conduct.

LAWYERS AND SEX

Among other things, Gratian's *Decretum* endorsed the established Church's position on marriage and sex: Marriage exists to produce children and to curb sexual temptation. (Oxytocin over testosterone.) However, his ideas on what elements were necessary for a valid marriage came with a bit more controversy. Gratian determined that freely given individual consent, generally, but not always, followed by coitus, was necessary for marriage. He merely left open the possibility that familial consent might be an additional requirement.

So what's the problem? The problem is that for hundreds of years marriage and sex were matters to be decided, for social-political reasons, by entire communities—primarily families and feudal lords (high-road brakes applied on low-road urges). Individual consent was not part of the picture and love was irrelevant. Romeo and Juliet deserved their tragic end. Furthermore, Catholic doctrine had historically separated the concepts of sex and marriage.

The role of sex within marriage was a matter of debate among theologians. This war of words, setting aside the no-means-no alternative (a "Gnostic" view of "defiled rubbing"), involved, in the Middle Ages, three different viewpoints. The most rigid was expressed by none other than a lawyer. Bishop Huguccio of Pisa (d. 1210), the greatest canonist of the twelfth century, took the view that every act of sexual intercourse, even inside marriage, involved sin, but marital sex was a venial sin and not a mortal one. The other prevailing viewpoints were: (1) sex within marriage is no sin, or at most a venial one; and (2) sex has an integral part to play in marriage, as long as it is not "excessive." This last viewpoint was, not surprisingly, the mainstream view. Gratian's *Decretum* followed St. Augustine's definition of sexual sins, distinguishing between natural sins (fornication and adultery) and unnatural sins (bestiality and homosexuality).

Sex and Marriage

The modern-day discussion of the role of sex in marriage has generally moved to how sex helps define marriage. Professor Robert P. George, a scholar of jurisprudence, has stated that "[m]arital acts, while (necessarily) reproductive in type, are not merely instrumental, as St. Augustine seems to have supposed, to the good of having children (or avoiding sin). Nor are they mere means of sharing pleasure or even promoting feelings of closeness, as many contemporary liberals think. Rather, such acts realize the intrinsic good of marriage itself as a two-in-one-flesh communion of person [meaning man and woman]." Thus the traditional sexual union can allow a man and a woman to experience their "marriage." All other sexual acts, although they may be fun, are arguably nonmarital.

Paul of Hungary, a Dominican and a law professor, defined the "sin against nature" in his 1220 work *Liber poenitentialis*. This sin was the wasting of seed outside its normal vessel—homosexuality, bestiality, and unnatural heterosexual intercourse—and was considered worse than incest because it violated man's relationship with God. Sin against nature, according to Paul, caused the destruction of Sodom and Gomorrah, the Great Flood, starvation, pestilence, and natural disasters, because it flies in the face of the natural order of things. It denies God's commandment to Adam and Eve to be fruitful and multiply. The punishment of the sodomite is irredeemable consignment to Hell—and if this position sounds a bit outdated or harsh, just consider some of the horrible modern-day rhetoric regarding AIDS.

Paul of Hungary reasoned that the sin against nature, somewhat similar to the ancient Greek point of view, is caused by excess: too much food, drink, and leisure—all of which leads to luxury and self-indulgence. Moral weakness. The antidote is prayer and fasting.

In addition to discussing the proper role of sex, it is important to recognize that the canon lawyers were in fact created by sex. This may seem obvious—but it's not. The point is about much more than where do baby lawyers come from. It has to do with the role of orgasmic sex in the creation of an entire class of people. As the first post–Dark Ages group of professional lawyers, the canonists give us a chance to bring together many of the important threads we have been exploring so far: threads that tie modern-day lawyers firmly to this group of medieval advocates and those advocates, in turn, to the Roman and Greek orators and rhetoricians.

In order for the human race to survive there has to be sex (at least as of this writing). And the role of the big "O" in sex appears to be one of inducement, as well as generating a certain level of commitment. The mechanism of orgasm is activated by repetitive, rhythmic stimulation (typically in four-four time, according to a lawyer-musician friend of mine), not unlike patterns or rituals. In fact it has been speculated that much of the neurological machinery of spiritual transcendence, often achieved through ritual, may have arisen from the neural circuitry that evolved for mating and sexual experience.

A ritual's ability to produce transcendent unitary states and immersion in something larger than the individual could be the result of the effect of rhythmic, ritualized behavior upon the hypothalamus (part of the ancient limbic system), the autonomic nervous system, and, eventually, the rest of the brain. Sexual bliss is also primarily generated by the hypothalamus. The ecstasies of sex, however, are generally the result of physical, tactile sensations, while transcendent experiences most likely depend upon the involvement of higher cognitive structures in the brain, especially those in the frontal lobe. Nevertheless, an evolutionary perspective suggests that the neurobiology of ritual leading to possible transcendent experiences arose, at least in part, from the mechanism of sexual response. And this point is certainly consistent with the fact that over the course of evolution, newer parts of the brain have seemingly built on, or in the case under discussion, taken input from, the older parts of the brain.

The upshot of all this neurobiology is that the connections between Greek myth (messages of the gods tucked away in the patterns of nature), ritual (responses to the gods in animal sacrifice), drama (tragedy and comedy), and the orators and rhetoricians are similar to the connections between Christian myth (Jesus), ritual (prayer), drama (mass), and the canon lawyers. And both the ancient orators/rhetoricians and medieval canon lawyers were made by sex. So there you have it: sex, sex, sex.

PRAISING THE LAWYERLY CANONISTS

In wrapping up this section on canon lawyers, it is important to heap some praise on the lawyerly abilities of those who devoted their energies to the classic canon law. As stated in *The Spirit of Classical Canon Law* by R. H. Helmholz:

> Whether one looks at their ability in mastering relevant authorities [like the ancient scribes], their proficiency in reasoning by analogy [like the Garden of Eden case compared to the London pig case], their skill in analyzing precedents [like the Roman jurists], their talent in drawing legal distinctions [like the Commentators], or their energy in working through a large body of law [like Tribonian and his crew], the canonists seem scarcely inferior to modern

lawyers. In some ways they were probably better, for at least in the United States there is now a widespread distrust of traditional methods of legal reasoning [such as Vinnie and Sal's defense of conflicting commandments] and a widespread confidence that other methods offer more [such as Vinnie and Sal's argument of economic efficiency]. Even leaving this American development aside, it is not clear that a simple comparison or analytical ability would put modern lawyers much ahead. If some of the distinctions the canonists drew seem forced and some of the categories they formulated seem artificial, and if the formalism of their approach to law is not quite congenial with our own, at the very least the modern observer can admire their skills as pure lawyers.

Amen.

CIVIL-LAW SYSTEMS

The French Revolution was based on the idea of establishing Utopia. And in Utopia there are no lawyers (unless you are a lawyer, and then there are only clients who love to pay for legal services). The leaders of the Revolution longed for a legal system that was nontechnical and straightforward, one in which the professionalism and the tendency toward technicality and complication commonly blamed on lawyers was eliminated. Consequently, the French Civil Code of 1804 was envisioned, not unlike the black rock of Hammurabi (except portable), to be a handbook for citizens: a *vade-mecum* drafted in a straightforward fashion so that it could be read and understood without having to consult lawyers or go to court. Utopia!

In contrast to the French Civil Code with its revolutionary, rationalistic, and nontechnical bent, the German Civil Code of 1896, *Bürgerliches Gesetzbuch,* was historically oriented, scientific, and professional. Hence, the Germans were convinced that it was neither desirable nor possible to eliminate lawyers. Clearly a sign of proper thinking.

While the drafters of the German code were influenced by the French code, they did not adopt the notion that law can be stated so that the popular reader would be able to correctly understand it—let alone be able to apply it to specific factual situations. The German view was that lawyers were necessary. Despite codification of the law, lawyers of the newly created nation-state of Germany were needed to interpret and apply the law. The code, with its abstract concepts and mathematical precision, therefore needed to be prepared not as a handbook for citizens but in a way that responded to the needs of those trained in the law. Wunderbar!

The various modern-day civil law systems resulted from the European movement for codification that erupted along nationalist lines in the late 1700s through the 1800s. These systems were, however, heavily influenced by post-classical Roman law—the main reason for including civil law in this discussion of medieval times. And it is this origin that is commonly thought to be the difference between civil law (practiced by civil-law lawyers) and the common law (practiced by common-law lawyers). This perception, however, is inaccurate. There is strong evidence that the English common law was not immune to Roman influence and therefore Roman law affected the course of English common-law history. In addition, it has been observed that the Roman law of the classical period was in many respects closer in character to the common law than it is to modern-day civil-law systems. These similarities include the fact that the common law, like roughly one thousand years of Roman law (510 BCE to 530 CE), was built mainly on the discussions and decisions of specific cases both actual and hypothetical and not on general rules laid down by a legislative body. Both the common law and Roman law focused on particular types of remedies rather than principles and rules. And like the Roman praetor and his Edict, the Chancellor in England and later the common-law courts issued a listing of the types of available remedies (the Register of Writs). The common law, like Roman law, divided legal actions into two stages: the first identified the legal issue involved in a dispute and the second was the job of a group of laymen, called the jury. Finally, the common-law system, like Roman law, developed two distinct bodies of law: the traditional rules, which became rigid and difficult to change, and the more flexible set of rules based on notions of fairness and justice, called equity.

The civil-law system, even though emanating from Roman law, seems rather alien to the common-law lawyer. The reason for this is that the characteristic external features of the civil-law system stems from a time after classical Roman law. One of the more jarring differences for the common-law lawyer is that the civil-law system (like the canon-law system) is codified—a notion typical of natural law thinking. This attempt at creating a statement of the entire law or at least a significant portion of it as a coherent systematic form is the product not of ancient Rome, but of eighteenth-century rationalism: a commitment to the objective study of the utility of legal rules in history and practice. In other words: belief in the possibility of discovering an absolute system of law based on pure reason—"first a bite of fruit and then make babies." The closest Roman law ever came to this approach was Justinian's legal compilation. He indeed decreed that his assemblage (*Codex, Digest,* and *Institutes*) contains the entire law. But except for the *Institutes* (which are a small portion of the whole), Justinian's "codification" of Roman law was neither systematic nor coherent—thus leaving lots of room for medieval legal scholars to work with. Civil law also contains, as a general rule, a sharper distinction between private and public law than exists under the common law. The first question a civil-law lawyer might be asked by a knowledgeable client is whether he is a publicist or a privatist; does the lawyer deal with cases in which one of the parties is a public authority. If a publicist, he will practice in a different set of courts, with different procedures, from those lawyers that deal with private law. Roman law distinguished public from private law but, like the common law, did not generally mark out two distinct bodies of law.

The civil-law notion of distinguishing between private and public spheres without creating distinct bodies of law can be seen in America—even though it is largely a common-law descended country. Legal scholarship has observed that nineteenth-century business interests both shaped the application of law in the private sphere to its needs and managed to derive the benefits of an anti-distributive ideology that existed in the public sphere. "Public law," at the time, was dominated by a conservative fear that legislatures might attempt to redistribute property rights for equalitarian ends, whereas "private law" was seen as tolerating and even encouraging disguised forms of court-sanctioned economic redistribution that actually increased inequality. These differences between the character of law's application to the public and private spheres were tied to an underlying conviction that the course of American legal change needed to be developed by the courts (common law) and not by legislatures (civil law). Legal thinkers of the nineteenth century—as well as a number at the time of this writing—saw a much greater threat of wealth redistribution by statutory interference with the economy than by the judiciary: a "democratic" institution versus an "aristocratic" institution.

From a lawyering point of view, the civil-law system seems to foster a purely deductive type of reasoning. This means that the lawyer proceeds from legislative rules, expressed in general terms, then considers the facts of the case, and finally applies the applicable rule to the facts in order to reach a conclusion. This form of reasoning has been said to lead civil-law lawyers to present arguments as if there can only be one right answer to any legal problem: The major premise is the statute, the facts of the case furnish the minor premise, and the conclusion inevitably follows. Any disagreement in the application of the law to the facts must therefore be the result of faulty logic by the other side.

More technically, the civil-law approach is patterned, ideally, after the way in which a neutral judge would approach a case: Find the applicable law, subsume the facts of the legal problem, argue for or against such initial subsumption by using the appropriate integration techniques, and consider the consequences of each possible decision, the possibility of "gaps" in the law, and whether, besides or in addition to the formal syllogism of scholastic logic, an analogy or other reasoning approach is possible.

It is important to appreciate, however, that somewhat similar to the common law, most civil-law codes acknowledge that they are incomplete. The reason for this is the recognition that in order to create a closed system, a code would have to anticipate every conceivable fact pattern that would, or could, ever occur. And as every lawyer knows (and is truly grateful for), each application of the law is unique—it's just that some applications are more unique than others. The Swiss Code, for example, expressly grants judges the authority, in certain circumstances, to make new law—at least with regard to the parties before the court. And the European Union, as well as the law of the European Economic Area, is made up of elements of civil law and common law.

It is also the case that Continental European lawyers are more generous toward their legal scholars than Americans are. This deferential attitude toward academic writing as a source of Law (i.e., *Recht*) has been said to be one of the most distinctive features of European, Latin American, and Japanese civil-law systems as opposed to the Anglo-American common law.

Ius Commune

The canon law of the Catholic Church, influenced by Roman law, was the first European *ius commune*. Its birthplace was Italy. The Roman law of Justinian, as massaged by the Glossators, Commentators, and Humanists, constituted the second wave of "common law." This synthesis of Roman law, scholastic jurisprudence, humanism, and a touch of canon law was the product of a small, scholastic world dominated by law professors. These academics, similar to the Roman jurists, knew one another's works and constantly referred to them. This closeness, in turn, gave rise to widely shared understandings on most legal matters, in contrast to the frequent guerrilla warfare that is carried on by many modern-day academics. In the mid-sixteenth century, a new legal science was pioneered by various German Protestant jurists and fleshed out during the next two centuries by jurists throughout Europe, both Protestant and Catholic. It differed from prior schools of thought (scholastic and humanist) in its methodology and drive to organize the law as a whole, as well as its desire to analyze and synthesize the various systems of law that prevailed in Europe: Roman, canon, royal, urban, feudal, and mercantile. This new legal science constituted the basis for the third wave of European *ius commune* of the sixteenth to eighteenth centuries.

This new *ius commune* was not only the "learned law" found in treatises, but was also actually used by the courts of various European countries in numerous cases where local statutes and customs failed to provide the needed law. In other words, a "common law" of the civil law.

The European *ius commune* faded from prominence sometime during the period from the French Revolution to the First World War. Among the causes of its rumored demise was the rise of rationalism and nationalism. This combination of "isms," in turn, led to a strictly positivistic definition of law. As a branch of legal philosophy, positivism sees law as three things: rules, sovereign authority, and enforcement by coercive state sanctions. Since these three elements, according to this category of positivism, are the distinguishing features of law, legislation is its basic source and form. Therefore, such things as custom and practice, precedent, and equity are subordinated or simply assimilated into legislation. In combination with the new legal science, this emphasis on legislation as the basis for law led to national codification of various branches of law—modern-day civil law. And since national codes were intended to contain the entirety of the law covered by the code, the *ius commune* seemed unnecessary. Nevertheless, despite massive assaults, the *ius commune* did not die but only went into a coma, from which it recovered in the latter half of the twentieth century.

XV

THE UNCOMMON COMMON LAW

IN CONTRASTING THE COMMON-LAW LAWYER with his civil-law counterpart, Roscoe Pound, a former dean of the Harvard Law School, had this to say:

> [B]ehind the characteristic doctrines and ideas and technique of the common-law lawyer there is a significant frame of mind. It is a frame of mind which habitually looks at things in the concrete, not in the abstract. . . . It is a frame of mind which is not ambitious to deduce the decision for the case in hand from a proposition formulated universally. . . . It is the frame of mind behind the sure-footed Anglo-Saxon habit of dealing with things as they arise instead of anticipating them by abstract universal formulas.

Among the nations of western Europe only the English, it has been argued, have managed to bring essential elements of "their customary legal system" into the modern world. These elements—the doctrine of precedent, jury trials, and the adversary system—are part of the English common law, a system stemming from a tradition of illiteracy and judge-made law that has managed to survive for centuries despite powerful critics and opponents along the way. At various times, proponents of absolutism, both royal and popular, threatened to sweep aside the substance of common-law rules; at other times, civil wars interrupted the operation of common-law courts.

It is generally thought that the English common law as distinguished from various ancient customs and practices had its start during the reign of King Henry II (1154–1189), the first Angevin king.

Henry sent out traveling judges to administer a law that would be "common" for all people in the kingdom—in other words, conformity enforcement. This approach had the effect of weakening the power of the nobles and the Church and enriching the king—since, in contrast to any rent-seeking activity of an Athenian, he was the sole private prosecutor and received property that was forfeited when someone was found guilty of a crime. Thus, such royal and centralized absolutism was, at least in the beginning, an antiaristocratic and antifeudal phenomenon. In fact one might argue that it was to some extent even democratic.

English *Common Law?*

> There are a number of other theories regarding the common law's origins. At least one scholar claims that prior to the Norman invasion, English common law did not exist; another theory holds that the main institutions of the common law were already latent in the laws of the preconquest Anglo-Saxons. And surprising to many is the strain of thought that Islam, through such substantive and procedural areas as action of debt in contract law, assize of novel disseisin in property law, and trial by jury, had a significant influence on the early common law's creation.

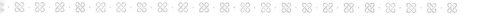

It is also the case that during or shortly after the reign of Henry II, lawyers started to appear in England on behalf of litigants. The development of these legal representatives is somewhat murky, but there is evidence that, at least by 1239, they appeared in two forms: pleaders and attorneys. Initially, both the pleaders—those who appeared in court and spoke for, or at least assisted, their clients—and the attorneys—those who took care of procedural matters and managed their clients' litigation—were, for the most part, amateurs. With the rise in the complexity of the law, litigants began to ask relatives, friends, and neighbors for help—somewhat like ancient Greek litigants who sought out the help of speechwriters (*logographoi*) and supporting speakers (*synēgoroi*). Over time, however, some of these pleaders and attorneys, as a means of earning a living or supplementing other income, began to repeatedly assist or represent litigants, thereby developing an expertise. There is also evidence that court clerks rendered legal assistance as a means of adding to their income. It is emphasized, however, that prior to 1640 (and in most cases much later), it was rare for defense counsel to even be present at criminal trials in common law—the accused, as in ancient Greece, normally conducted his own defense. And on the attack side, prosecution was carried out not by an official royal prosecutor, but by the victim or his relatives or by representatives of organizations concerned with enforcement of public order and morals.

By the reign of Henry III (1216–1272), there is abundant evidence that the increasing expertise of pleaders and attorneys gave rise to the professional serjeants and attorneys in the Court of Common Pleas and other royal courts, primarily Exchequer Chamber and King's Bench. These legal professionals then greatly expanded in number during the reign of Edward I (1272–1307), referred to as "the English Justinian." This growth (and the resultant rise in public criticism) followed from the numerous statutes that were passed and that, in the aggregate, had a significant affect on almost every point of law, both public and private.

There have been many forces that have helped to preserve the key features of the English common-law system. Two deserve special mention. The first is that early maturity made it a system of technical complexity before the end of the thirteenth century. The 1189 treatise called *Glanvill* discussed thirty-nine writs; about one hundred years later, there were 471 different writs. Law cases had become technical, and pleading back and forth incisive and subtle. As a result (and this is the really good part), laymen could not hope to carry out their own litigation without professional help from serjeants and attorneys. Any landowner who went to court in an assize land case or to a central court in Westminster without legal assistance was either very foolish or too poor to afford the help.

The appearance of a legal profession in England was soon followed by the appearance of the Inns of Court. Judges were selected from the ranks of the legal profession, and students, pleaders, attorneys, and judges formed a professional community with an interest in perpetuating a legal system they had learned about at the Inns. It was at these "law schools" that they learned to think in the patterns contained in formulas of the common-law writs, and in time, the successful lawyers and royal judges of the Common Pleas, King's Bench, and Exchequer formed a small, homogenous group. The common law, largely beginning with the reign of King Henry II, is the expression of the cognitive models of that community and a testimony to the power of subcultures. And the lack of any perceived need to systematize the common law by reducing it to a code is a reflection of the group's homogeneity—not unlike the jurists of classical Rome.

In fact, starting with imperial Rome, the jurisconsults' authority became grounded in professional prestige enhanced by their connection with the imperial government. The jurists became a distinct professional class, in contrast to simply being members of the ruling class (as had been the case during the Republic). Evidence for this new class consciousness, like its later appearance among the English bar, is found in the rise of shared mental models. Their writings frequently cited the opinions of their colleagues, expressing agreement or dissent, but never paid the slightest attention to legal views expressed by those outside their own circle. They even developed, not unlike the law French of the English bar, a linguistic style of their own. There are therefore clear similarities between the rise of the Roman jurists and the rise of the common-law lawyers.

And certain modern-day scholars have pointed out (not always in a good way) that modern-day legal academics often display traits similar to those of the ancient Roman jurists. For instance, the academic "contributory relations" during President Roosevelt's New Deal was certainly a play for prestige enhancement through connection with the government. Legal academics have also separated themselves from the practicing bar (like the jurists who distinguished themselves from Cicero), thereby becoming a distinct professional class. And members of this distinct lawyer subclass often write law review articles and books seemingly for each other (frequently citing each other) in a linguistic style that is impenetrable should the typical judge or lawyer happen to wander into this strange world.

The second factor involved in the common-law system's preservation is also related to its early maturity. Medieval common law was at its core land law, with its rules, first enforced during the reign of Henry II, fleshed out over time as if by an invisible hand. This maturation of the common law was especially true during the reign of King Edward I. Edward, not unlike King Lipit-Ishtar, specifically provided for the transfers of owned property and for the creation of long-term family property arrangements by means of conditional gifts.

ROMANS, ANGLO-SAXONS, ISLAM, AND THE BIRTH OF THE COMMON LAW

The common law system did not grow up in a vacuum, of course, but to what extent did Roman law influence the course of English legal history? Legal scholarship has provided an inconclusive answer to this question. Certain scholars on the subject see the Roman influence upon English law as significant, while others have concluded that in England, Roman law led to nothing—except in academic circles. Setting aside the extremes, there is evidence that Roman law, through the medium of canon law, at least influenced the course of English legal history. For example, the template for the medieval English Exchequer of the Jews was likely the Roman *fiscus judicious,* dating from around 70 CE, and the English medieval Jewry was governed in accordance with a Roman nomenclature prevalent among Romans centuries earlier. Even the official chest in which English rulers made Jewish lenders keep their debt instruments appears to have originated as a depository in use among the Jews in the 300s.

The point has been emphasized by various scholars that "Roman law" is a fluid concept, meaning that a body of law as rich, ancient, and widespread as Roman law could not possibly have been constant throughout its long history. It may be that certain academics who minimize the effect of Roman law on English legal history overlook the possibility that Roman-law concepts easily blended into the English legal structure. As highlighted in our prior discussion on civil law systems, there are a number of striking similarities between the common law and the Roman law of the classical period.

Looking at the issue of Roman law influence on the English common law in somewhat more depth, a fundamental proposition is that little to nothing of Roman law survived the withdrawal of the Roman troops from England in the fifth century. The basis for this proposition is that the later wave of Anglo-Saxon invaders were "barbarians" and knew nothing of Roman or canon law. Thus, unlike southern Europe, England, with regard to Roman law, became virtually a clean slate.

In the late sixth century, the Anglo-Saxons began to write down their laws, with the credit for the earliest written collection of Anglo-Saxon law (c. 595) going to King Aethelberht of Kent (560–616). The content of these "Dooms," or judgments, shows little or no hint of Roman law. And unlike those on the European Continent, they were not even written in Latin—the good king, even though a convert of St. Augustine of Canterbury, penned his Dooms in Old English. Additionally, these early laws, influenced by the Franks, generally followed the protasis/apodosis format discussed in Part I, as in, *"gif thuman ofaslaeh, XX scill"* ("if somebody cuts off someone else's thumb, then he shall pay 20 shillings compensation"). Not much difference between King Hammurabi and King Aethelberht—or Johnnie Cochran!

During the first century after the Norman Conquest of 1066, there were further attempts at stating the law—using more and more complex sentences. One such attempt was the so-called *Leis Willelme,* consisting of ten extracts that appear to have been borrowed from Justinian's *Digest.* The text is a French compilation that scholars date somewhere between 1090 and 1170. It was not, interestingly enough, an official document, but appears to have represented an effort to set out, for practicing lawyers, a few principles on Roman law. (The Romans, or at least their laws, have now clearly returned to the island.)

One of the most important early law treatises, *Tractatus de Legibus et Consuetudinibus Regni Angliae,* is popularly known as just *Glanvill.* It was assembled at the end of the reign of King Henry II, probably between November 1187 and July 1189, and focused on practice before the central royal courts: how to start a lawsuit and, surprisingly, how to keep it moving. The treatise, divided into books and chapters, was written in Latin and shows that the author, who may or may not have been the busy Ranulf de Glanvill, had considerable knowledge of Roman and canon law. There are no direct citations to either type of law, but it is clear that the author was well versed in both, along with possibly being touched by a sprinkling (or more) of Islamic law. In fact, it has been noted that the book, whose very title and preface showed Roman influence, would have bewildered any reader ignorant of Roman law.

Of particular interest to us is the fact that Glanvill's treatise, based entirely on a collection of writs, describes both the appointment of a lawyer and the writ for a lawyer to act in court on behalf of his principal (i.e., the client). That is, the litigant wanting to be represented by a lawyer had to personally appear in open court in order to make such a request. It was not until the reign of Henry III that individual lawyers gained the right to simply show up in court, either with regard to a particular matter (as a special counsel) or on behalf of a client for numerous matters over a period of time (as a general counsel).

With regard to Roman law, the prologue to *Glanvill* is a reworking of the prologue to Justinian's *Institutes*. The author, however, did not simply copy the *Institutes* but attempted to make it fit with his perception of English conditions—somewhat like the Commentators, who attempted to create from the revived Roman law a contemporary "common law" for the emerging European states. And where there were no native terms for procedural processes employed in the royal courts, *Glanvill* used Roman law terms.

The second major treatise on the practices of the central royal courts is ascribed to Henry de Bracton, Chief Justice of the Common Pleas, and is titled *De Legibus et Consuetudinibus Angliae* (*On the Laws and Customs of England*). It is commonly known simply as *Bracton*. The influence of the "learned law" is even more evident in *Bracton* than in *Glanvill*. Bracton's treatise, written in Latin with a sprinkling of English, is arranged according to the scheme of Gaius's *Institutes*: persons, things, and actions. Furthermore, the *Institutes* are extensively cited, along with Justinian's *Corpus* and the *Decretals*. In other words, heavy doses of Roman pagan and Catholic Christian law.

And now for an interesting turn of events—Islamic law's possible influence on the common law. The possibility of kinship between Islamic law and the common law can be seen, at a high level of abstraction, in the argument that Islamic law, like the common law, promotes a reactive state (versus activist state—as in Hobbes's idea that power rules) that, in turn, promotes individualism, touched with a strong desire for social justice. In making this argument it is necessary, however, to distinguish between Islamic religion and Islamic law, not unlike the point made by some that it is necessary to distinguish between Christianity and constitutional, statutory, and common law. The Islamic law that influenced (or perhaps even created) the early common law, by way of North Africa and Sicily, was secular, not canonical. Thus, according to one legal scholar, "It was concerned with civil sanctions for failure to do one's duty, not with moral sanctions for having a bad intention." It was therefore "a system focused on ensuring that an individual received justice, not that one be a good person."

In Islam, God (Allah) revealed His law through the Qur'an and the Sunnah. It is from these sources that law could be developed through legal reasoning expressed in legal opinions (*fatawas*). Thus both Islamic and early common law appealed to a law higher than the state, melding together traditional sources with custom, necessity, and preferred or dominant opinions among scholars.

On a less abstract level, various scholars have suggested that Islamic legal influence on the common law can be seen through the fact that the early English trusts closely resembled and probably derived from the even earlier Islamic *waqf* (a charitable institution) and the fact that there are numerous parallel institutions in Islamic and Western legal education, including, most important for our purposes, the *madrasas* in Islam and the English Inns of Court. One scholar has even gone so far as to suggest, with detailed supporting evidence, that the English common law, as an integrated whole, was a product of Islam. His evidence includes the "facts" that the royal English contract protected by the action of debt can be identified with the Islamic *ʿaqd,* the law of contracts; the English assize of novel disseisin, an action to recover lands of which the plaintiff had been disseized or dispossessed, can be identified with the Islamic *istihqaq*; and the English jury can be identified with the Islamic *lafif,* a body of twelve members drawn from the neighborhood who were sworn to tell the truth and to give a unanimous verdict, and not originally with the *Magna Carta.*

In a rather interesting turn of events, the Archbishop of Canterbury, in 2008, stated that "Shari'a law in Britain is unavoidable." Archbishop Rowan Williams told the BBC that for the sake of peaceful coexistence in a diverse society, British lawmakers should come to some "accommodation with some aspects of Muslim [Islamic] law, as we already do with aspects of other kinds of religious law." The fact is that certain concessions had already been made, such as a relaxation of the law on stamp duty in order to avoid it being paid twice when Shari'a-compliant mortgages are used. And husbands with multiple wives had been given permission to claim extra welfare benefits.

The Archbishop's statements, however, caused a bit of a fury. One editorial stated, "[S]hari'a may be a complex and convoluted legal system, but it means only one thing in the United Kingdom: oppression, barbarism and injustice.

This judgment may in itself be unjust, but the word is alien and, like 'jihad,' has taken on its own meaning." The word *Shari'a* may be alien, but, as can be seen in history, parts of Islamic law appear to have been well known and treasured in the West for centuries.

ALLOWANCES FOR LOCAL LAW

Lawyers in England were primarily drawn from the ranks of pleaders who learned the legal profession by apprenticeship, rather than at the Catholic-dominated universities. And the judges in the royal courts of Common Pleas and King's Bench were drawn exclusively from among the lawyers. Consequently, the practice of the common law became increasingly technical and its literature became, for almost 200 years, narrow and technical (and frequently in French!), in contrast to the academic breath that characterized many of the passages found in *Bracton*.

With regard to the English common law and local law, it is interesting to note that the common-law courts of medieval England took "judicial notice" of special or local custom, since the power to make and enforce law rested in multiple jurisdictions. One of the incidents of power granted by the king to rural vassals and chartered boroughs was jurisdiction over disputes. In rural areas, feudal customs were established and tried in the lord's court, which was attended by the lord's tenants.

This notion of custom might seem completely outdated in our modern era of extensive local, state, and national legislation. Such, however, is not the case. For instance, largely unwritten Native American tribal common law (composed of custom and tradition) still plays an important role in judicial decision making in tribal courts. In fact it might be argued that this use of tribal common law is an important part of resisting what Native American legal scholars have identified as an assimilationist discourse in Western jurisprudence. This discourse has been used, according to these scholars, to beat down Native American culture and thereby prevent the diversity of their cultures from becoming part of the official American culture. Consequently, Native Americans have struggled to preserve and protect indigenous discourses of law and justice by resisting the assimilationist tide of American law.

THE MAGNA CARTA

The Magna Carta is well known to British and American lawyers, particularly those who take an interest in constitutional questions. This "Great Charter," negotiated at knifepoint in 1215 on the field at Runnymede (a water-meadow beside the Thames River between Staines and Windsor), embodied a series of concessions extracted from King John by his Norman barons. It eventually became the first and foremost enactment in the English book of statutes, a declaration of Saxon independence—and remained there until the Law Reform Act of 1863. Embodied in its parchment-preserved provisions, composed of a preamble and 63 clauses (strangely enough, the exact same number of tractates that make up the Mishnah), are such lasting concepts as right of trial by jury and the ever-illusive right to a speedy trial. Of particular interest to our current discussions are Clauses 26 and 27, providing that when a man dies leaving a will (i.e., testate), his wishes should generally be carried out according to the testament's direction. And when a free man dies without a will (i.e., intestate), his goods should be distributed by his relatives under the supervision of the Church.

These testate/intestate provisions do not appear to be particularly radical to the modern way of thinking, but at the time of the Magna Carta, testamentary freedom was not generally recognized. The ability to will real property was, due to the importance of feudal ties, not fully adopted by the common law until the Statute of Wills in 1540. And the claims of a vassal's lord on the vassal's personal property were just as strong as those of the next of kin. The Magna Carta's provisions therefore represented a choice among competing rules. And it is from the canon law that one finds support for some of the choices that were made at Runnymede.

From a narrow perspective, English common law, as indicated above, was the body of law applied in a particular set of courts (i.e., the central royal courts of common law) in the absence of local custom, pleaded and proven. More broadly, the common law, however, can be seen as the custom of all England—the body of laws that applied throughout the country.

RETURN OF THE LEARNED LAW

During the sixteenth century in England there was, after 200 years of slumber, a revival of interest in the learned law. The common-law lawyers, in turn, felt the heat coming from various courts that more or less influenced this law—that is, canon and Romanist law. This competition, in turn, led to a strain in the relations between the common-law lawyers and the civil-law lawyers. Sir Edward Coke (1552–1634) and other great common-law jurists were vocal in their attacks on the presumptions of the "Roman idea" behind the civil-law concept. The common-law lawyers argued that the civil law's emphasis on rationality and on some intellectual elitist that was neither a legislator nor a judge, neither advocate nor prosecutor, invited absolutist monopolies on truth and justice. For Coke and others wedded to the common law, the search by the civilians for "universal law" seemed dangerously tied to the universal legal claims of the Catholic Church and therefore inconsistent with British nationalism. They also feared any encroachments on the institute that was perceived to be the ultimate guardian of private English rights, the Inns of Court.

Bleedings, Mercury, and Opium

This same type of intergroup tournament surfaced in "medical" science. Homeopathy had been developed by a German physician in the early 1800s. This approach to human diseases was so successful that by 1900 there were homeopathic medical schools and hospitals all across America. This success enraged the allopaths, with their long-standing belief in bleedings, mercury, and opium, and they waged war against the newcomers. The result was the founding of the American Medical Association and its efforts to purge the medical profession of their rivals.

This Us versus Them mentality deepened when, in the early seventeenth century, the common-law lawyers began siding with the forces opposing the monarch (especially those with papal sympathies), and the civilians tended to side with the crown. Engaging in a bit of leveling and sharpening, it became, in particular, a legal and personal rumble between Sir Edward Coke and Sir Francis Bacon. But even with the restoration of the monarchy in 1660, many institutions based on the learned law were lost in the scuffle or greatly reduced in power. Consequently, the common-law lawyers, at least with regard to England, were ultimately able to claim victory.

The English Revolution

The English Revolution of 1640–1689 established, for the first time, the supremacy of Parliament over the Crown and of the common-law courts over their remaining "Romanist" rivals. It also created a two-party system of Whigs and Tories, a socioeconomic transformation that established the predominance of the landed gentry and a rising merchant class over the royal nobility. A simultaneous religious transformation established the legitimacy of Calvinist belief-systems alongside a more liberal Anglicanism. And for our purposes, this English Revolution pushed along fundamental changes in legal philosophy, legal science, and criminal and civil law—all of which increased the importance of lawyers. God save the Queen!

The tension between the common-law-trained lawyer and the civil-law-trained lawyer continues to this day. It's not uncommon, for example, for an English barrister to argue a case before the Court of the European Communities at Luxembourg (where civil-law concepts prevail) and begin by setting out the facts that gave rise to the case. The judges will undoubtedly interrupt the barrister, asking what rules apply to the issue at hand. Somewhat frustrated, the barrister will wonder how the court could possibly understand the problem until the facts are presented.

The barrister's frustration stems from the fact that common-law lawyers are trained to begin with an examination of the facts. This examination then leads to an identification of the legal issue(s) bubbling up from the facts of the case. When on-point decisions can be found in earlier court cases (the doctrine of precedent), each lawyer will usually cite those cases that favor his client's position and emphasize the facts of his case relevant to those prior cases (analogical reasoning—generally based on a healthy dose of leveling, sharpening, and assimilating). Or if there is no favorable case law, the lawyer might resort to principles, policy, or morality in order to find legal meaning, as Adam and Eve's lawyers did, that advances his client's cause.

The civil-law lawyer, in contrast to this "inductive approach" (that is, going bottom-up from specific facts to general rules of law), frequently uses what seems more like deductive reasoning—top-down. He starts with a rule of law, often expressed in abstract terms, found in the applicable code, and then subsumes the facts of the case at hand to the rule in order to arrive at a conclusion. The reason for this approach is the civil-law notion that no rule of law can be recognized that is not in statutory form. Such rules can be subject to various kinds of interpretation, but the rules themselves remain unchanged until they are modified by legislation. This is not the case under the common law, in which judges, based on various fact patterns and typically using analogical reasoning, modify the law or, in some cases, create brand new law through inductive generalization.

CHRISTIANITY AND COMMON LAW

It has been said that the history of the English common law is largely embodied in the history of how the central royal courts came to ultimately dominate the entire system. The reason for this domination is that as the centralized court system developed, litigants frequently preferred to have their suits heard by the king's justices—who increasingly came from the rising gentry class—due to the inadequacies and prejudices prevalent in the local courts. (Not unlike the modern-day attitude that it is sometimes better to have a case heard in federal court than in state court.) In addition, the writs issued by the central courts had great authority since they were backed by the power of the king. As a result, many of the courts with which the English civilians were associated were abolished by the sixteenth and early seventeenth centuries, and those that survived were either taken over by common-law lawyers (who, after helping get rid of royals with Catholic leanings, became tighter and tighter with the king) or were, like the ancient Greek court of the *Areopagus,* deprived of a large part of their jurisdiction. Furthermore, training in the civil law and the *ius commune* was never a requirement for practice before the common-law courts.

The civil law and *ius commune* nevertheless seeped into the common law, despite claims of purity by Coke and others. Their respective influences came from the books that were available to common-law scholars, particularly due to the rise of the printing press, the interchanges between civil-law and common-law lawyers, and the institutions that applied the civil law and *ius commune*—especially the Church courts.

There is historical evidence that common-law lawyers, particularly during the late Tudor and early Stuart periods, actually used books from the civil-law tradition. This openness to Continental sources of law shows up in the common-law case reports. There are three areas, in particular, in which English common-law lawyers cited Continental sources: first, disputes regarding the rights and powers of the Crown; second, the origins of the privilege against self-incrimination; and third, the early history of the law on libel and slander.

Anglo-American courts through the centuries have repeated the observation that Christianity, and the Mosaic law in particular, is a part of the common law. It is a proposition that has been affirmed by some of the most highly acclaimed English and American jurists, such as Sir Edward Coke, Sir Matthew Hale, Lord Mansfield, Sir William Blackstone, and to some extent, Justice Joseph Story. The real question, however, is: Has Christianity always been part of the common law? The quick answer is no. There were certainly times and places in the British Isles where the "common law," broadly defined and existing in the form of early customs and practices, existed before Christianity was a known religion, particularly among its Celtic and early Anglo-Saxon peoples. How, then, did Christianity arguably become part of the common law?

Thomas Jefferson once argued that Christianity was incorporated into English common law by a seventeenth-century legal scholar named Sir Henry

Finch. Finch, according to Jefferson, used an English decision as the vehicle for accomplishing this task.

The 1458 decision involved the claim by a man named Humphrey Bohun that he, and not the Bishop of Lincoln, had the right to name a particular clergyman to a position (called *advowson* or the "right of a patron"). John Broughton, as Bishop of Lincoln, had failed to install Bohun's candidate because another church patron also claimed the right of a patron and presented another clergyman for the position. Under ecclesiastical law, the conflict was supposed to have been appealed to a special commission composed of six clergy and six laymen (an assize jury). Neither patron, however, requested the commission, and the Bishop, after six months of inaction, filled the vacancy with his own selection. In deciding for the Bishop, Chief Justice Prisot, a judge of the common-law courts, found that the Bishop had strictly followed Church procedures as embodied in ecclesiastical law.

Judge Prisot did not, according to Jefferson's line of reasoning, incorporate Christianity itself into his common-law-based decision but simply made reference to ecclesiastical law. However, some 150 years later, Sir Henry Finch (1558–1625) mistranslated Prisot's Latin phrases, contained in the decision, to incorporate the Christian Bible and its doctrines into the common law. Jefferson's claim was that in Finch's treatise entitled *Law, or a Discourse Thereof* (commonly called *Finch's Law*), Finch mistranslated and misinterpreted the case of *Bohun v. Broughton* by changing the phrase *en ancien scripture,* which does not mean "Holy Scripture" but merely the ancient written laws of the Church; which, as we saw in our discussion of canon law, is not the same as Scripture.

Jefferson, a confirmed Deist, went on to criticize a series of judicial decisions upholding Christianity as part of the common law. The bulk of these decisions were issued immediately following the publication of *Finch's Law* and extended throughout the late nineteenth century. The decisions, in large part, denied religious liberty to dissenters based on notions of blasphemy in the Anglican Church. These dissenters included Puritans and Quakers who came to America to escape religious persecution.

Certain legal scholarship indicates that Jefferson's argument may indeed point to the precise source of the incorporation of Christianity (in contrast to Christian principles) into the common law. At a minimum, he put his finger on the most widely printed sources that first announced such direct connection. And Jefferson pointed out how these mistranslations were used or misused to justify the oppression of religious dissenters by certain elitists in the seventeenth century.

However, Finch's arguable mistranslation of key portions of the 1458 *Bohun* case would not have amounted to much without the ability of seventeenth-century elites to control the printing and dissemination of law books such as Finch's. In other words, the incorporation of Christianity into the common law (along the lines of Jefferson's analysis) was not due simply to the individual efforts of Finch but most likely relates to the widespread dissemination of *Finch's Law* and the application of his concepts by leading jurists of the seventeenth century, particularly Coke and Hale. It was in fact Chief Justice Hale in his opinion in *Taylor's Case* (1676) who established the common-law crime of blasphemy based on Christianity, relying heavily on *Finch's Law* and the opinions of Coke, who had also been heavily influenced by Finch.

XVI

LAWYERS AND THE INQUISITION:
"Rack 'Em Up"

THE INQUISITION BEGAN as a discrete procedure in the decretal legislation of a former lawyer. This penitent was Lotario de Conti, Pope Innocent III (1160–1216), the most powerful of the medieval popes.

Heaven on Earth

All but one of the popes from the mid-twelfth to the early fourteenth century appear to have been trained as canon lawyers. The great majority of the cardinals were also lawyers. The reason for this was that by 1200 the papal Curia and the College of Cardinals acted as an international court of appeals for thousands of cases a year. The typical course of legal appeal was first to the consistory court of the archdeacon, then to the courts of audience of the bishop and archbishop, and finally to the papal court. It has been said that more time was spent on legal matters in Rome than on theological or spiritual matters.

At the start of his papacy in 1198, thirty-seven-year-old Innocent was faced with a church tainted by internal corruption. The accusatorial criminal procedure mandated by the *Decretum* was too cumbersome, too protective of a defendant's rights, and too reliant on the initiative of an individual accusator to work as an efficient tool for the punishment of misconduct by the clergy. The Pope therefore adopted and developed the procedure of inquisition as a means by which his appointed judges could investigate any rumor of misconduct. Innocent did not consider this procedure to be criminal in nature; the idea was to remove misbehaving clergy from their offices, but not otherwise to punish them.

In addition to internal problems, medieval Catholicism was threatened by various heresies including Catharism, a Christian sect that believed in two creators (one good and one with an evil grip on the world), gave a prominent role to women in its priesthood, and rejected all Catholic sacraments. In order to deal with such threats to its supremacy, the Church further refined its internal machinery. For example, Innocent III's nephew, Pope Gregory IX, turned to the Dominicans and Franciscans, who had popular support due to their restrained lifestyle, to act as shock troops in the Church's counteroffensive. The powers of the expanded Inquisition as a conformity enforcer were extensive. The inquisitors had jurisdiction over everybody in the area to which they were assigned, except the bishops and their officials, and were answerable only to the Pope. Their goal was to establish guilt or innocence by questioning and then attempting to persuade offenders to recant their heresy. If an inquisitor failed in his attempt to illicit repentance of the guilty party's Orwellian "crimethink," the heretic was turned over to the secular authorities for punishment.

Subtle Persuasion

The courts of the Inquisition could deal only with heresy, not "ordinary" crimes. And non-Christians, such as Jew and Turks, could commit blasphemy, a very serious crime that fell within the jurisdiction of both the spiritual and the temporal courts, but not heresy. The reason for this separation was the canonical principle that no person should be "forced" to embrace the Christian faith. But there was a difference between absolute force and conditional force. (Remember, as we saw in Part I, categorizing—good fruit/bad fruit—is an important part of traditional legal reasoning.)

The Inquisition, with its expanded powers, started acting on denunciation and in secret—no writs of *habeas* "you got the wrong guy" *corpus*. It employed full-time agents, part-time informers, and reformed heretics. (Some people in the United States, including many lawyers, see a bit of inquisition in the form of the modern-day Patriot Act and Military Commissions Act.)

In 1251 the Inquisition was given the go-ahead to use torture to arrive at the "truth"—meaning unconditional submission to Roman dogma. Pope Innocent IV, however, authorized its use only if the torture did not lead to mutilation, bleeding, or death, and inquisitors could only attempt to illicit a confession, not merely inflict pain. Since they had no legal training, inquisitors were not permitted to pass sentence but had to accept the judgment of bishops and professional lawyers.

In contrast to the many run-of-the mill heretics discovered by the Inquisition, there were few trials for heretic/Satanist witches before 1300. One reason for this involved the nature of the judicial process. An accuser was required to provide the evidence and to seek to convince the judge of the accused's guilt. If argumentation failed, ordeal by fire, water, or combat might be invoked. If, however, the accuser ultimately failed in his proof, he might suffer the same punishment he had sought for the accused. The burden of the process and the serious consequences, if the prosecution was unsuccessful, made finger-pointing problematic. As a result, "victims" of witchcraft tended to take matters into their own hands and organize lynchings.

As previously discussed, the twelfth century witnessed the reintroduction of Roman law concepts into Western culture. From this foundation emerged a systematic and coherent code of Church law, the canon law, that replaced the existing fragmentary and sometimes contradictory literature. In turn this surge in the law augmented the judicial process of the system of inquisition. Along with the use of torture, the enhanced inquisitorial process helped ensure more frequent confessions. The removal of the possibility of penalty for unsuccessful accusers encouraged accusation. Roman law also promoted the use of harsher penalties. The law codes of the twelfth and thirteenth centuries sanctioned the use of burning for witches and sorcerers. The processes of inquisition, versus private trial, were used by both the Church and state in numerous campaigns aimed at dealing with dissenters—including that unrepentant dissenter, Galileo. And the use of prosecutors (i.e., lawyers) in this process was not uncommon. I am sure, however, that they tried not to enjoy it—at least too much.

And in the spirit of tradition, lawyers have continued to be involved in attempts to squash "offensive" religious practices—such as those of Santeria.

In 1987, Ernesto Pichardo, a high priest of the Santeria religion, sought to establish a church in the city of Hialeah, Florida. The problem was that Santerians, claiming to follow Old Testament practices, consider animal sacrifice an important part of their religion. The community, however, did not consider this to be true religion but "heresy"—and called in the lawyers.

Alden Tarte, a lawyer representing residents seeking to shut the church down, did not mince words: "Santeria is not a religion. It is a throwback to the dark ages. It is a cannibalistic, voodoo-like sect which attracts the worst elements of society, people who mutilate animals in a crude and most inhumane manner." The Hialeah city attorney was, however, a bit more diplomatic: "The community will not tolerate religious practices which are abhorrent to its citizens."

According to one legal scholar, "Pichardo thought that Hialeah's actions amounted to a modern-day inquisition. And so it seemed. The city had obviously responded to a religion it abhorred with vehemence and intolerance [not unlike the medieval Church]. It passed four ordinances in an effort to outlaw Santerian practices, rituals that all agreed were central to adherents' religious beliefs, beliefs that were sincerely held." It appears that it's one thing to kill a chicken in a slaughterhouse and quite another to sacrifice it on the altar of religion.

So there you have it—some lawyers, Middle Age and modern, love a good inquisition: so rack 'em up.

XVII

EVEN A DIRTY RAT DESERVES A LAWYER

In the district of Autun, France, in 1522, the villagers were out-raged that rats had eaten the barley crops. So, they did what civilized people often do—they sued. The ecclesiastical court, after a proper investigation of the crime, delivered a summons to the rats, ordering them to come forward and stand trial. Court officials went to areas where the thieving rats were thought to live, and like God calling out to Adam and Eve, served notice with trumpets and loud and solemn voice.

The bishop's vicar, before whom the complaint had been initially presented, recognized that the accused might not be able to afford counsel and therefore appointed a local jurist named Bartolomée Chassenée to defend the rats. When the defendants failed to show, young Chassenée argued to the court that there had not been proper service of process because, in fact, the reputation of *all* rats in the com-munity was at stake and so *all* rats, not just those alleged to have eaten the barley, deserved to be informed of the action. The court agreed and the parish priests announced a new summons, preached from every pulpit in the diocese of Autun. The rats, despite the warnings to attend, still failed to show. Chassenée then argued that because the rats were spread across the countryside, they needed more time to make their way to court. Having bought a second procedural reprieve for his clients, Chassenée pressed for equal treatment under the law.

He pointed out to the court that a summons implies the full protection of the law while a defendant is on his or her way to court. His clients were anxious to defend their good name but, according to Chassenée, were afraid that they would be attacked by hostile cats. Furthermore, the cats were hardly neutral in the dispute since they belonged to the plaintiffs. It was simply too much to expect that his clients should risk death in order to obey the summons.

A default judgment was eventually granted to the rats, and the ingenuity and learning Chassenée displayed in defending his rodent clients established for him a solid reputation as a criminal defense lawyer. Ah, the majesty of the law.

The Autun indictment was not an isolated case. Records indicate that trials of animals, sometimes represented by counsel, took place throughout Europe and elsewhere from the ninth through the nineteenth centuries. Individual animals were tried—generally for killing a human—in various courts pursuant to legal precedents dating back to the biblical Book of Exodus. And like the rats of Autun, various types of animals were tried in groups as public nuisances.

Although on the surface the trial of an animal, individually or in a class action, appears to be rather silly, it was not a game. This point is underscored by the fact that such proceedings cost the community lots of money. As indicated above, most, if not all, of the animal defendants lacked the money or sense to hire a lawyer. Consequently, defense lawyers (who do not generally work for free—just ask O.J.) had to be hired by the community. In addition, individual defendants had to be fed while confined in jail at the community's expense, and the executioner, if a death sentence was handed down, had to be paid just as he was for any other execution. It certainly would have been easier to just forgo due process and hang the alleged offender from the nearest gallows.

Despite the cost and effort, communities all over Europe looked to the avenue of a trial, both secular proceedings—used to punish animals for criminal acts—and ecclesiastical proceedings—used to rid a region of infestation by threat of anathema or other type of "excommunication"—in order to bring offenders to justice. It appears, without any assurance of truth, that by integrating animals and insects within the scheme of law and justice, such trials allowed the various communities to affirm a rationale under, and to assign a role for animals and insects in, the hierarchy of God's creation. In other words, an attempt was being made through legal proceedings to carry out the requirements of God's universals of truth and justice—an extreme form of conformity enforcement. (Remember it was not just Adam and Eve; there was also the snake.) An animal that killed a person created a tear in the fabric of the cosmos—something that could not be ignored any more than if the killing had been by a human. It was about the act—not the intent. This universalization of *ius naturale* was in fact embedded in the *Corpus iuris civilis.* Justinian's work provided that Law "is not peculiar to the human race, but applies to all creatures which originate in the air, on the earth and on the sea."

Consider a 1750 trial in France. In Vanvres, a man named Jacques Ferron and his female donkey were discovered in the act of copulation. Both the man and the donkey were charged with bestiality and the man was sentenced to death. The donkey, however, was acquitted. The neighbors and parish priest, presenting the defense, focused on the fact that the animal was the victim of violence and therefore had not freely participated in her owner's crime (foreshadowing a type of psychological abuse defense). As supporting evidence, the donkey's advocates presented to the court a signed statement. The signers swore that they had known the donkey for four years, that she had always shown herself to be virtuous and well-behaved, both at home and abroad, and that she had never been involved in a hint of scandal. This community statement of the donkey's virtues, but not of Ferron's, appears to have had a decisive influence on the court's judgment.

✿ · ✿

A Vice-Ridden Mare

Mr. Goad's mare was not quite so lucky as Mr. Ferron's donkey. In 1673, Benjamin Goad of Massachusetts, "being instigated by the Devil," committed the "unnatural and horrid act of Bestiality on a mare in the highway or field," in the "Afternoon when the sun being two hours high." Goad was sentenced to hang until dead. The Court of Assistants also ordered "that the mare you abused before your execution in your sight shall be knocked on the head."

✿ · ✿

In contrast to bestiality and murder cases, there were trials of large groups of pests. These groups, like the Autun rats, were generally accused of creating a hardship in the community or of being a public nuisance. In such cases, the pests' counsel often used a biblical defense: "My clients, your Honor, were merely obeying God's command to be fruitful and multiply." Their lawyer, in waxing eloquent, thus served the function of participating in a public discussion regarding the roles and relationships among God, man, animals, and plants. This was, as discussed in Part I, a possible way to have framed the case involving Adam and Eve. Rather than God versus "man," Vinnie and Sal might have focused the High Court's attention on the roles and relationships between and among God, "man," animals, and fruit. (Not unlike, by the way, modern-day structural lawsuits involving endangered species, wilderness, and the development of natural resources.)

Because of the ritualistic role served by these group and individual trials of animal defendants, attention to procedural rules, a mixture of Roman law and canon law, was of great concern. For example, in a fourteenth-century Swiss case brought against a swarm of Spanish flies, the judge ordered the appointment of counsel to represent the flies due to their small size and the fact that they had not yet reached their maturity.

The important rule of law aspects involved in this Swiss case can be seen by contrasting it with a summary sentence issued by St. Bernard of Clairvaux (d. 1153). In this much earlier case, Bernard, while dedicating a new monastic oratory, found that his discourse could not be properly heard because of the racket being made by "an incredible multitude of flies." Exasperated, and unable to think of any other remedy, the good saint excommunicated them. The next morning the unrepresented flies were found dead—victims of Bernard's anathema.

In somewhat the same fashion as the Spanish flies, the 1519 trial involving a pack of field mice in western Tyrol ended with an agreement that the mice would be moved to a new tract of land. The mice's lawyer demanded that the court provide for his clients' safe passage to their new location by protecting them against harm or annoyance from cats, dogs, and other predators. The lawyer was persuasive. The judge agreed to the advocate's safe-conduct request, but only for the weakest and most vulnerable of the field mice. The judge also softened the sentence of immediate and perpetual banishment by ordering that "a free safe-conduct and an additional respite of fourteen days be granted to all those which are with young and to such as are yet in their infancy; but on the expiration of this reprieve, each and every [mouse] must be gone, irrespective of age or precious condition of pregnancy."

In a world of dangers, diseases, and high death rates, the philosophical backdrop to the animal and insect trials grabbed the attention of many great thinkers, including St. Thomas Aquinas. Thomas opined that if animals are regarded as God's creatures and employed by Him as agents for execution of His judgments, then cursing them constitutes blasphemy. If, on the other hand, they are treated as lesser, nonrational creatures, then cursing them is futile and therefore wrong. But this did not mean, in Thomas's opinion, that animals and insects should be left alone. In his *Summa Theologiae* he concluded that vengeance could properly be visited on animals in order to punish their owners and in "horror of sin" (act—not intent). "And while recognizing that irrationality ruled out punishment," according to one writer, "he made clear that God could be asked to curse, or athematize, an unwitting agent of Satan.

The only precondition was that it had to be made clear that the target was the demonic possessor rather than the possessed creature itself."

The argument that animals are God's creatures and act as His agents intrigued a number of defense lawyers. At many of the animal trials, these lawyers, in priestlike fashion, argued that because the pests were clearly sent to punish sinful humans, they should be regarded as agents of God and therefore it is blasphemous to prosecute them: Humans may have moral authority over nature, but God has moral authority over humans. Repentance would consequently be the only effective means of fending off the pests—for only then might God, in His mercy, remove the scourge.

Bankers as Agents of God?

The "not guilty—sent to punish sinful humans" defense might be useful to a modern-day, Big Business wrongdoer under criminal indictment. Financial crises have been described throughout the ages as a type of plague. And plagues are, traditionally, punishments from God. Thus we have: A plague is a punishment from God; a financial crisis is a plague; therefore a financial crisis is a punishment from God. The wrongdoer's defense can now be fully established—in fact, it is put together by the prosecutor. Do you see it? The defendant does not have to attempt to prove his innocence, but simply relies on the hard work of the state (to show, beyond a reasonable doubt, that he *is* guilty of causing a financial crisis). His lawyer, extending her index finger to point at the prosecutor, then tells the court that the state is persecuting God!

This argument appears to have rarely been successful. After all, God gave humans dominance over nature and therefore legal authority—right? The logic of repentance, however, did prevail in the Saint-Julien weevil trial; at least, in the first trial of these destructive creatures.

It appears that weevils had been destroying vineyards in the French village of Saint-Julien. The prosecution of the pests ended up being divided into two trials, spaced about forty-one years apart. The first complaint was made by the Saint-Julien wine growers in 1545. Attorneys were hired to defend the insects. After presentation by both sides, the ecclesiastical court dismissed the case. The court's May 8, 1546, proclamation specified public prayers as the first step. The required ritual then included three consecutive days of High Mass followed by a religious procession around the vineyards. The court recorded that the prayers did the trick—the weevils disappeared. The court viewed the insects as God's creatures and, consequently, their destruction was a sign sent from Heaven to humankind that the moral accounts were not in balance. The medium is, after all, the message.

During April of 1587 the weevils returned, arguably wreaking more suffering as punishment for human sin. A new trial was held. Because the original defense lawyers had died, the petition requested that new counsel be appointed to defend the weevils in excommunication proceedings.

The weevils' new attorney, Pierre Rembaud, answered the complaint with a plea to dismiss the case. Rembaud argued, based on the book of Genesis, that the lower life-forms were created before man and that God blessed all the creatures of the earth. As a result, the weevils, according to Rembaud, had a prior right to the vineyards: a sort of vested property rights defense—and a seeming end-run around a difficult causality issue. Additionally, Rembaud, on behalf of his clients, contended that because animals and insects could only be subject to *ius naturale* and instinct, bringing them within human jurisdiction pursuant to *ius gentium* was unreasonable.

The prosecuting attorney presented a document setting out the misery suffered by the poor, innocent villagers as a result of the ruthless weevils. Defense counsel requested, and was granted, an adjournment in order to review the document. In the meantime, the village's lawyer, François Fay, offered his reply. He argued that although the pests were created before humans, they were still made subservient to the needs of humans who were given dominion over the earth by its owner—God. In other words, although the weevils came first, God granted them no property rights in the vineyards but vested all such rights in the villagers—subject, however, to His paramount title. Thus the weevils were trespassers and should be punished. In response to Fay, another lawyer for the insects, Antoine Filliol, responded by arguing that the subordination of lower life-forms to man did not confer a right on man to excommunicate the insects.

In this vein he emphasized the argument that animals and insects could only be subject to *ius naturale*. Filliol's argument, like Fay's, recognized a hierarchy and order to the world, but positioned God as the only dominant adjudicator.

While the lawyers wrangled, sanity finally prevailed: The villagers decided to set aside land outside the vineyards for use by the weevils. The townspeople drew up a proposed contract with the weevils. The agreement described the designated land, and reserved for the villagers the right to pass through it (in legal terms, an easement) and to make use of the surface water concurrently with the weevils. Additionally, the town was to retain the right to take refuge on the land during time of war and the right to extract minerals as long as the insects were not harmed.

The village's counsel made a court appearance and demanded enforcement of the contract. The defense requested time to review the agreement to see if it was fair to the insects. When the court reconvened, the weevils' attorney, Filliol, objected to the proposed terms on the basis that the land offered to his clients was sterile and not suitable for the weevils' subsistence needs. The village's lawyer insisted that the land was more than suitable. In order to resolve this technical dispute, the court engaged experts to examine the area and to submit a written report regarding the land's fitness as a home for the weevils (a procedure, except for the defendant-weevil part, that is often used in complex modern-day litigation).

The irony to all of this is that the final decision of the court is lost to time—apparently insects destroyed the final page of the trial record.

From a modern perspective, all this attention paid to the trial of weevils seems incredibly foolish and adds nothing to the reputation of lawyers—or at least nothing good. But consider the possibility, as hinted at earlier, that the prosecution of animals and insects that violated self-evident laws (e.g., "Thou shall not covet thy neighbor's property" or "Thou shall not kill") was not really about punishing the offender but about incorporating the human and nonhuman within one community of truth and justice. The seemingly petty attention to procedural detail insisted upon by the lawyers might not have been merely clever tactics but a statement about the fact that truth and justice are universal. A statement that judicial procedures, established by God in the Garden of Eden, are grounded in the *ius naturale*—reasoned entailments from conceptual metaphors about how to keep the universe in moral balance.

This metaphorical notion of universal truth and justice, both procedural and substantive, appears to still be with us—or at least some of us. There is, for example, a growing sentiment to give chimpanzees legal standing, specifically including the right to have suits filed in their names in order to seek protection of their interests. And just like the animals and insects discussed above, the chimps, contrary to the *Planet of the Apes*, will most likely not be able to take such action on their own. This means, you guessed it, calling in the lawyers!

According to one newspaper report, a national coalition of research and advocacy groups has drafted model legislation to allow nonprofit groups to petition courts to act as guardians for any chimpanzee "subjected to the willful use of force or violence upon its body." This type of proposed legislation has received support from at least one Harvard Law School professor. United States constitutional scholar Laurence Tribe has argued, grounding his argument on an existing metaphor, that courts already recognize corporations as juristic, or legal, "persons." And if society is going to give incorporeal things rights, why not extend the legal definition of "persons" to the species whose DNA is closest to man? Or, stated in the form of a classical analogy: Corporations are to persons as chimp DNA is to human DNA.

There are in fact lawyers who represent pets facing execution for attacking humans. The arguments raised by these lawyers on behalf of their animal clients often have a tone very similar to that of the European lawyers of centuries ago.

XVIII

INNS OF COURT:

The Early English Law Schools

Sir Walter Raleigh, the tall, elegant sycophant of Queen Elizabeth, is famous for having popularized potatoes and introduced England to the pleasures of tobacco (for which a number of modern-day class-action lawyers are eternally grateful). But he was also trained in the law.

Raleigh, like many other up-and-coming men of the Elizabethan Era, came from the western part of England (i.e., the Cornish and Devon areas). His family had done well from the loot received after the political destruction of many of the monasteries. Nevertheless, as a younger son, Raleigh was expected to go out into the world and make his own way. He started at Oxford but left around 1574 after only a short time in order to fight in France on the side of the Huguenots (French Protestants). On his return to England, he decided it would be helpful to his future to study law at the Middle Temple—yes, a temple! In order, however, to understand what this temple was (and still is), we have to look at the Inns of Court.

Raleigh's Family Money

In 1509, the year of King Henry VIII's coronation, several million acres of land in England were under the Catholic Church's control.

This wealth was the accumulation of nearly 1,000 years of gifts and pur-chases. It was an inviting target for a government that had declared itself free from the Church and had already taken steps to discredit a celibate clergy and the monastic life. In 1536, armed with carefully collected data on the wealth of the various monasteries, King Henry VIII (or more specifically Henry's chancellor, Thomas Cromwell) had his allies in Parliament introduce an act dissolving all monasteries worth less than 200 pounds. Those mon-asteries worth more than 200 pounds were subsequently dissolved on an individual basis between 1538 and 1540. By 1554, most of the monastic hold-ings had been sold to private parties primarily from the rising gentry class—leading not only to the rise of Parliament and constitutional government but also creating lots of conveyancing work for attorneys and solicitors.

⊠ · ⊠

Historically, the Inns were not merely law schools, or trade unions, or social clubs, but all three. This combination was exactly what was needed by an up-and-coming gentleman. The notion of the "all-round gentleman" started in Italy in the early 1500s and had spread to England by the time of Raleigh. This concept meant that the medieval separation between ecclesiastical education and that of a knight was scrapped. Consequently, in Raleigh's Elizabethan Eng-land a gentleman was educated in both writing and fighting. He was expected to learn Greek and to know modern languages, to dance and to make music, to read and to write poetry.

And the English concept of a gentleman added to the Italian ideal the notion of the "governor." In order to achieve this enhanced ideal, it was thought that along with literature and philosophy, the Tudor gentleman should know something about the law so that he might serve the commonwealth as a judge, magistrate, officer, or administrator—a scalar distribution of social responsibil-ity. This is the reason Raleigh enrolled in the Inns of Court.

The exact origin of the Inns is unknown. There is speculation that they were established during the reign of Edward I (1272–1307) in order to stabi-lize the legal profession which, due to the King's sweeping legislative reforms, had experienced tremendous growth. The earliest surviving records, however, begin in 1422 and concern Lincoln's Inn. These records, called the Black Books of Lincoln's Inn, begin in the same year as the death of Henry V—the hero king who led his men to victory over the French in the battle of Agincourt.

Rather than stabilization of lawyers (a virtual impossibility), there is the theory that the Inns started as clubs, offices, and lodging houses for lawyers coming to London for the then relatively short law terms. During the time when the courts were closed, these facilities were used for the instruction of pupils like Raleigh. What is known is that by the fifteenth century a whole legal quarter had sprung up along the suburban boundary between the commercial City of London and the Royal City of Westminster, where the judges sat in the king's palace.

A Room at the Inn

It is believed that education became an important part of the Inns as a consequence of two events: (1) The universities, controlled by the Catholic Church, taught only canon, civil, and Roman law, and the Inns were therefore needed in order to provide education in the English common law; and (2) after much prompting, the Inns adopted academic requirements for "call to the Bar," and it was after this that legal education flourished. With regard to the first event, both canon and civil law, for example, were taught at Oxford and Cambridge from the thirteenth century on. There is also some thought that the change from Latin to French separated English legal education from Continental influences and led to the development of the Inns.

Until the English Civil War, instruction at the Inns was mostly oral. This instruction, conducted by the governing body of a particular Inn of Court, took the form of "readings." These were lectures in which learned lawyers (as opposed to institutionalized academics) expounded on the common law around a set curriculum of medieval statutes, such as Francis Bacon's six lectures at Gray's Inn on the Statute of Uses, glossed with examples and questions. Their central importance, according to legal scholarship, is that what was said embodied contemporary understandings of the common law to the same extent as case law did, and therefore the bright-line, modern distinction between academics and case law did not exist. The readings were also supplemented by discussions and mock trials. Since the readings and moots were central to the intellectual life of the Inns, all members of the Inn were expected to participate. The aim was the demonstration of the intellectual ability to manipulate principles, rules, standards, and arguments (i.e., logic, legal reasoning, and rhetoric). In other words, to eventually become mini Vinnies and Sals before the Law Lords.

The Inns, at least initially, were not limited to prospective professional lawyers. These private corporations also catered to wealthy young men, like Sir Walter Raleigh, who desired to acquire just enough legal knowledge to manage their estates, act as justices of the peace, or obtain employment in public ser-vice. The main purpose of the Inns, however, was to provide legal education for apprentices who were studying to become serjeants, the predecessors of the modern-day barristers. These students frequently entered as young as sixteen and essentially grew up within the confines of a particular Inn. It could take as long as a dozen years to be admitted to the Bar (in contrast to the puny three years of legal education currently required in America).

It became customary for the *apprenticii* to attend the morning hearings of the various courts in Westminster Hall. The students would sit and listen to the "pleadings," which were the core of the judicial process. There was no writ-ten evidence; all submissions and subsequent arguments were presented orally. Reports of these conversations, however, can be found in the Year Books. For example: "My client," an attorney pleads, "is a poor man and knows no law," to which the judge replies, "It is because he knows no law that he has retained you." The Year Books (c. 1290–1535), which are essentially student notes, even record how a judge winked at a lawyer in order to signal "the best procedure for him to follow."

After the students returned from Westminster to the various Inns, they would debate the pros and cons of the arguments and procedures raised in the cases they had heard argued. The *apprenticii* were instructed in both theory and practice, learning the principles that constituted the foundation of English common law.

It is clearly the case that, due to the lack of printed books, these students greatly depended on senior practitioners who carried the law in their collec-tive consciousness—what has been called, with regard to various types of close-knit groups, "institutional transactive memory." It was the older generation that owned the manuscripts and embodied the common law's oral tradition, not unlike the Oral Torah passed down to the priests and rabbis. Furthermore, instruction by speaking and listening constrained unorthodox legal interpreta-tions. This was due, in large part, to the fact that the novices could not counter pronouncements made by their instructors with textual authority. The minds of young students, not unlike as in the findings of current chimp research, were therefore molded almost exclusively by the sounds and facial expressions of the teachers who controlled the future advancements of the newcomers. And imi-tation, in and of itself, does not generate any new information.

The English Civil War broke many of the traditions of the Inns, and attempts to reestablish the old order after the return of Charles II, in 1660, failed. The framework of readings and mock trials deteriorated. The use of books took over and students no longer depended upon lectures but "read for the Bar." Printed law books allowed a greater measure of individual and small group study. Legal education gradually went underground and private instruction became an accepted method of learning the law. Consequently, the Inns steadily lost their influence on the professional lives of lawyers and simply became dining clubs.

The Inns of Court, despite the winds of change, continued their gentlemanly approach to the training of lawyers and judges. However, the pace of English society was picking up steam and the spirit of reform was taking hold. By the end of the eighteenth century, formal legal education at the Inns was out of touch with the social and economic needs of students and therefore essentially went defunct.

However, soon after the middle of the nineteenth century, examinations for "call to the Bar" (in American English, "admittance to the bar") were gradually introduced and the entire court system was overhauled in the 1870s. Serjeants-at-law, the historic upper class of medieval lawyers, had been losing ground to the Queen's Counsel and were finally stripped of all their privileges. And, after considerable debate by a committee of the House of Commons, legal education at the Inns was resurrected, perhaps due in no small part to the competitive ass-kicking the Bar was receiving at the time from the Law Society and its educational program for attorneys and their articled clerks. The Inns formed the Council of Legal Education and its Inns of Court School of Law.

Although there were once many Inns, only four still exist: Lincoln's Inn, Gray's Inn, and the twin Temples. It is said that each Inn has its own distinct personality.

LINCOLN'S INN

Thomas More, educated for several years at Oxford (where canon and civil law were taught) went on to study the common law at Lincoln's Inn.

The Inn's history is obscure. However, by the time of More's arrival in 1496 it was already prosperous, housing an excellent library. In addition, a new hall had recently been built in red and damson brick, characteristic of late fifteenth-century buildings. The Inn had more than 100 members.

It has been observed that two historical events have, in particular, influenced the development of this Inn. The first is that Lord Chancellor Talbot, in 1734, established his court at the upper end of the Inn's hall, leaving only the lower part of the hall for dining and other aspects of the Inn's communal life. Thus from that time until the new Law Courts were opened in 1882, the Chancery judges sat within the Inn. This meant that Lincoln's Inn became a magnet for Chancery practitioners, that is, those lawyers involved in equity rather than common-law practice.

The second significant influence on the Inn was the building of a new hall. The cramped conditions led to the building, in 1843, of a large neo-Tudor structure with an excellent library annexed to it. Queen Victoria opened the new hall with great fanfare, which helped heighten the Inn's prestige.

GRAY'S INN

The glory days of Gray's Inn came under the Tudors. Its membership included Thomas Cromwell (c. 1485–1540, King Henry VIII's minister); Francis Bacon (1561–1626, philosopher, scientist, lawyer, and courtier to Elizabeth I and James I), who often strolled with Sir Walter Raleigh in Gray's Inn gardens; John Cooke (1608–1660, prosecutor in the trial of King Charles I, staunch Puritan and legal and social reformer); and others who were on the cutting edge of modern thought. During the Civil War its members were split almost in half between king and Parliament, and during the restless and conspiratorial England of the Restoration, the Inn was again divided.

By the eighteenth century Gray's was in serious decline, and by the middle of the nineteenth century calls to the Bar from the Inn numbered in the ones and twos. When the new Law Courts in the Strand were built between Lincoln's Inn and the Temples, the convenience of proximity to the courts from Lincoln's Inn and the Temples drew much of the practicing Bar to those locations. The chambers in Gray's Inn were largely taken over by solicitors and architects.

Eventually, however, scholarships were established, and moots, long abandoned in all of the Inns, were revived at Gray's Inn. Membership began to rise.

Historically, the Inn has been characterized by a certain informality among its members and a more intimate bond between judges, barristers, and students than that found at other Inns. The seating at the long refectory tables, not unlike the public mess halls of ancient Sparta, is by seniority in messes of four. There are complex rules governing the obligations of members to toast one another individually and collectively by messes. The standard fine for a determined breach of custom is a bottle of port.

The following story, illustrating the deep connection between the above dining traditions and legal education (with a not-so-subtle hint of sexism thrown in), is told by a modern-day barrister who undertook her training at Gray's Inn:

> Within your "mess" of four you had to toast each other in a special order and pass the port according to ship's rules. Breach of this etiquette entitled a diner to act as plaintiff and bring a charge against his colleague, who was then required to defend himself. The Senior in Hall sat in judgment.

I unwittingly became the recipient of such a charge, made by a blustering public-school boy. Fingers in his lapels, he denounced me for entering the hallowed halls inappropriately dressed. . . . I still remember my puzzlement and then mortification as the thundering cacophony built up in the Hall. Spoons hit the table and feet stamped the floor for what seemed like an eternity as they demanded a display of my clothing [an above-the-knee black crocheted dress worn under her legal, dining gown]. Finally, quiet was called for by our judge, who asked if I wished to defend myself.

I sat motionless, not recognizing the court, and maintaining my right to silence. Calls of "bad sport" went up, and then the Senior suggested that this was a case where the judge should have a view of the *locus in quo*. He requested that I come up to the front and, after hesitating, I obligingly mustered as much dignity as I could and complied. I was made to parade in front of him with neither of us exchanging a word. On my returning to my place he chivalrously found for me and awarded me a decanter of port.

During World War II the predominantly seventeenth- and eighteenth-century buildings of Gray's Inn were largely destroyed. The Inn, however, was faithfully rebuilt, starting with its well-loved Elizabethan hall.

THE TEMPLES

Located by the river Thames, the twin Temples (the Inner and Middle) have historically been very different in feel from Gray's Inn, set on the far side of Holborn Hill, and Lincoln's Inn, looking westward across Lincoln's Inn Fields. Gray's Inn and Lincoln's Inn were open, full of light and air. In contrast, the Temples developed as a maze of irregular courts and alleys, with the unique Round Church of the Knights Templar at its heart.

The founding date for the two societies is unknown. It is also not known why the Inner and Middle Temples coexisted as separate bodies or when lawyers started using the buildings, which had originally belonged to the Order of the Knights Templar.

INNER TEMPLE

Despite the differences in architectural feel between the Inner Temple and the other Inns, the structure of life has, from a historical perspective, essentially been the same. The senior members (the practitioners) concerned themselves with the instruction of the students, including one Mohandas K. Gandhi, by readings and moots. As recreation, there were elaborate masques and revels in the hall.

An interesting tension existed between the Inner Temple and the City of London. The City laid claim to jurisdiction over the Inn, a claim vigorously disputed by the Temple members. On at least two occasions, the Lord Mayor was invited to dine in the hall. He insisted, however, on coming in state and bore the City Sword aloft as a symbol of his authority. Each time the Sword was beaten down by the Temple's younger members. In January of 1679 a large fire broke out in the heart of the Temple, and the Lord Mayor decided that this was his chance to make good on the City's claim of jurisdiction. He arrived with Sword erect only to have it beaten down again when the Inner Templars turned their attention from the fire. The Mayor retreated to a tavern, having taken revenge by calling back the City's fire engines.

The Link Between Government and Money

The City of London is one square mile and occupies the oldest part of London, where the original Roman settlement grew up and the medieval city operated. The City includes the area along the north bank of the Thames roughly between Tower Bridge on the east and Saint Paul's Cathedral to the west. The Corporation of London, which dates back to the twelfth century, still owns a quarter of the land in the City of London.

In 1066 the City secured itself behind its thick Roman walls and refused to surrender to William the Conqueror. Gradually, however, the City reached an accommodation with the new monarch whereby it acknowledged him but continued to manage its own affairs through its corporate guild.

The road that runs parallel to the Thames and connects Buckingham Palace and Whitehall (representative of government) with the City of London (the center of commerce) is occupied by the Royal Courts of Justice. The judges, barristers, and solicitors are the lifeblood of these courts and have, over the years, often been called on to mediate between the government and financial institutions.

In contrast to the cloistered calm of Lincoln's Inn, the Templars were historically involved in the nitty-gritty of the law: broken contracts, street accidents, libel and slander, and crime. It was in this atmosphere that certain Templars pumped up their reputation by supplying copies of their speeches and cross-examinations to newspaper reporters. In contrast, it is interesting to note that the first American Bar Association Canons of Ethics provided, among other things, that the indirect advertisement of business by furnishing or inspiring newspaper comments concerning causes in which the lawyer has been or is engaged "defy the traditions and lower the tone of our high calling, and are intolerable." Interesting? The drafters of this 1908 code of ethics must have had the traditions of Lincoln's Inn in mind. My sense, however, is that the spirit of the Templars is ultimately unable to be contained—meaning that the self-promotion of lawyers is unlikely to die anytime soon.

There was also the staid side of Temple life. For example, after a sufficient amount of alcohol, everyone would stand on the tables, a sack of rats would be emptied on the floor, and terriers would be let loose to hunt the rodents through the chambers. And who said lawyers don't know how to have fun!

MIDDLE TEMPLE

Life at Middle Temple was very much like that of Inner Temple. Its focus was, and still is, its great Elizabethan hall with its double-hammerbeam roof and its intricately carved gallery. The hall's builder was Edmund Plowden, one of the great lawyers of his time. He received the degree of serjeant-at-law but, as a devoted Catholic, refused to conform to Queen Elizabeth I's established Anglican church. This refusal barred him from any future advancement. Thus instead of going to one of the Serjeants' Inns and becoming a judge, he remained a member of the Middle Temple and was put in charge of rebuilding the hall. His colored effigy tomb stands in the Temple Church.

Japan's first "barrister," Hoshi Toru, was educated at the Middle Temple. He had been an official of the Ministry of Finance in Japan, but upon his return from his legal education in England, Hoshi made the unprecedented decision of withdrawing from public service to enter the bar. This decision was highly disfavored by Japanese government officials and the case was ultimately resolved by creating, in 1877, a special category of *daigennin* (an in-court representative) called, "*daigennin* to the Ministry of Justice." This special category was, as suggested by Hoshi, modeled after Queen's Counsel in England. In this status it was possible for Hoshi to handle litigation for both private parties and for the government, just like Queen's Counsel.

It is also the case that of the thirty or so lawyers who were in active practice at the time of the American Revolution in Charleston, South Carolina, no less than twenty-four had been educated at the Inns of Court—most of them in the Middle Temple. In fact Middle Temple became the favored Inn of American-born students seeking a legal education in England.

The four Inns of Court are voluntary, unincorporated associations responsible for admitting students and calling them to the Bar. In addition to the Inns, the Bar's affairs are regulated by the Senate of the Inns of Court and the Bar. The Senate was formed on July 27, 1974, and assumed the functions of the former Senate of the Four Inns of Court and the General Council of the

Bar of England and Wales. Also, since 1974, the constitution of the Senate of the Inns includes a Bar Council that represents the Inns and acts autonomously in certain areas. One of the Bar Council's main functions is "to maintain the standards, honor and independence of the Bar, to promote, preserve and improve the services and functions of the Bar, to represent and act for the Bar generally as well as in its relations with others and also in all matters affecting the administration of justice." The present organizations were designed to centralize the various interests of the four Inns by applying uniform standards and procedures affecting the Inns' students and practicing barristers. In other words: a conformity enforcer.

XIX

LUCY IN THE SKY WITH DIAMONDS: SIR THOMAS MORE

OUR DISCUSSIONS SO FAR OF MEDIEVAL TIMES have been somewhat abstract. We have looked, in sweeping fashion, at the movement from the group to the individual; the rise of various "types" of law—canon, civil, common, royal, urban, feudal, mercantile, and the *ius commune*; the consolidation of power by the Catholic Church through such institutions as the Inquisition; the how and why of prosecuting and defending a rat; and the training of lawyers at the Inns of Court. It is now time to look at how these factors influenced the lives of real people and how their lives, in turn, influenced society.

In briefly looking at the life and death of the lawyer-statesman Thomas More, we will be able to see important threads of ancient, medieval, and Renaissance thought combining to create the fabric of the early modern period. More specifically, we will be able to see the cumulative influence of grammar, rhetoric, religion, philosophy, logic, dialectics, drama, and formal legal training on the formation and growth of the modern-day lawyer class.

Thomas More, the author of *Utopia,* was the son of a prominent judge. He was born in London on February 7, 1478 (or possibly 1477) and his father, John More, wanted his eldest son to follow him into the legal profession.

Thomas's grooming for the law started with his study of Latin grammar and composition at St. Anthony's School on Thread Street,

London. This foundational training led to the reading and contemplation of classical writers like Virgil and Cicero. More and his classmates were expected to be able to write Latin verse and to prepare various rhetorical topics in prose. The boys of St. Anthony were, in fact, noted for their prowess in public disputation and deliberation. On the eve of the feast of St. Bartholomew the Apostle, the young scholars of the various London grammar schools met in the churchyard of St. Bartholomew. They set up a wooden stage and disputed a chosen topic in Latin. St. Anthony generally presented the best scholars.

At about age twelve, instead of moving on to Eton, More was placed as a page in the household of King Henry VII's lord chancellor, John Morton—who was also Archbishop of Canterbury and, from 1493, a cardinal. This was a position of great honor for young Thomas. With the exception of King Henry VII, Morton was the most influential man in England.

After More served as a page for two years, the Archbishop sent him on to Canterbury College at Oxford in order to sharpen his skills in, among other things, rhetoric and logic. He was then, at about sixteen, brought back to London to study English law, first at New Inn (one of the Inns of Chancery) and then at his father's alma mater, Lincoln's Inn.

Upon entrance to New Inn, More was poised to acquire the basics of the law, its various procedures and precedents. But first he had to learn a new language: law French. English was used for general arguments in courts, but formal pleadings and the moot exercises were conducted in law French. The roots of this strange language started with the Norman kings and eventually developed into a hybrid form of speech suited only to the legal profession. A kind of evolutionary devolution.

More's advanced training, and immersion into the common law, started when he left New Inn and entered Lincoln's Inn on February 12, 1496. His father was a senior member of the Inn and therefore the young More, it has been speculated, would most likely have been enrolled as a matter of familial propriety and obligation.

Within the field of law, More was able to employ, in the context of a practical career, the things he had learned through the study of rhetoric, dialectics, and logic. There was also the advantage to be gained from his admission to New Inn and Lincoln's Inn—of being in the right social setting. The sons of other gentlemen and nobles were being educated in the various Inns, and therefore young Thomas was in the company of those who would someday administer the affairs of the crown and the nation. This was, on all levels, a time that demanded important social connections.

It appears that the role of lawyer was not something unhappily foisted on him by his father but, in fact, well suited More's temperament. He was a skilled actor and became an accomplished rhetorician, both important talents that stretch all the way back at least to ancient Greece. His writings demonstrate the inventiveness of his attacks against opponents. And as a forensic orator and later as a judicial officer, More was, by all accounts, as fierce as he was persuasive. He was also "a man for all seasons": his training in the art of disputation allowed him to persuasively argue any side of a question. In other words, More had, as one writer has observed, the makings of a perfect lawyer—skillful yet detached, cautious as well as theatrical, persuasive and practical in equal measure. But that was More the lawyer—not necessarily More the individual. Surprisingly, this distinction, as already suggested by Cicero, often exists.

After leaving the Inn, More quickly became a very successful lawyer, earning huge fees as well as becoming involved in public service. In 1504 he served as a member of Parliament. In 1510 he was undersheriff of the City of London. He later rose to be speaker of the House of Commons in 1523 and finally, upon the ousting of Cardinal Thomas Wolsey by King Henry VIII—for famously not securing an annulment for the King—Lord Chancellor of England from 1529 to 1532. In the context of the historic folding and unfolding of the priest–philosopher–lawyer sequence, it's interesting that, unlike Wolsey, More was not a clergyman. Chancellors, as keeper's of the king's conscience, had traditionally been clergymen; and it may well have been part of King Henry VIII's strategy, in attempting to win support for his various political policies from the House of Commons, to appoint a common-law lawyer. Many of the members of the Commons were, like More, similarly trained in the common law. They were also, like More, generally part of the rising gentry class, vested in land taken from the aristocracy and the Catholic Church, which had allied itself with the king. In any case, it has been pointed out that More's appointment marked the transition from a Chancery presided over by ecclesiastics to one administered by laymen and common-law lawyers. Here, indeed, is evidence that the king's conscience, like the law, was becoming increasingly secular.

You are most likely familiar with the story of Henry VIII and the founding of the Church of England. Unhappily married to Catherine of Aragon, daughter of the very Catholic monarchs Ferdinand and Isabella, Henry VIII assumed the "blasphemous" title of "Supreme Head of the Church of England" and then granted himself an annulment, making possible his marriage to Anne Boleyn. (It's good to be the king!) This was more than More could take and he promptly resigned his post as Lord Chancellor. More took the position that he was willing to swear to the royal line (the Oath of Succession), that is, to any children who would be born, but he was not willing to swear that Anne Boleyn was the rightful Queen of England until she was so designated by the pope. For such refusal he was tried in Westminster Hall, the center of English justice, and found guilty of high treason. He was beheaded on July 6, 1535, and canonized by the Roman Catholic Church in 1935.

It was More's friend Desiderius Erasmus of Rotterdam (1466–1536) who wrote: "The study of law has little in common with true learning, but in England those that succeed have a great position; and with good reason, for it is from their ranks that the nobility is for the most part filled." This viewpoint appears to have been somewhat true in Lord Chancellor More's case. It has been pointed out, however, that Erasmus was off a bit (even after setting aside his jab about worthless information). The truth is that lawyers did not easily enter the ranks of high nobility; at most they were usually considered to be of equal status with knights.

Learned, Anticlerical Minstrels

In the early days of the medieval university, there were wandering scholars (*goliardi*) who showed up singing their own scurrilous, anticlerical songs. These *goliardi* were not always welcome by the masters of the university. It was only later, in the humanistic age, that these wanderers became respectable. Erasmus was one of these. He was a Dutch apostle of moderation and a spokesman of Christian humanism. In fact it has been said that Erasmus was one of the most influential men in the history of western Europe—providing a link between one lawyer, Thomas More, and another quasi-lawyer, Martin Luther.

The utopian commonwealth part of More's famous book *Utopia* (literally meaning "no-place"), published in 1516, provides a key to why, even after becoming one of the foremost Englishman of his time, he never appears to have completely comfortable in the high ranks of nobility. More, in this part of the book, was concerned primarily with the problem of economics—particularly the evils of his own time. More had been a highly paid lawyer, yet he reported that in Utopia there is no money. His fictional traveler Raphael Hythlodaeus said of the Utopian people: "Their common life and community of living without any traffic in money, this alone, which is the ultimate foundation of all their institutions, overthrows all excellence, magnificence, splendor, and majesty—the true properties and distinctions of a commonwealth according to the common opinion." More, although not technically part of the priest class, was arguably more priest and philosopher at heart than practical lawyer—or politician.

Really Utopia?

It is interesting to note that More rids Utopia of lawyers with a marginal annotation from one of the book's protagonists, Peter Gillis, saying that they are all "useless." And so like Socrates and Plato, Saint Thomas More is not up for induction, anytime soon, into the lawyer hall of fame.

In contrast to More is one of American's most famous jurists, Oliver Wendell Holmes (1841–1935). Holmes advocated a "bad man" perspective for evaluating law. This perspective focuses on the "material consequences" of law practice rather than on its utopian possibilities. Now do you see why Vinnie and Sal *had* to be American lawyers?

XX

LUTHER AND CALVIN

The notion of law as a path to success is also evident in the life of Martin Luther, a key figure in the first Protestant Reformation.

Martin Luther

Luther was born in Saxony in 1483 and lived until 1546. For many years it was thought that he was the son of poor parents, but it was later discovered that his father was a miner in the Mansfield district of Saxony who eventually acquired furnaces and his own mine. Thus, rather than a peasant, Luther's father was a skilled workman on the rise and desired that his son achieve success by becoming a lawyer. Luther, in pursuit of this goal, entered the University of Erfurt, the most flourishing university in Germany, in 1501. He enrolled in the college of philosophy, which prepared students for law as well as theology (our recurring troika of priest–philosopher–lawyer). In addition to his scholastic studies, Luther, like Thomas More, read the Latin classical authors, such as Virgil and Cicero. He obtained his master's degree in short order, graduating in 1505 second among seventeen successful candidates. He then enrolled in the doctoral program in civil law. A successful legal career seemed to be just around the corner.

However, something happened to Luther that dampened his drive to practice law—he got religion. At 21, Luther rejected the world (not a particularly good thing for a lawyer to do) after being struck by the omnipresent hand of God. This feeling hit Luther one day after having nearly been killed by a bolt of lightning. At that moment of exaltation he had the feeling that God was in everything—except, apparently, the practice of law. Luther left the university and joined the Augustinian order of hermit monks at Erfurt.

⚅ · ⚅

Are We Really That Bad?

Luther often berated the legal profession for its avarice, apathy, and indifference to the demands of justice and the needs of society. For example, in 1544 he leveled the following criticism: "I shit on the law of the emperor, and of the pope, and on the law of the jurists as well." He also wrote: "Show me the jurist who studies to discover truth. . . . No, they study law only for the profit it brings them." Ouch! Nevertheless, some of his closest friends were lawyers, including Dr. Jerome Schurff (1481–1554), professor of canon law at the University of Wittenberg and Luther's eventual chief defense counsel at the 1521 trial in Worms on charges of heresy, and Johann Apel (1486–1536), professor of law and, from 1524 to 1525, the rector of the University of Wittenberg.

⚅ · ⚅

Although seeing mercantilism and capitalism as literally the work of the Devil, Luther did not give up on the law. While cloistered in the monastery, he continued his study of canon law. And in 1510 he traveled to the papal Curia in Rome to represent the Erfurt chapter in a legal dispute within the Augustinian order. This trip to Rome made a lasting impression on young Luther. Years later he still could clearly recall his shock upon seeing the worldliness of Roman prelates at this, the high point of the Italian Renaissance.

Even during his famous revolt against Rome, Luther, having left the monastery and joined the faculty of the newly founded University of Wittenberg, drew not only on his theological insights but also on his extensive knowledge of the canon law. In his famous "Ninety-Five Theses" nailed to the door of the Schlosskirche in Wittenberg on the evening of October 31, 1517, Professor Luther cited a number of abuses and injustices involving canon law. He also prepared, over the course of twenty years, a number of learned commentaries and sermons on the Torah. Luther frequently bolstered his writings on biblical passages with citations to and quotations from Roman law and canon law texts. He gave lectures and published pamphlets on various legal and moral questions involving such things as crime, property, usury, commerce, marriage, and social welfare. And he strongly supported the efforts of legal humanists to reconstruct the ancient texts of Roman law for use in the secular kingdom and to reform legal education in the German universities—an important factor in the rise of the lawyer class. Luther believed that the Church, on the other hand, should become invisible; that its entire asserted ecclesiastical jurisdiction, including legislative, judicial, and administrative power, should cease to exist. No priest, Luther wrote, is authorized to come between God and each person that seeks forgiveness for sin. In other words, ban Vinnie and Sal from the Garden of Eden.

CALVIN

Both the Protestant Revolution and capitalism were greatly influenced by a full-fledged lawyer: Jean ("John") Calvin. Calvin was born at Noyon, in Picardy, France, about sixty miles northeast of Paris, on July 10, 1509. Although born into a bourgeois family, Calvin was raised in aristocratic society and acquired the manners of that class. His father was secretary to the local bishop and attorney for the cathedral. As a result of these connections, Calvin was raised and educated in an aristocratic family who were relatives of the bishop. From the beginning, Calvin was designated by his father for the Church—but he never was ordained.

His early education was informal, and it was from his "adopted" family that Calvin learned good manners and acquired a taste for the humanities. He was eventually sent to Paris to study theology at the rigorous Collège de Montaigu. His father, however, had a falling-out with the bishop and directed Calvin to give up theology for the law. So in 1528, at the age of nineteen and in a time when children actually obeyed their parents, Calvin left Paris to study law at Orleans, and in 1539 he moved to Bourges, where, for the first time, he began to study Greek and to read the New Testament in its original language. He also acquired a working knowledge of Hebrew.

Unlike Luther, Calvin apparently discovered a bit of the divine in the study and practice of law, as well as in the activities of the rapidly expanding urban commercial bourgeois: a more kindly view toward wealth. His becoming a lawyer was in tune with the lay nature of what eventually became known as the Calvinist reform—as opposed to the clerical nature of Luther's reform. Whereas Luther drew most of his early reformers from the ranks of the Augustinian and Franciscan monks, Calvin's followers appear to have come from the humanists.

Calvin's religious views did, however, color his views about the legal system—particularly with regard to litigation. Unlike other leaders who taught that Christians owed no allegiance to secular law or magistrates, Calvin insisted that magistrates were ordained by God for human benefit.

On the other hand, Calvin had strong words for those who "boil with a rage for litigation." He saw these people as never being satisfied unless they are quarreling with others: "[T]hey carry on their lawsuits with bitter and deadly hatred, and an insane passion to revenge and hurt, and they pursue them with implacable obstinacy even to the ruin of their adversaries." (An attitude not unlike certain litigants in ancient Greece discussed in Part III—or numerous modern-day litigants that attempt to use the law as a weapon of vengeance wielded, of course, by their lawyers.)

The way in which Calvin rationalized his views on magistrates and litigation was to declare that lawsuits are permissible by Christians, but only if they are used rightly. From a plaintiff's point of view, only justice should be sought. Litigation should not be based on hatred or passion for revenge, both of which he saw as sins of moral weakness. And from a defendant's point of view, litigation should be without bitterness and carried out only with the desire to defend what is the defendant's by right.

PROTESTANTISM AND THE BEGINNINGS OF CAPITALISM

Arguably one of the most important factors behind the rise of the lawyer class in the early modern period flowed, strangely enough, from Luther's, Calvin's, and other Protestant reformers' emphasis on the individual and "his" need for grace. Everyone, in order to attempt to understand and receive grace, now had to be able to read the Bible. Both the invention of printing and the translations of the Bible into the various European languages, a rather dangerous activity, facilitated this important personal quest.

From this new self-centeredness arguably developed a connection between Protestantism and the rise of capitalism. For example, the German sociologist Max Weber, previously discussed with regard to the notion of "profession," stressed the point that the discipline a man must exert once he has freed himself from the support of the international church is very much the same as the self-reliance needed for success in a capitalist economy. On the other hand, it has been forcefully argued that it was not Calvinism's emphasis on the individual that contributed to the capitalist spirit, but its emphasis on community. While the individual may have had his personal concerns regarding divine predestination, Calvinism (as well as Lutheranism) was strongly communitarian. Therefore the spirit of Weber's capitalism in the seventeenth and early eighteenth centuries was arguably not the product of "secular asceticism" but of public spirit—reflected not in the individualist doctrines of predestination and calling, but in the collectivist doctrines of covenant and covenanted communities.

For our purposes, the important point is that a confluence of individualism, capitalism, and secularism, in varying degrees, existed in ancient Greece and Rome. And as we have seen, the result was that the Greeks had their orators and logographers (speechwriters), and the Romans had their orators and jurists. With an even bigger helping of these "isms" over the next several centuries, combined with communitarianism, traditionalism, and Puritanism, the early modern period gave rise to the conditions for a perfect storm: a tidal wave of full-fledged lawyers—and some of them, like John Calvin, were even men of God.

XXI

IN MERRIE OLDE ENGLAND NO LAWYERS ARE ALLOWED—

But Don't Get Too Excited

In England there are no lawyers—only barristers and solicitors. Barristers are "courtroom lawyers" (also referred to, as we saw with regard to the Inns of Court, as "the Bar"), and solicitors are "office lawyers." Various theories have been proposed as to the genesis of this division in the British legal profession.

One explanation is that "narrators"—a common-law pleader employed in the Middle Ages to tell the litigant's story to the court— were the first barristers. Then sometime between 1300 and 1400, a bifurcation point arose. The more able or prestigious of the narrators became known as *conteure* (a plaintiff "made his count") or *narratores*. The terms *conteure/narratores*, for reasons that are not exactly clear, were eventually replaced by the term *serjeant*. The serjeants-at-law, similar to the modern-day Queen's or King's Counsel, then formed the Serjeants' Inns in the 1300–1400s, from which, by the mid-fourteenth century, all judges were selected. The other category of narrators was known as either *apprentices* (from the French, *apprendre,* to learn) or students of the serjeants. This group formed the Inns of Court. However, despite distinctions in function among those who appeared in court, the legal profession was not strictly divided. In other words, all lawyers, except the serjeants-at-law, who had their own Inns, could freely associate at the Inns of Court. And although the Inns were responsible for the nomenclature "barrister" (from "bar(re)," as they were advocates and therefore plead at the bar), the Inns did not, as evidenced by Sir Walter Raleigh's attendance at Middle Temple, exclude nonbarristers until the eighteenth century.

It was sometime between the sixteenth and seventeenth centuries that a division between the barristers and the solicitors occurred. One theory has it that part of the division followed from the nature of the duties that became associated with solicitors, such as helping move a client's suit through Chancery, the courts involved in equity matters, since the Chancery clerks were not known for their diligence—or honesty. Two other types of lawyers also became recognized, attorneys and proctors, each with different tasks; historically the more important legal tasks were performed by attorneys. Their primary functions were to determine the legal theory of the case and to prepare the written pleadings. But it appears that there were some who even functioned, early on, as pleaders in various courts. This overlap with pleaders was, however, limited, and eventually ceased altogether. Attorneys and proctors eventually merged in 1739 into the Society of Gentlemen Practitioners to become part of the present-day job of solicitors. Thus over time, the attorney's function became distinct from that of the serjeant's and foreshadowed the eventual bifurcation of the legal profession into barristers and solicitors.

Another explanation for the division between solicitors and barristers focuses on the fact that by the end of the sixteenth century the complexity of the court system and an increase in business led barristers to take on more work than they could handle. Consequently, they stopped dealing directly with their clients and started to rely on lower-statused members of the law to inform them about the case prior to trial. This theory also adds the notion that the division in the profession was motivated by the Bar's desire to assert its intellectual and social superiority over the mechanics of the law.

But whatever the reason for the division between barristers and solicitors, a similar distinction made its way across the pond, at least for a while. A Virginia Act of 1732 made a clear distinction between attorneys and barristers or counselors by providing that the act "shall not be construed to extend . . . to any counselor or barrister at law, whatsoever." It has been surmised that this mention of barristers refers to persons who had been called to the Bar by one of the Inns of Court. And as stated by a legal scholar: "The distinction, which did not survive the American Revolution, is one of the earliest of its kind in colonial legislation and colonial court rulings."

So what caused the division to collapse? One guess might be America's split with England. But America could have developed its own inns of court. The actual reason is cost and numbers.

In England, as a rule, the client consulted an attorney or solicitor who, in turn, called in a barrister whenever he considered it necessary. The new Americans considered this simply a way to run up legal fees. It was also the case that there were relatively few lawyers remaining after the American Revolution. Estimates are that around 150 leading lawyers and another 200 lawyers of lesser standing left the country or simply retired from active practice as a result of the Revolution. In light of this exodus, it simply made no sense to carry on the distinction, and the fusion between barristers and attorneys became a permanent feature of legal practice in the United States. In fact the English attorney or solicitor, rather than the barrister, became the model for the American legal practitioner.

Modern-day English barristers generally practice in a set of chambers (the barristers' offices). The majority of these chambers are located in London in one of the four Inns of Court. London barristers practice in the Inns because of long tradition, as well as the subsidized rent and easy access to the courts. However, it is extremely difficult to get your name on one of those doors in the Inns since many more members of the Bar are created every year than there is space.

The average set of chambers consists of fourteen barristers. While the chambers are physically offices, they also describe the relationships of the barristers to one another. A barrister is known not only by his or her individual work, but also by association with a set of chambers. The reason for this is that many chambers have reputations for specializing in certain substantive areas of the law. Chambers also consist of shared library, secretarial, and clerk assistance. Work and fees, however, are not shared since partnerships are restricted by professional rule. In other words, a barrister must technically, but not metaphorically, work alone.

XXII

LEGAL DRAG

Having distinguished between barristers and solicitors, the important question is: What's up with the Vegas showgirl wig and gown?

For an answer to this question we set the way-back machine to the year 1660, the restoration of the English monarchy. Charles II, the son of beheaded Charles I, has returned to England from Europe and brought back with him the fashion of the court of Louis XIV.

Under the Sun King, the extravagance of Versailles was so great that it bankrupted a significant number of the nobility. Indulgence and wealth were essential in order to maintain the fashion set by the King. It was important, in this atmosphere of crass materialism, that even one's servants be dressed almost as eloquently as their master. Among such fashion excess was the powdered wig. For England, this accessory, in addition to covering up lice, is said to have been a marvelous way to help cover up the divisions in society that had emerged from a violent civil war between those who wore their hair short (the "Roundheads") and those who wore their hair long—a bit like the United States in the 1960s.

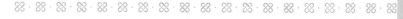

Roundheads and Cavaliers

The term "roundheads" seems to have come from the crop-headed city apprentices who supported Parliament, although there is a theory that the name came from a slighting reference by the Queen, Charles I's wife, to John Pym's round and balding head. (Pym was a Puritan squire, a member of Parliament.)

> The Whigs were the successors of the Puritan and parliamentarian "Roundheads" of Oliver Cromwell's time, and the Tories were the successors of the Anglican and royalist "Cavaliers" (probably a corruption of *caballero*— a Spanish trooper given to torturing Protestants). These two rival groups constituted the first party system of government in European history.

∷ · ✂

It has been argued that the court of Louis XIV was an important time and place in the development of fashion. Prior to this time, well-dressed men and women had a similar look. One of the major dividing lines between the sexes became the wig. In the latter half of the seventeenth century, this adornment, with its Samson-like quality, was a masculine privilege. To augment their natural hair, women wore false pieces, padding, wiring, and eventually powder, but rarely full wigs.

The barrister's gown and judicial robes had developed much earlier. By the time of Edward III (1327–1377), the fur and silk-lined robes were firmly established as a sign of high office.

Unlike judges with their various types of robes—black and scarlet, with or without some type of animal-fur adornment or lining—most modern-day barristers generally wear a black gown to court. Queen's Counsel gowns are made of silk. The plain black gown was adopted by a majority of barristers in 1685, when the Bar went into mourning at the death of King Charles II. This billowy black robe, received by newly minted barristers, is accompanied by a double-tabbed linen band that serves as a collar. The two tabs are said to represent the tablets of Moses—one good reason for not having black-robed, tab-wearing government lawyers in the United States, right?

The fact is that English barristers and judges began wearing wigs and robes because it was the fashion, and not just to intimidate their clients (or give them a good laugh). The reasons they have continued to wear them (although in ever-decreasing situations) are more complicated. It appears to be something deep, and perhaps Freudian, within the English psyche.

The wig has not always been associated with legal proceedings. The distinctive medieval legal headwear was the coif—a piece of white linen or silk that appears to have originally been designed to cover the tonsure of monks (that bald spot on the crown of their heads) who were acting in a legal capacity, a clear sign of the law's increasing secularization. Sir Thomas More's father, John More, when appointed a serjeant-at-law in 1503, was given a white silk coif that he was not permitted to remove—even in the presence of the king.

By the late sixteenth century all members of the English legal profession wore round, black caps with edges of the coif sticking out from underneath the cap. When wigs became the social fashion, "legal" wigs had a small version of the black skullcap and the coif sewn into them. Law students, not yet entitled to wear wigs, continued to wear the skullcap for some time after the introduction of wigs. This legal style for law students ended sometime in the early part of the eighteenth century.

By the end of the eighteenth century, the powdered-wig look, as a point of fashion, was beginning to fade. The wig makers, sensing a threat to their livelihood, started focusing on the legal profession as a specialty market—apparently figuring that lawyers were just pompous enough (or foolish enough) to continue wearing them. Humphrey Ravenscroft, a third-generation wig maker at the firm of Ede & Ravenscroft, developed and patented the "forensic" wig in 1822. This new and improved wig was made of white (instead of black) horsehair and did not uncurl, needed no powder, and was claimed to be able to retain its freshness indefinitely.

As wigs became unique to the legal community, they also became a means of distinguishing the various ranks within the profession. The higher up the legal totem pole you were, the bigger the wig you got to wear; the object was, and still is, to become a "bigwig." (Importance Is Big.) On ceremonial occasions, Superior Judges and Queen's Counsel, for example, wear full-bottomed or "spaniel" wigs. These are wigs that hang down over the ears like cocker spaniels. For general court activity, judges wear smaller "bob-wigs" with frizzed sides and a queue (pigtail) at the back. Barristers wear an even smaller wig (the "tie-wig"), with a few rows of curls at the sides and the back that usually do not fully cover the hair. Solicitors ("office lawyers") are required to remain wigless.

Interestingly, no codified legal rules require barristers to wear wigs and robes. It has been argued, with regard to judges, that the Judicial Rules of 1635, although not mentioning wigs and somewhat currently ignored, nevertheless established the exclusive right of the monarch to prescribe judicial dress. The argument has also been made that since the Anglican bishops had sought permission from the king before getting rid of their wigs in 1835, judges are required to do the same.

Wigs and Breeches in Parliament

For centuries, the Speaker of the House of Commons, like barristers and judges, wore wigs—along with breeches and full regalia. However, in 1992, the ancient custom of the wig was abandoned by Speaker Betty Boothroyd, the first woman Speaker in Parliament's 700-year history, and Speaker Michael Martin nixed the knee breeches and tights. With the current speaker (as of this writing), John Bercow, the traditional costume has been reduced to a simple black gown.

❈ · ❈

A few years ago, a push started in England to shed the Vegas showgirl attire, particularly the wigs. A study was conducted (pro-wig\anti-wig) and a paper prepared. The conclusion was pro-wig. Of those responding to the questionnaire, 67 percent favored retaining court dress in its current form. Approximately 15 percent favored abolition in all respects and the rest favored some simplification, including 14 percent who wanted elimination of the wig. The reasons for maintaining the status quo are interesting and seem to include the following:

1. Traditional judicial drag lends a sense of solemnity and dignity to the law—not unlike the vestments of priests as well as academics at graduation ceremonies;
2. Wigs and robes serve to disguise the appearance of judges and barristers—a type of caped crusader argument;
3. Wigs and robes tend to give judges and barristers a type of conformity that dilutes differences of gender, race and age—thereby creating a sense of fairness; and
4. Wigs and robes are a strong trademark look for the Bar and help define its relationship within the European Union, as well as making sure they don't look like American lawyers and judges.

Despite the results of the study, there was, during the first part of 2002, a proposed six-month experiment in wigless justice for all civil disputes. This move was a compromise aimed at settling a long-running dispute between solicitor-advocates, who are barred from wearing wigs, and the Bar. The solicitor-advocates argued that the barrister's monopoly on horsehair is discriminatory and breaches human rights.

With the threat of court action, the solicitor-advocates demanded that wigs should either be abandoned altogether or that they should also be allowed to wear them. Their point was that they should not be put at any disadvantage in court or seen as being of "lower status"—as illustrated by the joke that "the reason a barrister needs to wear a wig is so that the jury will know which side should win."

In 2008 the Lord Chief Justice of England and Wales announced a number of changes to court working (versus ceremonial) dress in the English and

Welsh courts. For example, the array of robes worn by High Court Judges, as alluded to earlier, has been abolished and replaced by a simplified robe. The wearing of wigs in the civil and family courts has been abolished. In addition, in April 2008, the Chairman of the Bar announced that, as a result of a survey of the profession, the Bar would recommend that advocates (a term that includes both barristers and solicitor-advocates) should retain their formal robes (including wigs) in all cases, civil and criminal—with possible exceptions in the County Court. In a letter to the profession, the Chairman said, in part, "Criminal barristers will keep wigs and gowns, and the Lord Chief Justice intends to keep the current court dress in criminal proceedings. The Bar is a single advocacy profession with specialization in particular practice areas. There is logic in having the same formal court dress, where formality and robes are required, for criminal and civil barristers."

PART VI

MODERN
TIMES

Wᴵᴛʜ ᴛʜᴇ ʀᴏʟᴇ ᴏғ ᴛʜᴇ ʟᴀᴡʏᴇʀ firmly reestablished by the Middle Ages, the issue of what law best served society floated to the surface, at least in the West. To a large extent the struggle over this issue involved the question of whether law is best entrusted to the realm of practical experience (promulgated by the common-law tradition) or the realm of academics (promulgated by the civil-law tradition). In Part VI we will see that this fight, particularly in America, did not die with the victory in England of the common-law lawyers over the civil-law lawyers. Instead, at least one important aspect of the intergroup tournament focused on the historic apprenticeship system that Dean Christopher Columbus Langdell of the Harvard Law School sought to uproot with his geometry of law. This system, stretching back into the mists of time, was premised on the assumption that the experienced practitioner is the best teacher of law. Langdell, as an academic, had to kill it. His competing approach needed to show that practical legal experience for a well-trained law teacher is not that important. To do this he proposed that law, properly understood, is a science and that its first principles, like the axioms of geometry, are intelligible even to the young and inexperienced. Rationalism over empiricism. Deduction over casuistry.

As a quick, but important, aside, the same spirit that animated Langdell's mathematized vision of law can be seen in the context of other disciplines, such as philosophy, as viewed by René Descartes, and linguistics.

Tʜᴇ Sᴄɪᴇɴᴛɪғɪᴄ Rᴇᴠᴏʟᴜᴛɪᴏɴ

Professor Zellig Harris (1909–1992) at the University of Pennsylvania became one of the leading figures in the school of linguistics called descriptivism. This view was strongly influenced by the developments that were occurring in a branch of mathematics called recursive function theory. The great mathematician Alan Turing, in 1937, showed that a "formal system" can be defined as any mechanical procedure for producing formulas. Turing's definition of "mechanical procedure" (read, write, or erase) became a driving force in the creation of computers and the science of artificial intelligence. Both of these developments captured Harris's imagination—which he passed on to his student, Noam Chomsky. Harris viewed the linguist, like the mathematician, as trying to develop a formal deductive system complete with axiomatically defined initial elements and theorems concerning the relationships among those elements—not unlike the way Langdell had viewed the law. Thus in language and law, metaphor is, based on this point of view, just pretty words.

With Langdell having, to some extent, tapped back into the mathematizing philosophy of Plato, there were those who, in contrast, argued that law and particularly the common law fit much more neatly into a framework similar to Aristotle's claims about the study of politics. The Philosopher, as you will recall, claimed that an understanding of political affairs can only be gained through long experience. The facts of political life are much too complex and disorderly to be derived by reason alone or from some simple set of axioms. He also believed that to make sound judgments regarding political matters, a person must possess not only theoretical understanding but also practical wisdom.

The debate at the time of Langdell and continuing on into the twenty-first century is not, however, simply law as art versus law as science. Even those who see law as science, or at least analogous to science, do not always agree about what type of science it is and what type of methodology is, or should be, applicable.

It was Galileo Galilei (1564–1642) who shattered the Aristotelian view of the universe with his skepticism concerning the possibility of arriving at certain truths through the senses, saying that our senses can fail us and our intuition is often untrustworthy. He saw observation, experimentation, and mathematics as the key to understanding the universe. "God hath made all things," according to Galileo, "in number, weight, and measure."

René Descartes (1596–1650) built on Galileo's skepticism of sense perception—adding a strong push for rationalism. His philosophy was an attempt to place all human learning on a rational basis modeled on geometry—or more specifically, analytic geometry. Descartes, a man of many talents, was also a lawyer. Eventually various philosophers, including Hobbes, Leibniz, and Spinoza, adopted the "mathematical way" (not unlike Pythagoras and Solon) as a means of attempting to achieve certainty not only in mathematics, but also in moral and political philosophy.

The mathematical way was indeed thought to be applicable to all branches of knowledge and it was generally accepted that philosophy meant knowledge that was certain—not just probably true. This belief raised the question as to whether or not there could be a true philosophy of law. Sir Francis Bacon believed that such a philosophy was possible and that it could be made to be certain, mathematical, if properly classified under a limited number of broad "maxims"—the root of his rumble with the common-law fundamentalist Sir Edward Coke. The truth of these maxims (stated in the "authority and majesty" of Latin) could, according to Bacon, then be tested against specific rules drawn from all parts of the legal system. Rules over rulelessness. And certainly Latin over English. Consequently, Latin rules.

This first wave of the modern scientific revolution was essentially Platonic. Absolute Truth exists and can be accessed, at least from a secular point of view, through what the mind, by observation, experimentation, and mathematics, is able to weigh, measure, and count—thus presupposing an invisible order and the complete objectivity of the observer. Aristotle's concept of a purposive and organic universe was rejected in favor of a morally neutral and mechanical one.

And in the political-legal arena, thinkers like King James I and his faithful Attorney General Francis Bacon, as well as others, defended absolute monarchy as a form of government that corresponds to the laws of motion followed by physical bodies. A major characteristic of this line of thought was the assumption, according to one legal scholar, "that the entire universe is based on a single explanatory model, that all phenomena—stars, billiard ball, forms of government [with absolute monarchy being the "natural" one]—follow the same basic principles. Bodin, Bacon, Descartes, Hobbes, Filmer, and others were all obsessed by this reductionist view."

However, during the course of the seventeenth and eighteenth centuries, the notion of certainty through induction came under fire. There were those diversity generators who began to see "truth" in probabilistic terms, as statistical reasoning—including, somewhat surprisingly, Sir Isaac Newton (1642–1727) and John Locke (1632–1704). Empirical science came to be viewed by many as designed not to show truth as certainty but only as more probable than not. A touch of Corax and Tisias. Thus the experimental method could only yield "moral certainty"; that is, a high degree of probability. As the empiricist David Hume (1711–1776) asked: What does it mean to "know" something by observation or experiment—that is, by induction? One answer is that like Big Pig in Part I, you can end up with an apple in your mouth roasting over a pit.

The growing split between scientific certainty, considered to be the first revolutionary change in Western scientific thought, and probability, considered to be the second revolutionary change, influenced the legal revolution of the seventeenth and eighteenth centuries. Certain lawyers and scholars had close ties to certainty and others to probability. These ties created an inner-group tournament that set lawyers in favor of probability, such as Sir Matthew Hale (1609–1676), at odds with followers of the mathematical way—followers like Thomas Hobbes, who, for example, attacked the unscientific character of the common law and the claims of its supporters. Hale did not, as some more modern legal scholars have done, simply concede that law is art. He argued instead that law is based on an empirical method similar in important respects to that advocated by certain leading natural scientists.

⌗ · ⌗

Hobbes and Headless Law

Hobbes (1588–1679) was violently opposed to antimonarchical philosophies and acts—like whacking off the head of King Charles I. Only a ruler with absolute power, Hobbes argued, can effectively restrain men from quarreling and exploiting. He seems to have considered the common law to be headless. In

fact it was Hobbes that inspired the tradition known as analytical jurisprudence that was later developed by Jeremy Bentham (a true hater of Blackstone and the common-law tradition) and his disciple John Austin. H. L. A.
Hart, the great twentieth-century legal philosopher, eventually pointed out
that the problem with the Hobbes-Bentham-Austin approach is that it fails
to fit the facts on the ground. This failure is because it does not take into
account the practical reasoning of people whose choices and actions create
and constitute the phenomenon of the law.

Despite Hobbes, the "science" of the common law remained a science
with its own subject matter and its own methods, including gobs of induction.
And despite Bacon, legal science could not seem to obtain certainty by use of
logic—at least in any overarching, formal sense of the word. Still it remained,
in the minds of many lawyers and scholars of the time, an empirical science: Its
principles, seen as universal and constant, were based on the empirical results of
past experience, and it could be made as coherent and as systematic as Roman
law and canon law had been made to be in previous centuries.

In the context of law and certainly economics, one of the most important
intellectuals of the eighteenth century was Adam Smith (1723–1790). Smith
was, among other things, an antimercantilist, and therefore hostile to the Big
Government that is needed to regulate trade. He demonstrated that economic
activity can be coordinated without central governmental planning and regulation, because there exists an equilibrium of independent producers and consumers that ensures a daily supply of the products that people purchase without the government directing producers and transportation companies to meet
such demand. And according to some scholars there is a Newtonian cast to
Adam Smith's invisible-hand concept. This is why the "discovered" equilibrium
point of supply and demand resembles the balance among the heavenly bodies
that Newton helped to explain in scientific terms.

The foregoing, however, expresses only the viewpoint that Adam Smith,
like many eighteenth-century intellectuals, was up to his eyeballs in the type
of thinking that had been responsible for Newtonian physics. There is a softer,
gentler side to Mr. Smith that is stressed by other scholars. These scholars can
also be found within the law and economics movement but point out that
Smith was essentially a moral philosopher, and thus recognized that markets
are moral instruments. As such, he demonstrated that social welfare concerns
need not be inconsistent with the desire for, and the promotion of, properly conducted free market capitalism. For Smith the market, efficiency, and
wealth maximization were never ends but only means to individual liberty and

freedom—both public values that are not subject to scientific analysis. It is only by ignoring Smith as a moral philosopher (and thus characterizing him as a "scientist") that one can believe that his philosophy is motivated by a theory such as wealth maximization, with its tendency to shove noneconomic values like liberty and freedom into a framework of cost-benefit analysis. In other words, the priceless, so that it can be "scientifically" analyzed, is given a price.

ART, SCIENCE—OR THE HIDDEN THIRD OPTION

It might be, in line with current concepts of chaos and complexity theory, that law is neither art nor science in the classical sense, but fractal. The study of chaos is not the study of nothing, in the sense feared by the ancient Greeks, nor is it the study of utter randomness, in the sense feared by many—it is the search to identify and understand nonlinear patterns, to understand that intermediate areas exist between large simple systems such as planetary motion and the unpredictable statistics of random individual behavior known as "organized complexity." From the mysteries of chaos, some scientific innovators have, in recent times, attempted to establish general principles that might be relevant to all problems of organized complexity. The study of chaos has revealed that many things—from the weather to the economy—are only superficially chaotic; nonlinear systems manage to produce their own brand of spontaneous order. And strangely enough the abstract, fractal patterns sometimes revealed in the context of chaos and complexity are often beautiful (art?) and very similar to one another—ranging, in their natural form, from clouds, coastlines, and cotton prices to earthquakes.

The key point about law possibly being pictured as a fractal is that while no legal situation is quite like another, there is arguably a limited set of key factors that resemble each other. It is therefore these recurring patterns that are worth discovering and studying—seemingly Christopher Columbus Langdell's point regarding the casebook method of study and his belief that to understand a branch of legal doctrine in a scientific fashion, one must begin by identifying the axioms on which that field of law is based by surveying the case law in that area.

But while academic analysis might reveal certain patterns in the highly sanitized context of reported cases, this does not mean that this type of analysis contains an algorithm for applying such patterns to that complex and interdependent legal system in the real world. As Aristotle argued regarding politics and Adam Smith, seen as a moral philosopher, argued regarding economics, it is perhaps experience and intuition that generally wins out over technical analysis because any legal analysis (given the often unpredictable variety of emerging patterns) can never be precise enough or conclusive. Analysis, whether of the facts generating a legal problem or of the cases reporting legal decisions, is therefore useful only as a supplement to such things as intuition and pragmatism grounded in such cognitive processes as basic-level categorization, radial categories, image-schemas, and conceptual metaphors.

Turing to the Far East for a second, "mountain big" is a complete Chinese sentence. Strange. There is no need in Chinese to use a verb (e.g., the mountain *is* big.) Thus according to one scholar, "the Chinese did not develop the idea of the law of identity in logic (i.e., an object is the same as itelf: $A = A$) or the concept of substance in philosophy. And without these concepts, there could be no idea of causality or science. Instead, the Chinese develop[ed] correlational logic, analogical thought, and relational thinking, which, though inappropriate to science, are highly useful to socio-political theory. That is why the bulk of Chinese philosophy is philosophy of life." It would also seem that such modes of thought fit well with law. If so, the irony in modern times may be that Western language and thought is naturally geared toward science and has struggled to find its place in law, and Chinese (Eastern?) language and thought is naturally geared toward law and has had to struggle to find its place in science.

The debate of law as art versus science—and if it's a science, what type of methodology applies—is one that rages on in academic circles with ever-increasing sophistication. The practicing lawyer, however, is generally not involved in (and perhaps not even aware of) this discussion. Notions of prudential versus scientific realism, law and economics, and critical legal studies are frequently said to have little place in the day-to-day world of a lawyer rushing to close a real estate deal, or arguing about the best interests of a child in a custody battle, or plea bargaining with the district attorney over a client's drug possession charge. This does not mean, however, that such debates are the same as arguing about how many angels can dance on the head of a pin. The reason is that theories of law and the practice of law are generally formulated and studied by law professors and taught to their students, who then go on to work in the private and public sectors of society. In its simplest terms, the academic and working world sometimes actually connect on abstract issues of what law is and what it ought to be.

✄ · ✄

Legislating Morality

At least one economist has observed that morality deals with how society ought to be and economics deals with how society is. Taking this as a starting point, it may be that the "problem" with law and the practice of law is that both zigzag, back and forth, across the "is" (descriptive) and the "ought" (prescriptive).

✄ · ✄

XXIII

THE QUICK RISE AND LONG FALL OF THE LAWYER CLASS IN AMERICA

IN WHAT HAS BEEN CALLED the "Era of Persuasion" (1521–1680), one of the selling points used by Captain John Smith, leader of the Jamestown party, for getting people to invest their money and risk their lives in America had to do with lawyers—or more precisely, the lack thereof. In 1614 Captain Smith sailed to the northern part of Virginia. He renamed the area "New England." Smith then prepared a promotional tract entitled *Description of New England* in order to entice the idle sons of English nobles and the poor of English cities to come and live in America. To the nobles this region, according to Smith, offered "employments for gentlemen": from fowling and fishing to hunting and hawking, and to the laboring class it offered a chance to grow rich, free of landlords and lawyers.

Setting a Bad Precedent

The Massachusetts *Body of Liberties* of 1641 prohibited anyone from accepting a fee to assist another in court. Although the legislature deleted this provision from its code in 1648, it later, in 1663, prohibited any "usual and Common Attorney in any Inferior Court" from serving in the legislature. In fact, distrust of lawyers permeated the seventeenth-century colonies. Both Virginia and Connecticut excluded them from their respective courts. The 1669 Constitution for the Carolinas called it "a base and vile thing to plead for money or reward."

In our hunt for the early lawyers in "America," we know that in the 1650s John Hammond practiced law in Maryland. Hammond was apparently a shadowy figure (a good start for the American lawyer class) who had lived in Virginia for twenty-one years. He won election to the House of Burgesses but was later expelled by his fellow burgesses for having a scandalous reputation that rendered him unfit to serve. Embarrassed by this loss of position, Hammond bought a plantation, where he farmed and practiced law.

Apparently his reputation had no effect (or at least no negative effect) on his ability to practice law. But after Protestants overthrew Lord Baltimore's government, Hammond fled to England. It was there that he wrote his treatise *Leah and Rachel,* which likened Virginia and Maryland to the two wives of the Old Testament prophet Jacob. His target audience was the poor and dispossessed, and his message was that anyone who chose to beg and steal in England when they could flourish in America suffered from stupidity. Remember, it was the Era of Persuasion.

The first woman lawyer in the colonies appears to have been Margaret Brent. She arrived in 1638 and quickly positioned herself to be appointed counsel to the Governor of Maryland. Brent was a very able litigator who handled 124 major cases for the Colony during an eight-year period. In court records and in person the colonists addressed her as "Gentleman Margaret Brent."

In every colony but Maryland, a wife could act as her husband's "lawyer." And women not only acted for and on behalf of husbands, they sometimes even acted on behalf of unrelated parties.

On August 1, 1684, for example, Volkert de Glabbais was represented before the Court of General Sessions of New York County by Anna Meynders, who acted as Glabbias's "constituted Attorney." On behalf of the client, Meynders cited English law in support of her argument—winning the case against a fairly renowned lawyer, Samuel Winder.

Despite Captain Smith's promise of a land free of lawyers, they were the most heavily represented group at the 1776 gathering in Philadelphia. Of the fifty-six men who ultimately signed the Declaration of Independence, twenty-five were members of the colonial bar.

If one stops and thinks about it, the role of revolutionaries is a strange one for a bunch of lawyers, since as a class they tend to be among the most conservative elements in a society. The reason for this is, of course, that legal training generally stresses respect for past and present institutions. There may even be a religious or patriotic tone involved. But the ultimate reason most likely comes in the form of dollars and cents. (I guess the practice of law has, over the years, made me more pragmatic—or is it more cynical? I get the two confused.) The truth is that there is generally not much money to be made in tearing down the very institutions that make the practice of law possible.

The question, therefore, is why? Why were so many of the leaders in the American Revolution lawyers?

In large part the answer to this question lies in the constitutional change that took place in England at the end of the French and Indian War, known as the Seven Years' War in Britain. After the end of this global conflict in 1763, the British government realized that Anglo-American relations had been left in an undisturbed "natural" state far too long and therefore instituted a policy of closer supervision and control over its colonies in North America. As a part of this policy, it was determined that the colonies should bear more of the administrative costs involved in running a colonial empire, specifically including support of the soldiers sent to protect them—the war having significantly increased England's national debt. The colonists, however, viewed a standing army as synonymous with a jackbooted, military dictatorship.

One step along the path of this new regulatory scheme was the Sugar Act of 1764. This Act provided a mechanism for raising or lowering the tariffs on sugar, molasses, and other commodities. The Act itself was not a problem, since colonial merchants had developed techniques for evading navigation acts. The real problem was that an earlier act provided that all violations of revenue acts, like the Sugar Act, could be tried in the admiralty courts without benefit of a jury. It was one thing to toy with local customs officials but quite another to deal with the British Navy—particularly without a jury of your peers backing you up.

The Birth of the Fourth Amendment

It was the one-two punch of the customs officials and the admiralty courts that really angered the American colonists. On the customs side, general warrants were conferred by Parliament on customs officials through Writs of Assistance. These general search warrants were used in an effort to stem the rampant smuggling operations that arose in the colonies in order to avoid the empire's restrictive trade laws. This was a period of mercantilism. The writs granted English officials wide discretion since the warrants did not have to identify the people covered or specify the property to be searched— nor were they limited by any probable cause requirements. And on the trial side, admiralty courts did not include the benefit of jury. The Fourth Amendment to the United States Constitution came about largely as a result of the English practice of issuing these general search warrants.

The Sugar Act and its enforcement mechanism upset the colonial merchants, to put it mildly. And the colonial lawyers, occupying one of the highest positions in pre-Revolutionary society, were connected with the mercantile families through marriage or kinship. Consequently, when the merchants got upset, the lawyers got upset.

The Stamp Act was the next step on the road to revolution. The British ministry, sensing resistance to the Sugar Act, attempted to find a tax that would be acceptable to the colonies. Parliament floated the notion of a stamp tax by the colonies a year prior to its passage in order to see if there were any objections or suggested alternatives. Silence.

The Act was therefore passed and imposed stamp duties on newspapers, deeds, wills, court pleadings, and all types of agreements essential to commerce. The interests of two of the most influential professions in molding public opinion were immediately affected by the tax: lawyers and newspaper publishers. Many of the documents prepared by lawyers were subject to the tax, leading many to believe that their businesses would be ruined. And a loss in earnings meant a loss in property, which meant an imposition on freedom.

The First Bar Association

A distinct bar association or bar organization appears to have been formed in New York as early as 1744 (disbanded about 1770). This association, called the New York Bar Association, was, to a large extent, responsible for instigating and supporting resistance to the Stamp Act.

A key to this doomsday outlook was that the fees lawyers could charge for various services were small and regulated by statute. Additionally, lawyers were often unable to collect their fees. Consequently, with the advent of the

Stamp Act, members of the Virginia Bar published a newspaper notice stating that they would no longer take cases unless the established fees were paid up front. The Act, however, presented another complicating factor for the bar. The stamps attached to the document showing that the tax had been paid had to be purchased with currency—a somewhat rare commodity in the colonies. In fact, lawyers' fees in some of the colonies were expressed and paid in tobacco or tobacco notes.

Opposition to the Act was strong, and not just from lawyers. The "Liberty Boys," after petitions to Parliament to repeal the offensive legislation went nowhere, forced the resignation of the stamp agents in all the colonies. They then prevented the landing of the stamps. But unlike such in-your-face opposition, a number of lawyers could not bring themselves to simply ignore the law. The sympathies, however, of many of those in the legal profession were with the colonial cause. Consequently, they reached a moral compromise (as is often the case with lawyers) and decided to conduct only that type of business that did not require stamps: a limited boycott. This watered-down approach to resistance did not sit well with some of the more aggressive factions. In the Boston area, for instance, a mob burned down a judge's home. Coming to court the next day in borrowed clothes, the Chief Justice of the Superior Court of Judicature of the Province of Massachusetts Bay carefully pointed out his personal versus professional opposition to the Stamp Act, and his awareness of what had provoked the violence. Cicero would have been proud.

Colonial opposition to the Act eventually caused the Superior Courts to close. In Massachusetts, while the courts were dark, the Sons of Liberty sought to reopen them without the use of stamps. John Adams appeared on behalf of the Town of Boston before the Governor in Council on December 18, 1765, and urged the governor to reopen the courts. Adams invoked British constitutional authority, citing from Coke's *Reports,* the Magna Carta, the law of nature, "the ancient Roman law," and even the great medieval source of the British constitution, Bracton's *De Legibus et Consuetudinibus Angliae,* in his argument that the Stamp Act was not binding on the colony because Parliament did not have authority to pass the statute. James Otis, Jr., greatly admired by the younger John Adams, also argued that the courts should be reopened, quoting from Coke's *Institutes.*

The court closures, besides possibly undercutting arguments regarding the Stamp Act's unconstitutionality, significantly affected the cash flow of legal professionals. Their primary source of income in colonial America was court appearances—and not, as was the case for the scribes of ancient Mesopotamia, transactional work. And as previously indicated, the fees that lawyers could charge for their services were often regulated by statute. The number of fees collected, for example, by Patrick Henry, admitted to the bar in 1760, fell from

557 in 1765 to 114 in 1766. It is no wonder that he finally yelled: "Give me liberty or give me death!" The legal profession indeed suffered along with all other colonists for their opposition to the tax.

Mere opposition to the Stamp Act was not enough, however, to incite the colonists to revolution. In order to accomplish this important step, a postulation of theories supporting radical change—a rhetoric of revolution—was needed, and it is here that the lawyers made a significant contribution.

A centerpiece of the legal and constitutional argument for revolution undoubtedly involved the virtues of common-law procedure. As discussed, violations of revenue acts could be tried not in the common-law courts of the Colonies, but in the English admiralty courts. And these proceedings were conducted without the benefit of a jury.

There were nevertheless a number of very prominent lawyers who could not support (arguably) illegal activities designed to overthrow a government. The notion of a radical lawyer was, for them, an attempt to force together two words that are conceptually contradictory. Of the fourteen active lawyers in the close-knit Boston legal community, for example, at least six were loyalists who eventually left the colonies. Indeed, acts of civil disobedience often raise deeply felt questions of right and wrong. There was, however, a sufficient number of able lawyers left in the colonies to help frame the relevant "constitutional arguments" and to help lead a revolution—including John Adams, Thomas Jefferson, John Jay, and Robert Livingston.

The bar also made a significant contribution to the events immediately after the Revolution by convincing the general population not to go to extremes—as was to happen with the French Revolution, which arguably resulted in not just a change in government but also in a dissolution of society. Consequently, when compared with other revolutions, America's generally lacked mob violence—like dragging dead bodies through the streets on the way to Utopia. This result was due, in no small part, to the influence of the lawyers who were in leadership positions and made public their belief in a pragmatic and orderly process.

One might think that the newly formed American nation would hold its lawyers in high regard for their risk taking. But *noooo!* The years following the Revolution were marked by a general animosity toward the legal profession— despite all the lawyer-signers of the Declaration of Independence. With the economy depressed, part of the reason for such dislike was lawyers' involvement in debt collection and property foreclosures (not unlike the activities involved in the subprime mortgage meltdown of the twenty-first century). Nasty business. In addition, some lawyers, although not Tories (English Loyalists) themselves, defended various Tories against state confiscation laws. Alexander Hamilton, in fact, built up his early legal career by representing such unpopular clients.

No Good Deed Goes Unpunished

New England farmers had expanded their production to meet food demands in other regions more affected by the Revolution. When farming resumed in other states, New Englanders had to hustle to meet mortgage payments on land they had cleared and planted during the Revolution. A wave of foreclosures and evictions resulting from the added competition spread across the western counties of Massachusetts, increasing animosity toward lawyers.

The ugly truth is that the swelling anti-lawyer contingency even suggested death to them all—at least figuratively. Popular writer Benjamin Austin wrote that the order of human species commonly known as lawyers had grown "not only USELESS, but . . . DANGEROUS," and therefore should be forever "abolished," replaced with a system of arbitration consisting mainly of responsible laymen. This push for arbitration, carried over from colonial times, was popular for several reasons. For one thing, it was less formal than a court proceeding, and hence was considered to be faster and cheaper. Perhaps even more importantly, it enabled merchants—who viewed the legal profession as being in the pocket of the landed elite—to avoid "Officers of the Courts and Lawyers who never Trade." In other words, the merchants viewed the lawyers as slaves to legal precedents born from a feudal, hierarchical Big Man society versus employing procedural and substantive laws that were efficient and effective for competitive private businesses and emerging capital markets.

It is interesting to note that the same push for arbitration, based on some of the same reasons expressed in early American society, has been gaining steam in modern times. But like other ancient species that have learned to survive massive change, lawyers are keeping pace. Thanks to law school classes, bar association training, and sheer necessity due to overloaded courts, many lawyers are no longer concerned that they will be considered a wimp if they say: "I'll see you in arbitration!"

RETURN OF THE LAWYER

Despite the post-Revolutionary ebb in the reputation of lawyers, the profession rose from its 1790 low point to a position, within three or four decades, of political and intellectual domination. Alexis de Tocqueville, the French chronicler, concluded that of all the classes and types of people making up America, the group most deserving of deference and respect were the lawyers.

This observation was made in the early 1830s but, surprisingly, not everyone has had the wisdom to adopt this enlightened point of view.

At the risk of further tempting the egos of the otherwise humble lawyers of America, I quote from Tocqueville's *Democracy in America*: "In America there are neither nobles nor men of letters, and the people distrust the wealthy. Therefore the lawyers form the political upper class and the most intellectual section of society. . . . If you ask me where the American aristocracy is found, I have no hesitation in answering that it is not among the rich, who have no common link uniting them. It is at the bar or the bench that the American aristocracy is found." Wow—this is good stuff.

But wait! On second thought, I sense a possible backhanded compliment. What exactly does Tocqueville mean that since America had no nobles or men of letters that lawyers formed the upper class and the most intellectual section of post-Revolutionary society? There is a certain "king of the village idiots" tone to this aristocratic Frenchman's observation. Nevertheless, a compliment *is* a compliment.

Additionally, viewing Tocqueville's observation in the best light possible, it appears that he might have been likening the lawyer class, scattered throughout American society, to that of the deposed but then still cohesive European aristocracies. The lawyers, like the aristocracies of Europe, injected into society an importance sense of stability that counteracted tendencies toward the quick fix, disorder, and "royal" or majoritarian oppression. Tocqueville saw that during democratic America's expansionist, equalitarian phase, a dangerous vacuum existed between the people at the base, all of them theoretically being equal, and the government at the top, which, though selected by the people, possessed threatening power. The lawyer class helped to fill this vacuum by standing between the people and their government, thereby keeping the full weight of political power from crushing the "common man."

This same type of sentiment has been expressed by more recent scholars. It has been observed that judicial liberalism, born in thirteenth-century England, is continually being played out through lawsuits involving the United States Constitution's Bill of Rights and the Fourteenth Amendment (enshrining the idea of due process and "legalizing" the Declaration of Independence's public virtue that "all men are created equal"). And it is the legal profession that is deeply involved in this important area. Whereas the English still have the monarchy, Parliament, the Church of England, and the distinctive institutionalized life of the gentry and other upper-middle-class people to act as a binding force (e.g., Sir Paul McCartney and Sir Elton John), the United States only has the Bill of Rights and the Fourteenth Amendment. Take away these important statements of due process and equality and the American system would arguably implode. The prospect of groups then splintering off into warring factions may be why the legal profession is more important in the United States than in any other country. Imagine that!

It should also be pointed out, in fairness, that Tocqueville might not have been so complementary of the legal profession if he had spent just a little more time in America. There is, after all, the retort of a Indiana lawyer made when opposing counsel repeatedly tried to build his case with citations from "the great English common law." "If we are to be guided by English law at all," the attorney snapped back, "we want their best and not their common law." There is also the case of Simon Suggs, who began his rise within the Arkansas bar by winning a law license in a Georgia card game.

As one might glean from the foregoing, the early American lawyer was generally not a learned doctor of laws; he was principally a man of action and cunning. And much of these street smarts were employed by an increasingly important segment of American society. In the period between 1790 and 1820 the mercantile class rid itself of its virulent antilegalism (developed due to the law's agricultural leanings), frequently manifested during the colonial period by the use of extralegal forms of dispute settlement. The bar, during this same period, finally got the message and became aggressive in shedding many eighteenth-century, anticommercial legal doctrines. As a result of these two factors, the leaders of the bar in the period after 1790 were no longer the land conveyancers or debt collectors, but the commercial lawyers.

$\otimes \cdot \otimes \cdot \otimes \cdot \otimes \cdot \otimes \cdot \otimes \cdot \otimes \cdot \otimes \cdot \otimes \cdot \otimes \cdot \otimes \cdot \otimes \cdot \otimes \cdot \otimes \cdot \otimes \cdot \otimes \cdot \otimes \cdot \otimes \cdot \otimes \cdot \otimes$

Book and Street Smarts

Early America didn't entirely lack high legal culture. There were Northern and Southern legal circles that pursued scholarship. A Boston circle pushed the study of Roman and civil law in its desire to raise the status of the legal profession and to help establish the model of university-affiliated legal education. For Southern lawyers who considered themselves Southern gentlemen, a scholarly approach to the law fit within their social environment. Many of these Southerners had been trained, primarily in Roman and civil law, in England, Scotland, Germany, and other European countries.

With regard to the bench, it is noted that in early post-Revolutionary America men were appointed to the courts not because they had been to law school or had any special legal expertise, but because of their social and political rank and influence. Starting, however, in the 1790s, judges began to withdraw from politics, to promote the development of law as a "science" known best by trained experts, and to limit their activities to the regular courts—which became increasingly professional.

$\otimes \cdot \otimes \cdot \otimes \cdot \otimes \cdot \otimes \cdot \otimes \cdot \otimes \cdot \otimes \cdot \otimes \cdot \otimes \cdot \otimes \cdot \otimes \cdot \otimes \cdot \otimes \cdot \otimes \cdot \otimes \cdot \otimes \cdot \otimes \cdot \otimes \cdot \otimes$

GOOD MORAL CHARACTER

With the rise of Jeffersonian and Jacksonian democracy, the political climate was generally opposed to the notion of government run by experts. (Some might agree that America has accomplished this goal—but not in the way envisioned by either Jefferson or Jackson.) This spirit filtered down into the legal profession and implied either limits on the power of the bar, or hosting, so to speak, an open bar. In fact, prior to the Civil War, several states abolished restrictions on entry into the legal profession other than that the entrant be of the age of majority and of "good moral character": a Moral Accounting in which virtues clearly outweighed vices. Other states were slightly more restrictive, adding the requirement of an apprenticeship as a condition to becoming a member of the bar. However, despite the bar's espoused new egalitarian spirit, the case of Thomas Addis Emmet (1764–1827) provides a pointed example of an attempt to exclude an applicant based on "lack of good moral character."

Emmet was born in Ireland into a family of stature. He received his doctorate in medicine in 1784 from the University of Edinburgh and set up a practice in Dublin. By his midtwenties, he was already the ex officio physician to the royal family. However, in 1789 his brother, who had shown promise in the legal profession, died. Emmet's father, as a tribute to his dead son, urged Emmet to raise his sights and become a lawyer. He agreed and studied at the Temple in London. By the early 1790s, Emmet was a member of the Irish Bar.

As it turned out he had a gift for oratory and an intellectual breadth that quickly earned him prominence within the legal profession. He also became embroiled in the nuances of the centuries-old dispute between Ireland and its English rulers. His legal talents made him one of the best-known defenders of Irish political dissidents, whose protests against Catholic disenfranchisement and other British wrongs were increasingly bringing them before the Crown on charges of sedition. And as chief counselor for the protesters, Emmet, in 1795, defended one of his clients against charges of treason for administering an oath of loyalty on behalf of the nationalistically oriented society of United Irishmen. The defendant was found guilty. Emmet, upon the court's delivery of the verdict, called for an arrest of judgment and then launched into an eloquent oration, ending with the swearing of his own allegiance to the society. This bold move convinced the court that the mere act of administering or taking the oath of a reformist organization should not be interpreted as treason. The client received only a small fine.

Emmet became a god of the Irish nationalist movement and was placed on the United Irishmen's directory. His affiliation with this group had, however, negative personal consequences. In an effort to help neutralize Irish dissent, the English placed Emmet under arrest without bringing charges—a slight variance on Shakespeare's "advice": "The first thing we do, let's kill all the lawyers." He was later released from prison on the condition that he never return to Ireland. So in 1804 he and his family left for New York City.

Emmet found himself welcomed in the city's more liberal quarters. But New York's conservative Federalists thought that his involvement in Irish protest against the Strict Father Figure labeled him a dangerous subversive and an unfit candidate for the practice of law in America. In other words, he "lacked good moral character." Eventually, however, Emmet won admission to the bar and went on to become a very successful lawyer in his adopted country.

Explosive Lawyer Growth

There were some tendencies during the colonial period for creating a small, exclusive guild of legal professionals. The pressure of American practical politics, however, eventually won out, as noted earlier, and the doors to the bar swung wide—at least for male WASPs. In 1740, there were about 15 lawyers buzzing around Massachusetts (population 150,000). In 1790, there were 112 lawyers; in 1800, 200; in 1810, 492, and in 1840 there were 640 lawyers in the state.

The above statistics are not meant to imply that lawyers took no steps, beyond the gate-keeping function of Moral Accounting, toward limiting their numbers. After all, competition can be tough on earnings. The New Hampshire State Bar, for one, adopted elaborate rules in 1788 and again in 1805 regarding lawyers. These rules provided, among other things, that legal apprentices without college degrees must qualify and gain admittance to Dartmouth College or be dismissed. Minimum tuition fees for lawyers' apprentices were also used by early bar associations to keep down the number of practicing lawyers.

Legal education was not very stringent. In fact, other than an apprenticeship requirement in some states, there were no formal educational requirements and no bar exam. The bar, therefore, became seen as a means for social advancement. A career in the law was, as is still somewhat the case, considered to be as a vehicle by which even a poor man's son might achieve wealth and position in society. The trick was, of course, that not everyone succeeded—but everyone of the right color, sex, and religion had at least a fighting chance. Consider, for example, that county lawyer named Abraham Lincoln.

Lincoln (1809–1865) was self-taught in the intricacies of the law. In response to Isham Reavis's inquiry to read law at Lincoln's office, Lincoln, Esq., advised Reavis that he was away too much to instruct him. Besides, as Lincoln said: "It is but a small matter whether you read with anybody or not. I did not read with anyone. Get the books, and read and study them 'till you understand them and their principal features; and that is the main thing. It is of no consequence to be in a large town while you are reading. I read at New Salem, which never had three hundred people living in it." The catch in Lincoln's simple advice is, however, that the law was then, as it is today, an intellectually demanding profession. A bright man like Lincoln could become a successful lawyer with little formal education—but the same might not be true for the Reavises of the world.

Lincoln, Esq.'s story was definitely not the rule. A person with a background like Thomas Jefferson's had the contacts, in addition to the intelligence and training, that were generally necessary for a successful practice. For example, of the 2,618 lawyers in Massachusetts and Maine practicing between the years 1760 and 1840, 71.4 percent had a college education.

A Slight Change in Standards

As late as 1951, 20 percent of American lawyers had not graduated from a law school, and half of those had not even graduated from college. But by 1960, college graduation, plus three years of law school, plus passing a state bar exam, plus satisfying a bar committee that you are of good moral character became the standard. This post-1960 part of becoming a lawyer I clearly remember.

There were a variety of practices available to lawyers of the day—even if there were not always a lot of clients. Some had a taste for the wild, wild West. These lawyers did not ask if a case was suitable work; if it paid in gold or goats, it was suitable. Many of them were engaged by eastern land speculators, a practice that involved the legal aspects of buying and selling land, including searching titles and the scribal work of preparing deeds. And if they weren't paid in money, they would take part of the action. Lawyers were also hired by local and eastern creditors to find and sue debtors.

In the eastern and southern states, there was much more chance of running into the pompous, traditional lawyer. These lawyers, from elite backgrounds, formed a small but sophisticated bar of commerce. They advised the large mercantile houses on matters of marine insurance and international trade. No poverty law. No criminal law.

Litigation concerning marine insurance often involved large sums of money and enabled America's first generation of commercial lawyers to become wealthy exclusively through the practice of law. For example, because of the money involved, Alexander Hamilton, after leaving the federal government in 1795 and before being shot dead by Aaron Burr, devoted much of his New York commercial practice to insurance cases. And Horace Binney, a lawyer with an extensive commercial practice, apparently rejoiced at the "unparalleled harvest to the bar of Philadelphia" resulting from the Atlantic sea war then in progress.

It has been estimated that in 1830, New York City, with a population of about 200,000, there were about 500 practicing lawyers. Almost all of these lawyers were sole practitioners. There were a few two-man partnerships but no firms of any size, in contrast to modern-day law firms with thousands of lawyers.

MODERN-DAY MEGA FIRMS

Even though the current trend is toward supersizing, big ain't always better. The reasons for this include the fact that Big is generally expensive. Despite talk of economies of scale, a modern-day law firm merger rarely results in significant downsizing or cost reduction—there is nothing to reduce. Law firms do not have sales forces to combine, a large advertising budget to cut, or physical plants to close. The only commodity a law firm has is lawyers and support staff: "thinking property." A firm that acquires hundreds of new lawyers cannot simply fire their secretaries, paralegals, or runners. And the newly merged firms rarely close offices, since the point of the merger is to have offices in different cities or countries.

✗ · ✗

The Secret of the Opulent Waiting Room

Have you ever asked yourself why it is that lawyers often have impressive waiting rooms and offices and doctors don't? I would like to tell you that it is because lawyers are smarter, more valuable, and therefore richer than doctors. I would like to. But the truth is that the opulence most likely has to do with signaling. The notion is that potential and existing clients will believe that only a "good type" would invest in expensive quarters. Doctors, by nature of the profession, are usually intrinsically thought of as good and therefore do not need to charge for the cost of a temple or cathedral. Think about sitting in a waiting room in physical pain versus sitting in a waiting room furious at your cheating spouse. I suspect that in the latter case, a bit of opulence might signal to you that "we" are going to nail the philandering rat to the wall.

✗ · ✗

The usual fallout of this increased firm expense is higher billing rates. The whole idea of size is to be able to run with the Big Dogs. And once a firm reaches that level of competition, its billing rates will also rise to the level of its self-perceived position in the legal community. Besides, the firm's clients, unlike Wal-Mart's customers, need to pay for the additional overhead that comes with the convenience of one-stop shopping in large and expensive quarters.

Big also tends to be slow. An increase in the number of lawyers and support staff almost always means more management committees, compensation committees, malpractice committees, opinion letter committees, and committees on the formation of committees. It is tough enough to deal with one or two lawyers involved in a transaction or court case; imagine dealing with a team of twenty.

Finally, the pressure on partners and associates to generate more billable hours also increases with size. As firms cross time zones, there is no such thing as 9 to 5. Forget the idea of part time as a solution to both practicing law and raising children; the "mommy track" is not a detour but a dead end—at least in many large firms. And the additional pressure on the lawyers flows out to the support staff. The general feel of the firm becomes one of hypertension.

Rise of the Billable Hour

According to *The Cheating Culture: Why More Americans Are Doing Wrong to Get Ahead* by David Callahan, it was not until the 1970s and 1980s that law firms started seriously tracking the billable hours of every lawyer and holding them accountable for their time. "A new bottom-line logic held that the hours each lawyer billed reflected his or her contribution to the firm's profitability." Consequently, billing expectations in many New York law firms rose to over 2,200 hours a year—leading to the temptation to simply make up the numbers. The legal bill sent to the client, however, is real. Trust me.

There is, however, one technique that some large firms have found to be helpful in relieving a bit of the pressure: "Skaddenomics." This is a term that entered the legal lexicon in the 1990s. As stated by one social critic, "[i]t referred to the increasingly common practice of billing clients for basic office expenses like faxing and long-distance calls at the kind of outrageous rates one might expect from a five-star hotel. [The law firm of . . .] Skadden, Arps happened to be among the worst offenders. . . . But many other firms engaged in the same practice. In the mid-1990s, [the law firm Cravath, Swaine & Moore] was charging clients $1.00 a page to send faxes, not including the long-distance charges. It charged 15 cents a page for photocopying, up to $91.00 an hour for proofreading. *The American Lawyer* [in an investigative article] estimated $6.6 million in revenue just from its secretaries."

EARLY AMERICAN LAW STUDIES

In the newly formed country of the United States of America, what law did the lawyers study and practice? In answering this question the first thing that should be pointed out is that its lawyers, as had been the case during colonial days, had no interest in attempting to understand and utilize the law of the various Native American tribes. None.

An Ancient Prejudice

Systems of American Indian justice have historically been devalued and marginalized (along with the legal systems of other "folk" societies) as "primitive," "illiterate," or otherwise less sophisticated than the Anglo-American legal tradition. Such attitudes are reinforced by the perceived reliance by Native American societies on oral traditions in contrast to written legislation and precedent, a theme that we have seen many times so far: the Oral Torah versus the Written Torah; the unwritten common law versus the codified civil and canon law; the unwritten English constitution versus the written American Constitution; oral evidence versus written evidence. . . .

The backbone of post-Revolutionary American jurisprudence was, in some form or another, the English common law. Americans kicked the collective butts of their overlords but kept their law, and to some extent their legal institutions (the jury system, for example). Modern scholarship has shown, however, that the early American lawyers were not fixated on the common law. They in fact looked to such sources as Roman law, civil law, and the *ius commune* and sometimes even threw canon law into their arguments. Pushing institutionalized legal education and acquiring a scholarly air played a large part in the fascination, particularly among the elite American lawyers, of looking to sources other than the common law.

But besides acting as a source of inspiration, did these non-common-law sources play any practical role in the development of American law? The answer, in broad terms, appears to be yes.

Scholarship has demonstrated that more than a few American lawyers of the immediate post-Revolutionary period knew and made use of the "civil law" in arguments offered in courts. The *Institutes, Codex, Digest,* and *Novellae* were frequently cited and commented upon. And English speaking civilian writers were also used as a source of American knowledge and usage of the continental *ius commune.*

It is interesting to observe that, with regard to sources of law, there does not appear to have been any particular geographic bias. The reported cases of northern states, like Massachusetts, evidence citations to civil-law authority with just about the same frequency as southern states such as South Carolina. The western states, like the great state of Nevada, were not even a gleam in Uncle Sam's eye. And by the time the West was carved up into states, the use of authorities drawn from the civil law was completely overshadowed by references to American cases. As a result, the law of the western United States was influenced by Roman and European civil-law concepts, with certain exceptions, through its adoption of earlier Eastern case, statutory, and constitutional law.

Dirty Citations

There does appear to have been an increase in citation of Roman law between 1825 and the start of the Civil War by various southern courts with regard to slavery issues. The Romans, like the ancient Greeks and Mesopotamians, were big on slavery—but not based on race; enslavement could happen to anyone. The *Lex Fufia Caninia* (2 BCE) established a quota for the number of slaves that could be freed by a will (this was repealed by Justinian); *Lex Aelia Sentia* (4 CE) regulated minimum ages for masters and slaves and prohibited manumission of slaves to the detriment of creditors; *Senatus Consultum Silanianum* (10 CE) permitted interrogation on public authority of slaves whose master had been killed.

In contrast to American cases stood the English common-law decision in *Somerset's Case* (1772). Lord Mansfield, Chief Justice of the King's Bench, held that a black slave brought into England from the colonies as a personal servant could not be forcibly taken from England back to the colonies since the common law did not recognize the status of chattel slavery.

There was not, however, a universal love fest between the American lawyer and the Roman and European civil law. A Kentucky lawyer, for example, took the opportunity in 1823 to contrast the purity of American institutions with the vice of the Roman system summed up in the personage of the decadent Emperor Caligula. And an Indiana lawyer, in an 1820 case, characterized the *ius commune* as the product of "the gloomy times of Popery." (I assume he was not Catholic.)

There appears to be three basic circumstances in which early American lawyers and judges resorted to the civil law in its broadest sense. The first was when the English common law was thought to be nonexistent, inconclusive, or "wrong" on a particular point. The second was when fundamental principles of justice were called into question. This reason for citing civilian writers, who had developed sophisticated legal systems from tenets of natural law, reaches all the way to the United States Constitution. Legal scholarship has argued that the Framers of the Constitution saw constitutions, in general, as expressions of a "higher law" and not just simply as an expression of the will of the people. (Many of the Founding Fathers, shocking as it may be, didn't exactly trust the *hoi polloi*.) According to this view, the United States Constitution should be read within the context of natural law in which fundamental rights, although perhaps not found in the document's exact words, are embedded in the spirit of its various provisions. And civil-law sources, according to this view, played a role in forming America's constitutional law, since many of the natural-law principles originated in European legal thought. Finally, the civil law was used by early American lawyers to pump up the volume of the common law. In general terms, a lawyer who believed that law is based on universal principles saw no reason not to delve into the extensive sources of Roman, civil, and canon law.

Having looked generally at the ups and downs of lawyers in America's start and the law that shaped their thoughts and practices, we will now get specific. This means taking a close look at how education, professional training, and economics actually worked in the lives of lawyers spanning the time period from 1743 to 1938. The lawyers to be discussed in some depth are names you may be familiar with: Thomas Jefferson, Daniel Webster, Abraham Lincoln, and Clarence Darrow.

XXIV

THOMAS JEFFERSON:

THE THINKING MAN
WHO THOUGHT ABOUT
"THINKING PROPERTY"

THOMAS JEFFERSON'S FATHER DIED while Jefferson was still a young man. While his death did not make Thomas rich, he nevertheless stood to inherit a significant amount of land. However, by the time Peter Jefferson's estate was divided up, Thomas ended up sharing half of the best land with his brother. In addition, his young mother had use of the main house and farm during her lifetime. These circumstances dissuaded Jefferson from immediately becoming a planter and pushed him in the direction of the law. Jefferson knew that someday he would own the patrimonial farm in the mountains at Shadwell and Monticello, but in the meantime a law practice would augment his agricultural income.

It was also the case that Jefferson's cousins and uncles, on his aristocratic mother's side, were among Virginia's most distinguished attorneys. And Jefferson had read John Locke's 1693 treatise *Some Thoughts Concerning Education,* which advised young gentlemen to study works on international law and legal philosophy (harking back to the notion of the "all-round gentleman").

Having carefully considered all these factors, Jefferson decided, following his attendance at the College of William and Mary, to pursue a legal education. (As an interesting aside: While at William and Mary, Jefferson's roommate was John Tyler Sr.—the father of lawyer-President John Tyler.) He was put in contact with a lawyer named George Wythe, who was later to become the first law professor in America and who viewed the study of law through a broad lens, encompassing not only the common law but also international and Roman law. At the time there were no law schools in America, and aspiring attorneys generally learned their profession by serving apprenticeships—that is, reading law and acting as an unpaid clerk.

A few Virginians, including Jefferson's cousins Edmund and Payton Randolph—Edmund Randolph later became the first U.S. attorney general—studied at the Inns of Court in London in order to qualify as English barristers. This course of legal education was also followed by Benjamin Franklin's son, William. The cost, however, was high and families were concerned about the possibility of their sons being corrupted. The Inns were located in the overgrown Metropolis of London, notorious for "abounding with every species of dissipation"—prostitutes, taverns, tailors, periwig makers, and dancing masters. And students were not provided with even the slightest form of collegiate discipline.

In 1782 Jefferson, a tall, lanky boy of nineteen, saddled up his horse and headed out for Wythe's brick mansion in Williamsburg, Virginia. Wythe was thirty-five, a self-taught legal scholar, with an imposing appearance. Over the next five years, Jefferson plowed through mounds of books from Coke to Montesquieu and also grew to become part of the family—the Wythes had no children of their own.

Jefferson could have chosen an easier route by studying with one of his relatives. In picking Wythe, Jefferson, however, sought to study law with a man who not only had one of the best legal minds in Virginia, but was also a self-taught classical scholar.

Jefferson was not Wythe's only famous student. John Marshall, the fourth chief justice of the United States Supreme Court, studied under Wythe. And Henry Clay, U.S. statesman, orator, and young Abraham Lincoln's role model, became Wythe's clerk thirty years later. In fact it seems that Wythe played a significant role in advancing the ideal of the "lawyer-statesman." This once-powerful image, not unlike the image of the "all-round gentleman," viewed lawyers as uniquely placed to function as highly trained and principled elites whose main role is to serve as protectors of American public virtues. (I suspect, however, that such things as lawyer-President Nixon's involvement in Watergate and lawyer-President Clinton's lying about his relationship with a White House intern have had some negative impact on the lawyer-statesman mythos.)

Jefferson, along with other young clerks, studied in a first-floor back room in Wythe's mansion. Wythe frequently took on students free of charge and spent time actually teaching them rather than simply loading them up with clerical chores. Along with the other students, Jefferson was expected to carefully study each stage of the cases taken on by Wythe. Wythe explained each step and as Jefferson progressed, Wythe gave him increasing responsibility for legal research in the provincial records and from Wythe's extensive library.

When the Williamsburg courts were in session, Jefferson carried Wythe's books and notes and stayed nearby in case Wythe needed something—like coffee. When Wythe went out to the county courts, Jefferson rode along.

Thank Heavens for Xerox and Computers

Robert Troup, who later tutored Alexander Hamilton in the law, explained in a 1780 letter to Aaron Burr why he had declined to study law under the same attorney Burr had: "[H]e is immersed in such an ocean of business," said Troup, "that I imagined it would be out of his power to bestow all the time and pain on our improvement we would wish." Troup was also afraid that he would be confined to the drudgery of copying. John Quincy Adams, future president of the United States and the son of lawyer-president John Adams, on October 2, 1787, expressed his assessment of this common clerkship task of copying: "I began to copy off, not a small volume, of forms for declaration. This is a piece of drudgery," he said, "which certainly does not carry its reward with it. . . ." Furthermore, even though those serving clerkships assisted with office drudgery, they were generally charged for the chance to work with and receive instructions from a practicing attorney. George Wythe was indeed an extraordinary teacher.

Jefferson's general method of studying was to take a blank notebook and write at the top of each page, in alphabetical order, the major topical divisions of the common law. Under the different headings, he wrote comments on what he considered to be the essential points of law as he read through various case reports, statutes, and treaties. On the opposite page he wrote the individual points of law. Jefferson started this process in 1762 and continued it for many years—even though he never relished the actual practice of law, nor, unlike some of us lawyers, felt the financial need to keep it up.

The bible of legal learning for Wythe and his students was Sir Edward Coke's *Institutes of the Laws of England*. The *Institutes* compiled over 400 years of English law, stretching all the way back to the Magna Carta. Sir Thomas

Littleton, a fifteenth-century English judge and knight, wrote a treatise perhaps somewhere between 1465 and 1475 on the law of real property, the core of the English common law, entitled *Tenures*. Then in the early seventeenth century, at the time of Queen Elizabeth and King James I, Coke, who had been appointed chief justice of the Court of Common Pleas in 1606 and chief justice of the King's Bench in 1613, brought Littleton's work up to date and expanded it. His famous commentary on Littleton, entitled *The First Part of the Institutes of the Lawes of England; or, a Commentarie upon Littleton, Not the Name of the Lawyer Only, but of the Law Itselfe,* was published in 1628.

Jefferson spent a year wading through Coke's notoriously difficult four-volume *Institutes,* which are laced with Latin and French and demanding in form, content, and length. As he wrote in a letter to a friend: "I do wish the Devil had old Coke, for I am sure I never was so tired of an old dull scoundrel in my life." Jefferson began with the *Commentary on Littleton,* which is part gloss on the land law and the English constitution (which, as far as I know, still has not been physically located), part exposition on principles of jurisprudence and interpretation, and part learned free-association.

Broaden Your Horizons

The general lack of diversification in legal study has posed persistent problems throughout the history of legal education. Coke's advice to prospective law students was to first attend a university and study subjects such as philosophy before studying law. This was advice that Jefferson followed with a vengeance—even while studying law.

Between the ages of nineteen and twenty-four Jefferson essentially trained to become a legal philosopher, studying up to sixteen hours a day. He read treatises on the common law (Littleton, Bracton, and Coke); on ethics, religion, and natural law (including Cicero); and on politics. In this context, it is interesting to note that when Jefferson set out to draft the Declaration of Independence, although having none of his books with him in Philadelphia, he drew freely from such political and legal scholars as Aristotle, Cicero, Grotius, Vattel, Burlamaqui, Domat, and Locke. For example, it has been pointed out by scholars that when Jefferson declared, in axiomatic form, that "all men are created equal" and are "endowed with certain inalienable rights" (evidence of the founding era's commitment to constitutional law based on natural law and rights), he was elaborating ideas that originated in classical Greek philosophy and were later shaped by Roman and European thought.

Jefferson followed his study regimen while many of his friends spent much of their time hunting, gambling, staking out western lands, and "wenching" among their slaves. Even the more serious students studied law for no more than a year or so. Future U.S. Chief Justice Marshall, for example, studied under Wythe for a whopping three months. Jefferson's seeming overkill stemmed not from fear about actual legal practice or about leaving his role as George Wythe's surrogate son, but from recognition of his good fortune at having the opportunity to study in Williamsburg.

After leaving Williamsburg, Jefferson, as stated by one legal historian, "was admitted to the bar of the General Court, the [Virginia] colony's highest, in 1766 [1767]. At twenty-three [twenty-four] he was the youngest member of the superior court bar, joining an elite group of only six other practitioners. In his eight-year practice he accepted more than nine hundred cases and provided numerous opinions, but like other practitioners of that time, he found it hard to collect fees [so what else is new?], which were fixed by statute and collectible only at the conclusion of a case." Jefferson collected only about £43 in fees in 1767, while approximately £250 owed to him for professional services remained unpaid. His most profitable year as a lawyer was 1770, when he collected about £531.

The primary focus of Jefferson's brief practice was in property law—yes, including slaves. Much of it involved traditional real property issues: acquiring and defending title. But he also used a fair amount of his legal skills in drafting instruments to control and transfer human property, much of "it" his own. He settled slaves on his daughters and sons-in-law's plantations when they married, bought and sold slaves through legally enforceable contracts, and drew up documents and provided legal advice for other buyers and sellers of "thinking property"—an extremely valuable "commodity" in antebellum America.

A Strange Distinction

Although not opposed to people owning people, Jefferson was generally opposed to people owning ideas. As a one-time U.S. patent commissioner, he thought ideas were "like air" and therefore should not be owned. Consequently, he rejected patent applications at the slightest excuse.

On the upside, Jefferson did become one of the small and unpopular group of attorneys who took slave freedom cases on a pro bono basis. Like a number of other lawyers, Jefferson was conflicted by the institution, opposing it on principle but owning slaves to run his plantation.

XXV

DANIEL WEBSTER (AND THE DEVIL)

Daniel Webster started his study of law in late summer of 1801, shortly after his graduation from Dartmouth. He, like Jefferson, was nineteen.

Also like Jefferson (and unlike our next case study, Abraham Lincoln), Webster apprenticed in a law office. He decided to study in his hometown of Salisbury, New Hampshire, with a neighbor by the name of Thomas W. Thompson. Young Webster studied at Thompson's office for about two years, reading a modest selection of treatises, such as those of Vattel, Coke, and the important addition to legal literature by Blackstone (in contrast to the numerous volumes consumed by Jefferson), and without much supervision (in contrast to George Wythe's hands-on approach). The interesting part of Webster's early studies was that he contracted a growing reservation about becoming a lawyer. He somehow came to suspect that his chosen career was too materialistic, but often not particularly profitable, and that it could frequently be intellectually dull. It occurred to Webster that he might not have what one scientist has called "optimum intelligence": "bright enough to see what needs to be done but not so bright as to suffer boredom doing it."

In 1804, Webster joined his brother in Boston. Despite his creeping concern about entering law, he arranged to study with the well-known lawyer Christopher Gore. During his nine months in Boston, Webster progressed more rapidly than he had in Salisbury. Under Gore's guidance, Webster was exposed to a wider range of materials, particularly in his mentor's specialty of maritime law. He also had the

261

advantage, being in the heart of Massachusetts, of observing some of New England's best attorneys in both state and federal courts.

Yet Another Category of Law

The law of the high seas and maritime commerce (admiralty) was a rival of the common law—recall, for example, the transfer of revenue act violations to the admiralty courts discussed earlier. Admiralty had an international tradition that was separate from the common law. As a result, the English courts of admiralty, starting in the sixteenth century, came into conflict with the common-law courts. In the United States, admiralty law remains a unique specialty, with its own licensing requirements.

Webster was admitted to the bar in the spring of 1805 and decided to set up his practice just down the road from his hometown. His office, in the village of Boscawen, New Hampshire, was a room that a merchant had added to his house. It was extremely sparse, with a bed in one corner and no books.

For two years Webster traveled the circuits of the country courts of common pleas in order to gain the experience necessary to practice in the Superior Court. In addition to the physical demands of travel, the bulk of this work was not particularly satisfying (confirming his worst fears, as well as a common modern-day complaint). It generally involved representing firms from Boston and Portsmouth that were attempting to collect payments from country merchants for goods the firms had sold to them. In one case Webster sued his own landlord, Timothy Dix, a local merchant, for overdue notes. Webster, however, eventually evened out accounts by representing Dix in a proceeding against his debtors.

In 1807 Webster moved from Boscawen to the comfort of Portsmouth. Debt collection, however, was still the main bulk of his work. He, in fact, handled several cases involving his new landlord, William Wilkins, who was eventually forced to close his store below Webster's office. Some of the actions were against Wilkins and some were on behalf of Wilkins against his debtors. Apparently the young Mr. Webster never met a conflict of interest that he couldn't overlook.

Webster's election to the United States House of Representatives in 1812 significantly affected his legal practice. The demands on his time forced him to take on an associate—young Timothy Farrar, Jr. Farrar managed the New

Hampshire office while Webster was in Washington. And his presence in the capital gave Webster the ultimate opportunity as a trial lawyer: practice before the United States Supreme Court.

In 1816 Webster started thinking about jumping into the thick of commercial activity: either New York or Boston. He eventually settled on Boston and set up shop near the hustle of banks, mercantile houses, and insurance companies. As an attorney and politician, Webster led the charge for his commercial clients. His fees, historically never totaling more than $2,000 annually, began to climb, providing him with an income between $10,000 and $15,000 per year.

The Era of Big Boston

Prior to the completion of the Erie Canal in 1825, New York City played second fiddle to Boston. The Canal made Gotham the entrepôt for the vast agricultural output of the Midwest, which flowed through the Canal to the Hudson River. These days, in a historical shift, there appears to be increasing pressure on Boston law firms to catch up with the big New York firms.

With the growth in America's economy came a rise in banking and a word that makes a lawyer's heart skip a beat: complexity. The financial institutions spawned new issues for lawyers such as Webster to explore, as common-law rules were modified by legislators and courts. The trend was not to regulate financial development but to stimulate it. And true to Webster's disposition to take on either side of an issue, he represented not only banks but also, occasionally, parties claiming damages from banking misbehavior. For example, he accepted the case of a client suing the Gloucester Bank based on its alleged carelessness in allowing theft and forgery of certain notes. He lost—the court ruled that it was not the bank's fault. Nevertheless, it was just this kind of case that eventually earned Webster the romanticized image of being a champion of causes for the common man.

In addition to banking law and a bit of criminal law, Webster handled a number of admiralty cases—undoubtedly due to the training he had received from Christopher Gore. This specialty led to a highly profitable business before the Spanish claims commission in the early 1820s.

The 1819 Florida Treaty provided that the United States was to assume its citizens' claims against Spain, up to $5 million, for the seizure of ships during the Napoleonic wars. The administration of this agreement was vested in a commission established by Congress. Webster, along with other attorneys, represented claimants and received a percentage of any awards. It is arguable that the large percentage fees were justifiable. Documentation of a claim was time consuming and difficult long after the actual seizures had taken place. In mid-1824, as soon as the final report of the commission was issued, Congressman Webster helped move an appropriation's bill through the House of Representatives, and then lawyer Webster collected approximately $70,000 in legal fees. Again, there was clearly no conflict of interest that Webster couldn't overlook.

It is, however, his practice before the United States Supreme Court that is Webster's enduring legacy as a lawyer. For the first twenty years of his thirty-eight years before the Court, he appeared before a court headed by the dynamic Chief Justice John Marshall (a student of George Wythe). The Chief Justice, along with former law professor Joseph Story, was a nationalist and protector of property rights against state infringement—and no friend of his relative Thomas Jefferson. With regard to questions of governmental powers, Webster's success rate, given his Federalist leanings, was high—specifically including his passionate defense of the autonomy of little Dartmouth College, a privately chartered institution, from virtual appropriation and control by the evil empire of New Hampshire; his defense of the Bank of the United States against the Anti-Federalists; and his victory in the Hudson River steamboating case. But starting in the mid-1830s, Webster began having much less success before the Jacksonian-dominated Court of Chief Justice Roger B. Taney. Taney and his associate justices were less disposed to favor broad, exclusive national power vis-à-vis the states or to sanction special economic privilege. So is the practice of law science or art? Or simply the luck of the draw?

⚘ · ⚘

Federalism versus States' Rights

In 1801, when John Marshall was appointed as chief justice by President John Adams, the Federalists (spearheaded by Alexander Hamilton) were just about finished as an organized political force. They were not, however, extinguished ideologically. Marshall, a Virginia Federalist, turned the United States Supreme Court into a Federalist redoubt, using the Court to rein in states' rights and to prevent local politicians from interfering with the sanctity of business contracts. The Litchfield Law School, located in Litchfield, Connecticut, provided a curriculum suffused with Federalist principles, ensuring that the defeated party's public philosophy remained an integral part of the county's discourse for generations to come.

⚘ · ⚘

Chief Justice Taney, one of the great justices in the history of the Court, is generally remembered for his decision in the infamous *Dred Scott* case. Dred Scott was a slave transported by his master from the slave state of Missouri to the free state of Illinois, then to an unorganized federal territory north of the old Missouri Compromise line, where slavery had long been prohibited, and finally back to Missouri. Following his return, Dred Scott sued for freedom on the grounds that once having set foot in free territory, he was free forevermore. When the case reached the United States Supreme Court, Taney declared the Missouri Compromise of 1820 to be unconstitutional and on that basis denied Dred Scott's claim that he was free by virtue of his having crossed over into the northern territories. In essence the Chief Justice, a strong proponent of states' rights, adopted the position that the federal government's role in the territories was limited to that of caretaker until such time as they were ready to be carved up into states. Only then, Taney asserted, would the citizens of the new state decide whether they were to be pro- or antislavery. It is also the case that the Court, for the first time, recognized that the Due Process Clause of the Fifth Amendment to the Constitution forbids government from interfering with people's liberty or property (remember, Dred Scott, a slave, was legally property) unless it has a very good reason for doing so.

And therefore, surprisingly, there is a direct connection between *Dred Scott* and the 1973 abortion case of *Roe v. Wade*. As pointed out by one legal scholar, the right of privacy, the guiding principle of *Roe,* is part of the Constitution's protection of "liberty" under the Due Process Clause.

XXVI

ABRAHAM LINCOLN:

THE MAN WHO MISTOOK HIS HAT FOR A FILING CABINET

ON AUGUST 4, 1834, Abraham Lincoln was elected to the Illinois House of Representatives from Sangamon County. He was twenty-five years old. Out of a total of thirteen candidates, four were chosen and one of them, besides Lincoln, was John Todd Stuart, a young Springfield attorney. Stuart had crossed paths with Lincoln during the campaign and advised him to become a lawyer, since it was the surest road to political success. Lincoln had, in fact, been considering the law for some time but had not pursed this career path due to his lack of formal education. It appears, however, that he had argued (without compensation) a few cases before New Salem's justice of the peace and had served on juries in Springfield—experiences that strengthened his interest in the legal process.

Lincoln was particularly impressed with the Springfield bar because many of its members had not gone to law school, or even to college. Encouraged by Stuart, Lincoln decided to launch into the study of law. He borrowed a number of books from the firm of Stuart and Drummond and went home to New Salem to start reading—at least until the legislature convened in December.

When the legislature adjourned in February 1835, Lincoln left the state capital of Vandalia and returned to New Salem to resume his studies. Many students of the law, as we saw in the case of Thomas Jefferson and Daniel Webster, read under the tutelage of an established attorney. Lincoln, however, toiled away on his own. He studied principally from Blackstone's *Commentaries*, Greenleaf's *Evidence*, Chitty's *Pleadings*, and Story's *Equity*. He often rehearsed cases out loud—analyzing a legal point, not unlike Vinnie and Sal, from various angles.

In March 1836, the Sangamon County Court registered Lincoln as a man of "good moral character." It appears that he was admitted to the bar, having received his license to practice on September 9, 1836, before Illinois instituted a bar exam. He then went right to work on his first case, involving three related suits over disputed farmland and oxen. His final step in becoming a lawyer did not take place, however, until March 1837. It was in that month that the clerk of the Illinois Supreme Court finally got around to enrolling his name.

John Stuart, who had come down to Vandalia to lobby for Springfield to become the state capital, invited Lincoln to join his law firm. Lincoln accepted. The day Lincoln arrived in Springfield, the local newspaper carried an announcement that Stuart and Drummond had dissolved their partnership and that Stuart was now practicing law with "A. Lincoln." Their office was located in Hoffman's Row across from the public square.

During the next four years the new partners got along well. Stuart coached Lincoln in the practical aspects of litigation and Lincoln drafted pleadings with precision. Their practice expanded—they once handled sixty cases in a single term of the Illinois circuit court.

In January 1840 Lincoln argued his first case before the Illinois Supreme Court, the highest court in the state. And by the end of his legal career he had participated in hundreds of cases before that tribunal—winning many of them.

Lincoln the Lawyer

Lincoln's legal skills have often been praised based simply on a numerical analyses of the number of cases he "won." At least one legal historian has pointed out that this is an unsophisticated approach to the question. The reason is that while Lincoln quantitatively won slightly more cases than he lost, sometimes the court compromised the issues so that a seeming loss was in fact a win and a seeming victory was in fact a loss. This observation highlights the fact that it is often hard to numerically judge the competency of a trial lawyer.

❖ · ❖

In May 1841 Stuart and Lincoln dissolved their law firm by mutual consent. The reason was that Stuart was constantly in Washington, leaving Lincoln to attend to the firm's bookkeeping and clerical chores, all of which he hated. Lincoln quickly moved across the street and formed a new partnership with Stephen T. Logan: Logan and Lincoln. Logan, a shriveled little man with frizzled red hair and a shrill voice, proved to be an excellent senior partner for Lincoln. He was precise and meticulous, with a broad command of the philosophical and practical aspects of the practice of law. Having practiced in Kentucky for ten years, Logan had moved to Springfield in 1833, served as a circuit-court judge, and became the leader of the Sangamon bar.

With their combined talents, Logan and Lincoln built their law firm into one of the busiest in Springfield. They all but monopolized litigation before the Illinois Supreme Court. Consequently, by the mid-1840s Lincoln was pulling in over $1,500 a year—just about the hourly rate of some modern-day New York lawyers.

❖ · ❖

Give Peace a Chance

Antebellum lawyers, who took their status as republican mediators seriously, were encouraged to run their offices like little chancery courts. American lawyers therefore frequently saw themselves as peacemakers and not as hired guns. Lincoln was no exception; he made every effort to settle matters outside the context of litigation.

❖ · ❖

Logan and Lincoln, in December 1844, dissolved their law firm by mutual agreement. Logan wanted to go into business with his son and Lincoln was tired of being a junior partner. The future president of the United States was now thirty-five and wanted to run his own firm.

Lincoln took on William Henry Herndon, nine years his junior, as an associate. Herndon had been studying law with Logan and Lincoln and had just received his license. It appears that Lincoln's main reason for taking on this inexperienced partner was his belief that Herndon would make an excellent office lawyer—meaning that Herndon would attend to case preparation while Lincoln rode the circuit, as well as bill clients, organize files, and handle all the other details that are generally necessary for a successful practice. Herndon was also a young politico and Lincoln, on the move from a leading member of his community to a full-fledged lawyer-statesman, was scheduled to run for Congress in 1846. He wanted the support of the younger Whigs and believed that Herndon might be influential with this up-and-coming group.

Due to Lincoln and Herndon's capacity for hard work, they were quickly handling over 100 cases a year and drawing in business on a regional basis. Lincoln's notion of Herndon as an organizer was, however, wrong. Dead wrong. The second-floor office of Lincoln and Herndon soon reached maximum chaos: papers were stuffed in drawers, piled in boxes, and stacked on desks and tables. The two partners constantly lost things and visitors often found Lincoln or Herndon thrashing about in search of documents. Lincoln even stored papers in his stovepipe hat; he once had to write a letter of apology when he got a new hat: "[W]hen I received the letter, I put it in my old hat and buying a new one the next day, the old one was set aside, and so the letter was lost sight of for a time."

Ridin' the Circuit

Touring around with the circuit judge from one county seat to another, as Lincoln and others did, helped maintain legal standards and kept alive a tradition of professional ethics. But with the rise of urban centers and the increasing importance of client-caretaking, the circuit bars substantially disappeared in the latter part of the nineteenth century. In part this helped to usher in what Roscoe Pound, former dean of the Harvard Law School, has called the "Era of Decadence" (1836 to 1870).

In the early 1850s Lincoln rose to the top of the Illinois legal profession despite his lack of neatness. (I take great comfort in this fact.) He had, by then, earned a reputation as a first-rate general practitioner and litigator, displaying a direct and simple approach to the practice of law, a talent with words, and an extraordinary skill in the organization of materials in order to clearly strike at the heart of a matter. And because of his ability to sway judge and jury, he represented people of all classes and became one of the most respected attorneys in central Illinois. He in fact developed a reputation as a "lawyer's lawyer" and argued appellate cases for other attorneys, including one oral argument before the United States Supreme Court. His annual salary rose from $1,500 a year in the mid-1840s to around $5,000 a year.

Illinois lawyers like Abraham Lincoln charged relatively modest fees and therefore depended upon handling a large volume of cases in order to generate income. Lincoln's three two-lawyer partnerships handled over 6,000 cases. The fee book for Stuart and Lincoln reveals fees ranging from $2.50 to $50.00. Logan and Lincoln received fees in the range of $10 to $100 for cases appealed to the Illinois Supreme Court. And the fees charged by Lincoln and Herndon were about the same as those charged by Stuart and Lincoln—despite Lincoln's increased experience as a lawyer and fame as a politician.

Shocking as it may be, Lincoln, like many lawyers, generally took on cases as they came to him, regardless of the "justice" involved. In other words, he did not practice law from a fully theorized perspective. (Few lawyers can afford this luxury—despite what their law professors may preach.) For example, in different cases he represented both sides of the fugitive slave issue. There were, however, times when he turned down cases because he was not comfortable with the possible consequences of his actions as an advocate. In one such situation, based on a type of means–ends analysis, he rendered the following advice to a man seeking legal assistance:

> Yes, we can doubtless gain your case for you; we can . . . distress a widowed mother and her six fatherless children and thereby get you six hundred dollars to which you seem to have a legal claim, but which rightfully belongs, it appears to me, as much to the woman and her children as it does to you. You must remember that some things legally right are not morally right. We shall not take your case, but will give you a little advice for which we will charge you nothing. You seem to be a sprightly, energetic man; we would advise you to try your hand at making six hundred dollars in some other way.

But whatever the cause, once he accepted a case, Lincoln, like Vinnie and Sal calling God to testify under oath, pursued it zealously. In selecting a jury, he was especially meticulous—analyzing prospective jurors with both practical logic and with his own biases. He once prepared, for example, a three-page annotated list of prospective jurors for a murder trial. Using the technique of categorization, he grouped fat men into the category of ideal jurors, believing that they were jolly by nature and therefore easily swayed. He rejected people with high foreheads because they had already made up their minds, and considered blond, blue-eyed men inherently nervous and apt to side with the prosecution.

⊠ · ⊠

Voir Dire Secrets

During the past two decades, an entire cottage industry has developed around the notion that an expert can predict what a juror will do based on demographic factors such as age, race, sex, and socioeconomic status. There are, however, still those lawyers that, much like Lincoln, rely largely on instinct and/or heuristics when selecting a jury. But whether based on "scientific theory" or "folk theory," the lawyer's job is to attempt to skew the normal distribution curve that society believes exists by averaging the views of twelve (and sometimes fewer) citizens.

Additionally, Lincoln's criteria of weight, forehead height, hair color, and eye color do not run afoul of any of the United States Supreme Court's principles of equality in jury selection—at least so far. Starting in 1880 the Court intervened in the process of jury selection by striking down, as a violation of equal protection of the laws, a statute prohibiting African Americans from serving on juries. And more recently, the Court has moved into the area of peremptory challenges (removal of a potential juror whom a lawyer suspects of bias but as to whom he cannot convince the judge that his intuitions are correct), prohibiting lawyers from discriminating in jury selection on the basis of race and sex.

⊠ · ⊠

Lincoln handled a wide range of cases, from murder and rape to divorce, wills, property matters, maritime law, and patent infringements (largely arising from rival manufacturers rushing to meet growing agricultural demands). And in criminal matters he might be found on either side of a case: serving sometimes as defense counsel and other times as court-appointed prosecutor. (As an interesting aside: Lincoln is the only United States president, at least so far, to be issued a patent: No. 6,469, for "A Device for Buoying Vessels Over Shoals," dated May 22, 1849.)

In the 1850s Lincoln became known as a railroad lawyer. This reputation started with his representation of the Illinois Central Railroad in *Bailey v. Cromwell.* In this case Lincoln persuaded the Illinois Supreme Court to exempt railroads from county taxes because they were "public works" and already paid taxes to the state. He and Herndon, from this point on, regularly defended the Illinois Central and various other railroad companies. It was a time of extensive railroad construction all over the Midwest and this growth created a lucrative area of legal practice for both Lincoln and Herndon.

An interesting footnote to the case of *Bailey v. Cromwell* is that Lincoln had to sue the Illinois Central for the bulk of his $5,000 fee. Lincoln apparently forgot the lawyer's most important credo: "Show me the money!"

XXVII

CLARENCE DARROW AND THE MONKEY MAN

IN OUR WALKABOUT OF MODERN-DAY LAWYERS and their history, it seems especially appropriate to take a look at Clarence Darrow (1857–1938) for two reasons: (1) Unlike the other lawyers we have just considered—Jefferson, Webster, and Lincoln—Darrow's fame rests not on being a president or a senator, but just a hard working trial lawyer; and (2) his involvement in the Scopes monkey trial helped focus public attention on the rise of science in defining the way twentieth-century humankind would come to view the world.

Clarence Darrow, at the age of thirty, closed his law office in Ashtabula, Ohio, and headed for Chicago. He had grown tired of his small-town practice and wanted to make a name for himself. Chicago, however, was full of ambitious lawyers. As a result, during his first year of practice in the Windy City he raked in about $300—but this was only a temporary setback. Darrow had two important things going for him: a penchant for liberal causes and strong oratory skills (i.e., rhetoric). Both of these attributes quickly brought him to the attention of Chicago's reform-minded citizens and into a power position among the local Democrats. By 1889 he was hired to serve as legal counsel for the city. Two years later he became legal counsel for the Chicago and Northwestern Railway.

Being egalitarian (although apparently not toward women) and antiestablishment in orientation did not, however, always mix well

273

with his tasks as a big-time corporate lawyer. Darrow, in defending the railroad in personal-injury suits, frequently found himself sympathizing with the plaintiffs, whom he saw as victims of corporate greed. He was not able, or at least not willing, to compartmentalize the contradictory moral demands of this representation from his personal feelings. This led to his break with Big Business in 1894—thereafter becoming, like Webster (at least in popular perception), a champion of people and causes. In that year workers at the Pullman Company's railcar plant near Chicago struck over a wage cut. As a gesture of sympathy, the American Railway Union members voted to stop working any trains using Pullman cars. This act, if carried out, would have had national ramifications. Therefore, railroad management and government authorities decided to seek an injunction designed to kill off any competing legal understanding of the Union's actions regarding the secondary boycott. Lawyer-President Cleveland in fact called out the troops, and the attorney general (who was a railroad shareholder) asked for an injunction against the Union president, Eugene V. Debs, calling on him to stop disturbing the railroads' business. At the time, courts were handing out labor injunctions like penny candy. Between 1880 and 1920, state and federal courts, in an attempt to avoid the cost involved in the form of a strike, issued almost 1,000 such injunctions—including one against the American Railway Union. But the Union continued the strike, and its president, Eugene V. Debs, was imprisoned. Darrow immediately resigned as legal counsel for the Chicago and Northwestern Railroad and enlisted himself in labor's cause.

Darrow was vigorous in his defense of Debs and the Union. His courtroom attack on railroad management proved so effective that the criminal conspiracy charges against his client were dropped. Debs, however, was found guilty of violating a federal injunction and sentenced to six months in jail. This fight firmly established Darrow as a champion of the working man and made him, for the next fifteen years, one of the best-known legal spokesmen for organized labor.

The Anti-Darrow

There was also a lawyer-champion for Big Business, union-buster and crime-fighter Franklin B. Gowen. Gowen, who started apprenticing with a coal trader and later turned to law, briefly served as district attorney of Schuylkill County, Pennsylvania. In 1867 he moved to Philadelphia to become legal counsel to one of the mighty railroads. Within a short time Gowen was no longer merely legal counsel but began running the Reading Railroad.

In contrast to Darrow, Gowen was a champion of the "gospel of Bigness" for American industry, vigorously fighting the coal miners' newly formed union. In fact, through a series of brilliant political moves he was able to convince the state and the general population that the Molly Maguires, who had for years tried to advance the interest of coal-mine workers, were in fact a secret organization of Irish Catholic terrorists. As a result, scores of suspected Mollies were rounded up and tried in the spring of 1879.

Now for the really good part: Gowen not only managed to have some of Allan Pinkerton's private detectives gather information on the Molly Maguires though undercover informers, and then use his private Coal and Iron Police to round up suspects, but he also arranged to have himself appointed as special prosecutor for the state of Pennsylvania.

Gowen appeared in court arrayed in formal evening wear and electrified the audience with his oration. He presented a case not just against five murder suspects but against all the Molly Maguires. And in order to get to the heart of the matter, he made sure to make his prosecution, at least by strong implication, against the miners' disbanded union. Gowen was so successful in his case that the press blamed the Molly Maguires for all the labor violence by miners during the hard-fought strike of 1875. And after a series of trials, twenty Mollies were hanged, and twenty-six more imprisoned.

❀ · ❀

But in 1911 Darrow's labor image was fatally tarnished by the *McNamara* case. Union organizers James and John McNamara were accused of masterminding a bombing of the offices of the anti-union newspaper, the *Los Angeles Times*. Darrow took up their defense.

It appears Darrow led the union rank and file, who had raised thousands of dollars to pay his fee, to believe that he thought the McNamaras were innocent. But at trial, the defendants, on advise of counsel, plead guilty. Even though the plea was the result of clear and convincing evidence that the McNamaras were guilty as charged, various labor organizations felt Darrow had betrayed them.

Like his early days in Chicago, this was only a temporary set back. By the early 1920s Darrow's legal specialty had changed from primarily civil to principally criminal. And in 1924, at the age of sixty-six, he reinvented himself (again) and took on a case that earned him the title of "attorney for the damned." His clients were Leopold and Loeb.

Nathan F. Leopold, Jr. and Richard Loeb, young men from wealthy Chicago families (and most likely lovers), decided to commit the perfect crime. Using the pretext of a kidnapping, they murdered a fourteen-year-old boy named Robert "Bobby" Franks in cold blood. Their self-proclaimed criminal genius was, however, lacking a bit in reality. When questioned by the police, they soon confessed. By the time Darrow took the case, the mission was no longer to get Leopold and Loeb off, but to save the two boys from being hanged.

The atmosphere in the community, and consequently in the courtroom, was strongly against his clients, due in no small part to their families' substantial wealth—the very reason they were able to engage a famous, high-priced lawyer. (Interestingly, the fact that they were Jewish did not enter into the picture—most likely because Bobby Franks was also Jewish.) Darrow, however, turned the wealth issue against the prosecution by arguing that had the two boys been from poor families, not a state's attorney in all of Illinois would have hesitated in dropping the death penalty for a guilty plea. In addition, he argued Leopold and Loeb's case with such passion, moving the judge to tears, that the court rewarded his efforts with life sentences for his clients.

⊠ · ⊠

The Chicago Way

There is some indication that the judge's tears during the Leopold and Loeb trial may have been helped along by a bribe paid to the judge out of Darrow's substantial fee. Darrow was not above paying a bribe or two in order to help a case move in the "just" direction.

⊠ · ⊠

Now for the crowning moment in Darrow's career—his loss to William Jennings Bryan.

In 1925 Darrow was sixty-seven and, in the sweltering heat of Dayton, Tennessee, acting as trial counsel for the high school teacher John T. Scopes. The issue involved the teaching of biological evolution.

Tennessee had passed the Butler Act, prohibiting the teaching of evolution in public schools. The American Civil Liberties Union, in reaction to this statute, announced its search "for a Tennessee teacher who is willing to accept our services in testing this law in the courts." Civic leaders in Dayton saw an opportunity to revive the town's sagging economy. In other words, law and economics Writ Large. They were, however, unable to convince the regular biology teacher to participate and so drafted John Thomas Scopes, a coach and math/chemistry teacher, into the cause.

The local judge called a special grand jury to indict Scopes. The relevant statutes, however, provided that a special grand jury could be called only if certain conditions existed prior to the time the regular grand jury was scheduled to reconvene. The applicable conditions did not exist but the teaching of evolution was a crime that simply had to be prosecuted—the maximum penalty being $100.

Shortly after the arrest of Scopes, Darrow was in New York. He read that democratic politician and Presbyterian William Jennings Bryan (1860–1925), at the request of a religious group, had volunteered to go to Dayton to assist the prosecution. It appears that Darrow's principal interest in the case was to bring to America's attention the program of Bryan and other Christian fundamentalists. He saw their agenda as a threat to education.

What is often not brought out in the telling and retelling of the Scopes trial, besides the fact that Bryan was a Democrat and an economic populist, are the full range of Bryan's motives for resisting the teaching of evolutionary theory to children. One was that during this time period, many evolutionists were pushing for changes in the law in order to allow for the forced sterilization of "inferior stock." In fact, not long after the Scopes trial, the U.S. Supreme Court, in sync with the great Progressive cause of eugenics, upheld a sterilization law in Virginia that eventually resulted in more than 7,500 sterilizations of "mental defectives." There is evidence that at least 60,000 forced sterilizations occurred in the United States between 1907 and 1960. This historical context certainly lends support and understanding to Bryan's concern that if humans are depicted as just another animal, they will treat each other as animals. After all, why allow inferior stock to breed?

The Designer-Baby Debate

Charles Darwin's half-cousin Francis Galton (1882–1911) started the eugenics movement with his forays into the inheritance of such characteristics as genius, feeble-mindedness, and criminality. In fact he coined the term "eugenics" ("good in birth" or "noble in heredity"). And according to one legal scholar, "the science of eugenics is likely to reappear [in the twenty-first century], albeit with a different appellation. The science of behavioral genetics might one day permit us, among other things, to design babies, enhance ourselves, and identify those among us who are prone to violence." A more modern way of viewing and dealing with Original Sin?

In line with this concern is the fact that the 1914 book allegedly used by Scopes, *A Civic Biology,* portrayed eugenics side-by-side with Darwin's theory of natural selection as a scientific method to improve humankind. Epilepsy and feeble-mindedness, according to the text, "are handicaps which it is not only unfair but criminal to hand down to posterity." Under the book's heading "The Remedy," students read that "if such people were lower animals, we would probably kill them off to prevent them from spreading." (Prior to the 1920 census, most people in the United States lived on farms; this subjunctive, casu-istic reasoning ["if/then"] probably didn't sound quite so repugnant to them.)

The point is that "legal" issues are not always as clear-cut as popular cul-ture sometimes portrays them. It is therefore important to keep in mind the rules of rumor and their effect on any relevant cost-benefit analysis and always ask yourself: What, if anything, has been leveled, sharpened, and assimilated? (Consider, for example, the so-called "Twinkie Defense" in the 1979 trial of Dan White for the assassination of Supervisor Harvey Milk and San Francisco Mayor George Moscone.) Inquiring minds should want to know.

Bryan had not tried cases for many years—in fact, he had not been all that successful as a practicing lawyer in Illinois or Nebraska in the 1880s. But the Scopes trial was not really a court case. It was a public forum: Part of the trial was even held on the courthouse lawn with a crowd of more than 5,000 in attendance, and around the courthouse there were banners and lemonade stands. Chimpanzees, said to be witnesses for the prosecution, performed in a sideshow on Main Street. The trial was somewhat in the same vein as the animal and insect trials discussed in Part V, in which the debate was over how society should view science and religion and how we should view each other. More than 100 magazine and newspaper representatives were present. Bryan was up for the challenge, having sharpened his oratory skills on the lecture circuit. His lecture tour on "The Prince of Peace" was said to have had men and boys clinging to the rafters when there were rafters, and to tree limbs when there were groves.

Darrow, on the other hand, was a seasoned trial lawyer and had been exposed as a boy to existing scientific theories. His father, the town's vocal atheist, had stocked the house with Thomas Huxley's books and books by and about Charles Darwin. And so the opposing intellectual and emotional forces that gathered in the little town of Dayton, Tennessee, were strong.

If I Were the King of the Forest . . .

William Jennings Bryan had been a Populist senator from the farming state of Nebraska and a perennial Democratic candidate for president during a con-sistently Republican era. He campaigned tirelessly for bimetallism, the use of both silver and gold as a monetary standard. And as a result, 76 percent of Nevada voters voted for lawyer-Democrat Bryan in the 1896 presidential election—though he lost to lawyer-Republican William McKinley.

Although Bryan continued to run for office, he never won a national election. However, with the election of Woodrow Wilson, the first Democratic president since the Civil War, Bryan was appointed secretary of state in 1913. He resigned in 1915 when it became clear that Wilson was leading the United States toward involvement in the war in Europe.

It is interesting to note that the cowardly lion in L. Frank Baum's *The Wonderful Wizard of Oz* (a satire of the U.S. monetary policy at the opening of the twentieth century) represents William Jennings Bryan. And you thought that it was just a kid's story.

The first round of confrontation concerned the fact that the judge had Brother Twitchell open court with prayer. After adjournment on the first day of trial, Darrow and the rest of the defense team went to the judge and objected to opening the proceedings by calling upon God. The lawyers for the prosecution appeared shocked at this objection. Prayer, in their opinion, could do no harm.

Prior to the start of the next session, Darrow renewed his objection to opening the court with prayer. The judge overruled the motion and promptly appointed a committee of church members to provide a preacher to begin each day with prayer. (The judge obviously desired to display his impartiality.)

Darrow realized from the beginning that the jury was not going to allow Scopes to get off scot-free. There were, however, questions to be argued regarding the statute's meaning, and the power of the legislature to make the teaching of evolution a criminal offense. Legal stuff.

Darrow's strategy, harking back to Aristotle, was to introduce expert testimony as to the meaning of the word "evolution" and whether the theory was inconsistent with "religion" under proper definitions of both words. The state of Tennessee, on the other hand, called a number of Scopes's students to the stand. These students told how Scopes had tried to poison their young minds and imperil their souls by telling them that life began in the sea from a single cell. On cross-examination, the boys admitted, however, that they did not see how Scopes's teaching had done them any harm. (In order that the student witnesses could honestly testify that Scopes taught them evolution, Scopes tutored them in the backseat of a taxi prior to the trial. This almost forgotten fact is a good example of how factual truth can yield to symbolic truth—which is, after all, the deeper meaning of the *Scopes* trial.)

The judge decided to admit, out of the jury's presence, one of Darrow's witnesses to give testimony on the meaning of the word "evolution" and to describe the process. The expert was Dr. Metcalf from Oberlin College. Then in a Perry Mason–like twist, Darrow called Bryan to the stand as an expert on the meaning of the word "religion." After a flurry of objections and arguments Bryan stood and said that he was perfectly willing to take the stand—provided that Darrow would do likewise. Darrow agreed.

Darrow started by probing into Bryan's qualifications to define religion—especially fundamentalism. Bryan testified to his lifetime of study, lecturing, and writing on Christianity and the Bible. In particular he pointed out that he had been active in getting the statute under which Scopes was charged through the Tennessee legislature and in urging the enactment of similar statutes in other states.

Darrow then proceeded to ask Bryan questions that brought out points illustrating the fundamentalists' ideas of religion: Was the earth really made in six days? Was Eve really made from Adam's rib? Was Jonah really swallowed by a whale? Bryan, according to Darrow, "twisted and dodged and floundered, to the disgust of the thinking element, and even his own people."

The next morning Darrow was prepared to continue his outdoor grilling of Bryan in front of thousands. The judge, however, announced that he had been thinking it over: Despite Bryan's willingness to take the stand, the judge had decided that the testimony was not relevant. Consequently, there would be no further examination of Bryan, and his prior testimony would be stricken from the record. Darrow later stated that the attorneys for the prosecution (one of whom, Sue K. Hicks, was apparently the "Boy Named Sue" of Johnny Cash's hit song) could see the effect Bryan's answers were having on their case and the public in general. They concluded that something had to be done and went to the judge. The court's ruling was also extended to exclude any further testimony by the defense's expert on the meaning of "evolution."

In the end, the court summarized the case by stating that the jury had the statute before them and had heard the testimony of the witnesses. The evidence showed that Scopes had told his students that life began in the sea and had slowly evolved into the various life forms, including human, that are upon the earth. The State had offered in evidence the first and second chapters of Genesis, and the jury, according to the judge, could decide whether these were in conflict with Scopes's teaching. Having leveled, sharpened, and assimilated the facts and the law for the jury, it took only minutes for a verdict to come back: "guilty."

Darrow, Bryan, and Intelligent Design

The judge deprived Bryan of the chance to examine Darrow. Bryan had spent years collecting highly speculative guesses of intellectuals relating to evolutionary theory. He had numerous examples of ludicrous materials that were widely available at the time, such as the development of the eye by chance as a light-sensitive freckle. Bryan would have undoubtedly used this material to illustrate that the highly speculative theories coming from the intellectual community should be critically evaluated. Not a bad idea—especially coming from a Bible-thumping lawyer.

It is also interesting to note, with regard to the eye, the difference in chance versus teleology. While the human eye might not have developed from a light-sensitive freckle, chance may still have played a role. On the other hand, some argue that the complexity of the eye is a clear sign, not of chance, but teleology. The fact that the simple parts of the eye function in an ingenious way is, in other words, proof of "intelligent design." And intelligent design means an intelligent "designer" (read: God). Hence the fight taken up by Darrow and Bryan continues on in the twenty-first century.

XXVIII

THE BREEDING GROUND FOR LAWYERS: LAW SCHOOLS

I⊤'s NOW TIME TO PULL BACK THE CURTAIN and take a peek at the breeding ground for most modern-day lawyers: no, not sex again, but exactly the opposite—law school. In order, however, to gain a deeper understanding of this institution and to bring together many of the concepts discussed so far, we will start at the beginning.

MESOPOTAMIA

Although it is perhaps not exactly mainstream thought, I have come to the conclusion that the first law schools were located in Sumer. While it is true that there were no tweed-clad professors molding students' minds to think along strict legal lines, these ancient schools arguably embraced some of the most important concepts underpinning law and what lawyers are all about: categorization, casuistic reasoning, narrative, and rhetoric.

The curriculum of these Mesopotamian schools, whether private or endowed by the "state" (for instance, Yale Law School versus the University of Michigan Law School), was divided into two main groups: semiscientific and literary. On the semiscientific side, the aim was to teach budding scribes how to write the Sumerian and Akkadian languages. To accomplish this difficult task, the teachers classified the vocabulary of the two languages into groups of related words and phrases, a task near and dear to the hearts of modern-day lawyers—grantor, grantee, consideration, "grant, bargain, and sell," habendum, reddendum, and so on, all magical elements related to the purchase and sale of real estate. And most important for our purposes, this system of instruction influenced what constituted a sign in nature from the gods and how it should be read and dealt with (as discussed in Part II). This semiscientific view—classifying and categorizing nature *is* science, though the part about the signs from gods isn't—also spawned the preparation of mathematical tables, the study of Sumerian grammar, and the eventual preparation of dictionaries.

On the literary side of things, the scribes, influenced by narrative and rhetoric and in turn influencing narrative and rhetoric, were steeped in studying, copying, and imitating a large and diversified group of poetic information: myths and epic tales in forms of narrative poems celebrating the deeds of gods and heroes; hymns to gods and kings; lamentations regarding the destruction of Sumerian cities; and wisdom compositions including proverbs, fables, and essays. All these tasks at least hint at various modern-day thoughts regarding law and literature; for example, that law is poetry (both being drenched in metaphor).

One of the specific semiscientific/literary skills required of an aspiring scribe was mastery of the legal terminology and clauses that he would use in recording a formal court case or in drafting a contract between private parties. In order to accomplish these important skills, the scribal curriculum often included a multitablet series of thousands of Sumerian and Akkadian legal terms and formulas of exercises that focused the student's attention on a narrow series of laws or contract formulas relating to a single theme. These lessons would be used to draft the contracts needed in daily life. In addition, there were those scribes at the top of their class, the law review elite of their time, who were chosen by rulers to help collect, organize, and publicize formal law collections and cases.

ANCIENT GREECE

In ancient Greece, what might loosely be considered law schools were wrapped up in the "universities": Plato's Academy, for example, nestled in the shady grove of Academus. And throughout various cities, particularly Athens, members of the Stoic school could be seen arguing points of law, rhetoric, and justice with Peripatetics (followers of Aristotle); Epicureans taking on Orphics;

the hippie-like Pythagoreans shuffling around with their long hair, capes, and sandals; and the iconoclastic Cynics sporting unkempt beards.

Various Sophists seem to have also provided instruction in the "practice of law." One such teacher was Protagoras (c. 480–411 BCE). Legend has it that a man named Euathlus persuaded Protagoras, the founder of sophism and the first teacher in ancient Greece to charge money for his lessons, to teach him rhetoric and argumentation. Euathlus didn't have the funds to pay Protagoras during the course of instruction but promised to pay the hefty enrollment fee after he won his first case. Protagoras agreed to the student loan and taught Euathlus rhetoric and argumentation—perhaps too well. Because the student tried to get out of the deal by refusing to accept cases, Protagoras was eventually forced to sue for the fee. The case was heard before the court of the Areopagus.

Protagoras's argument was that he would either win the case or lose it. If he won it, Euathlus would have to pay him by the judgment of the court. If he (Protagoras) lost the case, then Euathlus would have to pay him pursuant to the terms of their agreement, because Euathlus would have won his first case. So Euathlus must, according to Protagoras, pay either way. Brilliant!

The learned Euathlus, however, met his professor's argument with a counterattack. He argued to the court that "I will either win this case or lose it. If I win it, then I need not pay Protagoras by the judgment of the court. If I lose it, then I need not pay him under our contract [because Euathlus still would not have won his first case]. So I need not pay him either way."

And the answer is . . . ? It depends on whether or not you are speaking of logic or law. (They are not, as you know, always the same.) From the law point of view there are a number of solutions that are unavailable to the logician— such as, the contract could simply be reformed in equity and Euathlus ordered to pay *quantum meruit* ("how much was it worth") for the time Protagoras had devoted to his instruction. Nevertheless, reflexivity dilemmas as well as other types of logic problems pop up in the doing of law with surprising frequency. (Can a clause in a contract providing that the contract cannot be orally amended be, itself, orally amended?) Their importance, however, in defining the nature and practice of law often goes unnoticed—unless, of course, the lawyer has been lucky enough to have received his or her legal training from the likes of a Protagoras.

It has been observed that some of the Greek academics, in contrast to Protagoras, were not intensely focused on molding young minds around high concepts. Instead it appears that these luminaries frequently led their students into extracurricular activities. Cicero's son, Marcus, found that during his study-abroad program in Greece the professors invited him to more banquets than lectures. His oratory tutor became his drinking buddy—the stuff of certain teacher-student relationship rumors at my law school. They in fact became such close friends that Marcus rented him an expensive place on a street close to where he was staying.

THE ROMAN EMPIRE

For centuries, legal instruction in the Roman Empire was based on an informal, personal relationship between teacher and pupil—something that generally does not exist in modern-day American law schools. The pupil attended the teacher's consultations and joined him, together with other admirers, for discussions on legal issues. During the first century of the Common Era, these purely personal relationships developed into two distinct schools or sects. It has been speculated that their emergence was the result of an increasing tendency by the jurists toward a more definite professionalization.

The two schools were called the Proculiani and the Sabiniani (or Cassiani). Tradition has it that the eminent jurist Marcus Antistius Labeo, a contemporary of Caesar Augustus, was the founder of the Proculiani school and his contemporary, the technically weak but well-connected Gaius Ateius Capito, was the founder of the Sabiniani school. However, there is speculation that the organization of the schools might actually have been the work of three outstanding jurisconsults active during the middle of the first century CE— Sempronius Proculus, Marcus Massurius Sabinus, and Sabinus's successor, Gaius Cassius Longinus.

The organization and teaching methodologies used at these schools is not known in any depth. They seem to have been less concerned with substantive issues than with methods. According to one scholar, "The Sabinians tended to justify their opinion by referring to traditional practice and to the authority of earlier jurists [i.e., custom and practice]. They were primarily concerned with finding just solutions to individual cases, even if this meant abandoning logic and rationality. When interpreting texts, they were not worried if the same words were given different meaning in different texts [a nod toward pragmatism]. The Proculians, on the other hand, favored strict interpretation of all texts and insisted that words and phrases should, in every case, be given an objective, consistent meaning."

A specific example of a Proculian versus Sabinian controversy surfaced in the context of marriage. By the time of Caesar Augustus, a female had to be at least twelve years old to marry—but whether she had reached puberty was irrelevant. In the case of a male, however, he had to be fourteen and have reached puberty—at least according to the Sabinians. In fact, contrary to the Proculians, the Sabinians not only required that the groom be pubescent but they also demanded proof by physical examination. No puberty, no marriage.

It has been speculated that the Proculians and Sabinians were most likely not schools in any strict sense of the word. Rather than organized classes and methodical instruction, they were probably clubs of jurisconsults and their apprentices who gathered for informal discussions, through which opinions were exchanged and the young men informally trained. It is possible, with regard to this training, that there might have nevertheless been a certain amount of organization. It appears, for example, that leading jurisconsults succeeded each other as the heads of the two schools (like law school deans) and jurists were connected with either one or the other school, held together by bonds of personal loyalty.

Burden of Proof

> Even though "proof" was an important part of the Greek and Roman legal tradition, neither of these Western societies have a claim on its invention. Take the following middle Assyrian law (c. 1076 BCE, Assur): "If a man sodomizes his comrade and they prove the charges against him and find him guilty, they shall sodomize him and they shall turn him into a eunuch." There is, however, no indication as to how the charge was to be "proved" (victim testimony? physical examination? both?) or, if proved, who the "they" is that are to sodomize the defendant (the judges?). Nevertheless, the important point is that the ancient societies of the Near East recognized the importance of proof in legal matters long before the Greeks or the Romans.

The basics of legal education, prior to the fall of the Roman Empire, became increasingly formalized and were eventually taught in all the significant cities of the East and West. The most famous provincial school, as discussed in Part IV, was that at Berytus, on the Phoenician coast, which flourished for at least three centuries. This Harvard of the ancient Middle East is known to have existed in 239 CE and its start was perhaps even earlier—possibly during the reign of Septimius Severus (a native of Africa, of—no surprise here— Phoenician stock). There was also, like Stanford in the West is to Harvard in the East, a well-known law school in Rome.

Under Justinian, the length of law school training in the Eastern Empire was increased from a few years to five years—three years of formal instruction and two years of private study. The extra time was needed in order for students to digest all of the "new" law—the *Codex, Digest,* and *Institutes*—as the focus of training was on reading classical legal writings and imperial constitutions (both of which were embodied in Justinian's *Corpus*). In addition, Justinian's reform of legal education was of great importance to his government. The reason for this was that the law schools of the time focused not so much on training men to handle civil disputes, but on the training of civil servants to administer their responsibilities with efficiency and justice. Consequently, Justinian instructed his imperial lawyers "to regard the population paternally, to protect them against injustice, to take no bribes, and to show themselves equitable in their judgments."

The fact is, however, that even in the East knowledge of classical literature (or what was thought to have come from the classical period) by the average legal expert went into serious decline. But the lawyers of the East avoided a complete jurisprudential meltdown as a result of two factors: the ancient law school at Berytus and, from around 425 CE, the law school in Constantinople—resulting in the development of a "Byzantine legal science." Both of these schools, although originally private, were brought into ever-closer connection with the imperial government during the fourth and fifth centuries. Salaries for their "teachers of the universe," for example, appear to have been paid by the government after 425 CE. And in the fifth century certificates of attendance of law courses at one or the other of the schools were required by those who desired to practice before the highest courts of the Empire—those run by the *praefectus praetorios.*

It is also the case that during the eighth and ninth centuries, four Sunni (orthodox) schools of law came into being. These Islamic schools—Hanafi, Shafi'i, Maliki, and Hanbali—had their differences, but when compared to their similarities, the fissures were slight. And it was the Maliki school, which had spread out primarily over North Africa and Sicily, that represented the face of Islamic law to the West and arguably influenced and perhaps even created the early English common law.

AFTER THE FALL

With the fall of the Roman Empire, the West plunged into the Dark Ages. As a result, there were no longer law schools of any vigor. (Perhaps the Dark Ages, depending upon one's point of view, were not quite so dark.)

Western Europe, however, slowly dug itself out of this pit. In the eleventh century, the major law school was in Pavia, the capital of the Lombard kingdom—the old stomping grounds of the Teutonic "long beards." The focus of study and teaching for its jurists was on Lombard law as contained in the *Liber Papiensis,* a collection of the edicts of the Lombard kings prior to

Frankish conquest and of Frankish capitularies. Setting aside Jewish midrashic techniques, it appears that the jurists of Pavia were the first jurists to use the method of the gloss alongside the text. And on matters of substance, the competition at the law school was between those who adhered to the traditional understanding of the Lombard texts (called the *antiqui*) and those jurists who were characterized by their readiness to accept Roman law as a supplement to Lombard law (called the *moderni*).

According to one academic: "The jurists of Pavia did not give particular attention to the *Digest* [of Justinian], because Roman law was not their prime concern. Their concern was the law of the Lombard kingdom and their aim was to ensure that judges and advocates in the Lombard courts were properly prepared. They recognized the value of Justinian's texts indicating a sense of legal reasoning but they did not study those texts for their own sake. They were interested less in the juristic arguments of the *Digest* than with what could be gleaned from the Roman sources about the nature and purpose of the law in general."

After the West's rediscovery of Justinian's *Digest,* there were those, in contrast to the students and teachers at Pavia, who were very interested in this exotic text. These individuals were so intrigued that they started gathering together and hiring teachers to expound on its mysteries. The form of association for these students was a *societas,* a type of partnership. One of the teachers in great demand was Irnerius (c. 1060–1125 CE). Eventually, thousands of students from all over Europe flocked to him each year, as well as the other teachers who joined him. By about 1150, there were 10,000 to 13,000 law students in Bologna. Smell that smell.

As a means of protection against the civil disabilities of alienage, the students grouped together on the basis of their ethnic and geographical origin—composing in all approximately twenty "nations." The different groups (Franks, Alemanns, Angles, etc.) eventually consolidated into two corporate bodies: one comprising all students from north of the Alps (*ultramontanes*) and the other comprising all students from south of the Alps (*cismontanes*). Each of the two main divisions was further organized into a *universitas,* a Roman legal term meaning, essentially, corporation. The professors (*doctores*), were, surprisingly from our modern-day perspective, not members of the universities.

Another Division of Law and Logic

The other original European university was in Paris. This university, in contrast to the one in Bologna, was composed of groups of masters—generally requiring six years of study and twenty-one years of age for the liberal arts, and eight years of study and thirty-four years of age for a master of theology. Whereas Bologna was strong in law, both civil and canon, the university at Paris, grouped around Notre Dame, focused on theology and logic.

In a united "embodied" form, the students placed themselves in a much stronger bargaining position with the city government of Bologna. They also, unlike the largely failed radicalism of the 1960s, dominated the administration of the school.

The student universities obtained from the city of Bologna charters that permitted them to make contracts with the professors, regulate the rents of student lodgings, determine the courses to be taught, and set the rental and sales prices for books. The professors were paid directly by the students in their respective classes. And interestingly enough, if the students felt that they were not getting the bang for their buck, they had the right to refuse to pay that professor. There were also statutes that forbade professors from being absent without leave, and required a master who departed the city to post a deposit in order to ensure his return.

The professors eventually fought back, forming their own association—the *collegium doctorum* (the college of teachers). Members of this association had the right to examine and admit candidates for the doctorate, thereby controlling membership into the teaching guild. This power was later modified by the pope's decree that nobody at Bologna could receive the degree of doctor (and therefore teach) without being examined by, and without receiving a license from, the Archdeacon of Bologna. This church "license to teach" (*licentia docendi*) eventually became a requirement throughout Italy as well as elsewhere.

Focusing specifically on Italy, the jurist Pepo started conducting a school of law at Bologna in the mid-eleventh century. One of his students appears to have been the above-mentioned Irnerius, founder of modern Romanist legal science in the 1080s. It was during the time of papal and imperial conflict that Irnerius applied the scholastic method to Roman law, thus separating the science of law from the practice of law—not unlike what often happens in modern-day law schools. And of particular interest to our current discussion is the fact that Irnerius's patron was Pope Gregory VII's friend, Matilda of Tuscany. It appears that Matilda's concern for the papacy and the Church led her to suggest to Irnerius that he devote his life to the study of Roman jurisprudence. It may also be that Irnerius, who was officially appointed by the emperor as Professor of Roman Law at the University of Bologna, founded the school of Roman law (around 1084) at Matilda's suggestion.

Strange Bedfellows

The rebirth of law schools undoubtedly served the general needs of the papacy, which was engaged in codifying the canon law of the Church along Roman-law lines, as well as the needs of north Italian merchants who desired to recover the law of a commercial society. There was, however, a serious dark side to the establishment of such law schools—besides the creation of lawyers. The subject matter for study was Roman law in the textual form of Justinian's *Corpus*. This meant that all the old Roman disabilities against Jews, at least as embodied in the *Corpus*, were now closely studied in a revered, juristic text. The graduates of these law schools, who frequently went on to important jobs in the state and Church, were conditioned to claim that the Jews (who were doing reasonably well at the time) were evading the controls prescribed by the code and it was therefore time to crack down on them as the law demanded.

As a teacher of grammar, Irnerius initially concentrated on the unusual and difficult Latin terms found in the Roman texts. His discussions with other jurists centered upon the application of rules to particular fact situations. Irnerius, however, soon switched from just explaining interesting words to explaining whole passages—thus making the leap from grammatical to legal analysis. Scholarship has identified this shift in focus as the start of the tradition, very much a part of modern-day law schools, of specialist legal studies. Here were the first glimmerings of the university legal academic—and allegedly the invention of the word "baloney," meaning legal twaddle.

Even though the school was caught up in the excitement of newly discovered Roman law, canon law was soon placed along side civil law as a subject of study at Bologna. The primary teaching method of these canonists involved dialectical reasoning—that method that proceeds by questions and answers, allowing only (in its most restrictive sense) "logical" arguments. But lacking an authoritative body of texts comparable to Justinian's *Corpus,* canon law was generally considered to be inferior and unworthy of consideration as an autonomous discipline. This view radically changed, as least for some jurists, with the appearance of Gratian's *Concordantia Discordantium Canonum.* The *Decretum,* as discussed in Part V, superseded earlier canonist collections and was accepted as a subject worthy for glossatorial exegesis by canonists. The immediate reaction, however, by the dyed-in-the-wool civil lawyers to Gratian's work was to continue to treat canon law as a discipline inferior to their own. (A bit of tribal warfare.) In the opinion of the civians, the civil law provided all the techniques necessary for understanding any kind of law—including canon law.

MEDIEVAL EUROPE

The medieval law schools required the students, in the spirit of the Tanna'im discussed in Part I, to perform considerable feats of concentration and memory. They memorized a vast amount of laws, civil and/or canon, and had to be able to repeat them in the proper order—a lingering tie between law and magic.

It is noted that this medieval focus on memorization has fallen by the wayside. The modern-day law student is not expected to learn, by heart, the rules in force during his or her time as a student—with perhaps the sole exception of the popularized form of the R.A.P. (the rule against perpetuities). This type of factual knowledge would, even if it were possible to accomplish, be of little use in later professional life—since many of the rules will undoubtedly change. Instead the hope is that the student will gain an understanding of the structure within which certain fundamental rules, principles, and concepts are organized, the meaning of various concepts, categories and metaphors ("fruit of the poisonous tree," "under color of law," "marketplace of ideas"), and the relationships between and among them. In other words, the purpose of a law school education is not to teach law per se but to teach students to "think like lawyers"—to become Vinnies and Sals, for good or bad.

It has been observed that in old Byzantium there were most likely just enough qualified lawyers and magistrates to keep the system functioning. Thus a legal system as extensive as Justinian's *Corpus* could not truly be implemented in the expanded and much less homogeneous Western Europe of the early Middle Ages prior to the growth of law schools. It was not until the early thirteenth century that the supply of graduates receiving the degree of *doctor utriusque iuris* (doctor of both laws, canon and Roman) caught up with demand and the rediscovered Roman law system could be widely instituted. This point of critical mass occurred in Italy and France by 1250 and in Germany by 1450.

THE NEW SCIENCE OF GERMANY AND HOLLAND

Universities played a key role in legal education in Germany, in contrast to the apprenticeship/Inns of Court system that developed in England. The early law graduates typically emerged from the study of Roman law taught at the University of Bologna. They generally preferred employment at the emperor's court and the courts of the princes of the territorial states in Germany (not unlike the law students of the Roman Empire who found employment with the court of the Praetorian Prefect of the East). Starting, however, after the rise of the territorial states in the thirteenth century, princes began to establish universities in their own territories in order to meet the staffing needs for expanding judicial, financial, and economic institutions—Mesopotamian scribal schools all over again. These scholarly German universities taught Roman and canon law and were supported by the likes of Martin Luther. It is also interesting to note, with regard to our recurring theme of astrologer–priest–lawyer, that these medieval universities considered Roman law to be one of the classic faculties and therefore separate from theology and canon law.

In the sixteenth century, as previously noted in Part IV, there arose a new legal science, developed primarily in Germany by Lutheran jurists such as Johann Apel (1486–1536), Konrad Lagus (c. 1499–1546), and Nicolas Vigelius.

The Low Countries, after a series of revolts against their Spanish governors, formed the loosely structured Union of Utrecht in 1579. Each of these seven northern Dutch provinces retained its own courts and particular laws. Holland, with its technological innovativeness, was the leader, producing over half of the wealth of the United Provinces, and Amsterdam replaced Antwerp (which had previously replaced its rival Bruges) as the main trading center through which the trade of the Rhine Valley passed.

Along with the Low Countries' eventual domination of the world's commerce came the growth in universities. The first was established in 1575 at Leyden in Holland, where young John Quincy Adams later received some of his pre-law education. This institution's primary mission was to offer a Protestant counterattack to Louvain, the Catholic university in Belgium. It was in the Catholic southern Netherlands (the Spanish Netherlands) that inquisition had chilled the flow of any idea that appeared to threaten the traditional order of things. The faculty of law at Leyden was, from the start, given an important place in this counterattack. The symbolic representation of this elite fighting force's key role was displayed at the formal opening procession: The Holy Scripture and Four Evangelists were immediately followed, in symbolic form, by the Roman jurists Julianus, Papinianus, Ulpianus, and the frequently maligned Tribonian. Roman law—not canon law.

In addition to Holland, most of the major northern provinces also established universities with law faculties: at Franeker in Friesland (1585), Groningen (1614), Utrecht (1636), and Hardewijk in Gelderland (1648). And the law to be taught was primarily created by the Dutch professors, particularly those of Leyden, and by the judges of the High Courts of the provinces. Through their synthesis of a distinctly Protestant legal science and legal practice, the Netherlands led the rest of Europe in the seventeenth century.

THE BEGINNINGS OF MODERNITY

While schools teaching law—primarily Roman and canon law—in Scotland were founded in 1413 (St. Andrews) and 1451 (Glasgow), the depth of teaching was shallow. Consequently, students that desired to study law to any great extent were forced to go abroad, usually to Paris, Orleans, or Cologne. It was not until the eighteenth century that the teaching of law in Scottish universities began to expand and the practice of Scots seeking legal education abroad declined. David Hume (1711–1776), for example, went to Edinburgh University when he was twelve and studied there until the ripe old age of fifteen. His career began in commerce and law. The legal profession, however, gave him a certain feeling, and so at 23, the young Scotsman decided to devote his life to philosophy instead of continuing to feel nauseous. Additionally, with the Union of England and Scotland in 1707, the English common law seeped into (or perhaps more technically, back into) Scotland, resulting in a hybrid legal system that distinctively combined bits and pieces of Roman and English law.

As indicated, the basis of legal teaching in all universities was Roman and canon law. This was the case in continental Europe, as well as the British Isles. Only much later did the teaching of national law even make an appearance. Swedish law snuck in at Uppsala in 1620 and a chair of French law was created at the Sorbonne in 1679, but in many other counties, national law was not taught in the universities until the eighteenth century. It was not until 1707 that the *Deutsches Recht* (German Law) was taught at Wittenberg; national law was not taught in Spain until 1741; at Oxford, not until the Vinerian professorship of common law filled by Blackstone in 1758, and not until 1800 at Cambridge; and in Portugal, it was not until 1772 that Roman law and canon law lost the stranglehold they had on academics at the various universities.

Notably, admissions to the English Inns of Court (discussed in Part V) rose from about 100 per year in the 1550s to about 300 per year in the 1620s. In the period between 1570 and 1640, they enrolled almost 16,000 students and called to the Bar about 2,800 barristers. The scale of increase can be seen by looking at matriculation in the early sixteenth century. Lincoln's Inn, for example, recorded only 164 calls to the Bar in the period between 1520 and 1569, but 628 calls between 1590 and 1639. The Inns of Court together admitted just more than 1,000 in the 1550s and more than 2,700 in the 1610s.

THE LINGERING EFFECT OF THE INNS OF COURT

At this point we need to briefly consider the role of the Inns in modern-day legal training.

An aspiring lawyer in England usually completes his or her academic stage by obtaining a university or polytechnic law degree. This degree is the initial qualification for becoming either a solicitor (office lawyer) or barrister (wig-wearer). University or polytechnic law study is a three-year undergraduate program (in contrast to American legal education, which is postgraduate) consisting primarily of law courses. The focus is on the study of legal institutions (e.g., the court system) and the development of general principles of law. Instruction is usually formal lectures and tutorials. There is a less frequent use of the case method that is heavily relied upon in U.S. law schools, and few clinical or practice courses. A student who desires to be a barrister must then be accepted into one of the four Inns. This portion of the educational process is the vocational stage of British legal education required for entry to practice at the Bar of England and Wales (but not the "strange" hybrid legal system of Scotland). It consists of undergoing a period of training under the supervision of the Inns of Court School of Law, dining at the Inns, and passing the bar examination. Conducted mostly by practicing barristers (versus law professors), the practical exercises consist of advocacy, drafting, court attendance, and a course in professional ethics.

The final stretch for an aspiring barrister is an apprenticeship. This "pupilage" lasts for one year, during which a yellow-wigged barrister instructs the bar student—similar to what Thomas Jefferson underwent in carrying around George Wythe's books and getting his coffee.

As was mentioned in Part V, legal education at the Inns, after study and debate by a select committee of the House of Commons, was revived in the mid-nineteenth century. The Inns, by resolutions passed in 1852, formed the Council of Legal Education. And in response to criticism that legal education lacked standardization and rigor, comprehensive examinations for both barristers and solicitors were required for the first time.

CHINA'S CULTURAL REVOLUTION

Turning briefly to the Far East, the Great Proletarian Cultural Revolution of 1966 to 1976 was disastrous for traditional Chinese law—a consequence of closing law schools and eliminating virtually all legal professionals. It has been said that the most far-reaching consequence was the interruption of higher education that affected an entire generation. Law faculties were abolished and lawyers were "re-educated" by relocating them to farms and factories. The bright spot, for this virtually "lawless" nation, is that we're back! Several new law schools have opened. Tsinghua University in Beijing, for example, reestablished its law school in 1997 and completed an impressive building in 2000.

THE AMERICAS

In the New World, the first university was the University of San Marcos of Lima, founded in 1551. The second was the University of Mexico, created in 1553. In an effort to maintain European values, these "Universities of America" apparently employed not only professors of medicine, theology, and the arts, but also of law.

In the early part of North America's history, legal education, as has been discussed previously, consisted primarily of an apprenticeship system (or the Abe Lincoln–method of going it alone—one that, by the way, also worked out for lawyer-President James A. Garfield). The would-be lawyer often learned his profession by clerking for a number of years in the office of an established lawyer. This system worked well when things were relatively simple—simple law, simple lawyers. But as the knowledge base surrounding the law increased in amount and complexity, pressure for a more formalized, collective educational system grew. And so in 1779 the College of William and Mary, pushed by then Governor of Virginia, Thomas Jefferson, founded the professorship of "Law and Policy." George Wythe, who earlier had signed his name to the Declaration of Independence, filled the chair. This system of legal education reflected, in contrast to apprenticeship, a university-based model of legal education that concentrated not only on private law but also on constitutional and statutory law. Its broader perspective—although not yet established as a separate degree program—spread quickly to other schools such as Yale, Princeton, the University of Pennsylvania, and Brown—"culminating" in the founding of the Harvard Law School in 1817.

TRANSYLVANIA UNIVERSITY—SERIOUSLY

One of the most important post-Revolutionary law programs for the training of lawyers was founded at Transylvania University. Honestly. In 1799 George Nicholas, a student of George Wythe at the College of William and Mary, was appointed to a chair in law at Transylvania, located in Lexington, Kentucky. The University's law program was, not surprisingly, modeled on the chair at William and Mary; thus Nicholas was a "Professor of Law and Politics." Upon his death in 1800, Nicholas was replaced by another Wythe student, James Brown (not the Godfather of Soul, but the brother of Senator John Brown). Henry Clay, another Wythe protégé, succeeded Brown.

The Transylvania program proved to be a bloody success. By 1823, it boasted three teachers of law: Professor William T. Barry, a former U.S. senator and future member of President Andrew Jackson's cabinet; Professor Jesse Bledsoe, a former senator; and Horace Holley, the president of the University. And by 1830, Transylvania was, thanks to the efforts of the dynamic Henry

Clay as trustee and patron, the largest university in America, with more than 400 students. Following the tradition of George Wythe, Transylvania recruited public men to train a younger generation of republican leaders, preparing them for public life. The Civil War, however, drove a stake through its heart, and the school merged with Kentucky University in 1865. It returned to the Transylvania University name in 1908, but sadly, has no law school attached.

THE LITCHFIELD LAW SCHOOL

Yet another competing model of legal education in the emerging intergroup tournament was embodied in the Litchfield Law School, founded in 1784. This system, like the university-based model (whether integrated or separate), refined the apprenticeship approach to legal education. But in contrast to the university-based model, the Litchfield Law School had a narrower approach—with lectures centered on the common law, excluding criminal law and governmental agency.

The Litchfield Law School, located in Litchfield Connecticut, was founded by Tapping Reeve, a practicing lawyer who had realized that the most enjoyable part of his practice was the instruction of his clerks. The enterprise proved to be a temporary success and by the time the school closed the doors of its one-room white clapboard facility in 1833, more than 1,000 students had passed though its fourteen-to-eighteen-month curriculum of daily morning lectures, afternoon study period, and weekly moot court sessions.

The astonishing influence of the Litchfield Law School is evidenced by the success of its graduates. It has been said that in proportion to the size of the school's alumni, there has perhaps never been a professional school in America that has produced more graduates of public distinction. Its output included six federal cabinet officers, two Vice Presidents, more than one hundred Congressmen, twenty-eight U.S. Senators, fourteen state governors, three Justices of the United States Supreme Court, and thirty-four members of the highest courts in their respective states, including sixteen Chief Justices or Chancellors. In addition, the school's Federalist agenda seeped into many of its graduates, their respective communities, and the marketplace.

In 1797, after the tragic death of his wife, Reeve was ready to devote himself full-time to teaching the law. At this same time, however, a vacancy occurred on Connecticut's highest court and Reeve was offered the position. Despite some reluctance, he accepted and became a member of the Superior Court. This decision not only forced him to close up his law practice but also to find a partner to assist in managing the law school. He quickly settled on James Gould (1770–1838)—a smart young lawyer who had graduated first in his class at Yale in 1791 and who had been an outstanding student at the Litchfield Law School during 1795.

It has been observed that Reeve and Gould possessed exactly the right combination of personalities to make the school a success. Reeve was a brilliant man consumed by passion. He took people's problems to heart and argued their causes in the courtroom with a force unmatched by any of his contemporaries. He was also the town's beloved eccentric—a ruddy-faced, portly, absent-minded professor who was known to often misplace important legal papers and to wander down Main Street still holding the bridle of a horse that had broken free blocks before.

In contrast to Reeve's eccentricities, Gould was the peak of refinement and mental discipline. He was an exceedingly polished individual with dashing good looks. His in-court approach was philosophical but always to the point, and his ability to identify the central legal issue of a case in a matter of seconds was legendary.

The Eyes Have It

The skill of "thin slicing"—seeing the central issue immediately—is not limited to lawyers. As Malcom Gladwell in *Blink: The Power of Thinking Without Thinking*, has stated: "It is striking [. . .] how many different professions and disciplines have a word to describe the particular gift of reading deeply into the narrowest slivers of experience. In basketball, the player who can take in and comprehend all that is happening around him or her is said to have 'court sense' [not a bad phase to describe Gould's, Webster's, Lincoln's, and Darrow's abilities]. In the military, brilliant generals are said to possess 'coup d'oeil'—which, translated from the French, means 'power of the glance,' the ability to immediately see and make sense of the battlefield [not a bad phase to describe Demosthenes's and Cicero's abilities]."

It has been observed that the cultural forces that inspired the Litchfield Law School—namely a Federalist counteroffensive against mass democracy and economic uncertainty—ensured that it would have certain distinctive characteristics: institutional independence, a professional or post-collegiate character, a national student body, a vocational focus, and a religious/social/political spirit that transcended pure personal or pecuniary interests. This does not mean, however, that the worldly aspects of practicing law were overlooked. Young men and their families knew (or were properly informed) that a lawyer who received his training with a systematic guide to the "science" and practice of law had a significant advantage over his competitors.

The Litchfield Law School reached its peak of enrollment between the years 1813 and approximately 1825. During this period, enrollment generally ran between forty-five and fifty-five students. But with the establishment of Harvard Law School in 1817 and Yale Law School in 1826, Litchfield began to lose its ability to attract students. At the same time, Gould—now Judge Gould, having joined the Connecticut Superior Court in 1816—who had been the sole proprietor of the school since Tapping Reeve's retirement in 1820, was beginning to have health problems. In 1833 he retired and with him ended America's first venture into independent, institutionalized legal education.

The school's demise was a combination of factors: the permanent defeat of Connecticut's old-line political leadership known as the Standing Order; the rise in sectional tension, which dissuaded Southerners from sending their children north for legal training; the publishing of thorough commentaries on the law; the general relaxation in educational requirements for the admission to legal practice brought on by "Jacksonian democracy"; and perhaps most important, as indicated above, the proliferation of law schools affiliated with a university. In other words, the school's death was led by inner-judges activating their self-destruction machinery. And adding to the tragedy was the fact that Litchfield had sowed the seeds of its own demise. Its methods were copied and modified by other schools, primarily through Litchfield graduates, who were among the leading legal educators of the time.

THE DAWN OF THE UNIVERSITY SYSTEM

The Harvard Law School is the oldest existing "school of law" in the United States (as early as 1642, Harvard College offered lectures on "Ethieks and Politicks"). It was founded as an adjunct of what was to later become Harvard University, America's oldest corporation (chartered in 1636), and is credited with developing the "Socratic method" of teaching used by most American law schools. This method is a type of brain-salad surgery in which the professor, through a series of hopefully probing questions, challenges a student's analytic abilities.

As far as the record shows, Harvard Law School started with one student—Charles Moody Dustin. This number, however, dramatically increased to six during the school's first year, 1817–1818.

Harvard began its venture into structured legal education with the creation of the Royall Professorship of Law in 1816. Isaac Parker, who was Chief Justice of the Supreme Judicial Court of Massachusetts, was appointed to this chair. He was an early proponent of law as a separate and distinct area of study and outlined the separation of general or liberal arts education and legal education, with a liberal arts education as a prerequisite for law studies in the United

States. Parker, said to be good-natured but lazy, was given wide latitude in carrying out his role. The core requirement was to deliver a series of lectures covering law and government each week. They were conducted three or four times a week at the reasonable hour of ten o'clock in the morning, and appear to have been broad and rather shallow.

The first formal description of the school's method of instruction is set out in Professor Asahel Stearns's January 9, 1826, report to the Board of Overseers. This report highlights the following regular exercises:

1. Recitations and examinations with regard to several of the more important textbooks such as Blackstone's *Commentaries*. In these exercises the differences between the common law of England and American or Massachusetts law were brought out and discussed;

2. Written lectures on the law in which those parts of the United States system of jurisprudence that differ from the English system were pointed out;

3. A moot court in which questions were argued, frequently at length, before the professor, who rendered a decision. Professor Stearns specifically noted "that no other exercise is so powerful an excitement to industry and emulation or so strongly interests the students in their professional pursuits";

4. Debating clubs, including all the members of the law school, that met once a week in order to debate various questions (generally involving moral philosophy, political economy, or civil polity) with the idea of improving extemporaneous speaking; and

5. Dissertations by the student upon some title or branch of the law or the history of some department of legal or political science.

During its early years, Harvard Law School was a collegial place among its white male students (with emphasis on the white and male). The Ames Moot Court competition eventually became the intellectual equivalent of a school football team, and groups like the Pow Wow Club and Lincoln's Inn were important social organizations.

As can be surmised by the existence of a "Lincoln's Inn" and Professor Stearns's 1826 report, there was a strong English influence in the early days of the law school. This influence, however, tended to weaken at Harvard and throughout American jurisprudence as judges and academics adapted "English law" to the circumstances of a new continent and then to a different political system. The "heretic" St. George Tucker, for example, edited Blackstone's *Commentaries* in 1803, eliminating from this bible the most offensively royalist sentiments and adding notes on the few American legal sources then available.

Up to 1870, the date of the somewhat reclusive Christopher Columbus Langdell's arrival, Harvard Law School was largely a genteel enterprise with few objective standards. In general, what was required of a young man entering its curriculum was that he be of "good moral character"—meaning, basically, not female, African American, or a part of the Irish nationalist movement. It was thought that since all of the students were honorable gentlemen there was no need for tests designed to measure how much a student had learned. (Where was this enlightened notion when I went to law school?) All this changed under Langdell, who, looking like a Lombard jurist, wore a long white beard and often donned a dark eyeshade with green lining in order to cut down on the glare of the library's reading lamps. During his tenure as dean (1870–1895), the school's eighteen-month course of study was lengthened to two years and then, in 1899, to three; admissions standards were set and became increasingly rigorous; and the system of dreaded annual examinations of first-year students was instituted. Langdell also saw to it that the school's long-neglected library received attention, and by the early twentieth century its collection of legal writings had become one of the most distinguished in the country. At the time of Langdell's retirement as dean in 1895, the Harvard Law School had begun to set a new standard of excellence. Its success in the marketplace made the school, for good or bad, a frequently copied model for reforms at other American law schools—including adoption of a narrower model of legal education.

One of Langdell's greatest influences was not, however, the institutional structure of legal education, but the way in which law students were—and still are—taught. Even prior to arriving at Harvard, Langdell was convinced that the traditional way of teaching, whereby students were simply told the rules of law, was largely ineffective. The lazy Isaac Parker lecture method was out. Langdell maintained that the most important learning took place in the detailed "scientific" examination of actual reported court cases. Through this method a student, using his analytic powers, could discover not only the relevant rules of law but also the principles behind them—the *why* behind "don't touch the fruit." It has been noted, however, that this Langdellian transition to the case method was touched with a bit of irony. It was during this same period that the leadership of the legal profession was passing from courtroom lawyers to the office lawyers who sought to avoid litigation—focusing instead on boardrooms, corporate reorganizations, and deal making, subjects that are arguably best taught by tackling problems, not old cases.

Harvard's decision to employ the case method also constituted, at least implicitly, a refusal to train lawyers for, or even to acknowledge the existence of, all the new tasks needed for understanding statutes, administrative records, and procedures, the financial structures of corporations, and large-scale transactional work such as mergers and reorganizations. It turned a blind eye to the increasing complexity of late nineteenth-century society and the interconnectedness between business and social technologies. And even though the case method focused on litigation, it provided no training in actually conducting a trial, drafting pleadings and motions, or even in arguing an appeal—all the stuff young Jefferson learned from George Wythe.

The Dangers of Ill-Training (and Prejudice)

A number of Jewish lawyers from the Bronx and Brooklyn learned on-the-ground legal techniques in the 1950s and 1960s because of the narrow-mindedness of the lawyers of the time. As noted earlier, white-shoe law firms stayed away from hostile corporate takeovers and litigation in general. The old-line Wall Street firms, representing the country's largest and most prestigious companies, handled taxes and the raising of money, managed stocks and bonds, and made sure their clients were in compliance with federal regulations. This meant that "unfit" work was farmed out, and it was this work that was taken on by a number of bright, hard-working Jewish lawyers—outsiders to the establishment.

The 1970s, however, changed all this. Along with easier credit, relaxed regulations, and international markets, investors became more aggressive, and the result was a spike in the number and size of corporate takeovers—along with accompanying litigation and, most important, huge legal fees. But despite the potential competition, a number of Jewish lawyers and law firms thrived because they had already built up a substantial expertise in takeovers and litigation and were therefore prepared to assist a range of new clients.

In an 1894 paper delivered at a meeting of the American Bar Association, Woodrow Wilson expressed his disillusionment with legal education, especially the Harvard-initiated case method. According to one academic, Wilson, later to become America's twentieth lawyer-President, "warned against a narrow education that looked at nothing but the law and ignored the broader historical, economic, and sociological context in which legal development took place. He urged a broad liberal arts undergraduate program as the necessary prerequisite for law school, much like his own training at Princeton years earlier."

Most American lawyers probably remember their first day in law school when they were required, thanks to Langdell, to read not an overview of the law or of a particular area of the law, but a case. This is not something that could necessarily be said to be a logical starting point for the subject matter at hand. The feeling is a little like skipping algebra and geometry and starting with trigonometry. (The study of law, unless given over to the economists, never reaches the mind-boggling limits of calculus—OK, maybe there is the R.A.P., mentioned earlier, but modern-day lawyers have been desperately attempting to kill it.)

Additionally, Langdell was a common-law "top-downer," in which particulars are subsumed under general rules and high-order principles govern all lower-order functions. In reasoning from this acropolitan position, the lawyer or judge or law professor adopts or invents a theory about an area of law or law in general and then uses this theory to accept, reject, or amplify the decided cases in order to make them conform to that theory. For example, one might adopt the theory that the law should maximize efficiency and that a system of negligence law is economically more efficient than one of strict liability. Based on this general theory of law and specific theory of torts, the law, when moved inside a courtroom, should require proof of negligence. For Langdell, the leading cases (rejecting the "aberrant" ones, a luxury not generally afforded mathematicians or scientists), in line with the top-down approach, provided the means by which a person could discern the pure concepts of law. He believed law should be treated as a formal system composed of a set of concepts and rules. The lawyer, in Langdell's view, strives to discover them by studying decided cases.

Langdell's case method, despite its various problems, is a reasonable approach to "legal reasoning" and is therefore, at least arguably, a reasonable way to teach the law (supported by the fact that lawyers swing both ways, deductively and inductively—as well as abductively). Yet when Langdell instituted this approach in his course on contracts in 1870, most of the students revolted and classroom attendance plummeted. It appears that it is not always easy to lead a student to enlightenment—even at Harvard.

THE RACE PROBLEM

In addition to pedagogical disputes, American law schools have been caught up in problems of race—a persistent prototyping effect based on a tradition of prejudice. Young Thurgood Marshall (later a justice of the United State Supreme Court), for example, had originally wanted to attend the University of Maryland's law school. Marshall instead attended the segregated Howard Law School, where he was groomed by Dean Charles Houston. Later, when Marshall was a successful civil rights litigator, he and Houston took on the University of Maryland. While the school offered no legal education for African Americans, it did provide nominal scholarships so that eligible students could go to law school outside the state. In other words, study and practice law—just not here. However, one Mr. Murray wished to stay at the University of Maryland, and therefore filed suit—represented by the able Thurgood Marshall and his mentor, Dean Houston. Murray won before the trial court, and H. L. Mencken, Baltimore's famous man of letters, wrote that "there will be an Ethiop among the Aryans when the larval Blackstones assemble next Wednesday."

Marshall, pursuing an incremental attack on discrimination, went on to argue against the exclusionary ways of the University of Texas Law School. In this important case of the 1950s, Marshall convinced the United States Supreme Court that the makeshift African-American law school thrown together in an attempt to comply with the notion of "separate but equal" articulated by the Court in the 1896 case of *Plessy v. Ferguson* was objectively inferior to the facilities of the Caucasian law school. Chief Justice Frederick Vinson explained that "a school's alumni, its prestige and influence, and its history were all to be considered when comparing it with any other school." To coin a phrase: no kiddin', Colonel Mustard—just see how far you get with a silk-stocking, white-shoe law firm after graduating from West Undershirt Law School versus Harvard Law School. Separate is rarely equal.

TODAY'S U.S. LAW SCHOOL

In the United States today, the study of law, whether at Harvard or West Undershirt, is a three-year postgraduate course generally entered into after study in any number of fields. The possession of a baccalaureate degree after four years of undergraduate education (and an "acceptable" score on the law school admissions test, or LSAT) is generally mandatory in order to be admitted to an ABA/AALS-approved law school.

⊗ · ⊗

LSAT Origins

In addition to logic and analysis, the LSAT focuses on reading. But certain academics are concerned that abilities in logic, analysis, and reading are not sufficiently predictive factors for selecting students that will become successful and effective lawyers. They see psychological elements such as passion (Johnnie Cochran and Barry Scheck), engagement (Clarence Darrow), and the ability to see the world through the eyes of others (Abraham Lincoln) as equally important, along with practice-oriented skills such as influencing and advocating (Cicero), networking and business development (Quintilian), and strategic planning (Thomas Jefferson).

⊗ · ⊗

As discussed previously, this educational process is, however, a relatively recent addition to the practice of law, at least in America. Men like Abraham Lincoln could become successful lawyers with little formal education. In large part the reason for this was the low standard of education in nineteenth-century America. But as this standard rose, challenges to the exclusivity of the profession (translated into dollars) increased, and admittance standards for the profession followed. The beginning of this upward educational movement can be generally traced to the arrival of Langdell at Harvard. His program of educational reform was explicitly based on the premise, not of his invention, that law is a "science." This premise then led him to the conclusion that to become a lawyer, like becoming a scientist, required years of university training.

Blinded by Science

In addition to Langdell's influence at Harvard, legal education standards also began to increase with the rise of the Progressive Era (c. 1900–1917). It was during this Era that the bureaucratization of the state apparatus, the movements for civil service reform, and the articulation of legitimate principles highlighting the role of expertise all contributed to establishing the state's "neutrality." As a result, a favorable climate existed for asserting the legal profession's (scientific) neutrality and independence. And the growing reliance of the state on scientific and legal expertise operated as a professionalizing and distancing mechanism for the legal profession—including its educational process.

It is also interesting to note that the notion of "scientific" legal education, besides announcing law's neutrality and independence, was used as a marketing strategy by Harvard. In the early days, the law school was attempting to create a model of university-based legal training in the face of the long-standing apprenticeship system, the Litchfield Law School model, and influential foreign law schools. In light of these intergroup tournaments, Harvard used the concept of "law as a science" in order to describe a philosophy of legal education that focused not only on the fundamentals of running a law practice but also on providing training in a broad vision of the law—including the meta-law embodied in the law itself. Only a university-based program, according to Harvard, could provide both the practical and theoretical training necessary for becoming a well-rounded lawyer. And Roman and civil-law training constituted important additional modules to the school's business plan: a PR hook. The average practicing lawyer who could take on students would most likely not have the resources or training to teach his students either of these subjects—both of which, according to the hook, contained important information necessary for a firm scientific understanding of the law. Harvard, and those lawyers and legal scholars associated with the school, therefore flogged the importance of Roman and civil law and the school's ability, without the expense of going abroad, to satisfy this important aspect of a student's legal training.

It's possible that the big hook for the twenty-first century will be the flogging of "hard" science as part of the law student's education. This will not be the same pitch as "law as a science" but one that recognizes that neither a liberal arts education aimed, at least in theory, at preparing students to be critical-thinking generalists nor an education that focuses on giving students the nuts and bolts of legal practice is sufficient. The reality is that the law is an ever-increasing consumer of scientific products: DNA profiling (the O.J. Simpson case), paternity testing (Solomon and the two prostitutes), handwriting identification analysis (the Howard Hughes wills), fingerprinting, bite-mark identification, fiber analysis, hair analysis, tool-work identification, fire and explosion analysis, accident reconstruction analysis, gas chromatography, voice spectrography, global positioning systems (for real property descriptions and disputes), forensic linguistics, the challenges involved in defending DUI charges, et cetera, et cetera, et cetera. And how is a lawyer, besides relying on the TV show *CSI,* to understand the principles behind such scientific products and their application and misapplication to a specific case without at least some basic understanding of math—statistics and probability—and science?

The answer to this rhetorical question can be seen in the increasing cross-breeding between law schools and other university departments, as well as the staffing of law schools with scholars trained in other areas of study. Formal legal training has generally moved from apprenticeship to selected law classes offered within the university system to separate law schools (either associated or not associated with a university) to law schools that are quasi-integrated with various university departments—such as the economics department, the business department, the history department, and even schools of medicine. A growing consilience of knowledge.

Studly Science

It might be important for a lawyer to know whether or not, scientifically, stainless steel has any effect on the results of a breath test. A three-judge panel in Indiana decided 2–1 that the results of a breath test given to a woman suspected of driving while intoxicated were inadmissible because she had a foreign object in her mouth at the time the test was taken. The object? A stainless-steel tongue stud. While the main opinion stated that the defendant was not required to show that the stud affected the test results, the concurring opinion raised the legal-scientific point that the state (meaning the prosecutor) failed to show that the stainless-steel stud did *not* affect the test results. Science is indeed becoming an increasingly important part of legal work.

⌘ · ⌘

ASSOCIATIONS, EDUCATION, AND EXAMS

Professional associations in America, like the American Bar Association (ABA) and the Association of American Law Schools (AALS), do not directly control legal education. They do, however, exert a tremendous influence on its content and format. Specifically, the ABA grants accreditation to law schools that meet its standards (based on inputs into the educational process versus output of qualified graduates), thereby allowing its graduates to sit for bar examinations around the country. In June 2000, Nevada's new (and only—at least so far) law school, the William S. Boyd School of Law, for example, was granted provisional accreditation by the ABA's Council of the Section of Legal Education, with such accreditation to take effect after the Council's report to the House of Delegates at the ABA Annual meeting. The Council's decision was based on a positive recommendation from the ABA's Accreditation Committee, which in turn was based on a report from the ABA site inspection team that visited the school in November 1999. In February 2003 the school achieved full ABA accreditation and then turned its attention to gaining membership in the AALS. Following a site visit by an inspection team in April 2003, administrators of the university and the law school appeared before the Membership Review Committee of the Association in the fall. Based upon the Committee's positive report and recommendation, the AALS's Executive Committee approved the law school's membership in December 2003. This decision was then ratified by the House of Delegates of the Association in January 2004. At this annual meeting, the school popped the cork in order to celebrate its entry into the AALS.

But along with the power to grant accreditation is the power to take it back. In January 2004, Western State University College of Law in Fullerton, California, sued the ABA, alleging that the association was unfairly seeking to strip the school of its provisional accreditation. It appears that the ABA's House of Delegates had in fact been asked to remove Western State, a for-profit law school owned by Argosy Education Group in Chicago, Illinois, from the ABA's approved list.

Additionally, state bar associations, through statewide boards of bar examiners, are responsible for administering the bar examination, but not the education that leads up to the examination. Consequently, most law schools do not structure their curricula around the bar exam but approach the study of law from an academic viewpoint. This approach does not necessarily equip the law school graduate for the immediate practice of law—or for the bar exam. Practice skills are, in theory, acquired during employment, as the American viewpoint stresses the role of experience and training after law school as the means to becoming a competent lawyer.

Bar Exams Abroad

Associations and private practitioners in common-law countries have successfully campaigned for entrance exams, required by the state but administered by the profession. The medieval version of the modern bar examination was the judicial examination of all admission applicants pursuant to a 1402 English statute. In civil-law countries, a bar exam has historically been considered unnecessary, given the importance of the university as a gatekeeper. Law graduates did not have to take professional examinations in Switzerland until 1925 and in Brazil until 1963. In the Netherlands, Belgium, Spain, and Colombia there still are no requirements beyond a university law degree. And where examinations in civil-law countries are required, they are, as in Norway and the first examination in Germany, administered by the university itself or the state—not the profession.

The bar examination in Japan started in 1876. In 1880 the government took control of the examination system. This examination, which is a rite of passage into the *Nichibenren* (the Japan Federation of Bar Associations), is notoriously difficult. This process has given Japan one of the lowest ratios of "lawyers" (*bengoshi*) to population in the industrial world. It is important, however, to keep in mind that this ratio only relates to *bengoshi*—there are many other types of "lawyers" in Japan. (The various types of "lawyers" in Japan are discussed in Chapter XXXIII.)

Due to growing concerns regarding lawyer competency in general, many law schools have added clinical programs. These programs are classified as either "in-house" or external to the law school. In-house clinics allow students to practice and obtain instruction from faculty within the law school on cases that involve real clients. External clinics (called "externships") also involve real clients and cases, but they take place outside the law school in law offices or governmental agencies under a practicing attorney's or judge's supervision.

Much like the old Oral Torah versus the Written Torah argument, many law school graduates are shocked that "the Law" is not always written down in statutes, regulations, and court cases. In the "real world," unwritten rules and local customs, including relationships, power dynamics, and shared understandings between certain participants in the legal process, play an important part at the federal, state, and local levels. One suggested fix for this problem involves clinical legal education. Certain academicians have pointed out that clinical teachers can and should play a key role in preparing students to account for local legal culture and unwritten systems of practices in their future careers.

In broad terms, such preparation, it has been suggested, should include pointing out to students that unwritten rules and customs, as has been the case in many of the cultures that we have discussed in this book, are an important part of both procedural and substantive law. That is, "custom is king." Ferreting out local legal culture and then using it to the client's advantage requires the lawyer to use skills and realize values (including thinking and reasoning processes) that are different from the ones typically addressed in law school classes.

JAPANESE LEGAL TRAINING

The curriculum at Japan's advanced school for legal training, the Legal Training and Research Institute (run by the Supreme Court of Japan), is largely built around clinical programs. The year-and-a-half training period, which follows graduation from the law department of a four-year university and passage of the National Bar Examination, is divided into three terms. The second and lengthiest term is directed at field training. After the first term, which consists of three months of introduction to legal problem studies, legal writing and drafting of legal documents, and trial, each apprentice is assigned to a court for a period of six months, three months civil and three months criminal. This clinical program provides the student with knowledge and understanding of the judicial process. Another three months is spent at a district prosecutor's office. The final three months of the second term is spent as an apprentice at a bar association. And the third term is largely spent consolidating the student's learning from the field experiences.

XXIX

BROADS
AT THE BAR

W<small>HEN</small> G<small>RATIAN</small>, the great canonical legal scholar and monk, wrote: "The woman has no power, but in everything she is subject to the control of her husband," he was merely stating one of the absolute "truths" of the Middle Ages: the inherent and inescapable inferiority of women. The underpinnings for this notion came primarily from the teachings of the Church Fathers. Woman is the daughter of unrepresented Eve and therefore the source of Original Sin. She is inferior to man since she was created from Adam's rib, and evil since she was enticed by the serpent to eat of the forbidden fruit and caused poor Adam to be driven from the Garden. Women, Fruit, and Dangerous Things. Few people in the Middle Ages, at least those of the Christian male persuasion, seriously questioned the truth of this categorization of women. It was the punishment of stigma firmly applied. And because she is inherently evil, a woman needed to be disciplined. Such corrective measures included not only wife-beating but the inability of women to hold public office or serve as a military commander, lawyer, or judge. Secular law justified this view of women on two grounds: (1) that they are by nature light-minded, wily, and avaricious (unlike many lawyers), and (2) that they are of limited intelligence (body over mind).

A (Sort of) Apology for the Chapter Title

OK! I know "broad" is not a politically correct term but, as the father of two intelligent daughters, I wanted to get your attention through the use of this alarmingly alliterative allocation.

Prior to the rise of Christianity and its focus on Original Sin, there is evidence, as noted in Part II, of women scribes in Mesopotamia and ancient Egypt. And even better documented is the evidence that women served as advocates during Roman times. The public-spirited Afrania and Hortensia, for example, took on the role of both lawyer and orator in the late Republic. One should not, however, jump to the conclusion that the pagans of ancient Rome were an enlightened bunch. The truth is that very few women actually served as lawyers—due in large part to the objections that men had to women lawyers, namely that they could be too energetic (the discourse of the hysteric?). In ancient Roman-speak this meant that women were simply ill-suited to the "sit on a rock and think" practice of law favored by the jurists of the time (the discourse of the university). Again, for women it was the perception of body over mind.

A Dubious Distinction

This body-over-mind view of women has not been unique to religion or the law. The great movie director Erich von Stroheim, for example, once said in a meeting that all women are "whores." Louis B. Mayer of MGM expressed his disagreement with Stroheim by beating him, dragging him out of his office, and throwing his cane out after him. So as in religion and law, there have been those in the arts who have been willing to stand up and correct an ancient misperception. But, as Mayer said to his daughter, this did not mean that he thought women were capable of running a movie studio—only that not all of them are prostitutes.

Family members in early medieval England, as noted in Part V, sometimes acted as pleaders on behalf of a litigant. Spouses commonly appeared in this capacity. There is documented evidence that in 1185 a husband appeared on behalf of his wife. Some legal historians have stated that this right to appear as an "attorney" was not limited to men and that women, especially wives, appeared in such capacity. There is documented evidence of a woman appearing on behalf of her husband as early as 1198.

In addition to such early examples of women serving as "attorneys" on an informal basis, there are historical instances of formal female advocacy. The Judiciary records, for example, contain a report of a trial held on June 12, 1563, in which Lady Crawford appeared as advocate in the High Court of Judiciary in defense of a prisoner. Lady Crawford, in fact, obtained an acquittal for her client.

The Modern History of Female Advocacy

Pre-twentieth-century incidences of female advocacy are, however, rare. For example, the legal profession in the British Empire, for all practical purposes, was until relatively recently closed to women.

It was not until January 1920 that the King's Inns in Ireland admitted the first two women to the study of law. One of these students, Frances Kyle, distinguished herself by winning the then-leading scholarly prize for Irish law students. Both she and her comrade-in-arms were admitted to the bar in November of 1921—six months before the first Englishwoman, Ivy Williams, was admitted in England. And it was not until 1923 that the Irish legal profession welcomed its first female solicitor, Mary Heron. Even as late as 1991, only 18 percent of practicing barristers in England and Wales were women.

With regard to modern-day England, Bertha Cave, through some type of mistake, was allowed to join Gray's Inn in 1902. The benchers who ran the Inn eventually realized that an error had occurred and called for a special meeting. Cave's path to a career in the law was cut short by heavy legal reasoning along the following lines: There is no "precedent" for letting women in and therefore a woman should not be let in. An appeal before the Lord Chancellor and a tribunal of eight other judges confirmed the benchers' decision. Formalism at its worst.

In 1914, Miss Beeb, a brilliant Oxford scholar, applied for admission to the Law Society with the idea of entering "articles," the vocational training course for solicitors. The Society objected to this attack on its masculinity but was faced with a small problem. The Interpretation Act of 1889 provided that the masculine pronoun included the feminine and therefore the Attorneys and Solicitors Act of 1729, as well as subsequent legislation concerning admission and education, seemed to apply to both men and women. The Court of Appeals, however, had little problem getting around appearances and denied Miss Beeb the right to sit for the required initial examinations. When "necessary," the law can wreak hell on definitions.

Following the First World War, the tide of public opinion changed. But the only way to force change upon the English legal profession was by statute. So in 1919 the Sex Disqualification (Removal) Act was passed. It was this legislation that made possible Ivy Williams's call to the Bar by Inner Temple in 1922. The first woman solicitor, Carrie Morrison, who had been educated at Girton and with a first in the Modern Language Tripos, also qualified in that same year.

New Zealand has never legally prohibited women from practicing law. The first woman to set up a practice in that country was Ellen Melville. The year was 1909. But simply because there have been no statutes, regulations, or cases preventing women from practicing law does not mean that they have been truly free to set up shop. Remember: Custom is king. Scholarship has pointed out that women have historically felt discouraged from entering the profession in New Zealand, primarily due to the attitude of male lawyers. A study conducted by the Auckland District Law Society as recently as 1981 found that women still faced discrimination in the legal profession based on assumptions regarding their family responsibilities.

The earliest parts of the British Empire to abandon the closed-door policy against women and the legal profession were located in the outposts of Australia and Canada. Queensland, Australia, for example, set aside legal restrictions in 1881 and New Brunswick, Canada, in 1906.

WOMEN LAWYERS IN THE UNITED STATES

The first woman lawyer in "America," as noted earlier, appears to have been Margaret Brent. She arrived in 1638.

According to colonial records, Brent "was to be looked upon and received as . . . [an] Attorney" in the courts of Maryland. She started to act as her own lawyer as early as 1642, when she called upon the Provincial Court to assist her in the collection of some personal debts. From this beginning she soon appeared as an attorney for other parties—always discharging her duties with energy, devotion, and great ability. It was because of such professionalism that Governor Leonard Calvert frequently consulted her on political and legal matters, appointing her as administratrix of his estate. And it is in this capacity that her name (as his "Lordship's attorney") is frequently found in the early Maryland records. The high esteem in which she was held by her contemporaries can be seen in a letter signed by the entire General Assembly of Maryland and addressed to Lord Baltimore: ". . . we do Verily Believe and in Conscience report that it was better for the Collonys safety at that time in her hands than in any mans else in the whole Province."

Between 1642 and 1650 Brent's name appears no less than 124 times in the records of the courts of Maryland. She appeared, as noted above, *in propria persona* in courts for herself; as attorney general, administrator of Governor Calvert; attorney for her brother Giles Brent; by interpleaders; defenses at law, complaints against fugitive servants; warrants against the offender of his Lordship's custom laws; suing for damages in her estates and mill property in Kent, laying injuries at 3,000 pounds of tobacco and receiving 5,000. Brent, in fact, became involved in more lawsuits than any other colonial lawyer during her lifetime.

The first woman to take and pass a bar examination in the United States was Arabella Mansfield. She, however, did not attempt to practice law but remained an English and history professor at Iowa Wesleyan. Her point in taking the exam appears to simply have been to show that a woman could pass it.

The first woman law student in the United States enrolled in 1868, one year before Mansfield's Iowa bar examination. The student was Lemma Barkeloo, from Brooklyn, who traveled to St. Louis to get an education at Washington University's law school since no Eastern law school would admit her. She became a member of the Missouri bar in 1870 and was probably the first women in the United States to try a case. This seminal event took place in St. Louis, Missouri, in March 1870. The first woman on record, however, to have received a law degree was Ada Kepley from Union College of Law in Illinois (Northwestern). The year was also 1870.

In 1872 Charlotte E. Ray became the first African-American woman lawyer in the United States and the first woman lawyer in the District of Columbia. She was brilliant, a member of Phi Beta Kappa and an honors graduate of Howard Law School, which had opened its doors in 1869.

BELVA ANN LOCKWOOD

It is Belva Ann Lockwood who is responsible for opening up the United States federal courts to women lawyers and the first woman to argue a case before the United States Supreme Court. In 1873 Lockwood graduated from National University Law School located in Washington, D.C.—but only after overcoming a mean-spirited denial of her diploma. She had begun building her practice in the capital, even before officially graduating and being admitted to the bar, by representing clients in police and probate courts, as well as handling divorce and support proceedings. Lockwood also attempted to specialize in claims against the federal government. And it is in this area of the law that she ran into tremendous resistance—even with D.C. bar admittance in hand.

One day a client came to her office who wanted to file suit against the government for infringement of her husband's patent relating to the design of a torpedo boat. Lockwood was not admitted to practice before the United States Court of Claims and so with the assistance of A.A. Hosmer, Esq., she moved for admission. Hosmer presented the oral argument, where upon the chief judge of the Court of Claims, after looking Lockwood over, made the insightful observation: "Mistress Lockwood, you are a woman." The judge then continued the matter for one week.

After several more legal wafflings, the court finally denied Belva Lockwood's admission. Lockwood, however, did not give up. Instead of presenting the case of infringement herself, she prepared the legal briefs and trained her client, Charlotte Van Cort, to read the argument in court—not unlike the practice of the early Greek *logographers* discussed in Part III. Lockwood knew that this method of practicing law could not continue; the days of Lysias and Demosthenes were long gone and the days of unbundled legal services had not yet arrived. The case of *Raines v. United States* brought things to a head.

Mr. and Mrs. Raines disagreed about engaging "lawyeress" Lockwood. Mr. Raines believed that their case would be seriously compromised by engaging a woman. His wife was, however, determined to hire Lockwood. Lockwood convinced the Raineses that it would only be a short time before she would be admitted to practice in the federal courts. This good-faith belief was based on the wording of the federal statute dealing with admission to practice before the United States Supreme Court. The statute provided that "any attorney in good standing before the highest court of any State or Territory for the space of three years shall be admitted to this court when presented by a member of this bar." As Lockwood was to find out, "any attorney," as used in the statute, did not mean just "any attorney."

That Depends on What You Mean by "Person"

Gender discrimination certainly was not limited to the new world—a similar issue surfaced in Scotland when eighteen-year-old Margaret Hall requested permission, in 1900, to sit for the first of two required examinations given by the Examiners of Law-Agents. The organization refused, and Hall brought suit against the Incorporated Society of Law-Agents in Scotland. She based much of her case on the wording of the Law-Agents Act of 1873 that provided that "[f]rom and after the passing of this Act no person shall be admitted as a law-agent in Scotland except in accordance with the provisions of this Act." Hall pointed out to the court that "no person" applied equally to men and women—unless for some reason the court considered women not to be "persons" for purposes of the statute. As it turns out, the court agreed that "persons" included both males and females. However, the court went on to determine that Parliament, in enacting the statute, could not possibly have meant what it said. There is, after all, a difference between semantics ("sentence meaning") and pragmatics ("utterance meaning").

In order to start the Raineses' case, Lockwood went back to the United States Court of Claims to seek admission. She was again unsuccessful and had no other choice but to hand over the oral argument phase of the case to another lawyer. Lockwood later observed, "He said very badly in three days what I could have said well in one hour." In addition, the Raineses lost. This adverse decision set up the possibility of Lockwood arguing before the United States Supreme Court, with its admission standard of "any attorney in good standing."

In October 1876, with the Raineses' case accepted for hearing, Lockwood, through her attorney Albert G. Riddle (a former congressman and staunch supporter of women's suffrage), moved for admission to the United States Supreme Court. After some delay, the Court finally denied her admission, determining that "any attorney" does not mean exactly what it appears to mean to the untrained eye. Chief Justice Waite stated:

> By the uniform practice of the court, from its organization to the present time, and by the fair construction of its rule, none but men are admitted to practice before it as attorneys and counselors. This is in accordance with immemorial usage in England, and the law and practice in all the states until within a recent period: and the court does not feel called upon to make a change, until such change is required by statute, or a more extended practice in the highest courts of the States. . . . As this court knows no English precedent for the admission of women to the bar, it declines to admit, unless there shall be a more extended public opinion or special legislation.

News of the Court's decision outraged Lockwood and various other legal and social commentators. Myra Bradwell ridiculed the Chief Justice's opinion in the *Chicago Legal News*:

> The opinion delivered by Waite, C.J., refusing Mrs. Lockwood a license to practice in the Supreme Court of the United States . . . was unsound, and contrary to the practice of the court in every case since its organization. The same reasoning which the Chief Justice used to exclude Mrs. Lockwood, would compel every attorney who appears in the Supreme Court of the

United States to wear a gown and wig. Women have never been admitted to practice in Westminster Hall, and therefore Mrs. Lockwood is denied the right to practice in the United States Supreme Court. Counsellors have never been allowed to practice in Westminster Hall, and other superior courts in England, unless they wore gowns and wigs, and therefore it follows that they should not be allowed to practice in the Supreme Court of the United States without these necessary articles.

Belva Lockwood realized that her only avenue of recourse was Congress. She quickly drafted a bill specifically providing for the admission of women to the federal courts. The bill was submitted to the House Judiciary Committee by Representative Benjamin R. Butler. The bill, as well as a second draft, never got to the floor of the House. However, in April of 1878, the House finally passed Bill No. 1077: "An Act to Relive Certain Legal Disabilities of Women." Lockwood knew that there would be a battle in the Senate. She quickly mobilized grass roots support and lobbied senators in the corridors of the Capitol. And on February 7, 1879, "Lockwood's bill" was passed by the Senate and shortly thereafter signed into law by lawyer-President Rutherford B. Hayes.

AN INCREASE IN WOMEN LAWYERS

One of the most dramatic demographic changes in the American legal profession in the last several decades has been the increasing number of women. As late as 1971 women represented less than 10 percent of law students. However, by the end of the 1970s, approximately 34 percent of those enrolled in law schools were women. And the enrollment of women has continued to increase—currently reaching about 50 percent.

The Magic Pill

One reason for the rise in female law students has to do with the Pill. As stated by one economist: "Female enrollment in law and medical school soared as the [birth control] pill became available, because women knew they could qualify and establish themselves in a career without becoming a nun."

The number of women graduating from law schools and entering into the associate ranks of law firms has, however, failed to produce a corresponding percentage of women partners. In the intergroup tournament of male versus female, a principal reason for this failure appears to be that as long as there are two or three men among a firm's new class of associates with the skill and drive to become outstanding partners, there is no reason why a firm must choose to invest its scarce training resources on its women associates. Right? And, as noted previously, the path to partnership is largely tied to receiving this training. The law can indeed be an old boys club, and unfortunately, conscious and unconscious discrimination in mentoring also frequently extends to racial minorities.

The climb out of exclusion from the legal profession has not been an easy one for women. One reason is that law, as we have seen in our discussion concerning other times and places, has not been perceived as just another job, but as a profession with a special place and power—the power to control. This point is underscored by the fact that until the 1870s state laws denied women the right to practice law or even attend law school. These restrictions were reinforced by a professional culture dominated by white Christian males. This culture valued such things as competitiveness, physical courage, entrepreneurial skill, and oratorical prowess (i.e., rhetoric)—traits considered to be exclusively male. The problems Myra Bradwell faced with regard to her attempts to practice law illustrate this point.

MYRA BRADWELL

Myra Colby was born in Vermont on February 12, 1831. She attended school in Kenusha, Wisconsin, and graduated from the Ladies Seminary at Elyin, Illinois. She taught school for several years before marrying James B. Bradwell, an English immigrant journeyman who, like Abraham Lincoln, studied law during his spare time. James and Myra ran a successful private school in Tennessee for two years, and then moved to Chicago. James established a law practice with Myra's brother.

Along with raising four children, Myra Bradwell, in 1868, became the owner, publisher, and editor of the *Chicago Legal News.* This weekly journal was considered to be the most important legal publication west of the Alleghenies. And a special legislative charter permitted her, as a married woman, to own the Chicago Legal News Company, a publishing house that printed legal forms, briefs, and books, along with the weekly journal. The journal was extremely successful in part because by special state legislation it was permitted to act as a valid medium for the publication of legal notices, and that the laws, ordinances, motions, and court opinions printed in it could be used as evidence in courts. The Great Chicago Fire of 1871 destroyed the records and libraries of the entire Chicago bar, thereby dramatically increasing the paper's influence and circulation. Myra Bradwell became a wealthy women.

Legal Acts of God

In 2005, Hurricane Katrina decimated the legal system of the New Orleans area—obliterating courts and records. About a third of Louisiana's lawyers lost their offices, some for good. As stated by one newspaper reporter: "It is an implosion of the legal network not seen since disasters like the Chicago fire of 1871 or the San Francisco earthquake of 1906, events in times so much simpler as to be useless in making sense of this one."

Her ability to analyze and report on legal matters stemmed from her legal training. Bradwell had planned to help her husband in his law practice and therefore prepared for and passed the Illinois bar exam. In 1869 she applied for admission to the bar. The Illinois Supreme Court, however, denied her application. The court, at first, based its decision on the fact that she was married. It later got to the heart of the matter and denied her admission because she was a woman, married or not.

Bradwell appealed her case to the United States Supreme Court. Her lawyer, the prominent politician Matthew Carpenter, argued that practicing law is among the rights and privileges of citizens of the United States and that the Fourteenth Amendment to the United States Constitution prohibited Illinois from denying his client that right. In a 7–1 decision the Court held against Bradwell, finding that the practice of law is not among the privileges and immunities belonging to citizens of the United States (any more than voting, for example)—and therefore it is a privilege that the state could grant or deny. And indicative of the prevailing masculine viewpoint was Justice Joseph P. Bradley's concurring opinion in *Bradwell v. Illinois.* The Justice, somewhat like Gratian centuries earlier, opined: "The natural and proper timidity and delicacy which belongs to the female sex evidently unfits it for many of the occupations of civil life. . . . The paramount destiny and mission of woman [sic] are to fulfill the noble and benign offices of wife and mother. This is the law of the Creator." It seems clear that Justice Bradley wasn't interested in wrestling with the question of whether or not Bradwell was being arbitrarily denied a right to earn a livelihood practicing law—he had sex on his mind.

In 1872, seven years prior to passage of Lockwood's federal bill, Illinois changed its admission criteria in order to allow women into the bar, in large part due to the efforts of Myra Bradwell. Bradwell, however, did not immediately reapply for admission but instead devoted herself to the *Chicago Legal News,* professionalization of the practice of law, and legislation concerning women's issues.

WOMEN CHANGING THE BAR

Other than simply more lawyers, does it make any difference that there are an ever-increasing number of women lawyers? The answer is most likely yes. It is from the lawyer class that judges, law professors, and many legislators come. Many of these female interpreters share the belief, as evidenced by some of the legal literature, that the current position of women in society stems from a misogynistic tradition. They emphasize that people in power, primarily men, design norms and laws that become the status quo. Most of these feminist interpreters assert that the law has been largely spoken, written, practiced, and interpreted by men and therefore arguably depicts only the experiences of men. Additionally, feminists frequently point out that legal thought has been used as a means to subordinate women. Consider, for example, a law from the laws of King Ur-Nammu (approximately 2100 BCE): "A wife who chases and seduces a man shall be put to death, but the man shall go free." Arguably just a bit misogynistic.

One may believe that the law is the law and that it therefore makes no difference whether the interpreter is a man or a woman. But this viewpoint itself may be male. The fact is, as the ancient Roman College of the Pontiffs appreciated, that one's view of "the Law"—what is and is not good for society—seems to vary with who the person is and what he or she has experienced (a viewpoint apparently embraced by U.S. Supreme Court nominee Sonia Sotomayor). Because of this, not even all "feminists" share the same presuppositions or work toward the same goals.

It has been suggested that feminist scholars should focus on an analysis of law that probes the extent to which it is written by men and therefore defines the world as only men view it. In addition, feminist scholars should, according to certain commentators, investigate male methods of analysis and interpretation. It may be, for example, that originalism is a male method of interpretation. Originalism, in the context of the United States Constitution, comes in various forms but is generally the view that judges dealing with a constitutional issue should confine themselves to enforcing norms that are explicit or at least clearly implicit in the Constitution as understood by the framers of the document. Proponents of originalism argue that this interpretive method restricts judges to their proper role in a constitutional democracy. If, however, certain forms of reasoning or their application are "male" and given the fact that all the framers of the United States Constitution were male, the use of originalism arguably defines and implements only norms and values that are more distinctly male.

And speaking of norms and values, it is commonplace to see competition as intimately tied to the practice of law. It is therefore easy to see why "feminine traits" such as nurturing, caring, and giving to others make women less suited for the practice of law—especially litigation. Right?

Looking back to at least ancient Greece, it seems clear that the Greeks (especially the Athenians) liked to litigate, at least in part, because it was seen as a competitive enterprise. This same spirit, perhaps in a somewhat more institutionalized and instrumental form, seems to have carried over to the Romans. And there is no question that early Anglo-American legal practice was influenced by the deep roots of Greece and Rome.

However, perhaps modern-day legal practice, at least in the United States, is using the notion that the legal process is an adversarial, competitive process in a fundamentally different way than it was used in centuries past. In ancient Greece, Rome, and even early modern-day England and Continental Europe, most litigation was conducted by the parties themselves. As we saw in Part III, the Greeks thought it cowardly to have someone represent you in court—unless you were a woman, child, or incompetent. It was only with the rise of the Roman orators that the concept of full, in-court representation came to be accepted by the Western legal tradition—and then, only in certain cases.

There seems to be little doubt that the great Roman legal tradition helped lawyers eventually develop a class consciousness—though initially underdeveloped and screaming out for expansion. And what better way to expand consciousness than to grab for power? But from where? From whom? When faced with the ultimate power of politics and business, how was it possible for a bunch of lowly lawyers to be taken seriously? The answer, of course, was competition—something that both politicians and businessmen, in an ever more capitalistic society, could understand. But compete with whom? After all isn't the law (both with a small "l" and with a capital "L") ideally intended to help organize and promote efficiency in the realm of the already competitive worlds of politics and business? Does it make any sense to have lawyers competing with the very institutions and people they are suppose to be helping?

To further complicate the matter, this battleground is littered with procedural rules known only to lawyers that must be wielded in hand-to-hand combat between lawyers. If this notion is correct, think what has been accomplished: the lawyers are in competition not with the politicians or businessmen, but with each other. The power therefore to be gained (read: more money) flows from making sure that the path to resolution is neither easy nor quick, but always competitive. The Law is rational argument and Rational Argument Is War! As a consequence, "feminine traits" might indeed be a threat to this grab for power; nurturing, caring, and giving to others could seriously endanger cash flow.

Beaten by a Girl

The notion of lawyer versus lawyer appears to be one of the primary reasons that male lawyers, at least in the frontier West, fought against women practicing law. Arguments were made about women lawyers degrading themselves and contributing to the defilement of other women by dealing in court with the ugliness of human behavior (rape, sodomy, incest, murder). But it appears that a large part of the objection to admitting women to law schools and to the practice of law had to do with competition. Men were afraid of being beaten by a woman in the highly visible arena of the courtroom. After all, a woman lawyer would surely use her feminine charisma before an all-male jury in order to win. Remember poor Adam?

NOT JUST ANY CHIMP IN THE JUNGLE HAS THE RIGHT TO PRACTICE LAW

LAWYERS HAVE A SUBSTANTIAL MONOPOLY over the right to practice law, somewhat like the ancient priests' private line to the gods. In almost every state in the United States, this exclusivity is the result of statutes or court rules—hard-fought and won fair and square. In fact, the unauthorized practice of law, in most states, is a crime, which is a good way to make such services as inelastic as possible. California's Business and Professionals Code, for example, currently provides that the unauthorized practice of law constitutes either a felony or a misdemeanor, depending upon the circumstances. For a misdemeanor (first-time charge), a person can be sentenced to a stay in county jail, and be fined. For second-time offenders, the crime generally carries a mandatory sentence of at least ninety days behind bars.

What, however, is the practice of law? If, during a hands-on moment, Dr. Smith, a proctologist, tells his friend and patient, Pete Jones, that he is certain that it is illegal for Pete to shoot his wife's lover, has a crime been committed—the crime of unauthorized practice of law? Doubtful.

While not always clear, the unauthorized practice of law generally includes representing others before courts and administrative agencies, providing legal advice, and drafting legal documents for others. Examples of lay conduct that have been held to constitute the illegal practice of law include legal advice by an accountant to a client unrelated to auditing, bookkeeping, or tax return preparation; the preparation of legal documents (e.g., purchase and sale agreements, notes, mortgages) by a real estate broker; and legal advice by the owner of a secretarial service to persons seeking uncontested divorces.

LEGAL EXCLUSIVITY

The basic rationale for excluding lay individuals and organizations from the practice of law is that those in need of legal advice should be protected from possible incompetence and dishonesty. Consumers, the argument goes, do not have the ability to gather sufficient information in order to determine whether or not lay providers are competent (a technical question) or honest (a question of "good moral character"). The counterarguments are along the lines that providing lawyers with a monopoly results in consumers paying higher than necessary legal fees and that allowing laypersons and organizations to provide legal services would help fulfill the unmet legal needs of low- and moderate-income persons.

These very arguments for not restricting the practice of law were made in Japan during the early part of the twentieth century. Because the practice of law was largely unregulated, there was an arguable oversupply of practitioners; it's estimated that there were perhaps 20,000 people engaged in the "unauthorized" practice of law in Tokyo in 1929. Bills were therefore introduced in 1912, 1921, and 1925 making the unauthorized practice of law a crime. These proposals were met, each time, with strong opposition based on two grounds: (1) that it is difficult to define the "practice of law" once a narrow definition of advocacy is departed from, and (2) that people need to be able to turn to someone other than a lawyer to handle problems because of the expense associated with engaging a lawyer. In other words: Keep the marketplace for legal services as elastic as possible.

In ancient Rome, the strict formalism and ever-growing intricacy of the law made the advice of jurists indispensable. The upshot of that need was the formation of a distinct class of professional experts. However, unlike in the United States, Japan, and almost every other modern country, anybody could give legal advice in ancient Rome. And although available through apprenticeship or classroom study, no special training or examinations were required and the success of the jurist was left entirely to the marketplace (wide-open, economic elasticity). But, as in modern times, only those who had gained knowledge and skill, generally through education and experiences, could succeed.

THREATS TO THE PRACTICE OF LAW?

The unauthorized practice of law does not pose the same threat to all kinds of practice. The threat appears to be lowest to those areas engaged in by law firms representing Big Business and wealthy individuals. It seems to be highest to the practice of those lawyers involved in administering decedents' estates, organizing small businesses, handling divorces and child custody matters, and dealing with small real estate matters such as the buying and selling of homes.

Despite the threat, the ABA and other large comprehensive bar associations, starting a number of years ago, took a much less active approach on issues involving the unauthorized practice of law. The reason for this retreat seems to have been a reaction to the rising popular opposition to monopolies in general (remember Ma Bell?). In addition, attempts by bar associations to protect its members' monopoly might result in strong media campaigns by the opposition. Unbelievably, lawyers are not popular with every segment of society.

The current issues relating to lay legal technicians have, however, revived concerns about unauthorized practice with the ABA and some of the other major comprehensive bar associations. The term "legal technicians" refers to what are essentially paralegals and the issues involve whether and how extensively such technicians should be licensed to "practice law." There is growing interest-group and popular support for permitting legal technicians to handle certain types of legal matters independent of a lawyer as a means of expanding the availability of legal services at affordable prices.

Paralegals Practicing Law?

The number of paralegals in large law firms went from 14,000 in 1972 to 83,000 in 1989. Paralegals are now performing a substantial amount of the routine legal work, including drafting, basic research, and keeping track of documents, that was once the sole responsibility of law firm associates.

Despite the controversial nature of legal technicians, licensing proposals have generated considerable support in some state legislatures. And it appears that this support will only increase. This perceived threat to lawyers' practices, and arguably the quality of legal services generated by such licensing proposals, will likely draw bar associations ever deeper into the controversy.

An even more significant fight is brewing between accountants and lawyers over the practice of law. Congress passed legislation that, in certain cases, extends to clients of accountants practicing before the Internal Revenue Service the privilege of confidential communications historically enjoyed only by lawyers' clients. The extension of such a privilege to accountants raises questions about the basic difference between the two professions: an accountant's historic duty toward objectivity and public disclosure of financial information (a type of honesty-based code of ethics) and a lawyer's obligation to act as an advocate and to guard his or her clients' secrets (a type of loyalty-based code of ethics).

Many of the large accounting firms employ hundreds of lawyers in the United States, nearly all of whom work on tax matters. These firms insist that their lawyers are not practicing law. The reason for such denial is that the ABA Model Rules of Professional Conduct (as well as various state rules) prohibit lawyers from splitting fees and forming partnerships with nonlawyers. However, unlike nearly every United States jurisdiction, most European countries, following the economic principle of complements (like mac and cheese), either allow accounting firms to engage in law practice themselves or to affiliate with law firms. As a result, all the major United States accounting firms have significant legal practices throughout Europe with hundreds of lawyers on board.

The Multidisciplinary Trend

One of the current hot topics in lawyer governance is multidisciplinary practice. This type of practice was somewhat stymied when the ABA House of Delegates voted down a proposal in July 2000 for relaxed ethical standards permitting fee-sharing arrangements with other professionals. However, a number of firms have moved ahead without waiting for possible changes in ethics rules. They have used the law and started subsidiary businesses to get around prohibitions. Loopholes are not just for laypeople.

It has been argued that because elite law firms are locked into a path that leads them to offer increasingly specialized legal services at ever higher prices, these silk-stocking institutions will eventually lose out to international accounting firms in the competition to be the premier providers of legal and business services to Big Business.

The ABA, as might be expected, has raised its head and begun to take a hard look at the issue of accounting firms and the practice of law. One argument, at least with regard to client privilege, is for lawyers to focus on the traditional notion that the accountant's role is one of objectivity and not advocacy. Because of that, accountants can do work for clients with competing interests. After all, the numbers are the numbers—right? Conflict rules, on the other hand, generally prohibit an entire law firm from undertaking representation of a potential client with an interest that conflicts with an existing client of any lawyer in the firm. (I have run into this rule all too often and have longed for the days of Webster and Darrow.)

The same specter of intergroup tournament between lawyers and accountants also extends to lawyers versus financial planners, bankers (particularly investment bankers), and other businesses eager to help companies and individuals decide what to do with their money. These firms commonly employ not only finance specialists and accountants but also economists and even lawyers. Based on the economic principle of substitution, the potential for creating organizations that are competitive with those traditionally enjoyed by law firms is clear. And what about business owners who are willing to deal over the internet with an Indian or a Chinese lawyer, working at a fraction of the cost of a New York lawyer, who has familiarized himself with United States laws? Outsourcing isn't limited to blue-collar workers.

What Makes Lawyers Different?

With regard to legal monopoly over "the right to practice law" (a phrase containing a complex internal structure), one might ask: What makes lawyers different from other workers? Why not, for example, protect Pete Jones's statement to Bob, the brick mason, that he just finished walling in the body of his wife's lover and wants Bob's opinion on the technical and aesthetic quality of the brick work? The answer to such questions, besides the "fact" that Pete appears to be completely insane, can be approached by looking at what lawyers do.

In general a lawyer must have a good command of the relevant substantive and procedural doctrines applicable to his or her area of practice. An effective lawyer must, however, not only know the law but must also be a good judge of character, a quick and accurate calculator of costs and benefits (in the broadest sense of this economic concept), an empathetic listener, and a thorough deliberator who, as we have discussed a number of times so far, never loses sight of the important role that emotion plays in human affairs. In other words, a lawyer's work is often imbued with a deep and socially significant moral dimension—not always recognized by many lawyers—that does not exist in many other types of work.

But beyond such generalities, there is serious academic debate as to exactly what, if any, are distinctive lawyers' skills versus those, for example, possessed by economists, financial analysts, historians, literary critics, accountants, philosophers, linguists, or political scientists. Among the usual suspects, particularly where the common law is concerned, are (1) proficiency in a form of legal casuistry that involves such things as distinguishing cases (analogic reasoning) and recognizing significant facts (e.g., that Adam is not a pig—except perhaps to Eve); (2) a basic understanding of social science; and (3) proficiency at certain kinds of textual interpretation. And with regard to any society "advanced" enough to give rise to a lawyer class, it would seem that the ability to simply find the applicable law (acting as an "information broker") is an important skill. Individuals and businesses are subject to a ton of rules and regulations, and lawyers, hopefully in an economical fashion, can inform them about how to deal with the law.

One way to conceptualize these alleged lawyer skills is to think of law (laws or the Law) in terms of an asset. In theory, this asset, at least in most Western countries, is owned by the people. A community property. A lawyer has no more right to a reported case (case law), a statute (statutory law), or a regulation (regulatory law) than a nonlawyer. The nonlawyer can therefore use any or all of these components for himself. But the question is: Does his undivided ownership interest come with the right to sell or rent it to someone else? Where there are rules regarding the unauthorized practice of law, the answer is generally no. The reason is that the asset starts out as a bunch of scattered material; think of it in terms of building an apartment complex. Material needs to be located. Simply knowing that a particular pipe will be needed for the complex to be built takes skill. And what about blueprints and construction? Gathering the stuff and bringing it to the job site is only part of the task. Someone has to actually draw up the plans and have the skills to follow them in order to build the complex.

Without beating this analogy to death, the point is that many societies do not want people constructing buildings and selling them or collecting rents unless the structure has been designed and built by a licensed architect and contractor. Similarly, many societies do not want just anyone building legal structures for sale or rent. It is one thing for the roof to collapse on you and quite another to injure a purchaser or tenant. Therefore a person trained in such things as legal research, legal interpretive techniques, and legal reasoning can hopefully build a structure (e.g., a legal document or lawsuit) that in design, function, and stability is worthy of being sold or rented out. In other words, the law is a common asset composed of uncopyrightable components and each person can improve his or her interest by building a structure out of the bits and pieces scattered about (i.e., case law and statutes), but only a lawyer can sell or lease out the structure he or she has built.

REPUTATIONAL INTERMEDIARIES

Focusing for a few minutes on the business area, lawyers are frequently requested to deliver ("construct") legal opinions. Most of these opinions, although arising in a variety of contexts, are similar in form and frequently concern routine matters—including, for example, that the person who signed the agreement had the authority to do so. While a "legal opinion" is something that only a lawyer can give, the basic work necessary to give the opinion—that Mr. Smith, as XYZ Company's president, has the authority to sign the agreement on behalf of XYZ Company—can often be easily performed by a nonlawyer. So why is a legal opinion something lawyers have a monopoly on doing? Or, if special knowledge is not necessarily the reason for lawyers' monopoly on, at least certain aspects of, the legal opinion market, what is? One suggested answer is that service as a reputational intermediary is a defining aspect of lawyers' work; it defines because it separates lawyers and their products from other workers and their products. In fact it can be argued that acting as a reputational intermediary is an important part of the structure of the legal profession itself.

Legal Opinions, Ethics and the Definition of Torture

The rendering of legal opinions is not limited to business matters. Take, for example, the question (as of the date of this writing) of whether or not certain government lawyers who rendered an opinion on the legality of using harsh interrogation techniques violated legal ethics rules.

As we've seen throughout our discussions so far, lawyers do much more than simply advocate a client's cause. As stated by David Luban, a legal ethicist at Georgetown University: "The legal ethics rules [in the context of rendering an opinion] call on lawyers to be absolutely candid and straight up—not to spin the law the way they would if they were arguing in a courtroom, but to give more or less the same advice they'd give if they knew their client wanted the opposite." And this standard applies to the lawyers employed by the federal Justice Department's Office of Legal Counsel.

So the question is, with regard to harsh interrogation techniques (specifically waterboarding): Did Justice Department lawyers render an unbiased opinion on the definition of "torture"? Some critics say that the lawyers left out (due to sloppy legal research? on purpose?) relevant cases that would

have changed, or at least modified, the opinions that were ultimately rendered to the administration. On the other hand, as we have seen and as was
stated by Tom Morgan, a legal ethicist at George Washington University,
with regard to legal reasoning, "[t]he question of what cases are relevant
and what are not, is—to some extent—in the eye of the beholder." Consequently, the task for the Justice Department investigators who are exploring
the question of whether or not there was a breach of ethics will be to distinguish a legitimate judgment call from a blatant slanting of facts or law. In
other words: How much leveling, sharpening, and assimilating took place in
rendering the opinion?

But what exactly does "service as a reputational intermediary" mean? Consider a seller attempting to sell a business. The buyer will be naturally suspicious
of the seller and statements made by him. Why is he selling the business? What's
wrong with it? Suppose, however, there is someone engaged to verify, or at least
vouch for, the seller's information (e.g., render an opinion)—thereby lowering
the buyer's search and evaluation costs. This third party can offer its reputation
as a type of bond that the seller's information is accurate. In the world of law,
this third party is a law firm, or sometimes just an individual lawyer.

There is evidence that, depending upon the type of "reputational bond"
needed, not just any law firm or lawyer will do. The business world tends to seg-
regate reputational from non-reputational lawyers in certain high-dollar transactions. Call it product differentiation. For example, the elite and the "super-elite"
law firms are frequently picked to handle particular types of stock offerings. And
perhaps of no particular surprise, these silk-stocking firms, at least in the United
States, are almost exclusively located in New York City. The reason for this is not
necessarily related to superior knowledge, but simply location.

While the general belief is that the Securities Act of 1933 was all about the
benefits of disclosure and transparency in the marketplace (themes that have
certainly resurfaced in the early part of the twenty-first century), the truth is
that the Act severely limited the growing competition that was hurting top-tier
investment banks. Taking advantage of the stock market crisis, the old established New York City houses such as J.P. Morgan pushed for legislation that not
only mandated greater transparency and disclosure but also served their goals
of reducing competition in the underwriting business. The new legislation,
among other things, eliminated the possibility of underwriters selling securities
prior to the date agreed upon by the selling syndicate—a date controlled by the
lead underwriter, "someone" like J.P. Morgan. By preventing pre-offering solicitation, the lead underwriter eliminated competition within the syndicates and

thereby boosted profitability. This legislature favoritism toward the traditional investment banks was then enhanced by the Glass-Steagall Act, also of 1933, which forced their chief competitors, the commercial banks, to get out of the underwriting business (at least until the repeal of Glass-Steagall in 1999). All of this legislation greatly increased the degree to which a few traditional players dominated (and continue to dominate) the industry. And guess where their lawyers were, and are, located? You guessed it—New York City.

It also appears that the importance of reputational intermediary value for all but the "super-elite" firms is on the decline, a trend that is consistent with the changing market for legal services. A driving force behind this decline is the increasing openness in today's marketplace, including the death of Glass-Steagall (perhaps, in light of certain failures of capitalism, to be somewhat mourned), and the corresponding decreasing cost for direct information gathering and verification—what has been called the democratization of information. The fact is that clients can, on their own, sometimes cheaply acquire verification of what a seller is saying. This access to information, based on the democratization of technology, lessens various market frictions and consequently the need for the types of reputational bonding traditionally offered for "rent" by law firms.

Democracy in Action

A good example of this democratization of information is certain large U.S. natural gas and electricity marketers, who have launched their own Internet-based, over-the-counter energy (natural gas, power, and petroleum products) trading businesses. In this environment, it has been observed that greater standardization will become typical. Sales, operating, and other documents are available online and readily accessible to clients of natural gas and electricity marketers interested in expediting transactions (another crack in the 5,000-year scribal tradition). One consequence of this explosion of information and its access through the Internet will most likely be demystification of the law and, in the opinion of certain experts, an elimination of the plugging in of data into existing forms style of lawyering. For instance, there is a growing trend for legal services to be put up for bid on the Internet.

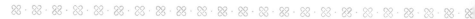

An important consequence of this waning reliance on pure reputational service in business transactions is the seeming breakdown of entry barriers based on inappropriate categories. An institution, such as a law firm, that is "renting" its reputation to clients will have a tendency to exclude those of race, gender, or socioeconomic background that are perceived as having a possible drag on the value of that reputation. Consider, for example, that of the 753,000 lawyers working in the United States in 1996, only 21.49 percent were female, 2.7 percent were African American, and 1.9 percent were Hispanic. If, however, the weakening of reputational services does not have a corresponding adverse effect on a law firm's bottom line, there should be, at least, no "economic reason" for continued discrimination.

XXXI

STEP INTO THE CONFESSIONAL
(Your Secrets Are Most Likely Safe)

THE ATTORNEY-CLIENT PRIVILEGE has existed for centuries and is in fact the oldest of the person-to-person privileges. Historians do not all agree, however, on why courts originally recognized the privilege. One theory is that it arose as a judicial extension of the right of individuals to avoid self-incrimination. Another possibility is that the privilege originally came from the notion of "honor among gentlemen." This justification is based on a lawyer's implicit oath of loyalty to the client, an obligation that would be breached if the lawyer disclosed the client's communications. This same notion of fidelity appears to have been the foundation for the attorney-client privilege in ancient Rome.

Later justifications for the privilege tended to focus not so much on honor or self-incrimination, but on utilitarianism. The privilege, according to this approach, is essential in achieving a social good because it induces clients to consult freely with legal advisers—something that is arguably important in a complex legal system. A 1776 English case, for example, adopted the effective-legal-assistance rational and explicitly rejected the honor-based justification, reasoning that the same rationale of "honor among gentlemen" might also justify the creation of a privilege for physician-patient relationships. Heaven forbid! What would doctors have to talk about at tea time? (The doctor-patient privilege appears to have first been recognized in a New York law of 1828.)

Modern-day justifications for the attorney-client privilege have focused on both the non-utilitarian (the right against self-incrimination and honor-based justifications) and the utilitarian (effective legal assistance) justifications that have competed for general acceptance throughout the history of the privilege. In the United States it appears that the largely unqualified obligations of loyalty to client interest and confidentiality concerning client information have enabled the legal profession to firmly attach itself to private industry. Where a country's ethical rules of conduct sweep in larger societal and third-party interests, the lawyers have not assumed the same central roles as representatives of Big Business.

PRIVILEGED INFORMATION

What exactly is a privileged communication? Consider, for example, fictional crime boss Tony Soprano, who put his nephew through some Ivy League law school for the purpose of consulting him from time to time about the best way to launder tons of ill-gotten gain. Are such communications protected from disclosure? The answer is most likely no. A lawyer is not permitted to assist a client in conduct that the lawyer knows is criminal or fraudulent, and the attorney-client privilege may not apply if the communication is made for the purpose of furthering ongoing or future conduct of a criminal or fraudulent nature (e.g., "Sal, I'm gonna grab some forbidden fruit tonight—can I stash it in your fridge?"). In contrast, consultations with an attorney after a crime or fraud has taken place remain privileged (e.g., "Sal, I took some forbidden fruit—can you help me?").

⊠ · ⊠

A Right or a Privilege?

In 2008 two attorneys knew that Alton Logan, serving a life sentence for the murder of a security guard, was innocent. The lawyers, however, kept silent because of the attorney-client privilege. It appears that their client, Andrew Wilson, had confessed to them that he shot the security guard but insisted that they only reveal this fact after his death. Wilson died in prison in 2007 and Logan, until his release on bail of a $1,000 (pending a new trial), had been in prison for 26 years. One of the lawyers told a news reporter that "[t]hey prosecuted an innocent man. How do you live with yourself having this secret? . . . I couldn't do anything legally or ethically. I represented Andrew Wilson."

But does Wilson's confession and insistence on silence until after his death constitute fraud? If a client is using an attorney's services to engage in crime or fraud, there is an exception to the privilege. It might be argued that knowing that an innocent man has been tossed in jail—based on your client's confession of guilt and refusal to confess to the authorities—constitutes, besides a moral injustice, a continuing fraud against the court or the innocent person. On the other hand, if the crime/fraud exception applies in this case, wouldn't the exception swallow the rule of confidentiality?

But how would a law enforcement agency ever know that Mr. Soprano consulted with his nephew-lawyer—his consigliere? This question gets to the heart of an interesting topic of legal discussion: whether the privilege extends only to oral and written exchange, or also, like the identity of a penitent in sacramental confession, protects the identity of clients, as well as fee information. This question stems from a fundamental debate over the purpose of the attorney-client privilege. In general, modern-day American courts tend to hold that the identity of a client (unlike the penitent) is not a "communication" entitled to protection. This conclusion is also true of fee arrangements, including the amount paid for services—even if it's a basket of fruit. The general acceptance of these rules indicates the dominance of the effective advocate rationale for the privilege (a utilitarian justification). The argument is that a lawyer will inevitably learn the identity of his client and the fee arrangement is something primarily generated by the lawyer—therefore there is no need for this information to be privileged. This utilitarian rationale, however, does not take into account the client's concern that he might compound his legal problems by having information provided to the authorities that could be used against him at some later date. Consequently, courts have also created exceptions to the "no privilege" rule that are aimed at protecting client identity and fees.

If our crime boss's actual communications are protected—dealing, for example, with a past crime instead of a future one—what good is just finding out his identity? It might be, for example, that an "anonymous party" (i.e., the crime boss) has paid the legal fees of a defendant charged with drug trafficking. The authorities might want to know who is paying the nephew-lawyer, and how much, on the assumption that the defendant has ties to that anonymous party.

The exceptions to the "no privilege" rule might be of some comfort to Mr. Soprano and his nephew. The first exception is referred to as the "legal advice" exception. It holds that such information as identity and fees are privileged when there is a strong possibility that disclosure would implicate the client in the very matter for which he sought legal advice. The second exception holds that the identity and fee information is privileged if it provides the "last link" in a chain of incriminating evidence that could lead to the indictment of the lawyer's client. This exception is called the "communication rationale" exception and protects information concerning identity and fees if disclosure would connect the client to an already disclosed and independently privileged exchange. Application of this exception comes into play, for example, in situations where the authorities already know enough information that disclosure of the identity of an anonymous client would connect him or her with a confidential communication that is separately protected by the attorney-client privilege. In this situation, the communication rationale exception prevents the disclosure of an identity that would effectively disclose the privileged communication.

It is possible that our nephew-lawyer might be able to find protection, in either or both of the exceptions, from being forced to disclose the identity of his uncle. In fact, the lawyer's life might depend upon fitting within one of the exceptions.

XXXII

BELLY UP
TO THE BAR

ONE OF MY FIRST JOBS AS A LAWYER was working for Mobil Oil Corporation. Proudly displayed on the walls of my tiny cubical in downtown Denver, Colorado, was the paper trail evidencing my right to practice law: college diploma, law school diploma, memberships in a state bar association and the American Bar Association. One night, while working late, a custodian for the building happened to notice the array of framed diplomas. In a somewhat excited voice he asked me about the certificate with the American Bar Association name embossed in large letters. I explained to him the purpose of the association and what one has to do to become a member. He listened politely and then with an air of disappointment said: "Oh, I thought you were a licensed bartender."

There are substantial variations among bar associations—of the lawyer kind. The two principal types are comprehensive and specialty. The ABA and the various state bar associations are examples of comprehensive associations. Specialty associations include such organizations as the Association of Trial Lawyers of America, the American Academy of Matrimonial Lawyers, and the American Immigration Lawyers Association. There are also bar associations in numerous countries throughout the world, as well as international associations. The Council of the Bars and the Law Societies of the European Union, for example, represents the interests of lawyers throughout Europe.

Many of the major American comprehensive bar associations were organized more than 100 years ago. The ABA was started in 1878 and now, with more than 400,000 members, it is the largest voluntary professional membership organization in the world. One of the first "American" bar associations (or at least law societies) was the Bar of Suffolk County Massachusetts in 1770, with future president of the United States John Adams as secretary. In fact, meetings of the Bar of Suffolk and bar rules, particularly regarding education and admission, extend back to 1759. Among the first state bar associations was the New York State Bar Association, organized in 1876, six years after the February 15, 1870, founding of the Association of the Bar of New York City. The Philadelphia Bar Association is considered to be the oldest *continuous* bar organization in the United States. Its articles of incorporation were signed in 1802.

State Bar Associations

The New York City association was the creation of a group of lawyers that met because of a December 1869 circular. This call to action was a response to the corruption and crisis in the city courts. This was the time of William "Boss" Tweed and justice in the Big Apple was rotten to the core. The Robber Barons of Big Business—John D. Rockefeller, E. H. Harriman, Jay Gould, et al., who owned about 45 percent of America's financial wealth—fought each other in the courts, obtaining injunctions and writs frequently purchased from corrupt judges. And on February 13, 1870, Dorman B. Eaton, a respected member of the legal community, was savagely beaten by a follower of Boss Tweed. This incident, more than any words on paper, called for action.

Why Play the Game if You Know Who Wins?

Even though some lawyers and their clients might have had a vested interest in making sure a corrupt system continued, this was arguably not the case for the bulk of lawyers. Uncertainty is an important basis for the decisions people (read: clients) make regarding how and when to invoke or turn to the law (read: hire a lawyer). If the outcome of the "game" is predetermined, why bother? In other words, the law is actively engaged (and, over the long run, lawyers are hired and paid) only when its effect is uncertain—as long as, like any game, there are rules.

Roscoe Pound, former dean of the Harvard Law School, labeled the years 1836 to 1870 as the "Era of Decadence" in the American legal profession. In his opinion, things started to turn around after 1870—the year of the New York City association's founding and the period of Langdell's tenure at Harvard. He also sang the praises of the ABA. According to Dean Pound, "Revival of professional organizations for promoting the practice of a learned art in the spirit of a public service and advancing the administration of justice according to law got its impetus as a country wide movement from the organization of the American Bar Association in 1878."

Membership in the earliest comprehensive bar associations was largely restricted to the more respected members of the profession. The goal was to purify the bar and redeem it from complicity in the piratical practices of certain of its business clients, as well as to distinguish the profession from both new-wealth businessmen and the growing number of immigrants within the profession. In other words, keep out the diversity generators. During the first year of the Association of the Bar of New York City, for example, about 450 lawyers joined. They were mostly well-to-do business lawyers from old-American stock—the profession's goodness-of-example. The Association continued as a highly exclusive organization well into the mid-twentieth century.

A majority of the state bar associations (which, besides the fifty states, include the District of Columbia, Puerto Rico, Guam, American Samoa, the Mariana Islands, the Navajo Nation, and the Virgin Islands) are unified. This means that a practicing lawyer in that "state" must be a member of the association in order to practice law. I am, for example, a card-carrying member of the Nevada Bar Association and on inactive status with the Utah Bar Association. And since such associations are mandatory (by statute or court rule), unified associations are generally more heavily regulated than other law-oriented associations. In contrast, membership in nonunified bar associations is voluntary. But even though voluntary, membership may sometimes be limited to members in a particular jurisdiction or those involved in a particular type of practice.

⚜ · ⚜

Volunteering at the Bar

How does a state come to have a unified bar—that is, whose self-interest is served by taking a voluntary leading role in advocating such an institution? One answer is that a part-time investment in bar association activities increases the chances that a lawyer becomes better known to other lawyers, thereby increasing the chances of being referred legal work—hopefully of the billable and collectable kind.

⚜ · ⚜

The unified state bar concept has been met with varying degrees of opposition. A bone of contention frequently has to do with positions taken by a bar association on public and professional issues. Consider, for example, an association that advocates a position on abortion or the unauthorized practice of law or the death penalty. Additionally, lawyers required to be members of the unified state bar sometimes object to regulated restrictions and obligations imposed on members and the amount (as well as the use) of annual dues charged by the association. At one point, opposition to the unified bar format became especially strong in California and Wisconsin. Pursuant to a legislative directive, an advisory plebiscite of all California lawyers was held in 1996 in order to determine if the unified form should be retained. Sixty-five percent of those voting supported the unified bar. And in 1988, the Wisconsin Supreme Court suspended mandatory lawyer membership in its state bar following a federal district court ruling that such membership violated the First Amendment of the United States Constitution. The Wisconsin Supreme Court, despite considerable resistance among lawyers, reinstated the unified bar in 1992 after the United States Supreme Court upheld the constitutionality of mandatory bar membership.

⊠ · ⊠

Anger at the Bar

In the fall of 1997 Governor Pete Wilson of California vetoed dues legislation for the bar and insisted on stripping the organization of any functions (e.g., political lobbying) other than admissions and discipline. (Unlike other states, the California legislature has the power to determine bar dues.) Leaders of the bar—which had, as of 1998, approximately 156,000 members—then scrambled to win support for a compromise bill that proposed splitting the bar into mandatory and voluntary arms, as well as reducing the mandatory bar's dues.

⊠ · ⊠

With regard to the rise of women lawyers, major comprehensive bar associations have made a special effort to fill leadership posts and other positions of responsibility with women. In 1995 Roberta Cooper Ramo became the first female president of the ABA, and women headed up the Connecticut Bar Association from 1992 to 1995.

Many bar associations have also actively fought gender discrimination within the legal profession. The ABA, for example, established the Commission on Women in the Profession in 1987. This commission, with Hillary Rodham Clinton filling its first chair, was formed to assess the status of women in the legal profession, identify barriers to their advancement, and make recommendations on how to eliminate any such barriers. Similar efforts have been made with respect to racial discrimination. The ABA initiated the Minority Counsel Demonstration (MCD) program in 1988 with a straightforward mission: "to create opportunity for minority attorneys to become fully integrated in the profession." In order to accomplish this, the MCD encourages participating businesses to retain minority firms and to ensure that minority members of large firms do some of their legal work. By stimulating demand for the services of minority lawyers at large law firms, the program seeks, among other things, "to increase the number of minorities they recruit, hire, retain and promote to partnership." The ABA's program has been said to be a resounding success. And in 2003 Dennis W. Archer became the ABA's first African-American president—the Association having formally lifted its ban against African-American lawyers in 1943.

There are currently thirty-eight states with continuing legal education (CLE) requirements for lawyers. In most of these states, the required hours of instruction each year is given by or under the auspices of a bar association. In recent years many CLE programs have been offered by the ABA, in conjunction with state and local bar associations. Some associations also administer specialist certification programs (e.g., family law) with instructional and examination components.

Bar associations have, particularly since Watergate, given extensive attention to encouraging and enforcing ethical and professionally responsible behavior by its members. This attention includes

- Developing and interpreting standards of professional conduct for lawyers;
- Disciplining lawyers who violate standards of professional conduct, including the possibility of disbarment;
- Emphasizing "professionalism": civility in a lawyer's relationship with opposing counsel and judges; curtailing overly aggressive and confrontational tactics in litigation; and checking excessive concerns with profitability;
- Protecting and expanding the legal monopoly lawyers have over the right to practice law;
- Providing needed legal services to the poor at little or no cost to the client, specifically including the possibility of mandatory pro bono work; and
- Improving dispute resolution, including making recommendations regarding judicial selections and alternatives to litigation (called alternative dispute resolution), helping shape procedural rules,

and influencing substantive law reform in nearly every field of law:
(1) evaluating bills before legislative bodies; (2) studying and reporting
on troublesome legal problems; (3) lobbying; (4) filing *amicus curiae*
("friend of the court") briefs reflecting the association's preference
on matters that arise in the context of litigation (e.g., cases involving
inappropriate lawyer advertising); and (5) sometimes initiating a
lawsuit (e.g., issues including the unauthorized practice of law).

The Long History of Legal Ethics

The first general code of professional ethics appears to have been the London Ordinance of 1280. This ordinance formalized the regulation of admission to practice before the London courts and enumerated various forms of
prohibited misconduct (toward both the courts and clients). In the United
States, the first bar association code of ethics was adopted in Alabama in
1887. By 1908, twenty-six state bar associations had adopted codes of ethics,
and the American Bar Association Canons of Ethics (a national code of ethics
for lawyers) was adopted in 1908. And the Council of the Bars and Law Societies of the European Union has plans to create a pan-European code. If all
goes as planned, the code would bring more than 700,000 European lawyers
under a common code of legal ethics.

XXXIII

A LAWYER BY ANY OTHER NAME SMELLS JUST THE SAME

Hᴀᴠᴇ ʏᴏᴜ ᴇᴠᴇʀ ᴛʜᴏᴜɢʜᴛ ᴀʙᴏᴜᴛ ᴀʟʟ ᴛʜᴇ ɴᴀᴍᴇs ꜰᴏʀ ʟᴀᴡʏᴇʀs? No, not those names—but ones like attorney, attorney-at-law, counselor, and advocate.

The Old English word for a then ill-defined lawyer was forspeaker (*forspeca* or *forspreca*). Latin, however, had already developed a number of more finely tuned words. For example, "advocate" was related to the Roman *advocatus,* and "proctor" to the *procurator.* The *advocatus* and the *procurator* also have ties to the Catholic Church. The ecclesiastical *advocatus,* like the common-law serjeant, denoted a pleader, and the *procurator,* acting as an agent for a client-principal, plied his trade in the Church courts before he became an "attorney" in matters relating to civil, common, and admiralty law.

At Ease, Serjeant

"Serjeant" is not a term that many people (even most lawyers) recognize as being associated with the American legal profession. But the Supreme Court of New Jersey in 1755, for example, set up an

345

order of serjeants. There were initially twelve. They were recommended to the Governor by the judges and were called up by writ as in England. The order, however, was abolished in 1839.

❈ · ❈

The word "attorney," in use in England by the time of Bracton, comes from the Classical Latin word *torno* (to turn on a lathe) through Old French *atorner* (turn to, arrange) and *atorne* (one appointed). The Norman-French spelling of the word was influenced by the law-Latin word *attornatus*. An attorney, in old British usage, represented clients in legal matters but generally left the court work to others. The Brits, at least for the time being, have dropped this usage of the word—which is now filled by the "solicitor," a word that comes from the Norman *solicitor,* by way of the Classical Latin *sollicitare* meaning to stir up. (No comment is necessary.) At one time, the attorney operated at common law and the solicitor in equity.

The attorney-at-law distinguishes himself or herself from the attorney-in-fact, who does not have to be licensed to practice law. The attorney-in-fact acts as someone's agent (e.g., a son acting on behalf of his aged mother).

There are unresolved questions regarding the origin of the words "bar" and "barrister." It is known that the barrister's ancestor is the thirteenth-century student "pleader" (French via Latin) known as the *apprenticius ad barram* (apprentice at the bar). The bar likely refers to the railing in court, as in "before the bar."

"Counsel" comes from the Latin *consilium,* and "counselor" (as in "see you in court, counselor") is traceable to Latin *consiliator.* A *consilia,* for example, was a new type (or technically a retooled type) of jurisprudence that arose between about 1320 and 1600. These were legal briefs that litigants requested from famous jurists and submitted to the court for consideration. A confluence of juristic opinions, along with the money to pay for them, could affect the decisions of judges. In canon law, cases raising particularly serious or novel questions could, at any stage of the proceedings, be referred to distinguished canonists or law faculties, whose *consilia* were influential and sometimes even binding in the Church courts.

The notion of *consilia* also existed in America. Daniel Dulany the Younger, for example, is considered by many to be one of the greatest pre-Revolutionary lawyers, educated at Eton and Cambridge, England, and called to the Bar in 1746 by Middle Temple. Upon his return to America he was admitted to practice in 1747. He eventually gained a reputation as an oracle of the law, unrivaled in legal knowledge. In fact, cases were even sometimes withdrawn from Maryland courts, and once even from the Lord High Chancellor of England, to be submitted to him for his expert opinion and decision. Some of these opinions, like *consilia* and the opinions of Roman jurists, carried such great weight that they were included in the official *Maryland Reports* upon their first printing. (Just imagine the press if the U.S. Supreme Court solicited the opinion of a law professor—even if she was tenured at Harvard.)

"LAWYERS" AROUND THE WORLD

Around the world the notion of "lawyer" is expressed in a wide variety of names. In Japan, for example, there are the *bengoshi*—private practitioners who have graduated from the Legal Training and Research Institute. The *bengoshi*, who came into existence with the Lawyer's Law of 1893, were preceded by the first class of legal representatives in Japan, the *kujishi* (innkeepers) and then by the *daigennin* (advocates). The Germans have the *Anwälte* (private practitioners) and the *Syndici* (house counsel). In Italy you will find the *procuratore* and the *dottori commercialisti*. Spain has *abogados* (private lawyers), *procuradores* (attorneys who draft pleadings), *notaries, registrars, fiscales* (prosecutors), and *abogados del estado* (government lawyers). And in France there are *officiérs ministériels, avoués* (official representatives of parties responsible for procedural formalities in courts of appeal), *juristes d'entreprise, notaries, agréés, conseils juridiques,* and *avocats* (with the functions of *conseils juridiques* and *avocats,* after an unsuccessful attempt in 1971, finally merging in 1992).

Some parents are so inspired by the name that they end up using it on their kids. California birth-certificate information from the 1990s, for example, shows three children named "Lawyer."

XXXIV

LAWYER ADVERTISING

IN THE EARLY DAYS OF AMERICA there was no such thing as in-house counsel, a lawyer employed by a company with a lock on all its legal work. Consequently, almost all lawyers were constantly seeking new business. This meant advertising. While there were no legal constraints on advertising, there were some technical ones, such as the absence of phone books, radios, TVs, or the Internet. There were, however, business cards and newspapers, both of which were frequently used—along with circulars, city directories, and banquet programs. But word of mouth was often the best way to attract clients. And what better way to spread the word than through flamboyance and courtroom antics? Keep in mind that, along with there being no radios, TVs, or blogospheres, many people could not read, but everyone could appreciate the tragedy and comedy of a good trial—even if they had never heard of the ancient Greeks.

The Illinois circuit court where Abraham Lincoln conducted most of his trial work illustrates this point nicely. In the spring and the autumn, circuit judge David Davis opened his court in Springfield, Sangamon County, and then moved around a circuit comprising 12,000 square miles in the rural heartland of Illinois. Davis and his band of traveling lawyers provided a sought-after source of entertainment. Consequently, farmers and villagers often flocked in to watch the human drama.

Lawyer advertising has become more and more popular as a marketing tool over the past thirty years. Many lawyers are no longer content to simply place ads in newspapers and the phone book. They now resort to billboards, mass mailings, radio, the Internet, TV commercials, and even Christmas cards.

With lawyers becoming more aggressive in their attempts to solicit clients, states have become concerned. The question, however, is to what, if any, extent can states regulate lawyer advertising without violating the "right of free speech." Up until the mid-1970s, the First Amendment of the United States Constitution was believed not to provide any protection for commercial speech (e.g., "hire me"), in contrast to political speech (e.g., "vote for me"). The United States Supreme Court, in 1976, changed this view of the First Amendment by finding that commercial speech sometimes provides the public with important information and therefore should be given constitutional protection—at least to some extent. Then in 1977 the Court held that advertising by lawyers should be included in the category of commercial speech. The court cases in reaction to this decision have prompted state regulation of lawyer advertising so as to prevent in-person solicitation (since lawyers have a strong presence) and false or misleading communications (since lawyers can be extremely tricky).

A number of scholars have taken the position that lawyer advertisement and solicitation have historically been seen as antithetical to the notion of legal practice as an esteemed profession. In 1925 the American magazine *Lawyer and Banker,* for example, stated that it was unethical for a lawyer to advertise and emphasized that this "prohibition is well known to the legal profession and is ancient."

If "ancient" means ancient Rome, then this statement may not be exactly true. One of the most pervasive and characteristic elements of Roman society was the *clientele*—the relationship between persons of unequal social statues. A person became the client of a patron in any of several ways. But no matter how it happened, the client looked to the patron for legal protection, food and money, and a sense of contact with some sort of power. In turn the client owed the patron obligations that varied with the individual but that almost always included the duty of accompanying him each morning on a stroll through the Forum in order to display the patron's following to the entire city. Shocking as it may be, most of the high-profile orators and jurists had their *clientele*— bought and paid for. And what better way to advertise and solicit the business of those with high-profile legal problems than to have a large group of clients following you through the streets of Rome? Or, for that matter, Reno, Nevada!

Additionally, as we saw in Part V, the Templars were not above boosting their reputations by supplying copies of their speeches and cross-examinations to newspaper reporters. So much for "ancient."

An important question is whether or not information available to the public through lawyer advertising (as well as legal directories, referral services, the Yellow Pages, copyrighted pleadings, "brand names," and reputation) is an adequate basis for selecting a lawyer. It has been argued, particularly with regard to selecting a trial lawyer, that attorney advertising influences decision making but does not really provide the kind of information that results in an informed choice. Attorney advertising theoretically provides information to the public about the attorney's services and fees. Most of it, however, is designed simply to attract clients and not to provide an assessment of an attorney's abilities or competency.

XXXV

THE CARE AND FEEDING OF LAWYERS

OR, "SHOW ME THE MONEY!"

IN SEPTEMBER 1997, lawyers for the major cigarette companies stood before a federal judge in Texas and swore that their clients would never settle the state's multibillion-dollar Medicaid lawsuit. Five months later, the industry clients agreed to settle the case for $15.3 billion payable over 25 years. And the really good news is that the judge awarded an unprecedented $3.3 billion in legal fees to private lawyers representing the state. Yes, $3.3 billion!

While the Texas governor congratulated the state's attorney general for his outstanding victory, he had this to say about the legal fees: "Outrageous!" (By the way, the governor just happened to be George W. Bush.)

Robbing Peter to Pay Paul

The gurus of law and economics might point out that this tobacco settlement, along with many other similar lawsuits and settlements, is an example of deliberate obfuscation. While the lawsuit and settlement were described in terms of "damages" and "settlement payments," the reality is that there is simply a new national tax increase on each pack of cigarettes—in other words, a tax to be paid by smokers, the very group supposedly being benefited by the settlement.

⌘ · ⌘ · ⌘ · ⌘ · ⌘ · ⌘ · ⌘ · ⌘ · ⌘ · ⌘ · ⌘ · ⌘ · ⌘ · ⌘ · ⌘ · ⌘ · ⌘ · ⌘ · ⌘ · ⌘

CONTINGENCY FEES

Even at the hourly rate of a New York lawyer, it would take a lot of lawyers a lot of time to generate billable hours of more than $3 billion. The secret, however, is to simply take a percentage of the client's recovery. This way the lawyer has the chance of working out a settlement without years of dragging the case through the courts and quickly grabbing onto a pot of money—and also seeing that justice is done. This method of sharing the wealth (and risk) is called the "contingency fee," frequently used in class-action lawsuits.

The Roman Empire, in fact, developed an arrangement similar to a contingency fee called *redemptio litis.* The lawyer, pursuing litigation under this arrangement, would pay a plaintiff for the right to act as his *procurator* in the lawsuit. The understanding was that the *procurator* would keep any money obtained in the action from the defendant. *Redemptio litis* was, however, considered to be contrary to good morals. (And keep in mind that the Romans were a bunch of pagans!)

In American legal practice, the contingency fee, like numerous other legal concepts, has its roots not (at least directly) in ancient Rome, but in England. Unlike, however, the United States, the English, from the thirteenth century on, have attempted to prohibit the financing of litigation by a lawyer taking a share of the recovery. But they have not simply relied on the social forces of good morals, as was the case in Rome. Instead, the English have done the Christian thing and enacted statutes. This offensive activity in Brit-speak is called "champerty." And by the seventeenth century, English society was pressing down hard on it.

Scholars have surmised, based on the various statutory prohibitions, that risk sharing between lawyer and client once played a significant role in English legal activity. The practice appears to have been particularly prevalent with solicitors and their "ancestors." These wigless lawyers, however, rarely occupied lofty positions on high court benches or in Parliament. Such heights, as we have seen, were generally reserved for the more "elite" members of the legal profession like barristers. And the barristers, unlike Mr. Abraham Lincoln,

Esq., always collected their fees up front. They also seldom had contact with clients or the responsibility for starting litigation. It is therefore not surprising that the practices of the lowly solicitors might be frowned upon.

⚔ · ⚔ ·

Tort Reform?

Contingency fees are also prohibited as being incompatible with the ethical stature of a profession in a number of other countries, for example Australia, Germany, and Spain.

In tenth-century Iceland, the solution to the problem sought to be covered by the contingency fee was simply to make tort claims transferable. In contrast to the common law, an alleged tort victim could sell his claim to a neighbor with sufficient resources to prosecute it. Such transferability also arguably solves problems associated with tort damages for loss of life and provides a superior alternative to the class action. Interestingly enough, ancient Iceland did not have a lawyer class.

⚔ · ⚔ ·

But simply pooh-poohing a particular legal practice is generally not considered sufficient. In order to satisfy the deep psychological foundations of the law, there needs to be an articulated social, economic, or political reason behind the pooh-pooh. In the case of contingency fees, the argument was put forth that such an arrangement was a danger to society since it might encourage feudal lords to abuse the system in furtherance of power and property. A systemic evil. There is, in fact, some evidence that the rich did engage in, or at least encourage, litigation designed to undermine neighbors. The argument, however, was generally poppycock. The real reason for prohibiting contingency fees appears to have been a growing antipathy among the upper crust to litigation—particularly where the case was filed against one of their own by an aggrieved commoner. (A clear sign that we are no longer in ancient Greece.) In fact, limiting access to the courts is a theme running through English legal history. In contrast, Americans have traditionally loved to see the rich pay for their sins—or at least alleged sins.

AMERICAN LOVE OF THE TRIAL

The French chronicler Alexis de Tocqueville, besides possibly designating the lawyer as "king of the village idiots," observed that in early nineteenth-century America virtually every serious question eventually became a lawsuit. This method of attempting to solve problems speaks volumes about the society's receptivity to "law talk" and legal solutions. Americans also rejected English reticence about the right to counsel. Even before the adoption of the United States Constitution, Americans insisted that someone accused of having committed a felony had the right, assuming he could afford one, to be represented by a lawyer. The English, during this same time period, refused to recognize any such right.

On the civil side of things, Americans rejected (and still generally reject) the English notion of the loser paying not only the judgment but the attorney fees of his victorious opponent. This potential payment burden does not jibe with America's ideas of easy access to the courts, and the fact that lawyers are an important resource to which the all people should have access. God bless America!

There are, however, a number of problems (besides how to spend $3.3 billion in legal fees) lurking about in the dark corners of a contingency-fee arrangement. For example, what if the client, after the lawyer has put in countless hours on a case, decides to fire the lawyer and settle it himself? Or what if the client simply will not settle—despite the fact that the lawyer has come to realize that recovery at trial is becoming less and less likely?

The Contingency Gamble

There is also the obvious problem, at least from the lawyer's perspective, that the lawyer who loses has spent time and money on the case and does not receive a dime. Due to this harsh result, one New York lawyer reportedly took action. After losing a contingency-fee case, the lawyer demanded a fee from his client anyway. He also wrote to the client's father and threatened that the father would be subpoenaed if the fee was not paid.

The New York State Bar rewarded the lawyer's aggressiveness by suspending his license to practice law for six months. The lawyer then appealed to the United States Supreme Court. The Court declined to grant a hearing. In addition the Court took the opportunity to issue an order barring the lawyer from appearing before it until further notice.

The fact is that the client almost always retains the right to fire his or her attorney, as well as the power to make or accept a settlement offer. The American Bar Association's Model Rules of Professional Conduct provide, for example, that "[a] lawyer shall abide by a client's decision whether to accept an offer of settlement of a matter." For this reason a lawyer generally cannot include a provision in a retainer agreement preventing the client from settling without the lawyer's consent or allowing the lawyer to settle without the client's consent.

The Philadelphia Bar Association's Professional Guidance Committee wrestled with the ethical aspects of a contingency-fee clause that required the client to reimburse the lawyer for costs advanced in a case if (1) the client fired the lawyer; (2) the lawyer sought to withdraw for "just and adequate" reasons; or (3) the client rejected a "fair and reasonable" settlement offer.

The Committee said that a lawyer could require client reimbursement of costs under circumstances within the control of the client (discharge of the lawyer) or under the supervision of the court (withdrawal of the lawyer). But the Committee was troubled by the scenario in which a lawyer seeks to withdraw simply for "just and adequate" reasons. This is because once settlement of a lawsuit is proposed, an attorney should generally not be allowed to impose last-minute pressure on the client to come up with funds on the eve of trial. The Committee determined that the possibility of an eleventh-hour demand raised the specter that an attorney might force the client to accept a proposed settlement.

The ethical aspects of contingency-fee provisions have not been confined to Pennsylvania. A lawyer in Oregon, for example, proposed (as a standard term in his contingency-fee agreement) a provision that if a client rejected a settlement offer that the lawyer deemed reasonable, the lawyer was entitled to the agreed-upon percentage of the rejected settlement amount plus an hourly fee that kicked in when the client rejected the offer. The Oregon State Bar Association, passing on the coercion issue, held that the provision could very well make an otherwise lawful fee "clearly excessive" or "unreasonable." The ethics opinion did not, however, come to the conclusion that all uses of split contingent/hourly fee agreements are necessarily unethical.

In a class-action antitrust lawsuit involving the auction houses Sotheby's and Christie's, a "novel procedure" was used to select the plaintiffs' top-dog legal counsel. The presiding judge held an auction (rather ironic given the business of the two defendants). He required each bidding law firm to set a base dollar amount for recovery. Any settlement below that base amount would result in no legal fees being paid to the lawyers. One-quarter of any recovery above that amount would go to the lead counsel, in addition to fees and expenses. The winning bid was $405 million. The judge, in addition to the bid, took into account a firm's ability to achieve the stated goal. In the end the settlement was $512 million (divided equally between Sotheby's and Christie's), producing an excess of $107 million from which lead counsel's fees and expenses were deducted.

And at 25 percent, the lead counsel earned $26.75 million. The judge observed that the contingency fee at "5.2% of the [total] recovery . . . is among the lowest fee awards ever made in comparable litigation on a proportionate basis."

Before leaving the area of contingency fees, it is noted that one of the least litigious countries in the industrialized world also embraces this concept. The Japanese courtroom attorney (*bengoshi*) is generally paid an initial fixed "retainer fee," calculated as a percentage of the amount alleged in the complaint. He is also usually entitled to a "success fee" calculated as a percentage of the recovery resulting from the, hopefully, favorable judgment or settlement (a payment scheme currently being pursued by certain United States law firms). The contingent portion of the attorney's fee, however, rarely reaches the high percentage common in American legal practice.

OTHER METHODS OF PAYMENT

Since lawyers are nothing if not imaginative, there are a number of other methods for compensation other than by contingency fee. There is always the good old standard of hourly rate. A Connecticut judge, however, recently found it a bit unreasonable to charge clients $250 per hour for the services of an attorney only three years out of law school—especially when the law firm was paying the young attorney less than $25 per hour. And as competition for legal business increases, firms that desire to maintain their position in the marketplace have started offering various types of "alternative billings." These alternatives include such payment methods as fixed-price and incentive-fee. The main thrust of these new schemes is to price and deliver legal services on the basis of their perceived value to the client—a consumer surplus that hopefully makes the client happy.

Business clients, in particular, like value billing because they can base their decisions on known or reasonably estimated legal costs. In addition it is easier for them to compare the price of one firm against that of another.

⊠ · ⊠

The Fixed-Fee Revolution

What about establishing set statutory amounts that lawyers can charge for particular tasks? An Act of May–June 1674 in Maryland, for example, provided that the fee for arguing a case before the Provincial Court was 400 pounds of tobacco, the fee in the High Court of Chancery was 800 pounds, and the fee in the County Courts was 200 pounds. And in February 1675, a further Act for Regulation of Attorneys Fees was passed. This new Act reiterated the provisions contained in the prior Act—but lowered the maximum permissible lawyers' fee for an action in the County Court to sixty pounds of tobacco. (You may recall from our earlier discussion on the Stamp Act that this payment method, given the shortage of hard currency in the colonies, created a problem in purchasing the stamps that were supposed to be attached to various legal documents. Hence, legal fees and revolution.)

Under traditional hourly billing, charges for legal services consist of fees based on the time spent on the project, plus costs (e.g., long-distance phone calls, copying, and mailing)—without, hopefully, the "Skaddenomics" component. The principal downside of this method is that it can be seen as rewarding inefficiency, at least until the client decides to change lawyers. Billings and profits go up as more time is spent on projects. Consequently, long and redundant legal language will most likely occur, as it did in Merrie Olde England, when lawyers charged by the page. While charging by the hour versus the page provides a less direct incentive to be verbose, it still supplies a strong incentive to show that size matters. In contrast, when lawyers are paid on a contingent- or fixed-fee basis, their writing generally gets to the point rather quickly.

The economic relationship between profit and time changes under value billing. This is because the lawyer's charges are based on perceived value to the client rather than on the lawyer's costs. Cost control therefore becomes critical. The price of the services is a constant and every dollar of cost saved translates into another dollar of profit for the lawyer.

One of the cutting-edge attempts to reduce legal costs involves the Internet. There are a number of existing and planned Web sites where potential clients can package up legal work and solicit bids from law firms in an online auction. The idea of these "B-to-B" e-commerce sites is for the participating firms to bid against each other in order to drive down the cost of legal services.

One such Web site developer has observed that clients all too often hold "beauty contests" among a small number of law firms they already know. There are, however, scores of other law firms that most likely are qualified and willing to complete on price—but never get a foot in the door.

All of this talk about multimillion-dollar contingency fees and billable hours might give one the impression that all lawyers make fabulous sums of money. The truth is that if you want to be part of the upper economic crust, become a movie or rock star—not a lawyer. According to *Forbes*'s 2008 list, "lawyer" ranks seventeenth of top-paying jobs. The average pay for lawyers, according to the list, is $118,280. Medical specialists took the top nine spots. Anesthesiologists, with an average salary of $192,780, were first, followed by surgeons, with an average salary of $191,410. Executives were tenth, and airline pilots were eleventh. The reason for lawyers' relatively low ranking is that the legal profession, at least in the

United States, appears to teeter somewhere between oligopolistic and monopolistic competition—with perhaps an increasing tendency toward the former. The following highlights some of the highs and lows of lawyer earning power over the late twentieth and early twenty-first centuries in the United States:

1. The U.S. Census Bureau computed that the median income for all lawyers in 1993 was $72,144; in 2008, according to *Forbes,* it was about $118,000.

2. The IRS, in 1993, received returns from 28,990 partnerships, which had a total of 138,855 partners. These lawyers reported a net average of $135,020—substantially more than solo practitioners at an average net income of $46,995. The median for the 515,000 salaried practitioners was $58,200, breaking down into $60,892 for the 360,000 male lawyers and $49,816 for the 155,000 female lawyers.

3. The 1,059 partners in New York's ten wealthiest firms averaged about $1,043,201 in 1995. In comparison, the 1,125 lawyers in the top ten firms in Washington, D.C., where everyone is a lawyer, averaged $418,480; next in line were the 1,263 San Francisco Bay Area lawyers at $339,418. And in 2002 the average partner at the white-shoe law firm of Cravath, Swaine & Moore took home nearly $2 million in bonus pay—loads more cash than its 2007 announcement of special bonuses for associates that ranged from a mere $10,000 to $50,000. (But these "special bonuses" were in addition to the traditional year-end bonuses of $60,000.)

   For 2007 the profit-per-equity-partner winner was Wachtell, Lipton, Rosen & Katz at $4.48 million. Its nearest competitor was Cravath, Swaine & Moore at a measly $3.3 million average profit per equity partner.

4. In 1995 the median compensation for chief legal officers of Big Businesses was $222,000—a number well above the average. The general counsel at Avon Products, for example, made $405,768; Campbell's soup gave its top lawyer $625,209; and Johnson & Johnson paid out $873,375 to its chief legal eagle. And chief legal officers and general counsel in legal departments of more than twenty-five lawyers made, according to one survey, a median of $645,000 in total cash compensation in 2007. Median cash compensation ranged from $285,000 for companies with $300 million or less in gross annual revenue to $740,000 for those with more than $10 billion in gross annual revenue, according to another survey. This pay was, of course, separate from any stock options.

5. Google's chief legal officer made a salary of $450,000 in 2008. But that measly amount did not include the $5.12 million, which included $1.38 million in bonus and $3.29 million in stock and option awards.

This top legal eagle earned nearly $11.9 million by exercising options and stock awards. In comparison, the average total compensation (including pay, bonus, and the value of long-term incentives) for chief legal officers of large companies for 2008 was approximately $2 million.

6. In 2007 the starting salaries for first-year lawyers at most of the 200 largest firms nationwide averaged $160,000—along (sometimes) with such perks as candied apples, pet insurance, concierge services, home mortgage guarantees, and on-site tailoring. (The 2009 "recession" undoubtedly put a crimp in such starting salaries and perks.)

7. Ending this somewhat random list on a sobering note, a 1995 survey done by the *National Law Journal* showed that Florida's Broward County started its prosecutors at $25,000. In Texas, the attorney general's office began its new hires at $30,492. Chicago's beginning public defenders got $32,772—not bad compared with Western Kentucky Legal Services lawyers' whopping $24,200. And the median starting pay for prosecutors in 2006 was $46,000, and $38,000 for legal services lawyers.

Society's Popular Misconceptions

People also tend to think that drug dealers make loads of money. As stated, however, by the authors of *Freakonomics—A Rogue Economist Explores the Hidden Side of Everything*, "a crack gang works pretty much like the standard capitalist enterprise: you have to be near the top of the pyramid to make a big wage." For example, the leader of a Chicago "franchise" (J.T.) made about $100,000 (tax-free) per year, not including various off-the-books money he pocketed. And the gang's top 20 bosses (comprising "the board of directors"), to whom J.T. reported, earned about $500,000 a year. On the other hand, J.T.'s three officers each took home $700 a month (about $7 an hour) and his foot soldiers earned a whopping $3.30 an hour—less than the minimum wage.

One difference, however, between being a lawyer and a crack dealer is that while you might have a one in four chance of being "dissed" as a lawyer, you have a one in four chance of being killed as a crack dealer.

LAWYERS FOR FREE

Yes, many lawyers perform legal services for free. Surprise! In light of the legal profession's "special calling," lawyers are encouraged (and sometimes, as previously noted, required) by bar associations to help meet the needs of those who cannot afford to hire a lawyer. And in order to link up with the nobility of those Roman jurisconsults who dispensed legal advise for free, such modern-day assistance goes by the fancy Latin name *pro bono.*

Pro Bono over No Bono

In 2008 and 2009, in a response to the economic downturn, more U.S. law-yers have "volunteered" for pro bono work. Several law firms switched lawyers with idle time to helping low-income clients. For example, the Dechert law firm moved seven associates to full-time pro bono work due to the slowdown in structured finance. At Akin Gump Strauss Hauer & Feld, pro bono hours rose to 85 hours per lawyer through September 2008 as compared to 69 hours per law-yer in 2007. The fact is that for idle lawyers, pro bono is better than "no bono."

An interesting example of this lawyer-for-nothing occurred in the case of former Illinois Governor George Ryan. The Chicago law firm of Winston & Strawn took up the governor's defense on fraud and corruption charges that stemmed from his tenure as Illinois secretary of state. And the cost of this pro bono effort to the firm? $10 million plus! In fact, during the trial the firm asked the trial judge to allow jurors to know that their client was paying noth-ing for his defense. The reason for this request (besides good publicity) was that the defense team was worried that the jury would view the high-powered firm's participation as an indication that the ex-governor was rich. One prong of the defense strategy was to argue that the ex-governor lived in a simple manner belying prosecution arguments that he had received cash from influence seek-ers. (By the way, the verdict was guilty on all 21 counts.)

A mass example of pro bono work occurred when 350 lawyers descended on the small West Texas town of San Angelo in 2008. The reason for this locust of legal talent involved representation of 462 children and their parents caught up in the raid of a polygamist sect's compound. This raid triggered one of the largest child-custody cases in U.S. history. And the attitude of one of the Texas attorneys involved in helping to sort out the complex issues involving parent–child–state interests exemplifies the highest tradition of the bar: "We've got a saying in this pro bono business here that it's 'billable hours for your soul.'"

XXXVI

THE WORD

Wₕₐₜ ABOUT THE LANGUAGE OF THE LAW—that customary language used by lawyers? Do lawyers derive the same kind of ecstatic joy from the language of statutes, case law, court documents, and contracts as a Muslim before the Qur'an or a Jew before the Torah? Or, if not exactly joy, do they at least get some type of perverse pleasure?

It is important to recognize that the way lawyers talk and write is not conditioned only by the law. The prevailing language must be considered. England, as we saw in Part V, is the oldest extant common-law jurisdiction and English, due in no small part to the Black Death, is its official language. This confluence of factors has certainly influenced the barristers and solicitors of England, as well as the lawyers of America. In fact, while it may not seem like it, the great bulk of words used by English and American lawyers are just ordinary English. There is a point, however, at which language used by lawyers (and judges, and most definitely by law professors) departs from common speech. Examples of this turn include the use of common words with uncommon meanings (e.g., "instrument" meaning not a violin but a legal document); the use of Old English and Middle English words once in common use, but now rarely used (e.g., "aforesaid" and "forthwith"); the use of Latin words and phrases (e.g., *corpus delicti*); the use of Old French and Anglo-Norman words that have not been adopted into general usage (e.g., "estopped"); the deliberate use of words and expressions with flexible meanings (e.g., "on or about"); attempts at extreme precision of expression (e.g., "and for no other purpose"); and the use of formal words and procedure (e.g., "may it please the court," and "the truth, the whole truth and nothing but the truth, so help me God").

CHARACTERISTICS OF LEGALESE

There are other characteristics that set off the language of the law from ordinary speech, as well as from other specialized speech—a truth that stretches all the way back to the Sumerian scribes and their training in legal terminology. The language of the law tends to be wordy, pompous, and frequently dull. This indictment of dullness even applies to such documents as the Emancipation Proclamation written by lawyer-President Abraham Lincoln. It has been observed that unlike, for example, the rhetorical heights of the Gettysburg Address, the Declaration is stiff, having all the zip of a bill of lading. But it is also the case that the Gettysburg Address "merely" dedicated a cemetery, while the Emancipation Declaration affected the legal status of millions of people. And if the goal of scientists is to say much with little ($E = mc^2$) then all too frequently, the goal of lawyers is to say little with much.

Making the Extraordinary Ordinary

Karl Marx, reporting for a London newspaper, understood the importance of what Lincoln had done in writing the Emancipation Proclamation—and, almost as important, why he did it the way he did. Marx observed that the "most formidable decrees which he hurls at the enemy and which will never lose their historic significance, resemble—as the author intends them to—ordinary summons, sent by one lawyer to another."

The wordiness of legal speech and documents is sometimes not just sheer pomposity but is actually a means of attempting to cover up a tautology. It has been pointed out, for example, that when Blackstone, in his *Commentaries,* stated that no man could be a tenant at sufferance against the king because the king could not be guilty of laches, what was really being said was: (1) the king cannot suffer a tenant at sufferance because he cannot be guilty of laches; and (2) because the king cannot be guilty of laches, he cannot suffer a tenant at sufferance. In other words, once it is decided that the king cannot be guilty of laches (an equitable statute of limitations) and that laches is something that is necessary for the creation of a tenancy at sufferance, then it follows tautologically that no man can be a tenant at sufferance against the king. The use of lots of words by Blackstone to back up the point makes it seem, however, that some kind of deep logic is involved—or at least more than mere power politics.

But it is important to note that "tautology" is not necessarily a dirty word. Mathematics is all tautological. Every conclusion follows completely from its own premises. Arguably a good thing. There is, however, a big difference between a mathematical theorem that has no direct connection to the real world or even one that arguably has an unreasonable effectiveness and a law or legal decision, wrapped up in a tautology, that seeks to deny real people real property rights. Arguably a bad (or at least a misleading) thing.

IT'S ALL IN THE PRESENTATION

It is also important to consider how the lawyer delivers his or her words. Like anyone in the communications business, "the medium is the message" (at least to some extent), and it certainly affects the message conveyed. Reflecting back on ancient Greece, the oral transmission and interpretation of law was significantly affected by shoving it into a phonetic alphabet. And both oral and written law, as presented in the law courts, were affected by the development of drama—tragedy ("goat song") and comedy.

But as Quintilian recognized, not every way of presenting "the word" is equal. There is vividness to consider. And vividness is tied up with the various modalities of linguistic communications. The prevailing view is that these modalities are each controlled by a different center in the brain: linguistic, paralinguistic, and nonlinguistic. The linguistic deals with the spoken or signed word. The paralinguistic involves any part of vocal behavior that affects the communicative content of an utterance but is not part of the linguistic system—for example, intonation, stress, rate, pause, pitch, and rhythm. (Think Johnnie Cochran in front of the O.J. Simpson jury propounding a type of coherence theory of truth: "If it doesn't fit, you must acquit.") And the nonlinguistic concerns gestures, posture, facial expression, gaze, head and body movement, and proxemics—any part of body behavior that affects the communicative content of an utterance but is not part of the linguistic system. So while the increase in choice for presenting "the word" may seem like a good thing, it also increases the pressure on the lawyer to get it "right."

For the modern-day lawyer the choices for presenting "the word" have only expanded. She can now consider such things as oral argument versus written argument, oral Q and A versus written Q and A, photographs, tape recordings, handwritten material, printed material, videos, and all kinds of electronic data—all submitted, distributed, displayed, or projected in the trappings of a legal drama. In other words, there's been a marked increase in dramatic "props."

OLD FOREIGN LANGUAGES

It has often been said that almost all of the English words that have a definite legal meaning are in a certain sense French. The importance of French words to the language of the common law is undoubtedly significant, but overemphasizing its influence discounts the contributions of Old English, as well as adaptations directly from Old Norse and Latin. For example, an Old Norse "crook" is the same as an Old English "hook"—a bent piece of metal. Middle English, through the process of semantic drift, later used "crook," among other things, to mean trickery or deceit. By the fourteenth century, the two words were joined to form "by hook or by crook." Later, hook meant to steal, and a hooker is still a "thief" (of sorts).

Some other examples of the Old English–French–Latin connection involve the fact that Mr. and Mrs. Smith in Old English "buy" a "house," but in French they "purchase" a "mansion." In French they take "possession" of their home, but in Old English they "own" it. The Smiths live in their home with their Old English "child," their French "infant," and a Latin "minor."

Keep in mind that such connections are not, however, just some weird fetish of lawyers. When ordering at a restaurant you most likely don't say, "I'll have the pig." Instead you politely order the pork. And you probably don't ask the waiter, "How's the sheep?" but inquire about the mutton. The reason for both of these, among many others, is that the English-speaking serfs, who lost at the battle of Hastings in 1066, tended the pigs and sheep, and the victorious French nobility ate pork (*porc*) and mutton (*mouton*).

A Likely Story

One of the valiant, but strained, defenses of law French made by such lawyer-apologists as Sir Edward Coke was that it was an easily learned tool of unequaled linguistic precision, necessary to fix the precise meaning of legal terms securing property and liberty. Nonsense! The reasons for using law French had to do with keeping the law mysterious and maintaining control over it.

Latin was at one time the language of all official documents in England. Even after English became generally used, Latin maxims, which were originally precepts of Roman law or inventions of medieval jurists, survived. There has been a recent push, particularly in England, to do away with Latin phrases in court proceedings. And interestingly enough, Latin was already abolished once from the law courts. An act passed by Parliament in 1730 did away with law Latin (and law French) in legal proceedings. Lawyers then faced the challenge of rendering certain Latin phrases into English. Such phases as *nisi prius* (unless before), *quaere impedit* (wherefore he hinders), and *habeas corpus* (you should seize the body) all caused great difficulty. According to William Blackstone, such phrases were "not capable of an English dress with any degree of seriousness." The withdrawal pains were simply too great. And so after much begging and pleading an act was passed in 1732 that allowed lawyers to attack and parry in a classical language once again.

Another reason for lawyers to cling to Latin phrases was not simply to impress the "common man," but that various phrases had been used for so long that many of them had acquired subtle meanings that could not be easily captured in an English translation. For example, *res ipsa loquitur* (a phrase from Cicero: *res loquitur ipsa, quaesemper valent plurimum*) translates to mean "the thing speaks for itself"—a group of words that provides little insight into the true significance of the Latin phrase. In the law of negligence, *res ipsa loquitur* refers to situations in which a court is prepared to draw an inference of negligence against a defendant without hearing detailed evidence of what he did or did not do.

Another argument for use of a "dead" language like Latin or law French is its claimed resistance to change. In other words, the language is no longer susceptible to the vagaries in usage that "plague" every living language. Consequently it is ideally suited for usage in fixed legal terminology. The problem with this argument is that it is unrealistic to believe that legal vocabulary, whether in a dead or living language, can or even should achieve such rigidity. Legal vocabulary comes from society and its institutions, both of which frequently change (via, as we have seen, diversity generators and resource shifters), resulting in the meaning of associated concepts also changing. Witness, for example, the current fight over the word "marriage."

Latin plays a significant role in certain fields of endeavor—medicine, for example. The law's dependency on Latin phrases is, however, arguably outdated. There is a story that in a civil case arising in England from a 1984 miners' strike, a judge rebuked counsel for the plaintiff: "Is your client not aware of the maximum *ex turpi causa non oritur action* [a participant in wrongdoing cannot bring an action based on that event]?" To this question counsel dryly responded: "The people of Barnsley are speaking of little else."

✞ · ✞

Doctors as Interpreters

Because the treatises of Galen and other Greek physicians came into the hands of medieval healers, Greek, along with Latin and Latin words with

Greek endings, plays a significant role in the technical language of Western medicine. About three fourths of Western medical terminology is of Greek origin and one fourth is Latin.

· ※ · ※

There are a number of reasons why legal language clings to archaic vocabulary and grammar:

- Like most major religions, the law tends to venerate authoritative texts. Just as the Qur'an, for example, is the authoritative source of religion for Islamic believers, constitutions, statutes, and judicial opinions, sometimes written hundreds of years ago (and almost exclusively by men), are the primary sources of law for the legal profession. The United States Constitution is certainly revered by many American lawyers, even though (or perhaps somewhat because) parts of it have become difficult for citizens to understand.

- The words and phrases of legal texts have frequently been the subject of authoritative interpretations over the years. This is certainly the case with the United States Constitution. Consequently, rewriting a statute or constitution tends to bring into question the applicability of legal decisions that have attempted to clarify what the text means and how it should be applied in particular situations.

- In the practice of law the safest course of action, for both the client and the lawyer, is usually to follow that which has been previously tested. In other words, if a particular word, phrase, or legal structure has past muster in an earlier legal proceeding, it should work (at least from a malpractice perspective) again.

- It is more convenient and economical for lawyers to use existing forms. Many law firms, like ancient Mesopotamian scribes, have built up large collections of documents that were drafted in the past and that can be used as a starting point for future deals. Consequently, the tendency is to perpetuate the same (and often stilted) language. Why reinvent the wheel?

- Archaic language tends to give the legal system a sense of timelessness and therefore something deserving of great respect—not unlike the laws of Lipit-Ishtar (Akkadian) being written in the "dead" language of Sumerian.

- Finally, archaic language also helps justify the profession's monopoly on the "practice of law." Like the astrologer and priest discussed in Part II, the layman must rely on the professional in order to obtain an accurate reading of the legal document's hidden meaning.

It is important to stress, with regard to this last point, that it is not just archaic language that creates reliance, but language in general—especially where it takes on legal meaning. As was the case in various ancient civilizations and cultures previously discussed, words, spoken or written, contain power. And lawyers, with their super-secret access to words that have legal meaning, are perceived to possess powers that mere mortals can only dream of. This magical charge, in turn, can be used by lawyers to cause the legal and political machinery of a society to do their bidding. And the means by which all of this is accomplished is frequently through sophistry and verbal skills (rhetoric) that are perceived as some type of trickery. It is no wonder that the word for lawyers is not always love.

XXXVII

COMPETENCY AND THE LEGAL WARRIOR

W HAT CONSTITUTES "COMPETENCY"? One definition is "an individ-ual's capacity to perform a particular task in an acceptable manner." With regard to lawyers, the American Bar Association's Task Force on Lawyer Competency has listed seven fundamental skills (exemplars added in parentheses):

1. Analyze legal problems (Vinnie and Sal);
2. Perform legal research (Roman jurists);
3. Collect and sort facts (Cicero);
4. Write effectively (both in general and in a variety of special-ized lawyer applications such as pleadings, opinion letters, briefs, contracts, wills, and legislation) (Lysias);
5. Communicate orally with effectiveness in a variety of set-tlings (Demosthenes);
6. Perform important lawyer tasks that call on both communi-cation and interpersonal skills (Abraham Lincoln):
   (a) interviewing
   (b) counseling
   (c) negotiating
7. Organizing and managing legal work (Tribonian).

The Difference Between Lawyers and Computers

There is a growing amount of research on the question of whether techno-logical change is "skill-based" or not. It is far from obvious whether it matters what the average worker knows about his or her craft—particularly given the rise of computers. After all, the unit that applies the technique, be it an artisan, a large industrial plant, or a household, does not need to know the epistemic base in question. Instead what it needs is the wherewithal to carry out the rules and instructions of prescriptive knowledge. This competence is normally much less encompassing than the epistemic base. With regard to legal practice, propositional knowledge is relatively thin (as compared, for example, with physics) but prescriptive knowledge is relatively expan-sive. What this means, from a competency point of view, is that in the area of legal practice, propositional and prescriptive knowledge are closely tied together; the "unit" (i.e., lawyer) that applies the technique should know something about its epistemic base. I believe that much of that epistemic base, grounded in cognitive theory, comes from other disciplines such as economics, politics, history, morality, linguistics, mathematics, philosophy, logic, psychology, and sociology.

TRIAL COMPETENCY

With these factors in mind, let us first take a look at another skill: trial com-petency (Darrow). The issues involved in this task can be brought into sharper focus by comparing two different systems of legal practice: English barristers/solicitors versus American lawyers.

On the English side of legal practice, barristers, as we have seen, are restricted from direct access to potential clients. This appears to be a key fac-tor in attempting to ensure quality courtroom performance. Barristers obtain clients through solicitors and barrister clerks, all generally male. This practice encourages clerks, acting as market intermediaries, to match up the right bar-rister for a particular case. The reason for this is that the solicitor wants a satis-fied client and the barrister clerk is frequently paid a percentage of what the barrister brings in. And these economic incentives might, in turn, be argued to put solicitors and clerks in the position of wholesalers that reduce a consumer's search costs for quality services.

It is also the case that barristers, in general, have a very focused practice, namely advocacy. It is the solicitor who receives the client calls, interviews witnesses, prepares pleadings, and generally investigates a case—the fact gathering and sorting emphasized by Cicero. After reviewing a solicitor's papers prepared on a case (called a "brief"), the barrister then advises, counsels, and if necessary, dons his wig and gown.

Barristers are also, at least in theory, relieved of the day-to-day tasks of managing a legal practice. The barrister clerk distributes work to the various barristers for which he or she works, arranges the calendar, keeps the books, and negotiates and collects legal fees. As indicated above, solicitors refer cases to the barrister of his or her choice. The initial contact, however, is with the barrister's clerk. If the barrister is available and an acceptable fee is negotiated by the solicitor and the clerk on behalf of the barrister, the solicitor sends a brief to chambers.

Just a Few More Differences Across the Pond

Though in England a "brief" is a written case summary for the guidance of a barrister, in the United States it is a written argument to the court. This is just one example of the different dialects of legalese in various English-speaking countries.

Another difference is that, historically, barristers do not discuss payment for services—their clerks do it—and they do not sue to collect fees. The underlying notion is that barristers are not involved in a trade. In fact, on the back of the barrister's gown is a little pocket that in earlier times enabled him to be paid without actually seeing or handling money, at least in the client's presence.

In contrast to the barrister/solicitor system, there is no official division between attorneys engaged in litigation and other attorneys (e.g., transactional lawyers) within the American legal profession. Nevertheless, some American lawyers do consider themselves to be advocacy specialists. And large law firms develop litigation departments, thus attempting to keep the space between propositional and prescriptive knowledge (i.e., trial theory and technique) as narrow as possible.

This informal division between transactional and litigation counsel does not, however, ensure that a particular lawyer possess all the skills required to perform effectively in a given case. Neither professional rules nor statutes restrict them from working directly on all aspects of a case, from analyzing legal problems to negotiating a settlement. Even more importantly, a specialty in litigation is not required for an American lawyer to engage in trial practice. And unlike solicitor and barrister clerks who help clients generally get to the right barrister, clients in the United States may end up hiring a lawyer that lacks the training to properly handle the particular case at hand.

The client may believe that because the lawyer has passed the appropriate bar exam he or she is competent to appear in any court. This belief is laced with danger. An American lawyer may appear in any court, provided he or she has passed the appropriate bar exam and the court has recognized the lawyer's admission to practice before that court. Bar examinations, however, do not generally test the skills necessary to ensure courtroom competency. After the bar exam is passed, admission to practice in most courts, including the United States Supreme Court, is pro forma.

IMPORTANT LAWYER TRAITS

Beyond mere competency, the question is: What makes a lawyer a good lawyer? There is speculation that perhaps the low opinion of lawyers held by (some of?) the public might arise from the public's inability to know or understand what makes a lawyer a "good lawyer," let alone a really good lawyer—the ultimate lawyer. The following, drawing on our 5,000-year journey, are arguably important traits:

THE GOOD LAWYER IS ETHICAL. HE OR SHE MAKES CLEAR AND UNEQUIVOCAL ETHICAL DISTINCTIONS—EVEN IN THE FACE OF DIFFICULT QUESTIONS.

Does this mean that contrary to popular opinion, lawyers, at least the good ones, are secular priests shining their moral beacon into the dark corners of society? The answer is generally no. The modern-day concept of morality generally relates to a set of rules concerning right and wrong that lacks a means of enforcement. The concept of ethics is generally grounded in relatively clear and teachable rules about relationships with others. In the case of lawyers, a violation of the rules of legal ethics can indeed bite him or her on the tuchus. This is why, as we saw earlier, the ABA is concerned with how lawyers carry out their role as lawyers and not, as is the case with the pope, about the morals of lawyers. The bar generally does not care if a lawyer is committing adultery with his neighbor's wife as long as he is doing a good job for his clients (*arēte;* not sainthood).

German Capital Crimes

> In sixteenth-century Germany, the imperial *Constitutio Criminalis Carolina* (1532), as well as the *Bambergensis*, was concerned with reforming the procedural and substantive law applicable to capital crimes. These crimes included unnatural sex acts, pimping, and violations by attorneys of their duties to clients.

However, it has been pointed out that a key social contribution of lawyers involves (or at least should involve) helping clients live up to their best instincts and deepest moral values. This type of role, separate and apart from professional ethics, does require advocates to pass judgment and to identify ways of harmonizing client and public interest. Even profit-driven businesses often need (think Enron and a number of banks and brokerage houses in the 2009 "recession") and want counselors who, like secular priests, help prick the "corporate conscience." A type of absolute empathy plus moral instruction.

A GOOD LAWYER SHOULD BE ABLE TO HEIGHTEN, OR AT LEAST ATTEMPT TO HEIGHTEN, THE CLIENT'S LEGAL CONSCIOUSNESS.

This is not the same as conscience but has to do with the way in which people see the law—particularly as it applies to their particular case.

Certain scholars have argued that there are three predominant types of legal consciousness—three different ways in which people see their relationships to the law. The first has been called "before the law." In this form of consciousness, legality is experienced as if it were a separate sphere from ordinary social life: something "out there" that exists as a formally ordered and rational system of rules and procedures. In the second, "with the law," consciousness envisions the law as a game, a loosely bounded arena in which preexisting rules can be used and new rules, if necessary, can be invented to serve the widest range of interests and values. It is an arena of competitive tactical maneuvering where pursuing self-interest is expected and those who have the skill and resources to play the game well have a much better chance of coming out on top—a modified

Athenian approach. And the final form is the somewhat Kafkaesque "against the law." Here people feel a sense of being caught within the law, or being up against it. Their response is therefore to try to find moments of respite from the power of the law, using whatever form of resistance might be available: foot dragging, omissions, and small deceits.

It would seem that the lawyer, through good communications with the client—talking and, the more difficult part, listening—can expand the client's legal consciousness; after all, the client has paid for enlightenment. In the case of "before the law," the lawyer might help the client, for example, see that there is a big difference between the formal institutional apparatus of law (mounds of papers, courtrooms, reporters, armed bailiffs, and judges in black robes looking down from on high) and the discrete, often disjointed, and sometimes contradictory aspects of the law itself. Thus the law is not a thing separate from the social world but is very much a human and contingent enterprise—a product of the mind. And where it is clear that the client sees the law primarily in gamelike terms (as did many of the ancient Greeks), the lawyer can explain the basic rules, normative framework, and possible endings of the agonistic game that the client is about to play.

It has been suggested that the law, at least in modern American legal ideology, is made up of a weave of both "before the law" and "with the law." In other words, at any moment the law has the feel of being both a transcendent object and a game. And out of this interplay, the third type of consciousness often arises: "against the law." Legality's power rests on its ability to be played like a game that draws from and contributes to everyday life and yet exists as a realm removed from and distant from the ordinary affairs of particular lives; this dichotomy can breed distrust. It is the good lawyer that can artfully help the client reach the highest level of integrated consciousness involving "before the law," "within the law," and "against the law."

Video Killed the Radio Star

With the increase of pictures in newspapers, magazines, and books, along with movies and television and especially the Internet, the routine imagination of large masses of people has become pictorial versus verbal. The influence of books has thus receded—along with people's attention span. This means that people's capacity to concentrate, indeed to listen, is on the decline. This may mean that we are heading into an age of MTV lawyers arguing their MTV clients' cases to MTV judges and juries—with the result that the practice of law will become much more about rapid sound bites and flashes of color than about detailed analysis.

A GOOD LAWYER HAS INSIGHT AND SAVVY WITH REGARD TO PROBLEMS, CLIENTS, AND ISSUES.

The crux of this trait is the ability to get at the heart of a problem and to anticipate what is to come next, so that the lawyer hopefully can lower the fixed costs—time, effort, opportunity costs, and anticipated regret—that the client will "pay" in deciding how he or she wishes to proceed. This skill does not necessarily have to be inborn but can be acquired by the lawyer through experience, listening carefully to others, and observing.

Notably, the ability to anticipate can be seen in chimpanzees—but not just any chimp. Researchers have found that it takes about twenty years to learn how to hunt. Youngsters carefully observe the most skilled hunters and model their own techniques on theirs. And what is it that distinguishes the most skilled? Anticipation. The top chimp hunters, not unlike good lawyers, have the ability to anticipate the actions of their intended prey, and what's more, to anticipate the effect that the actions of others will have on the behavior of the intended prey. And there you have it: It is not by instinct that chimps and lawyers such as Lysias acquire the important skill of "double anticipation," but through experience and observation.

THE GOOD LAWYER IS IN TUNE WITH THE SOUND, SMELL, TASTE, AND FEEL OF WORDS.

This trait is not simply the ability to write with clarity or grammatical excellence, but also involves the ability to read into a sentence its important implications. This is a trait that I have found sometimes causes tension between lawyer and client—the sometimes difficult issues concerning "what if this happens" and "what if that happens." The lawyer wants to cover possibility after possibility—which can, in the long run, save the client time, money, and heartache—and the client sees needless words and mounting legal fees. The key to resolving this tension is that the good lawyer, based upon an understanding of the law and practical experience, can quickly hone in on the truly important "what ifs" and propose practical solutions.

In addition, there is a growing awareness of the connection between law and linguistics. It has been said, for example, that language is an "ideal code." It is, according to this line of thought, the very type of thing that is sought for in the law: sufficiently flexible in order to accommodate new situations and yet rigid enough to provide predictive power. Linguists have made considerable progress in finding and analyzing predictable order in the seemingly infinite variety of speech. The same exploratory methods that have enabled linguists to make scientific progress can, according to the movement of law and linguistics, help lawyers find and analyze predictable order in complex textual issues—for example, in statutes, regulations, and contracts.

⊠ · ⊠

The Linguistic Imagination

It is indeed the case that a good lawyer is a careful and resourceful reader. Therefore, in addition to linguistics, legal scholarship has pointed out that immersion into poetry and other difficult imaginative literature can be an important related source in the study of law (with, for example, conceptual metaphors constituting a point of connection between the two disciplines). Certain legal academics have pointed out that the one thing lawyers are particularly trained to do is to think about imaginary future cases. The ability to fashion hypothetical cases and to explore them technically and empathetically is arguably the lawyer's professional forte.

⊠ · ⊠

Simply stated, linguistics is the scientific study of human language. And the importance of this study to the law was recognized by the ancient Greeks in their trivium of the linguistic arts. This "art," in modern times, has generally been deepened and refined into a number of different areas—including logic, syntax, semantics, and pragmatics.

Consider, for example, how the lawyer in the following story uses his insight into logic in order to allay his client's fears:

A prisoner appears before a hanging judge for sentencing. "I am not allowed to dispense cruel or unusual punishment," the judge begins, rather inauspiciously. "The harshest punishment I am permitted to recommend is hanging by the neck until dead. The gallows it must be then. Beyond that, my only freedom is in setting a date for your hanging. I am of two minds on that.

"My impulse is to order an immediate execution and be done with it. On the other hand, that might be an undeserved kindness. You would have no time to contemplate your impending doom. I choose instead this compromise: I sentence you to hang at sunrise on one of the seven days of next week. I further instruct your executioner to make certain that you have no way of knowing in advance on which day you will be hanged. Every night, you will go to sleep wondering if the gallows awaits the next morning, and when you do walk the last mile, it will come completely as a surprise."

The prisoner was taken aback to find his lawyer smiling at this incredibly cruel sentence. When they got out of the courtroom, the lawyer said, "They can't hang you." He explained: "You are supposed to be hanged at sunrise on one of the seven days of next week. Well, they can't hang you on Saturday. It's the last day of the week, and if you aren't hanged by Friday morning, then you can know with utter certainty that the day of execution is Saturday. *That* would violate the judge's plan of not letting you know the day in advance."

To this the prisoner agreed. The lawyer continued: "Therefore, the last day they can hang you is actually Friday. Fine. But look—they can't hang you Friday either. Granting that Saturday is *really* out of the question, Friday is the last day they can hang you. If you make it to breakfast Thursday morning, you will know for a fact that you are to die Friday. And *that* is against the judge's order. Don't you see? The same logic rules out Thursday, Wednesday, and every other day. The judge has outsmarted himself. The sentence is impossible to carry out."

The prisoner rejoiced until Tuesday, when he was awoken from a deep sleep and sent to the gallows—quite unexpectedly.

THE GOOD LAWYER CAN PREPARE AND PRESENT A POSITION.

This trait is related to the previous discussion regarding savvy. It is not enough to be able to argue a point—particularly if it is an unimportant one, or the wrong one. The good lawyer can present the most important points in an effective manner.

It has been observed that by engaging in legal practice, a lawyer should constantly be learning and growing, not just in the ability to recite black letter law, but in the ability to create the law of each case. It may be that a "bad lawyer," even when surrounded by a superabundance of legal precedent, is one who is unable to successfully "invent" the law of the case at hand. Put another way, without an algorithmic-like connection between the hypothetical meaning of the law itself and the demands of a particular case, persuasion by a lawyer involves some measure of invention in the form of representing the relevant law and the facts at issue. The bad lawyer is simply not able to perform this task effectively.

This point, I believe, deserves emphasis. It seems to me that the good lawyer is able, using all means at his or her disposal (including the "scandal of induction"), to assemble the law applicable to the client's case—Vinnie and Sal on steroids. Such activity may require more than simply trying to find a case, statute, or regulation. It might mean drawing on cognitive science, religion, philosophy, literature, economics, linguistics, history, statistics, sociology, physiology, et cetera, et cetera, et cetera. And it is not enough just to construct a product out of raw intellectual material. The product must be attractively packaged, marketed, and sold. In other words, the good lawyer, using legal reasoning—inductive, deductive, abductive, and perhaps most important, metaphorical—and rhetorical skills, must convince the other side, the judge, and the jury that this product is sound and worth buying. And that the other side's product is like an eight-track tape player in a digital world.

This point may be a bit jarring—prompting such responses, even this late in the book, as what about Truth! Justice! Reality! But consider what Kurt Gödel did to such "absolutes"—or at least truth and reality, arguably foundations for justice.

Working in Vienna in the 1930s, Gödel, through sublime and devastating logic, came up with his incompleteness theorem. In so doing, he shattered the convictions of steely-eyed mathematicians by demonstrating that even in very basic systems like arithmetic, statements can be made that can neither be proved nor disproved within the rules of that system. Thus, even a consistent numerical system composed of a finite set of axioms and rules of inference can generate formulas that cannot be proved—except by importing axioms from outside the system. And worse yet, his proof is not confined to mathematics. Reality, Gödel demonstrated, is a construct, not a given. Consequently, no finite language or system can capture all "truth."

The truth that we can dismiss the possibility of absolute Truth (at least in the practice of law) has been clear to many lawyers over many centuries—without the help of the brilliant and very odd Kurt Gödel. Remember, for example, the rhetoric in Part III on rhetoric. Additionally, this is why good lawyers, even if they have not always been honest about it, have seldom been afraid to look outside their given legal system, turning to religion, philosophy (specifically logic), history, sociology, psychology, economics, myth, fairy tales, voodoo, and so on, in order to construct the reality, the truth, and even the justice that is called for by a particular matter. The trick is to create the legal reality that fits snuggly (leveling, sharpening, and assimilating) within the constructed reality in which the lawyer finds herself. This is not, however, always an easy task—particularly if you're Vinnie or Sal before the High Court.

A GOOD LAWYER IS ABLE TO PROPERLY ORGANIZE AND ANALYZE FACTS.

It is an important fact that facts are important in performing most legal tasks, and therefore they must be obtained, arranged, and assessed. This often difficult and tedious task must be conducted in order to, among other things, help identify the relevant legal issues, assess which cases are sufficiently factually (and conceptually) analogous, and determine which statutes may be applicable. Facts, however, rarely arrive in logical order. They are often messy and need to be arranged in a manner that is suitable for use by the lawyer in advising the client or in presenting a case to a judge or jury. Furthermore, not all available facts are legally determinative. In other words, not all of the facts (no matter how important they seem to the client) will raise legal issues or will influence the outcome of the lawyer's analysis. But which ones to keep and which ones to throw out—that is the question.

In fact, that is the question for both lawyers and infants. Researchers have demonstrated that a significant aspect of focused attention is the ability to ignore nonsalient or distracting information. It has been established that controlled attention and inhibition develop significantly in the first five years of life. For a child, the origins of this ability lie in the ability to focus on the emotional content of the caregiver's message and to ignore the misleading elements. And for the lawyer, the origins lie in the ability to focus on the legally relevant content of the client's message and "ignore" all of the misleading stuff.

THE GREAT LAWYER ALWAYS SEES BOTH SIDES OF A DISPUTE.

By this I mean that he or she *really* seeks to understand the other side's position and attempts to educate the client regarding that position. Clients are often surprised at the strength of the opposing case when they get to court, and a great lawyer will prevent that surprise from happening. This skill is a key part of the creative design and construction of a case since it represents the disruption of stubborn, habitual patterns of thinking. It can allow the lawyer to see avenues that he or she may not have otherwise considered.

The public frequently sees a lawyer as a gladiator ready to destroy the enemy. In my experience this search-and-destroy attitude generally ends up costing the client lots of money. Keep in mind Edward Gibbon's observation, quoted in Part IV, regarding Roman lawyers "who conducted their clients through a maze of expense, of delay . . . ; from whence, after a tedious series of years, they [the client] were at length dismissed, when their patience and fortune were almost exhausted." War is frequently expensive and not always satisfying.

You Can't Please All the People All the Time

A trial lawyer must appear as a friend to the jury—there must be rapport— and he must come across as treating witnesses fairly. Badgering or humiliat- ing the other party, while perhaps satisfying to the client, can often alienate the jury—as well as piss off the judge. Thus, despite the adversarial process of a trial, an effective advocate can use non-adversarial techniques to his or her advantage.

THE GREAT LAWYER IS ABLE TO CRITIQUE HIS OR HER OWN POSITION (NOT JUST THE OTHER SIDE'S).

Based on an objective evaluation of a position, great lawyers are able to con- cede that which must be conceded in order to strengthen their position. They do not just claim that their client is good, but instead present a reason for the judge or jury to believe that the client has a redeeming quality that makes him not worthy of being hanged—as in Darrow's representation of Leopold and Loeb.

THE GREAT LAWYER POSSESSES DEEP AND EXTENSIVE KNOWLEDGE BASED ON PERSONAL EXPERIENCE AND LEARNING.

Only experience (contrary to Langdell) *and* learning (in not just law but a broad range of subjects) can generate high levels of creative and reflective thinking in the practice of law. According to two scientific scholars, "an exten- sive and accurate vocabulary is a *sine qua non* of any writer or lawyer, as is outstanding manual coordination for a surgeon or sculptor, or excellent skills of spatial analysis for an architect or fighter pilot. But these abilities are only preconditions for developing high intelligence in those fields, not intelligence itself. They will become part of deep intelligence only when a person uses them to gain knowledge and experience in a particular field and then operates cre- atively and reflectively in that field."

THE GREAT LAWYER HAS A REFINED SENSE OF JUSTICE—EVEN IN THESE CYNICAL TIMES.

As pointed out in the Opening Statement, the reason for the general fascination with lawyers is not simply that they are fascinating people (although some are) but because we believe they know where the bodies are buried. And swirling around the crimes and civil wrongs in a society is the range of human motives—hatred, envy, revenge, greed—arguably a large part of why practicing law has historically been considered a profession. Few motives, however, drive a person more than being unjustly accused. This fact is the reason that even a small injustice can cause a strong reaction.

The Physical Effects of Injustice

Is injustice simply an abstract problem? The answers appears to be no. Volunteers in an experiment on stress, for example, were asked to defend themselves against a false accusation of shoplifting. Scientific measurements showed that the volunteers' immune and cardiovascular systems mobilized in a potentially deadly combination. The immune system secreted T lymphocytes, while the walls of blood vessels emitted a substance that binds to those T cells, setting in motion the formation of artery-clogging plaque on the endothelium. Injustice (among other sources of stress) appears to be tied to a physical distress-to-endothelium chain reaction.

THE GREAT LAWYER EMBRACES MEANINGFUL EVALUATION OF HIS OR HER ABILITIES AND FAULTS. EVALUATION IS ACTIVELY SOUGHT THROUGH PEERS, CLIENTS, AND INTROSPECTION.

The devilish aspect of such evaluation is that a lawyer's greatest strength may be his or her greatest weakness. Consider, for example, the high-IQ lawyer who analyzes every possible issue with extreme precision—all of which is completely incomprehensible to the rest of us mere mortals. Such precision, and its accompanying complexity, may be acceptable coming from an Einstein, but not from a lawyer who is trying to convince a jury or drafting an agreement that others have to live with.

It has been said that in the end the most important test for evaluating a lawyer is the following: Would you refer your mother to this lawyer in a matter involving utmost confidentiality and in which her life hung in the balance?

CLOSING ARGUMENT

Stepping over the bones of *Ardepithecines, Australopithecines, habilis*, Cro-Magnons, and mere *Homo erectus*, we started our search with *Homo erectus legalus*. I quickly admitted that the remains of this silver-tongued devil have eluded me. True. But after sifting through the debris, we are nevertheless able to bring together, I believe, bits and pieces of not just the "mere" interpreter but the actual prototype lawyer: He was most likely a he (hence the *erectus* part of the Latinate), Mesopotamian, from the land of Sumer, and worked for a temple or a king. He wrote in cuneiform on clay tablets, using a reed stalk cut obliquely on one end. He spoke Sumerian and most likely worked while squatted on his haunches, almost totally nude (hence the *Homo legalus* part of the Latinate). In other words, the first "lawyer" was a man who lived c. 3,000 BCE.

This scribe, like the proverbial first bacterial cell from which all subsequent life on earth descended, generated and was generated by his environment. And most importantly, he reproduced—asexually.

The general school curriculum for these early scribes, as we saw, was divided into two primary groups: semiscientific and literary. The semiscientific side developed from the practical need to teach scribes how to write, using multitudinous signs, the Sumerian language. In order to accomplish this difficult task, the teaching scribes derived a system of instruction using classification (a darling of modern-day legal systems) of Sumerian language into groups of related words and phrases.

These Sumerian schoolmen (and apparently some women) also created highly sophisticated study approaches to grammar (syntax) and mathematical tables.

With regard to the literary side of things, the curriculum evolved into studying, copying, and imitating literary compositions, poems, myths, epics, laments, and hymns. In other words: religion and art. It appears that the legal tradition grew out of both the semiscientific and the literary. This part of the curriculum, as we saw, embraced law collections ("codes"); "advice" by kings on specific legal topics (*misharum*, edicts); and the drafting of private and public documents that included contracts, wills, adoptions, loans, land boundaries, administrative texts, and international agreements.

Lawyers, however, are not just about law. They are therefore not Sumerian or Akkadian. They are not just about philosophy or rhetoric and therefore not Greek. They are not Babylonian, Assyrian, Egyptian, Roman, Jewish, Christian, or Muslim—and therefore not scribes, priests, oracles, or scientists. They are, in broad strokes, some of each. In a word, they are mutts.

The interesting thing, however, is that the tangled bloodlines do not mean that lawyers are the embodiment of the chaotic. Au contraire! The lawyer class, or perhaps more technically, classes (e.g., American lawyers, English barristers and solicitors, *bengoshi*, *Anwälte*, elites, solo practitioners, government lawyers, academics), seem to be a prime example of spontaneous emergence of self-organization—and subsequent suborganization.

The study of complexity has built on the insights gained by radical scientific innovators who are teasing out the secrets of chaos theory—nonlinear dynamics dealing primarily with functions in which a small input can lead to a disproportionate response. "The straw that broke the camel's back." One of these insights is that complexity is about emergence; how, for example, groups behave quite differently from the aggregation of their individual characteristics. In combining individual units often what emerges is something completely unexpected and different. Step into Albert Einstein's shoes for a moment and engage in a Gedanken experiment, a thought experiment in which a physicist sets up a scenario and tries to solve it using the laws of the theory he is testing. For example, let's examine the difference in the town of Lawless, Nevada, with one lawyer versus two. The phenomenon of self-organizing system becomes key. The reason, as we have seen in many cases throughout this book, is that although the system starts out in a random state, it soon organizes itself into a large-scale pattern: the Lawless School of Law; the Lawless Bar Association, the judge of Lawless, the courthouse, the court clerk. . . . As we have seen, the individual components (paganism, Judaism, Christianity, Islam, rhetoric, drama, philosophy, politics, law, economics, history, linguistics, and on *ad infinitum*) making up the lawyer class at various times and places are numerous and often seemingly unrelated to, and sometimes in conflict with, each other—muddled metaphors. Yet somehow spontaneous emergence of self-organization has occurred, or what I like to call, using more technical terms, the "poof theory of lawyers."

It is also pointed out by scientists that self-organizing systems, though often complex, are also adaptive. In the case of lawyers it is hard to argue that they are not complex. Recall that twelfth-century judges and the United States government in both the twentieth and twenty-first centuries wanted to (and still frequently wants to) prevent lawyers from complicating various proceedings. And given their emergence from complexity, we have seen how lawyers are highly adaptive to their surroundings: scribes drafting contracts in cuneiform, ancient Greek speechwriters preparing legal arguments for clients, Roman orators and jurisconsults shaping the rule of law, canon lawyers working within a highly religious environment, common-law lawyers shaping property and contract law for use in emerging markets, and civil-law lawyers packing the law into organized codes.

It is also the case that complex systems can be poised on the "edge of chaos," creating an interesting state somewhere between order and disorder, between stability and transformation. But surrounding this dynamic tension is structure. Any self-organization must have, as an aspect of its structure, boundaries. In the case of the lawyer class (or classes), we have seen that the question of boundaries has manifested itself in intergroup tournaments among lawyer subgroups: common-law lawyers, for example, versus civil-law lawyers, and intergroup tournaments between lawyers and various outside boundary-encroachers, like accountants, financial advisors, investment bankers, real estate brokers, and the ultimate weapon of mass destruction, artificial intelligence.

Lawyers are not just about law, any more than mathematicians are just about numbers or investment bankers are just about bags of money, and therefore this book has not been about law per se. Nevertheless, we have looked at law (or more precisely, legal systems) from many angles: Mesopotamian, Grecian, Roman, Jewish, canon, common, civil, and so on. One reason for this has been that it is difficult to talk about lawyers in any meaningful way without discussing law. And whether or not law, at its heart, is grounded in politics or economics (the usual suspects) or something else like religion, race, or sex, it appears to come from and to reflect those things that are important to a particular society: morality, religion, science, technology, wealth, race, gender, art, and language, for example. It is for this reason that a lawyer, by nature, is a scavenger—rummaging around in the length and breath of physical and social technologies.

Chaos theory tells us that the idea of sensitivity to exact initial conditions takes into account the history of a system or a particular aspect of that system.

If this notion applies to a legal system, then the system can be seen as evolving and therefore any given starting point—for example, messages from the gods, declarations of a king, or proclamations of a pope—can be seen as having embedded historical information, as well as information about the future. And who better to pry out such information (particularly in the best interest of a paying client) than a lawyer? As we have seen, nothing escapes this mutt's attention: religious analysis of law, political analysis of law, philosophic analysis of law, psychological analysis of law, moral analysis of law, social analysis of law, historical analysis of law, linguistic analysis of law, economic analysis of law, and so on—even sometimes, at least hopefully, legal analysis of the law. Consider, for example, the 1859 murder trial of Daniel Sickles, a congressman from the State of New York.

Sickles's young wife took a lover, Philip Barton Key (the son of Francis Scott Key, composer of "The Star Spangled Banner"). When Sickles discovered that his wife, Teresa Bagioli Sickles, was singing the national anthem with someone else, he shot Key to death. The defense team had few "legal" arguments at their disposal. The best that they could come up with was temporary insanity—a fairly weak defense under the circumstances. But like Vinnie and Sal, and the Simpson dream team, Sickles's lawyers thought and worked creatively. They pushed not a psycho-philosophically abstract issue of mind, but a strong social argument: Key had deceived and betrayed Sickles. He had taken something that did not belong to him—Sickles's wife. (Brilliant! A combination of thou shall not covet and thou shall not steal.) And for his treacherous actions and thoughts Key deserved ("legally") to die. The jury agreed and quickly acquitted Sickles. Ain't love grand.

Lawyers are not ordinary mutts. They seem to have evolved, at least in many modern-day societies, into highly efficient scavenger-mutts that are able to pry lose "necessary" information from that system popularly known as "the law." In fact they have been largely created and nurtured by that very same system—in other words, birth by feedback and growth by grazing. Thus vagaries of human beliefs, attitudes, emotions, and goals that make up a complex legal system (of which "the law" as rules and regulations is only one aspect) both make up and sustain the lawyer class. This does not mean, however, that both legal systems and the lawyer class are examples of irregularity and randomness. If chaos theory is correct, then like any complex system there is an underlying order to both law and, shockingly, lawyers. An interesting question, however, arises: Is the underlying order (whatever it may be) the same in the case of law and lawyers? The answer, at least in the early part of the twenty-first century, appears to be no.

As we have seen, law has historically been viewed as one of the principal means of arriving at right answers. Throughout life's seeming "chaos," the gods, for example, left messages that needed to be discovered, understood, and acted upon. Properly done, the "right answer" was discovered and humankind was spared for another year. Or if not through divine messages, the right answer is found by reason, or logic, or scientific methodology. Lawyers simply want to understand the "why" of things. The draw of reason, however defined, is therefore just as compelling to the lawyer as it is to the normal person. Reason is a force—in the sense that reasoned argument is war. And because conflicts abound, the right solutions to problems and conflicts are highly valued. But besides being a human being, the lawyer seems to have emerged (the "poof theory") from the same initial conditions that give rise to her operative legal system. This means that lawyers, as humans, crave order based on "right" solutions, and at the same time, are, as legal professionals, the creation and "diviners" of chaos—thus charged with digging through the appearance of irregularity and randomness to find order and patterns (particularly when being paid to do so by a client).

The catch, however, is that the order and patterns (contrary to Langdell's dream) are not found, except in very broad terms, using linear techniques. And even though there are times when nonlinear mathematics provides glimpses, the day-to-day work of lawyers does not appear to be solvable even by such sophisticated automated techniques. As one academic has rhetorically argued with regard to the claims of economic analysis of the law: "[I]f all important human values can be reduced to supply and demand curves, and if only the changes 'at the margins' count, and if all preferences are to be measured in money and only those with money can vote their preferences, and if all factors such as fairness, justice, and equity are considered to be inherently accounted for by the market, why not just use computers as a substitute for courts? A finder of fact [i.e., judge or jury] would still be necessary, but once the facts were known the answer would be obvious. The computer could perform the proper economic analysis and generate answers efficiently." Ahhh . . . sure. It would seem that this type of skepticism about computer-generated legal answers is the reason why lawyers are not yet slated for structural unemployment and continue to hold on tight to the basics of their "craft" accumulated over 5,000 years: writing, categorization, interpretation, drama, rhetoric, oratory, syllogisms, analogies, metaphorical reasoning, and so on. As a result, modern-day lawyers often seem strikingly similar to ancient lawyers in what they do and how they go about doing it. Contrast this, for example, with a typical modern-day research scientist and Thales. My guess is that there are vast differences.

Before discussing one of the most significant exceptions between the modern-day lawyer and the ancient lawyer, we need to briefly discuss "efficiency" and its relationship (or lack thereof) to chaos theory.

One of the key concepts regarding capital markets involves the efficient capital market hypothesis (ECMH)—at least in current, mainstream economic thought. This hypothesis holds that a market is efficient if the prices of the goods sold in the market fully reflect all available information about those goods. (This was arguably not the case, as you will recall, with regard to the forbidden fruit.) "All available information" is generally understood to mean, in the case of weak-form efficiency, past prices, and in its semistrong form, all publicly available data. Strong-form efficiency, arguing for the absorption of all information, both public and private, has generally been discredited. What this means, if one accepts ECMH, is that an analyst, using prices and other publicly available data, cannot easily find "undervalued" stocks. The reason for this is that all such data is already ("efficiently") reflected in a stock's price.

Recent developments in mathematics and physics have, however, called into question even the weak form of the ECMH. The reason for this lies in the fact that ECMH is built on linear mathematical models.

These models, according to some theorists, have become obsolete as a result of recent advances in the mathematics of nonlinear dynamics and theoretical and applied physics. The growing indication is that there is nonlinear dependence in the public capital markets. Thus, such markets are to some extent inefficient, and they are inefficient based on deep structural forces.

So what does all of this have to do with lawyers? The answer is that the "lawyer market," seemingly contrary to chaos theory but true to the scavenger-mutts thesis, embodies both weak-form efficiency and semistrong-form efficiency. That is, all information that is publicly available is, at least theoretically, fully reflected in the value of the lawyer class. This "efficient marketplace of lawyer techniques" hypothesis holds that specified information sets (e.g., writing, categorization, interpretation, drama, rhetoric, oratory, syllogisms, analogies, metaphorical reasoning) are fully reflected in the value of the lawyer class as a whole. But even if this is true, it does not provide a basis for determining what it means for any such information to be "fully reflected" in such value. The answer to this inquiry lies in the "simple" fact that human nature has arguably not changed, at least significantly, over the 5,000 years of legal practice. Consequently, the same basic techniques that worked for the ancient lawyer also work for the modern day lawyer—at least so far.

The interesting thing about all this is that the information sets themselves (categorization, interpretation, rhetoric, etc.) do not appear to be nonlinear. In other words, there seems to be a linear independence between the value of the lawyer class and the information sets. Consequently, the relationship between such information sets and the value of the lawyer class do not follow chaos theory. On the other hand, the content of these information sets do change—and sometimes radically so. Such changes have a nonlinear dependent impact on the value of the lawyer class. And so true to their "muttness," lawyers are arguably both linear and nonlinear at the same time.

A key aspect in the evolution of the lawyer class has to do with representation. Today it seems perfectly natural that a person pressing or defending against a legal matter has a right to have a lawyer speak for him—particularly in court. And when the lawyer opens his mouth, he generally speaks for and on behalf of the client.

But there has not been, as we have seen, a historic acceptance of having someone speak for and on behalf of another person. This was particularly true where the speaker was operating before a court of law, whether in Sumer, Akkad, Babylon, Assyria, Egypt, or Greece. It was not until the rise of Rome and its increasing constitutional, political, economic, social, and legal complexity that representation came to be generally accepted. And with this acceptance came the right to openly practice legal ventriloquism: the art form in which the dummy's lips do not move.

The complication with this art form is that the dummy (client) has a brain—sometimes one that is bigger than the ventriloquist's (lawyer's). This complication can translate, as we have seen, into problems between the litigants themselves and between the client and the lawyer. Thus the lawyer's words may have weakened or undermined the client's claim or defense and the client may then have an action against the lawyer—handled by a lawyer, with the errant lawyer most likely represented by a lawyer. And there you have it: lawyers all the way down.

In line with chaos theory, we have also seen that there is, at least historically, a strong feedback system between the lawyer class and that class's working legal system. Recall the Mesopotamian scribe's influence on the legal forms used in Sumer and Akkad; the Greek orator's refining of "acceptable" arguments; the Roman jurisconsult's influence on the rule of law; the canon lawyer's shaping of rules and procedures; the English lawyer's influence on the common law; the civil-law lawyer's influence on the formulation of various continental European codes; and, in return, the feedback of etched-in-stone statutes, rhetoric, the rule of law, canonical decrees, cases and codes on scribes, orators, jurists, canon-law lawyers, common-law lawyers, and civil-law lawyers. And this autocatalytic feedback loop, the hallmark of a nonlinear system, operates on a nonproportional relationship between cause and its effect. In the case of a lawyer and her operative legal system, this means bits and pieces of her class contribute to the legal system and bits and pieces of that system contribute to the class, which in turn contributes to the system, which in turn. . . .

But it appears, however, that the legal system has a much greater influence on the lawyer class than the lawyer class has on the legal system these days: a type of one-way power law effect. The reason for this is that legal systems reflect those things that are important to a particular society—and while some lawyers (particularly law professors) may believe that they are the arbiters of what is important, the reality, as we have seen, is far more complex. Take for example the triumph of secular law in England and the virtual eradication of the canon-law lawyers, or the rise of the common law and the elimination of civil-law lawyers from Britain.

In carrying out their task of prying out information imbedded in a particular legal system, a question is raised regarding the shelf life of any such information. In other words, is there any benefit in struggling with Mesopotamian or ancient Roman legal systems? Or for that matter, why should a lawyer ever consider modern-day legal systems that are foreign to her own? The answer to these questions has to be looked at from at least two perspectives. With regard to the main focus of this book (a brief 5,000-year history of lawyers) the answer is found in myth, the Torah, the Bible, the Qur'an, the Magna Carta, the U.S. Constitution, and the importance of tradition. From this perspective, the importance of Mesopotamian and ancient Roman legal systems is the key to the overarching lawyer class's narrative—both its accuracy and, more importantly, its legitimacy. With regard to the secondary focus of this book (legal systems), the answer is arguably found in perspective. It is sometimes necessary, as we saw with Gödel's incompleteness theorem, to step outside a system in order to prove or disprove a particular statement within that system. Additionally, René Descartes' fundamental division between mind and matter (the I and the world) created the tenacious belief that the world can be described objectively—that is, without ever considering the observer. Both the theory of relativity and quantum theory have proved that this classical ideal of a completely objective science cannot be maintained when dealing with the extremely large or the extremely small. In other words, neither the observer nor her perspective can be ignored. This is not only true in physics, but arguably it is also true with regard to law, legal systems, and the social realm in general.

Is the lawyer class (however defined) a living organism? The answer, given the awful stench of no, is hopefully yes.

Certain scientists have suggested that the defining characteristics of living systems can be seen by looking closely at bacteria. This simplest of all living systems displays the following general characteristics: membrane-bound, self-generating, and having a metabolic network that is organizationally closed. By analogy (one of the basic reasoning techniques, as we have seen, of lawyers), it would appear that the lawyer class displays these same basic characteristics. We have seen, for example, that Mesopotamian scribes walled themselves off from others by the specialized nature of their training and work. This same type of membrane generation was also present in the case of Greek orators, the Roman jurisconsults, canon-law lawyers, common-law lawyers, and civil-law lawyers. And it continues on, at least so far, in the twenty-first century.

It is also clear over the 5,000-year history of lawyers that they have been self-generating—sometimes against all odds and sometimes like rabbits. Stepping back to the Mesopotamian scribes, we saw the scribal schools; and in the case of the English Inns of Courts, we saw generations of lawyers received their training at the knees of seasoned readers. And the king of self-generation has to be the American lawyer, with his numerous law schools spread out across the land.

Finally, with regard to a metabolic network that is organizationally closed, we have seen that everywhere from Mesopotamia to modern times, scribes, orators, jurists, barristers, solicitors, *bengoshi*, and lawyers have used various techniques to effectuate organizational closure. Such techniques have, as we have seen, included scribal schools, guilds, social status, rhetorical training, apprenticeships, law schools, bar associations, and licensure.

With regard to the network itself, in the context of bacteria, there are several types of highly complex macromolecules: structural proteins, enzymes (acting as catalysts of metabolic processes), RNA (messengers carrying genetic information), and DNA (storage for genetics information and responsibility for a cell's self-replication). In the context of lawyers, metabolic network would appear to be the relevant legal system, with all its complexity. It is also the case that the cellular network is materially and energetically open. This openness to the external environment allows the cell to produce, repair, and perpetuate itself—operating far from equilibrium (on the edge of chaos) where new structures and forms of order may spontaneously emerge. Similarly, a vibrant legal system, acting as its lawyer class's metabolic network, appears to be open to the external environment of politics, social norms, economics, religion, psychology, sociology, and so on, leading to its development and evolution that in theory leads to a particular lawyer class's development and evolution.

Assuming that the lawyer class is (or at least, in certain societies, can be) a living organism, the question arises as to whether or not this organism has cognition.

It has been argued that cognition, the process of knowing, is the activity involved in the self-generation and self-perpetuation of living networks. Based on this viewpoint, it appears that the lawyer class historically, and certainly presently, possesses cognitive function. Lawyers (individually and in groups) undeniably interact with their environment—sometimes even aggressively so. But are they conscious? A trickier question.

There are vigorous debates over consciousness (particularly where lawyers are concerned). However, there appears to be a growing consensus among cognitive scientists and philosophers on two important points: (1) that consciousness is a cognitive process, emerging from complex neural activity; and (2) that there are two basic types of consciousness. The first type, known as "primary consciousness," arises when cognitive processes are joined by basic perceptual, sensory, and emotional experience. The second, moving beyond most mammals, is "higher-order consciousness" and involves self-awareness—in other words, a concept of self.

In the case of lawyers, it seems that even the ancient scribes possessed a "self-awareness" of their work and place in society. In other words, among them, there was a certain reflective consciousness: a group mind aware of specialized knowledge. For example, in ancient Egypt each year the tax inspectors and their assistants would spread out across the countryside and measure, assess, and collect taxes. The author of the New Kingdom schoolbook, a scribe, tells the reader about the typical farmer:

> When he reaches his field he finds it broken up. He spends his time cultivating but the snake follows him. It eats the seed as he sows it on the ground and he does not see a single green blade. . . . Now the tax collector lands on the river bank. He surveys the harvest. He is attended by bailiffs [literally, doorkeepers who control the government supplies at state warehouses] with staffs and Nubians with clubs. They say to him "Give us grain!" but he replies "There is none." The farmer is beaten savagely, he is tied up and thrown into the well where he is ducked head first. His wife is tied up in his presence and his children are bound in fetters. His neighbors abandon them and run away. When it is all over, there is still no grain.

The reason for this tale of the farmers' plight was simple: to persuade its young readers to follow the best occupation in the world—that of the scribe. A reflective (class) consciousness indeed, spiced with a hint of social elitism.

A number of scientists have observed that the process of categorizing various experiences is a fundamental part of cognition at all levels of life. Animals, for example, categorize food and noises that sound like danger or sex (or dangerous sex). And in the case of human beings, we not only categorize experiences, but also use abstract concepts to characterize our categories.

It appears that humankind's concepts arise, at least in part, from our neural structures and bodily experience and that some of these embodied concepts are also the basis of certain forms of reasoning—many of which are employed by lawyers. Recall, for example, our syllogism about Socrates.

Cognitive researchers have pointed out that humans tend, due to our particular neural structures and bodily experiences, to distinguish between "inside" and "outside." We tend to visualize this spatial relationship in terms of a container with an inside and an outside (a boundary). This mental image is grounded in the experience of having a body that acts as a container and thus becomes a certain form of reasoning. Imagine a sprig of hemlock inside a cup which itself is inside a bowl. In the Socrates syllogism we saw that the argument seemed conclusive because, like the hemlock, Socrates was within the "container" (a category) of men, and men were within the "container" (a category) of mortals. The syllogism has therefore been argued not to be a form of disembodied reasoning, but grows "organically" out of human, bodily experience. It is no wonder that lawyers, charged with convincing human beings of particular propositions, have gravitated to the use of syllogism as a form of legal reasoning.

The fascinating thing is that this same explanation appears to apply to many other forms of reasoning—for example, analogy (a favorite among the lawyer class) and metaphorical reasoning (Law Is a Path; Justice Is a Blind Lady Holding Scales and a Sword). The structures of bodies and brains determine, according to this line of thought, the concepts that can be formed and the reasoning that can be engaged in—at least if one intends to be persuasive.

And speaking of legal reasoning, we should not forget the importance of rhetoric to both legal reasoning and the rise of the lawyer class. We have spent a great deal of time stressing the rise, adaptation, and application of rhetoric (one of our linearly independent information sets) in carrying out that important lawyer function of persuasion (discourse of the hysteric) and education (discourse of the university)—both in breeding new lawyers and handling clients. But this is only a piece of the power pie. We have also seen that, unlike the rhetoric of the literary critic, the lawyer often backs up her rhetoric with threats of sanctions ("we'll sue you"), referred to by some as coercive power (tapping into the discourse of the master). And certainly in obtaining clients, retaining clients, legal fees, and settling legal disputes, the lawyer's rhetoric is spoken in terms of financial incentives and rewards, referred to by some as compensatory power (taking on the discourse of the analyst).

In the end, perhaps the most important questions raised about lawyers are, What do they do? and, Is what they do good or bad?

As we have seen (at least I hope), the answer to these two questions is more than simply that lawyers file frivolous lawsuits for their own financial gain and, therefore, what they do is bad. Very bad! The more complex answers arising from our 5,000-year swath of time is that lawyers are involved in redistributive, rent-seeking activities (which might, depending upon the circumstances, involve a good thing); facilitating economically productive activities like transfers of property, information brokering, contract formation and enforcement, dispute resolution, and fighting against unproductive rent-seeking activities; and the creation of nonmarketed social goods such as individual rights, free speech, and due process of law.

In the early 1990s, Professor James Gwartney became involved in the preparation of the annual Economic Freedom of the World Index. When asked what surprised him the most in preparing the Index, he responded: "It turns out that the legal system—the rule of law, security of property rights, an independent judiciary, and impartial court system—is the most important function of government, and the central element of both economic freedom and a civil society. It is far more statistically significant than the other variables." He went on to point out the fact that a number of countries lack a decent legal system. As a result, these countries suffer from corruption, insecure property rights, poorly enforced contracts, and an inconsistent regulatory environment—and consequently score low on the Index.

As we saw, with regard to the United States, lawyers played an important role in framing the legal and political arguments for separating from England, in keeping mob rule to a minimum before, during, and after the Revolution, and in framing a written constitution. Based on their legal training and experience, these lawyers helped advance a constitution grounded in separation of powers and thereby created a strong, independent judiciary with an important role for lawyers to play as officers of the court. Arguably a good thing.

And so, what if Adam and Eve had hired a lawyer? Would Vinnie and Sal have saved their clients—and in the process, all humankind? Or would they, and all of us, be in a lonelier and drearier world—frozen at the moment of creation without a fall from which to be redeemed? Personally, I don't know the answer. What I do know is that like most lawyers, Vinnie and Sal would have been creative and resourceful in advocating for their clients. Lawyers are, if nothing else, both mutts and scavengers. But in the end, questions of law and justice are, in my opinion, much too important to be left to lawyers alone.

APPENDIX A
A WHO'S WHO

A

Accursius ("Accorso di Bagnolo") (c. 1182–1263 CE) was an Italian jurist and referred to as the "Idol of the Jurisconsults." He is most noted for his organization of the glosses and for arranging into one body the tens of thousands of comments and remarks upon the Emperor Justinian's Code, Institutes, and Digest. This compilation, entitled *Glossa Ordinaria*, is commonly known as the Great Gloss and was completed at about 1230. The Gloss grew to be the starting point for every exegesis of the *Corpus Iuris* and was even given force of law in some jurisdictions. The authority of the Gloss is probably due to Accursius's very exhaustive coverage of the civil law. Modern research has shown that Accursius's work contains nearly 100,000 glosses.

Adams, John (1735–1826 CE) after graduating from Harvard in 1755 and a stint as a schoolteacher, signed a contract with a young Worcester attorney, James Putnam, to study law "under his inspection" for two years (1756–1758). Putman's fee was $100, payable when Adams could "find it convenient." Adams was admitted to the Massachusetts bar in a ceremony before the Superior Court at Boston on November 6, 1759, and in a matter of weeks, at age twenty-four, he took on his first case. Adams went on to become America's first lawyer-President.

Adams, John Quincy (1767–1848 CE) was a lawyer and the sixth U.S. President, and a diplomat involved in many international negotiations, helping to formulate the Monroe Doctrine as Secretary of State. He was a leading opponent of slavery and argued that if a civil war ever broke out, the president could abolish slavery by using his war powers.

Aeschylus (525–456 BCE) was born in Eleusis. Both Aeschylus and his brother, Cynegirus, fought at the battle of Marathon, where Cynegirus was killed. In 484 BCE Aeschylus won first prize at the Festival of Dionysus and four years later, at the age of forty-five, he fought at the battle of Salamis. Eight years later, in 472 BCE, Aeschylus again won first prize at the Festival of Dionysus, this time for a tragic trilogy that included *The Persians*, his play about the important battle of Salamis.

Aeschylus is said to have introduced a second actor into the play itself—in contrast to the traditional single figure representing a god or a hero and the chorus representing the people. And once there were two actors interacting with one another, true drama (tragedy and comedy) was born—an important step in the rise of the lawyer class.

Afer, Domitius (d. 60 CE) was an orator and advocate, born at Nemausus in Gallia Narbonensis. He flourished in the reigns of Tiberius, Caligula, Claudius, and Nero. At one time he was one of the most celebrated orators in Rome. However, in his old age, Afer lost much of his reputation by continuing to speak in public, thus giving life to the saying that old lawyers never die, they just lose their appeal.

Afrania, Gaia (d. 48 CE) was born into the gene Afrania, an old plebeian family. She was married to a man (Licinius Buccio) who had climbed the *cursus honorum* to enter the Senate at a time of social and political upheaval (i.e., the breakup of the Republic and warring military commanders such as Marius, Sulla, Pompey, and Caesar). During this chaotic time, Afrania did not wait for male kin to protect her interests, as was traditional, but argued cases before the *praetor* herself. And by all accounts her legal knowledge and rhetorical ability were successful.

Alciato, Andrea ("Alciatus") (1492–1550 CE) was an Italian jurist and writer. He is regarded as one of the founders of the French school of legal humanists.

Al-Shafi'i, Muhammad ibn idris (767–820 CE) was an Arabic jurist. According to Al-Shafi'i: "God [Allah] has not permitted any person since the Prophet's [Muhammad's] time to give an opinion except on the strength of established legal knowledge" and "legal knowledge after the Prophet's death includes the Qur'an, Sunna, consensus, narrative, and analogy based on these texts."

Antiphon (480–411 BCE) was probably the first speechwriter, wrote speeches for the Assembly and for the law-courts (with a specialty in homicide). At least one scholar has characterized speechwriters like Antiphon as "our first media experts and spin-doctors."

Apel, Johann (1486–1536 CE) was a Lutheran jurist and professor of law and, from 1524–1525, the rector of the University of Wittenberg.

Aquinas, Thomas (1225–1274 CE) born in Aquinaum, a city located on the road between Rome and Naples, into an aristocratic Neapolitan family, was a thirteenth-century philosopher and Catholic theologian. He joined the newly founded Dominican Order, studied under Albertus Magnus at Cologne, and afterward taught at Paris, Rome, and Naples. His principal work was the *Summa Theologiae*, which is a systematic exploration of philosophy (as it existed in the thirteenth century) and theology. Aquinas was the first person to attempt the assimilation of natural law with secular justice. Before Aquinas, natural law (for example, in the hands of Cicero) was something of an obscurity, permitting arbitrary and ambiguous application in various circumstances. Aquinas attempted to integrate the principles of natural law with the realities of the human condition. In so doing, Aquinas believed he was accomplishing for Christian thought what Maimonides (1135–1204 CE) the great medieval scholar, philosopher, and codifier in *Moreh Nebuchim* (*Guide of the Perplexed*), had tried to do for Jewish thought (but not always appreciated by faithful Jews): namely, to achieve a synthesis (or at least an integration and reconciliation) of revealed faith and the best science known at the time (which was essentially the Aristotelian system that had just become available through translation in the mid-twelfth century).

Arion (625–585 BCE) was the first to convert the dithyramb—a passionate choral hymn sung in honor of Dionysus, the god of wine, usually featuring around fifty men and boys—into a literary form and recite in it at Corinth. Aristotle claims that Arion's dithyramb developed into Greek tragedy.

Aristotle (384–322 BCE) was a philosopher and scientist of ancient Athens. He was born in Stagira, Macedonia, and did not come to Athens until he was seventeen. His father, Nicomachus, was the personal physician to the king of Macedonia, Amyntas III, who was the father of Philip of Macedon and the grandfather of Alexander the Great. After Aristotle was left an orphan, he was sent to Athens for his education. There he joined Plato's Academy as a student.

Augustine (Augustine of Hippo) (354–430 BCE) was a philosopher, rhetorician, and theologian. St. Augustine is noted for formulating the doctrine of Original Sin and the concept of "just war" that influenced Catholic and Reformed theology.

Augustus, Caesar (63 BCE–14 CE) born with the name Gaius Octavius Thurinus, was adopted by his great uncle Julius Caesar (44 BCE) and renamed Gaius Julius Caesar. After 27 BCE he took on the additional name Augustus (Gaius Julius Caesar Augustus). He became the first emperor of the Roman Empire (the Roman Republic having collapsed) and ruled from 27 BCE until his death.

Austin, John (1790–1859 CE) a jurist, is noted for his publications on the philosophy of law and jurisprudence. He became a Professor of Jurisprudence in the University of London in 1826. Austin's publications include *The Province of Jurisprudence Determined* and *Lectures on Jurisprudence*.

B

Bacon, Francis (1561–1626 CE) was the son of Sir Nicholas Bacon, Lord Keeper of the Seal (the Queen's legal officer), and Lady Ann Bacon. In 1573, at the age of twelve, the young Bacon entered Trinity College at Cambridge (which had been enriched decades earlier by land grants from Henry VIII). He quickly tired, however, of the university's sterile intellectual atmosphere with its devotion to either religious instruction or rhetorical logic. This meant that Bacon spent most of his time preparing for "disputations," which were competitions with other students over syllogisms. And so in his spare time he studied the intricacies of the Aristotelian universe. Three years later, in 1576, he followed in his father's footsteps by entering Gray's Inn. He was called to the Bar in 1582.

Barkeloo, Lemma (d. 1870 CE) was the first woman to be admitted to a United States law school. She traveled from Brooklyn, New York, to the Law Department of Washington University in St. Louis in the fall of 1869, after she was refused admission to Columbia and Harvard law schools. Although she did not graduate, Barkaloo was admitted to the bar of the Supreme Court of Missouri in March 1870, and appears to be the first woman in the United States to try a case in court.

Bentham, Jeremy (1748–1832 CE) English jurist and philosopher, was born in London, England. He studied at Oxford University before qualifying for the bar. His father hoped that Jeremy would become the Lord Chancellor of England, but his son never actually practiced law, complaining that the "Demon of Chicane" was rife in the legal system. He therefore chose to concentrate on legal theory rather than its practice. His writings have spread wide and deep in the areas of political, economic, and legal thought.

As a utilitarian (but not the founder of utilitarianism) and a vigorous advocate of codification of the law, Bentham wrote about the disadvantages and irrationality of the common-law approach. Consequently, he had an intense dislike for William Blackstone and Blackstone's love of the English common law.

Bernoulli, Jakob (1654–1705 CE) was a contemporary of Sir Isaac Newton and, like him, worked on the foundations of calculus. Bernoulli's approach was to derive "moral certainty" (in essence, being as sure as one can be) from multiple examples, an approach that is analogous to the notion of limits in calculus. One can, for example, never know with absolute certainty the slope of a smooth curve at a given point, but one can achieve an increasing level of "moral certainty."

Binney, Horace (1780–1875 CE) graduated in 1797 from Harvard College and later became the attorney general of Pennsylvania. He was a leader of the bar in the United States, and his most famous case, in which he was unsuccessfully opposed by Daniel Webster, was *Vidal v. Girard's Executors*. His argument in the case influenced the interpretation of the law of charities.

Blackstone, William (1723–1780 CE) was a Fellow of All Souls College, Oxford, who became a barrister of the Middle Temple on November 28, 1746. He practiced as a barrister with only moderate success, but was a man of broad interests—for example, he wrote a treatise on architecture. When the Vinerian professorship of common law, endowed by Charles Viner (who had chambers in the Temple (King's Bench Walk) but was never called to the Bar), was founded at Oxford in 1758, Blackstone became its first holder. He also served for nine years as a member of Parliament and sat as a judge of the Common Pleas. He is said to have not been an avid politician—but, with Tory inclinations, he opposed the repeal of the Stamp Act.

Blackstone's most enduring achievement was his *Commentaries on the Laws of England*, published in four volumes (1765–69). It has been said that this work not only made the study of law in England more respectable but it helped create the American legal profession.

Brandeis, Louis D. (1856–1941 CE) was from a trading Jewish family of Kentucky and is considered to be one of the best students of the English common law ever to have attended Harvard Law School. After graduation he decided not to become a law professor but went into a law partnership with a classmate. The partnership was successful and Brandeis made quite a bit of money practicing corporate law—becoming known in Boston as "the people's attorney" through such acts as skewering J. P. Morgan over his stewardship of the New Haven Railroad. He became a friend and close adviser to Woodrow Wilson, who in 1912 became president of the United States. In 1916 Wilson, as a lawyer turned educator turned politician, nominated Brandeis to the U.S. Supreme Court. And despite strong anti-Semitic fervor and rightist prejudice, Wilson prevailed in his appointment of Brandeis. Brandeis became the first Jew to sit on the high court—and perhaps the greatest judicial policy analyst of his age.

Bradwell, Myra (1831–1894 CE) was a teacher, a publisher, and an attorney. In 1869 Bradwell applied for admission to the Illinois bar. The Illinois Supreme Court, however, denied her application. She then appealed her case to the United States Supreme Court, but lost. While Bradwell's case was on appeal, Alta M. Hulett applied for admission to the Illinois bar and was also denied. Hulett took her cause to the legislature, drafting a bill providing that no person be discriminated against in any occupation, except the military, on account of gender. With Bradwell's assistance, Hulett succeeded in getting her bill passed and became the first woman lawyer in Illinois (1873). In 1892 Bradwell received her license to practice law.

Brent, Margaret (1601–1671 CE) was the first woman in the North American Colonies to act as an attorney before a court of the common law. She entered more lawsuits than anyone in Maryland, although she was much more of a businesswoman than a lawyer.

Bryan, William Jennings (1860–1925 CE). Following high school, Bryan entered Illinois College and studied classics, graduating as valedictorian in 1881. He studied law at Union Law College in Chicago. He practiced law in Jacksonville (1883–1887) and then moved to the boomtown of Lincoln, Nebraska. He became the Democratic Party nominee for president of the United States in 1896, 1900, and 1908 (losing each time), but eventually became the Secretary of State under President Woodrow Wilson.

Budé, Guillaume ("Budaeus") (1468–1540 CE) was a legal humanist and is known for his superb scholarly abilities exhibited in the two works he produced on law and classical antiquity. Most noted is his influence on the revival of Greek studies in France and in persuading the king to establish the Collège de France.

Burlamaqui, Jean-Jacques (1694–1748 CE) was a Swiss scholar. His chief works are *Principes du droit naturel* (*Principles of Natural Law*) (1747) and *Principes du droit politique* (*Principles of Political Law*) (1751). He held a chair at the University of Geneva. It was from Burlamaqui's understanding of natural law (based on "voluntarism") that Thomas Jefferson gleaned the right to pursue happiness (i.e., the phrase "pursuit of happiness"), which he saw as being achieved as a result of humankind's commitment to reason.

Burr, Aaron (1756–1836 CE) was a lawyer and third U.S. Vice President. He served in the New York State Assembly from 1784 to 1785 and was appointed New York State Attorney General. Burr shot and killed Alexander Hamilton in a duel.

C

Calvin, John (1509–1564 CE) was jurist and theologian. He was instrumental in the development of the system of Christian theology later called Calvinism. In 1536 he published the first edition of his *Institutes of the Christian Religion.*

Capito, Gaius Ateius (c. 30 BCE–22 CE) was a jurist in Rome during the reign of emperors Augustus and Tiberius. He was said to be the "founder" of the Sabinians and was granted the *ius respondendi*, although he is cited only once by other jurists of the classical period.

Cardozo, Benjamin N. (1870–1938 CE) was Chief Judge of the New York Court of Appeals until his appointment in 1932 to fill the seat on the United States Supreme Court left vacant by Justice Oliver Wendell Holmes' retirement. He is remembered for his significant influence, mostly based on his decisions during his eighteen-year tenure on the New York Court of Appeals, on the development of American common law in the twentieth century.

Caro, Joseph (1488–1575 CE) was a codifier and mystic who lived in Turkey and Israel. In putting together the *Shulhan Arukh*, Rabbi Caro frequently relied on court decisions. Hundreds of decisions by Rabbi Isaac ben Sheshet Perfet (known as the Ribash, 1326–1408 CE) chief rabbi of Algiers and head of its rabbinical court, were incorporated into the code.

Cato the Censor (234–149 BCE) strongly resisted the introduction of Greek culture into Rome. He, along with other Romans, was angered by the moral degeneration represented by virtuous Roman matrons painting themselves with imported cosmetics, by the adoption of Greek literary activity, and by the infiltration of the Bacchic cult—seeing it as bad for public morals. This anger became the impetus behind the senatorial edicts that expelled two Greek Epicurean philosophers in 173 BCE and any remaining philosophers and rhetoricians in 161 BCE. Cato's goal was to return to the primitive simplicity of a primarily agricultural state.

Catus, Sextus Aelius Paetus (fl. 198–194 BCE) was elected Roman Republican consul in 198 BCE. He is known today for interpreting the Twelve Tablets.

Cave, Bertha (c. 1900 CE). With regard to Cave's trouble in pursuing a legal career, the *British Journal of Nursing* of December 5, 1903, says it all:

> On Wednesday a special tribunal, composed of the Lord Chancellor, the Lord Chief Justice, and Justices Kennedy, Wright, Walton, Farwell, and Joyce, met at the House of Lords to consider an appeal by Miss Bertha Cave. A law student, whom the Benchers of Gray's Inn have refused to call to the Bar.
>
> The proceedings were private, and lasted less than ten minutes, but at the close a representative of the London News Agency was informed that

after Miss Cave had addressed the tribunal the Lord Chancellor said there was no precedent for a lady being called to the English Bar, and the tribunal were unwilling to create such a precedent.

It is said that Miss Cave will now try to get her name placed on the rolls as a solicitor.

A representative of Gray's Inn has stated that the objection of the Benchers was based on the simple grounds that when the Inn was founded the possibility of lady students was never contemplated. The statutes of the Inn, therefore, while containing no definite bar against women, ignore the sex so absolutely as to leave the Benchers, in their opinion, no power to admit a lady. It is really a sex problem.

Charondas (dates unknown) was a lawgiver of Catania in Sicily. There is some evidence that he was a pupil of Pythagoras (c. 580–504 BCE). His laws, originally written in verse, were adopted by the other Chalcidic colonies in Italy and Sicily.

Chassenée, Bartolome (1480–1541 CE) published *A Treatise on the Excommunication of Insects.* This 1531 treatise, in discussing the full range of issues that can arise during the trial of "insect animals," cites, among other relevant anathemas found in the Bible, God's cursing of the (unrepresented) serpent in the Garden of Eden.

Cicero, Marcus Tullius (106–43 BCE) is considered to be one of Rome's greatest orators and prose stylists. He championed a return to the traditional republican government. His career was marked by inconsistencies and a tendency to shift his position in response to the political climate. For more information on Cicero, see Appendix B.

Clark, Marcia Rachel (1953– CE) is best known as the lead prosecutor in the O.J. Simpson case. She attended the University of California at Los Angeles for her undergraduate degree and then earned a juris doctorate at Southwestern University School of Law. She was admitted to the State Bar of California in 1979 and joined the Los Angeles District Attorney's office in 1981. Following the Simpson case, Clark, along with Teresa Carpenter, authored a book, *Without a Doubt,* about the case. The book deal was reported to be worth $4.2 million. Clark was on leave from the District Attorney's office following Simpson's acquittal in 1995, and she officially resigned in 1997.

Clay, Henry (1777–1858 CE) was the founder and leader of the Whig Party. He worked diligently to defend the Kentucky Insurance Company and saved it from an attempt, in 1804, to repeal its charter.

Cochran, Johnnie L., Jr. (1937–2005 CE). Besides representing O.J. Simpson and other notables, including Sean "Diddy" Combs and Michael Jackson,

Cochran represented hundreds of downtrodden clients. He first made a name for himself in Los Angeles, by taking on the Los Angeles Police Department in a series of high-profile police-brutality cases.

Coke, Sir Edward (1554–1634 CE) served as a jurist until 1616, when, due to his continuing quarrels with King James I, he was dismissed from office. The chief bone of contention between them was Coke's belief that the law of James's predecessors (the Tudors, the Plantagenets, the earlier Normans, and even Anglo-Saxon rulers) remained in force. From 1616 to his death in 1634, Coke spent his time as an MP and wrote treatises on the common law. Coke's influence continued well past the seventeenth century. His most famous work, *The Institutes of the Laws of England*, is still used in the study of property law.

Coke was extremely vocal in his attacks on the presumptions of the "Roman idea" behind the civil-law concept. Like other common-law jurists, he argued that the civil law's emphasis on rationality and on some intellectual elitist that was neither a legislator nor a judge, neither advocate nor prosecutor, invited absolutist monopolies on truth and justice. After being called to the Bar in 1598, Coke was a highly successful practicing lawyer; a local judge in Coventry, Norwich, and London; a professor ("reader") in the Inner Temple (his alma mater); Solicitor General (1592–1594) and Attorney General (1594–1606); Chief Justice of the Common Pleas and then the King's Bench; an influential Parliamentarian; and author of the seminal *Institutes* (imitating Justinian, who had imitated Gaius) and *The Reports* (a systemization and organization of the Principle of English law as they arose from various cases—especially pre-Tudor cases).

Coke (pronounced not like the popular drink but "Cook") accepted the notion that the ancient Britons wrote their law in Greek. There is no surviving evidence of this practice. Coke's reason for the alleged practice is, nevertheless, interesting. His explanation is that the ruling class used to do it in the Greek tongue in order that the law might not be made common among the vulgar (i.e., known among the common people).

Constantine (306–337 CE). It was the Emperor Constantine who established a new capital for the eastern empire—a New Rome. And the east/west division became permanent when, in 395 CE, Theodosius I divided the Empire between his two sons, Arcadius (ruling the Greek East from Constantinople) and Honorius (ruling the Latin West from Rome).

Cooke, John (1608–1660 CE) was probably one of the first Anglo-American lawyers to champion the obligation of free legal services. Cooke, the prosecutor of King Charles I, proposed that barristers should make it a professional obligation to donate 10 percent of their time to pro bono work—a proposal that was greeted with stony silence by the English Bar.

Corax ("Corax of Syracuse") (5th century BCE) is said to have lived in Sicily during the time that the tyrant of Syracuse, Thrasybulus, was ousted and a democracy formed. Under Thrasybulus, the property of many citizens had been seized. These people flooded the courts in an attempt to recover their property. Corax devised an art of rhetoric in order to permit ordinary men to increase their odds of victory in the courts. His main contribution was in structuring judicial speeches into various parts: prose, narration, statement of arguments, refutation of opposing arguments, and summary. His student is said to have been Tisias, who brought Corax's teaching to Athens.

Cromwell, Thomas (1st Earl of Essex) (c. 1485–1540 CE) was a jurist and a statesman who served as King Henry VIII's chief minister from 1532 to 1540. In 1524 he became a member of Gray's Inn.

Cujas, Jacques ("Cujacius") (1520–1590 CE), a French legal expert. He was a prominent legal humanist who sought to abandon the work of medieval Commentators and to concentrate on the correct text and social context of the original words of Roman law.

D

Dalrymple, James, 1st Viscount Stair (1619–1695 CE). It was primarily through Stair's treatise, *The Institutions of the Law of Scotland, Deduced from Its Originals and Collated with the Civil, Canon, and Feudal Laws, and with the Customs of Neighboring Nations*, that Scots law was systematized and Scotland was heavily influenced by Roman law.

Darrow, Clarence (1857–1938 CE) was a famous American lawyer with cases ranging from murder defenses to fighting for labor and the rights of workers. He is considered to be one of the greatest criminal defense lawyers in American history. Darrow is most noted for defending two teenagers, Leopold and Loeb, against the death penalty based on murder charges and for defending the evolution-teaching John T. Scopes in the so-called Monkey Trial. One of the legends about Darrow's prowess as a defense attorney involves Williams Jennings Bryan, who was assisting the prosecution in the John Scopes trial. It is told that during Bryan's closing argument Clarence Darrow purposely diverted the jury's attention by placing a piece of piano wire through his cigar, lit it, and puffed furiously throughout Bryan's closing. The gathering ash on the end of the cigar refused to fall, transfixing the jury as they watched the cigar intently, wondering when the voluminous ash would finally cave in. When Bryan's argument ended, Darrow pulled out the wire and let the ashes fall.

Darwin, Charles (1809–1882 CE) appeared on the scientific scene with *The Origin of Species* and a claim for evolution (natural selection) as the mechanism for how life forms change. The year was 1859. The concept of evolution was generally condemned by organized religion as heretical, notwithstanding the fact that Darwin in the closing lines of his book attributed the entire evolutionary flow of life to "its several powers having been originally breathed by the Creator in a few [life] forms or into one."

DeLancey, James (1703–1760 CE) was born in New York City. He went to school in England, attending Corpus Christi College, Cambridge, before studying law at the Inner Temple. Having been admitted to the Bar in 1725, he returned to New York to practice law and entered politics. In 1733, upon the removal of Chief Justice Lewis Morris, DeLancey was appointed to serve as chief justice of New York. He presided over the 1735 trial of printer and newspaper publisher John Peter Zenger.

Demosthenes (382–322 BCE) was the son of a wealthy knife maker, also called Demosthenes, who died when Demosthenes was only seven and left a large inheritance. The guardians put in charge of the young Demosthenes by his dying father embezzled from the estate. When Demosthenes was old enough to know what had happened, he spent years suing his guardians—and they suing him. He ultimately, however, made his own fortune as the owner of a furniture workshop with twenty slaves and gained fame as a rhetor—sometimes, according to Plutarch, preparing pleas for both parties to a dispute.

Descartes, René (1596–1650 CE) was a French philosopher, mathematician, scientist, and writer. He is considered to be one of the guiding lights of the Industrial Revolution. Descartes' "geometrical method" involved breaking down any situation or operation into its smallest constituent parts, and then attempting to deal with each part mathematically. Descartes believed that this process would always be possible if the parts were small enough.

Domat, Jean (1625–1696 CE) has been called one of the greatest French jurists and systematizers of the law. His book, *Les lois civiles dans leur ordre naturel* (*The Civil Law in its Natural Order*), combined in one system the materials of Roman law and French legislation and decisions. Domat was a close friend and literary executor of Pascal, the famous French philosopher and mathematician (1623–1662). *Les lois civiles*, published in two volumes between 1689 and 1694, was designed to provide Domat's children with a scheme for understanding the civil law. William Strahan translated Domat's work into English (1722). This translation influenced not only Thomas Jefferson but also other American revolutionaries and early American jurists such as John Jay; Ralph Assheton, the distinguished Pennsylvanian jurist and judge of the Pennsylvania Court of Chancery (1730–1735) and later the Pennsylvania Court of Common Pleas (1738–1746); and Jasper Yeates, Associate Justice of the Supreme Court of Pennsylvania (1791–1817).

Donellus, Hugues (1527–1591 CE) was a French law professor and legal humanist. One of his most important insights was that classical Roman law as elaborated through particular forms of action and therefore legal debate had actually centered on procedure and not rules of substantive law. And while teaching at Leyden in Holland he raised and explored the important question: What's the relationship between individual rights and the procedural means for enforcing them? In exploring this question, he came to see the law as a system of rights and actions. He criticized Justinian for merging actions with obligations. Donellus's analysis, for the first time, divided private law into substantive law (subjective rights) and civil procedure.

Draco (7th century BCE) was the first legislator of ancient Athens. Around 620 BCE a group of elites commissioned Draco to assemble a code of laws aimed at controlling the masses. His "code," inscribed on four-faced wooden blocks, decreed death the penalty for almost every offense.

Dulany, Daniel (the Younger) (1722–1797 CE) was a legislator who was elected to the Maryland General Assembly and became the Mayor of Annapolis. He studied law at Middle Temple and was a noted opposer of the Stamp Act. Dulany argued against taxation without representation and wrote the pamphlet, *Considerations on the Propriety of Imposing Taxes in the British Colonies.*

E

Emmet, Thomas Addis (1764–1827 CE) was an Irish-American lawyer, a politician, and New York State Attorney General from 1812 to 1813.

Erasmus, Desiderius (1466–1536 CE) was born the illegitimate son of a cleric and a widow. He was sent to a school in Deventer that was run by the Brethren of the Common Life, a pietistic lay order that stressed morality and good works—deeply influencing Erasmus's Christianity. He was ordained a priest (1492), but disliked the clerical life and instead pursued a career as a scholar, teacher, and writer.

F

Fay, François (16th century CE) and Petremand Bertrand were the prosecutors in the 1587 CE trial of the weevil infestation of the vineyards of Saint-Julien, France. Concerned over clever arguments presented by the defense, Fay summoned the villagers and suggested a compromise—a piece of land outside of town be given to the weevils.

Ferne, John (c. 1510–1609 CE) was a writer on heraldry, a genealogist, and an eminent common-law lawyer. He graduated from St. John's College, Cambridge (1572), appears to have studied at Oxford, and was admitted to Inner Temple (1576).

Filliol, Antoine (16th century CE) and Pierre Rembaud were the defense attorneys who defended weevils in their second trial for infestation in 1587 CE in Saint-Julien, France. Upon being presented with prosecutor François Fay's compromise of a piece of land outside of town, Filliol required the proposal to be put in writing and demanded time enough for deliberation before he gave his opinion on the prosecutor's suggested compromise.

Finch, Henry (1558–1625 CE) was a seventeenth-century legal scholar and lawyer.

Flavius, Gnaeus (censor 312 BCE) was a Roman legal writer and politician who was the first to make public the technical rules of legal procedure that determined what legal acts might be done on which days and the form of words that had to be used to state a claim or make a defense. Until then, the rules had been kept secret by the patricians and the pontifices so that they could maintain their advantage over the plebeians. For the first time the Roman people could learn the *legis actiōnēs* required to maintain legal proceedings. Flavius's work was later known as the *Ius Civile Flavianum*.

Frankfurter, Felix (1882–1965 CE) was one of President Roosevelt's trusted advisers. As a professor at the Harvard Law School, he pushed a number of his students toward public service with the New Deal administration. And following the death of United States Supreme Court Justice Benjamin W. Cardozo in 1938, President Roosevelt appointed Frankfurter to the Court.

G

Gaius (full name unknown, d. after 178 CE) was a teacher, possibly at Berytus. His book, *Institutiones*, was directed at students—posing "Socratic" questions and often giving the contradictory opinions of his predecessors before offering his own resolution.

Galilei, Galileo (1564–1642 CE) was first enjoined by the Church in 1616 from publicly supporting Copernicus's theory of Helios-Centrism. He was later tried (largely for having failed to live up to his agreement not to teach or advocate Copernicanism), in 1633, by the Inquisition and required to kneel and read aloud a recantation saying that he "adjured, cursed and detested" the theory that the Earth moves in orbit around the Sun and spins about its own axis.

Gallus, Gaius Aquilius (ca. 116–before 44 BCE) was a Roman jurist, a politician, and a teacher. He also was a pupil of Quintus Mucius Scaevola. He is noted for his devotion to the duties of a Roman jurist and his expertise in the law.

Galton, Francis (1882–1911 CE) was Charles Darwin's half-cousin, and it was Galton's forays into the inheritance of such characteristics as genius, feeble-mindedness, and criminality that started the eugenics movement. In fact, he coined the term "eugenic" ("good in birth" or "noble in heredity").

Gandhi, Mohandas K. (1869–1948 CE) was one of the most respected spiritual and political leaders of the 1900s. He studied law in London (Inner Temple) and returned to India in 1891 to practice. In 1893 Gandhi accepted a one-year contract to do legal work in South Africa and stayed for twenty-one years working to secure rights for Indian people. He promoted nonviolence and civil disobedience as a way of obtaining political and social goals through a method of action called *Satyagraha*. He developed this method of action based upon the principles of courage, nonviolence, truth, and a belief that the way people behave is more important than what they achieve. More than once Gandhi used fasting to impress upon others the need to be nonviolent. He was assassinated in 1948 at the age of 78 by Nathuram Godse, who opposed Gandhi's program of tolerance for all creeds and religion.

Glanvill, Ranulf de (1130–1190 CE) came from a wealthy landowning family. In 1163 he was appointed sheriff of Yorkshire. In 1174, while sheriff of Lancashire, he was selected to head the troops who met and defeated the invading Scots at Alnwick. This heroic effort gained Glanvill favor with King Henry II, and in 1180 he became chief justiciar of England (the king's chief minister responsible for legal and financial business). Glanvill, although less favored by Richard I, accompanied the King on his crusade to Acre (the great fortress port on the Mediterranean), where he died of illness.

Gore, Christopher (1758–1827 CE) was a prominent lawyer, Federalist politician, and diplomat. In 1778 Gore was considered to have studied law according to the rules of the Suffolk bar since July 1776—although his main activities were actually those of a patriot rather than those of a law student.

Gorgias (c. 487–376 BCE) was a pre-Socratic philosopher and rhetorician. He was a native of Leontini in Sicily. Along with Protagoras, Gorgias was part of the first generation of Sophists. His chief claim to fame is that he brought rhetoric from Sicily to Attica.

Gould, James (1770–1838 CE) was a lawyer and a law professor at Litchfield Law School, America's first law school.

Gratian (c. 1095–1150 CE) was a Camaldolese monk and legal scholar. He produced the *Decretum Gratiani* (c. 1140 CE)—the first comprehensive and systematic legal treatise in Western European history and a work that was central to the development of classical canon law.

Gregory I (590–604 CE) was one of the foremost papal legislators. Pope Gregory's knowledge of important aspects of secular law followed from his own background, which, shocking as it may be, most certainly included studies in the law. Before entering a Gnostic order, he had served in 573 CE as the highest administrative and judicial official of the city of Rome.

Gregory VII (1073–85 CE) as part of the Investiture Conflict (a long conflict between the popes and the German emperors over the question of whether the emperor and other princes had the right to invest an abbot or bishop with the ring and staff of his office) succeeded in freeing the Church from the temporal control under which it had lived since the late Roman Empire. The Investiture Conflict gave rise to a barrage of pamphleteering from the pope's and the emperor's respective sides—thus giving rise for people trained to present and refute argument by "logic" and "authority."

Grotius, Hugo (1583–1645 CE) a leading Dutch Protestant jurist, became famous for his 1625 treatise, *De iure belli ac pacis* (*Concerning the Law of War and Peace*) a book systematizing and expanding upon the ideas of, among others, the Jesuit Francisco Suarez and the Italian bartolist Alberico Gentili (Regius professor of civil law at Oxford and an adviser to King James I), on the law of war and peace. His writings reaffirmed and secularized the doctrine of natural law (based on "intellectualism") during the seventeenth and eighteenth centuries. He revived the Ciceronian idea of natural law and its underlying optimism about human nature. In doing so, Grotius "liberated" this concept of law from any remaining dependence on ecclesiastical or papal interpretation. He fashioned a bridge from the Christian Commonwealth of the Middle Ages to a new interstate society. Grotius has been called the "Father of International Law." Scholarship has also suggested that Grotius might also be called the "Modern Father of Natural Rights," since he influenced all of the major rights theorists of the seventeenth century—including Hobbes, Locke, and Domat.

H

Hale, Matthew (1609–1676 CE) whose father gave up the practice of law because of moral scruples against the then "required" practice of submitting false pleadings, was critically important to the development of English jurisprudence. He has been said to be the greatest common-law lawyer since Coke—and was ready to appear on behalf of Charles I at the king's trial for alleged mass murder, treason, and tyranny had he been called upon. His *History of the Common Law of England* (first published in 1713), although imperfect and fragmentary, was the first attempt at a history of the common law as a whole. There is little doubt, however, that even though a graduate of Lincoln's Inn, he was also a student of Roman law. He was justice of Common Pleas (1653–1657) under Oliver Cromwell, Chief Baron of the Exchequer under the restored monarchy of Charles II, and from 1671 until just before his death in 1676, Chief Justice of the King's Bench. Although deeply religious, Hale asserted that law should be tested by reason. And his test of reason was distinctly instrumentalist: laws are made not for their own sake but for the sake of those who are to be guided by them, and though laws are and ought to be sacred, if they are not useful they must be amended or replaced. The question was, and still is, what is meant by "useful." Useful in maximizing wealth? In redistributing wealth?

Hamilton, Alexander (1755–1757 CE) was the first U.S. Secretary of Treasury. He was one of America's first constitutional lawyers, cowriting the *Federalist Papers* (a primary source of Constitutional interpretation). Hamilton was shot and killed in a duel by lawyer-Vice President Aaron Burr.

Hamilton, Andrew (1676–1741 CE) was a Scottish lawyer in Colonial America. He is best known for his legal victory on behalf of printer and newspaper publisher John Peter Zenger.

Hammurabi (c. 1792–1750 BCE) was the sixth king of the First Dynasty of Babylon (a dynasty that ended about 1600 BCE). King Hammurabi's 300 law provisions constitute the most famous "code" outside of the Bible.

Hancock, John (1737–1793 CE) was a prominent patriot of the American Revolution and served as the president of the Second Continental Congress. He was also the first governor of the Commonwealth of Massachusetts and is most remembered for his large and stylish signature on the United States Declaration of Independence.

Hart, H.L.A. (Herbert Lionel Adolphus) (1907–1992 CE) was a legal philosopher and is noted for his contributions to political philosophy. He was a Professor of Jurisprudence at Oxford University and authored, *The Concept of Law*. Hart was instrumental in developing a sophisticated theory of legal positivism within the framework of analytic philosophy.

Hayes, Rutherford B. (1877–1881 CE) had a sixteen-year law career (1845–1861) that involved a series of law partnerships and high-profile cases. He was the first lawyer-President to have graduated from Harvard Law School—President Obama is the second.

Henry of Bratton ("Bracton") (d. 1268 CE) while intensely committed to the common law, was schooled in Roman and canon law at the University of Paris. He took holy orders in the 1230s (mostly just so that he could be a student at the University of Paris) and held several ecclesiastical posts. He knew the *Corpus Iuris Canonici*, that is, the *Decretum* and *Decretals*. Bracton also studied the works of Azo (1170–1230 CE) one of the early professors at the University of Bologna and a great exponent of civil law. In addition to serving as a Judge of Assize, Bracton was appointed as a Justice of Eyre of the King's Bench for a short period during the reign of Henry III and was a member of the group of legal advisers in the King's Council. Bracton was the last of the great English ecclesiastical lawyers of the Middle Ages. He wrote just before the establishment of pure secular law schools in London.

Henry, Patrick (1736–1799 CE) was an American Revolutionary and is most noted for his "Give me Liberty, or give me Death!" speech. He was vehement in his denunciation of corrupt government officials and, along with Samuel Adams and Thomas Paine, is remember as one of the most influential advocates of the American Revolution.

Herder, Johann Gottfried von (1744–1803 CE) was a one-time student of Immanuel Kant. In the eighteenth century there was no movement for German, Italian, or Slavonic national unification. There was no sense among the people of national unity and no sense, for example, of loyalty to Germany versus the dynasty of the king. (In fact, King Frederick the Great of "Germany" spoke French.) All of this started to change as a result of the intellectual and emotional revolution started by Herder. He laid down the criteria by which a People or a Race could be defined. According to Herder, *das Volk* must have a shared body of myth, a shared language, a shared homeland, and even a shared body type. And this new national consciousness (e.g., *das Vaterland* and the Aryan Race) as the focus of national life, eventually had political consequences—even though Herder's own conception of nationalism was cultural and not political.

Hicks, Sue Kerr (1895–1980 CE) was a jurist who practiced law and served as a circuit court judge in Tennessee. He was a co-instigator and prosecutor in the 1925 trial of John T. Scopes, a Tennessee teacher accused of violating Tennessee law forbidding the teaching of the theory of evolution. Named after his mother, he was apparently the original "Boy Named Sue" of Johnny Cash's hit song.

Hobbes, Thomas (1588–1679 CE). Hobbes developed a complex system of thought in which man was reduced to a state of nature and then reconstructed. From a law point of view, Hobbes sought to vindicate the English Parliament's authority to legislate for the common good—without being hamstrung by the supposedly firm principles of the common law. He wrote, for example, that Coke's conception of law as artificial reason (i.e., reason that is brought into being not by nature but by human effort and human art) was untrue since law does not originate in lawyers' or judges' reasoning, or indeed in reason at all, but in the will of the sovereign. Hobbes looked to introspection as the source of genuine understanding.

Holmes, Oliver Wendell, Jr. (1841–1935 CE) is one of American's most famous jurists, serving on the Supreme Court of the United States from 1902 to 1932. He advocated a "bad man" perspective for evaluating law. This perspective focuses on the "material consequences" of law practice rather than on utopian possibilities. Holmes is noted for his concise opinions and is one of the most widely cited United States Supreme Court justices in history.

Hortalus, Quintus Hortensius (114–50 BCE) was a Roman orator. At nineteen he made his first speech at the bar. His reputation as an advocate was made by his successful defense of Nicomedes IV of Bithynia (one of Rome's dependents in the East). It was lost, however, by his defeat in defending Gaius Verres against Cicero as prosecutor (the case that made young Cicero's reputation). Hortensius's daughter, Hortensia, was also a successful orator.

Hortensia (1st century BCE) was the daughter of the orator Quintus Hortensius Hortalus and achieved a reputation for eloquence for her only recorded appearance, in 42 BCE, before the tribunal of the Second Triumvirate composed of Gaius Julius Caesar Octavianus, Marcus Aemilius Lepidus, and Marcus Antonius. In this case Hortensia appeared on behalf of the wealthy elite matrons of Rome (a type of class action), 1,400 of whom were to be taxed to support the war against the assassins of Julius Caesar. The main thrust of her argument questioned the fairness of a war tax levied against women who did not have the vote and who had lost their male protectors.

Hotman, Francois (1524–1590 CE) was a French Protestant lawyer and writer, associated with the legal humanists.

Huguccio of Pisa (1190–1210 CE) was one of the greatest canonists of the twelfth century. Bishop Huguccio was the author of a famous etymological dictionary.

Hume, David (1711–1776 CE) was an empiricist and as such, the only important kind of statement for him was one about matters of fact, which are not necessarily true. It is the answer to such a question that tells one something new about the world. Any real knowledge comes in this form, according to the empiricists, and such statements are based on observation, not pure reason.

Huston, Charles (1895–1950 CE) studied at Dunbar High School, Amherst College, and Harvard University Law School. In 1935 he was recruited to establish a legal department for the NAACP. And in 1936 Huston appointed Thurgood Marshall as his assistant. Over the years Houston and Marshall used the courts to challenge racist laws involving education, housing, and transportation. Houston was also a law professor and dean of Howard University Law School.

Huxley, Thomas Henry (1825–1895 CE). In 1860, Huxley attacked the religious notions of man's origin with a vengeance. An idea attributed to the Bible, but not actually found in Genesis, purports to show that each species is a special creation unto itself. This notion was in direct opposition to Darwin's concept of the gradual evolution of species. For Huxley, "Darwin's bulldog," the scant fossil record, which today has been greatly enhanced and brings certain aspects of Darwin's theory into doubt, was absolute proof that Darwin had "guessed" correctly.

Hyperides (390–322 BCE) was a logographer (speechwriter) in ancient Greece who studied under Isocrates.

I

Innocent III (1198–1216 CE) is said to be one of the greatest legal innovators to occupy the papal throne. It was during Pope Innocent III's reign that the zenith of papal monarchy was achieved. The concept of papal sovereignty reached its height with Innocent's emphasis on the pope as entrusted to rule not just the Church, but the world, all as the vicar of Christ. In order to properly administer the comprehensive supernational society he had achieved, Innocent III reorganized the papal Curia (Court), establishing three separate divisions: the Chancery, dealing with official documents; the Camera, dealing with finances; and the Judiciary, dealing with the law.

It was Pope Innocent III who, looking at the letter of the law (and perhaps the fact that earlier King John had made nice with him and subjected all of England and Ireland to the papacy), granted the King's appeal and excommunicated the Norman barons who forced him to sign the Magna Carta, suspended the archbishop that sided with the barons, and declared this first version of the Great Charter invalid. The Pope, from a Roman/canon-law perspective, determined that the Charter, obtained by coercion, violated the political order of the world. Thus from a technical canon-law perspective, King John was absolved of his oath to observe the Magna Carta based on the Church's claimed reserve power to dispense with the binding charter of oaths (even if the oath was given under duress). Fortunately for England, John was dead a year later. His son and successor, Henry III, required a regent. The boy king and his regent compromised with the barons and, under some duress, the regent twice confirmed the Charter. Henry III, upon formally ascending to the throne, reissued the Charter in a special ceremony.

Irnerius (c. 1050–after 1125 CE) was an Italian jurist and founder of the school of Glossators. Justinian's *Digest* (the *Pandects*) was taken to the emperor Clothaire where it was arranged by Irnerius.

Isaeus (c. 420–350 BCE) was a Greek orator and a professional writer of forensic speeches, confining himself to the area of property claims and legacies. He is credited with over sixty speeches (all written for clients), eleven of which have survived in their entirety. They are the oldest documents in the world that exhibit in detail the workings of a testamentary law. It is said that even the great Demosthenes associated with and received help from Isaeus. He had the reputation as being a "lawyer's lawyer."

Isocrates (436–338 BCE) was a Greek rhetorician and one of the ten Attic orators. During his working life, he was probably the most influential rhetorician in Greece. It appears that Isocrates' teacher was Tisias, whose teacher was Corax of Syracuse, who was the first to formulate a set of rhetorical rules (5th century BCE).

J

James I, King of England (1566–1625 CE) fought against Calvinist, antimonarchical views, as well as claims of papal supremacy and the notion that law makes the king, and not the other way around. His weapon of choice was the position that God, as the creator of natural order, appoints monarchs to carry out His will on earth. Thus kings derive their power directly from God (a position supported by certain lawyers of the time—for example, the king's faithful attorney general Francis Bacon). And just to prove that he was right, King James enforced his theory, sometimes harshly, against all who dared to oppose it.

Jay, John (1745–1829 CE) was an American politician, statesman, revolutionary, diplomat, Founding Father, and President of the Continental Congress from 1778 to 1779. As governor of New York, he was the state's leading opponent to slavery.

Jefferson, Thomas (1743–1826 CE) was the third U.S. President (and the second lawyer-President), principal author of Declaration of Independence, and one of the Founding Fathers. He served as Governor of Virginia during the

Revolutionary War. And prior to becoming president he served as the first U.S. Secretary of State and the second U.S. Vice President.

Judaeus, Philo. See Philo of Alexandria.

Judah (Jehudah) ha-Nasi (c. 135–c. 220 CE) was a Palestinian Jewish communal leader (*tanna*). He occupied the office of patriarch (*nasi*). Tradition has presented him as the redactor of the Mishnah. And it is interesting to note that Judah ha-Nasi's final compilation of the Mishnah (the culmination of the process that began with Rabbi Akiva) took place on the heels of Gaius's completing his *Institutes* (a seminal work) in Rome, apparently intended to act as an elementary textbook for lawyers.

Julianus, Salvius (Julian the Jurist) (c. 100–170 CE) was a Roman jurist, public official, and professor at Constantinople. In about 130 CE he was charged with revising and rearranging the *Praetorian Edict*. His most noted work, however, is the *Digesta*, a systematic treatise on civil and praetorian law.

Justinian I ("Justinian the Great") (483–565 CE) was a Byzantine emperor from 527 to 565. He initiated a total overhaul of the empire's legal system. In the *Corpus Juris Civilis* his commissioners assembled a systematic exposition of the basic legal texts and the essential interpretational literature that summed up the great heritage of Roman law and preserved it for transmission to later generations. The *Corpus Juris Civilis* is still the basis of civil law in many modern states.

K

Kant, Immanuel (1724–1804 CE) was an eighteenth-century German philosopher from the Prussian city of Königsberg. He is considered to be one of the most influential thinkers of modern Europe and of the late Enlightenment. As a leading philosopher of retribution punishment, Kant stressed, for example, the imperative of maintaining equality among offenders.

Kelsen, Hans (1881–1973 CE) was born in Prague to Jewish parents and moved to Vienna with his family when he was two years old. Upon graduating from the Akademisches Gymnasium, he studied law at the University of Vienna, taking his doctorate in 1906. In addition to being a full professor at the University of Vienna (1919), a judge of the Austrian Constitutional Court (1925–1930), a professor at the University of Cologne (1930–1933, until the Nazis came to power), a professor at the Gradate Institute of International Studies (1934–1940), a professor at the University of California at Berkeley, and a visiting professor of International law at the United States Naval War College, Kelsen wrote a number of influential books. His main legacy is as the inventor of the modern European model of constitutional review.

Kent, James (1763–1847 CE) was Chief Justice of the New York Supreme Court, Chancellor of the Court on Chancery, first professor of law at Columbia College, and author of *Commentaries on American Law*. While preparing to give a series of public lectures he studied, in the original, the works of Bynkershoek, Cicero, and Quintilian. It was this type of intellectual rigor that eventual led Kent to write his classical treaties—said to have done for American jurisprudence what Blackstone did for England's.

Kepley, Ada Harriet Miser (1847–1925 CE) was born in Somerset, Ohio. Her family later moved to St. Louis, Missouri and in 1867 Ada married Henry B. Kepley, who had his own law practice in Effingham, Illinois. At Henry's urging, Ada attended the Union College of Law (now Northwestern) from 1869 to 1870. At Union College she earned her bachelor of law and became the first woman to graduate from law school in the United States.

Kopernik, Mikolaj ("Copernicus") (1473–1543 CE) was a physician and a canon lawyer. It was Copernicus who came to the startling realization that the earth is not at the center of the universe, but, with the other planets in our solar system, revolves around the sun. And in the spirit of full disclosure, Copernicus has not been the only lawyer to mess up the cosmos. Edwin Hubble, a lawyer turned astronomer, "revealed" that the universe is not just resting in eternal comfort but is actually expanding.

Kyle, Frances (20th century CE) was one of the early modern-day lawyers. She distinguished herself by winning the then-leading scholarly prize for Irish law students and was, in November of 1921, the first Irish woman admitted to the bar.

L

Labeo, Marcus Antistius (d. 10 or 11 CE) was a Roman jurist. Perhaps his most important contribution was the *Libri posteriores* (so called because it was published after his death), which contained an organized compilation of Roman law.

Lagus, Konrad (c. 1499–1546 CE) was a professor, politician, and legal practitioner who combined Roman-law and canon-law sources. Previously these sources of law had been analyzed separately: the Roman law texts being read in courses in Roman law and written about by Romanists and the canon-law texts being read in courses on canon law and written about by canonists. Lagus appears to have been the first jurist to present a compendium of concepts and rules of law drawn from both systems.

Langdell, Christopher Columbus (1826–1906 CE) studied at Phillips Exeter Academy (1845–1846), at Harvard College (1848–1860), and at Harvard Law School. From 1854 to 1870 he practiced law in New York City—until his appointment, at the recommendation of James Coolidge Carter (a famous legal practitioner and jurisprudent), in 1870 as Dane Professor of Law. He thereafter became Dean of the Law Faculty of Harvard. His legacy is largely based on his influence of methodology for the teaching of law. Prior to Langdell's tenure, the primary method was by lecture. In other words, students were told what the law is. Langdell, in contrast, pushed the idea of teaching law through a dialectical process of inference called the case method.

Leibniz, Gottfried Wilhelm (1646–1716 CE) after graduating from the Nicolai School at the age of fifteen, enrolled at the University of Leipzig to study philosophy. He wrote his master's thesis on the relationship between philosophy and the law, and received his degree in 1664. In 1666, Leibniz, one of the co-discoverers of calculus (Isaac Newton being the other), received his doctorate in law from the University of Altdorf.

Lincoln, Abraham (1809–1865 CE) was the sixteenth U.S. President. Before his presidency he had been a country lawyer and an Illinois state legislator. He introduced measures that resulted in the abolition of slavery, issuing the Emancipation Proclamation in 1863 and promoting the passage of the Thirteenth Amendment to the United States Constitution.

Lipit-Ishtar (r. c. 1934–c. 1924 BCE) was the fifth ruler of the First Dynasty of Isin, a city that rose to power in southern Mesopotamia after the fall of the Third Dynasty of Ur (founded by King Ur-Nammu). King Lipit-Ishtar promulgated a set of laws written in Sumerian—which by his reign was a dead language (in the same way that Latin, for example, is a dead language—but not to lawyers). It appears that the laws of Lipit-Ishtar (as well as those of Ur-Nammu) are premised on a new idea: that law can be used to transform a society.

Littleton, Thomas (c. 1422–1481 CE) the son of Thomas Westcote (a king's servant in court) and Elizabeth de Littleton, had a distinguished legal career. In the 1440s he began holding county offices. He served, for example, as Undersheriff of Worcestershire. In about 1450 he was elected Reader at the Inner Temple. He became a Serjeant-at-law in 1453 and a judge of the assizes (a French word for "sitting") on the northern circuit in 1455. He was made judge of the Court of Common Pleas in 1466 and served until 1481. Littleton was knighted in 1475.

Livingston, Robert (1746–1813 CE) was an American lawyer, politician, and diplomat from New York. He was a member of the committee that worked on the Declaration of Independence.

Livy (c.59 to 17 CE.) was a Roman historian who wrote a monumental history of Rome and its people, *Ab Urbe Condita* (*From the Founding of the City*).

Locke, John (1632–1704 CE) was an English physician and political philosopher whose *Second Treatise of Government* (1690) is considered by many to be the most important document in the literature of constitutional democracy. Locke's theory, for example, that humans have certain inalienable rights that cannot be infringed upon by the state appears to have significantly influenced Thomas Jefferson's drafting of the Declaration of Independence. And his views on the social collective's right to dictate and modify the (preferably written) terms of its governance led America's Founding Fathers to compose and seek ratification of one of the most famous of all social contracts: the Constitution of the United States of America.

Locke stressed that all men are equal because they are equal in the eyes of God and that property rights need to be limited to the extent that they threaten this God-given dignity. In other words, Locke's concept of property was bounded by a divinely established natural law. This concept, more frequently seen in its various secular versions, continues on in certain modern-day concepts of property law.

Lockwood, Belva Ann (1830–1917 CE) was an attorney, teacher, author, and politician active in working for woman's rights. She holds the distinction of being the first woman attorney given the privilege of practicing before the United States Supreme Court when, in 1879, she was victorious in getting a bill passed by Congress.

Longinus, Gaius Cassius (1st century CE) was a prominent Roman jurist—a pupil of Massurius Sabinus, with whom he (and perhaps not Gaius Ateius Capito) founded a legal school (the *Sabiniani*). He was the grandnephew of Servius Sulpicius Rufus and nephew of Gaius Cassius Longinus, one of Caesar's assassins. His principal work is the *Libri (Commentarii) Iuris Civilis* in at least ten volumes.

Luther, Martin (1483–1546 CE) began his study of law in 1505 in accordance with his father's wishes. Within a year of receiving his degree his life took an unexpected turn and he became a monk and a professor of theology. His ideas started the Protestant Reformation.

Lycurgus (c. 800–730 BCE) was the legendary lawgiver of Sparta. He is said to have established the military-oriented reformation of Spartan society in accordance with the Oracle of Apollo at Delphi.

Lysias (c. 459–380 BCE) was the son of Cephalus, a native of Syracuse (a Greek colony on the island of Sicily) and a prosperous arms manufacturer. Cephalus had been recruited by Pericles to come and live in Athens. At age fourteen Lysias and his brother, Polemarchus (later executed during the Thirty Tyrants' reign of terror), went to Thurii (a colony founded in southern "Italy" in 444 BCE by Athens) to study philosophy and eloquence (apparently, at least in part, under the tutelage of Tisias, a teacher of rhetoric). Later Lysias assembled his own school, but was outdone by Theodorus, another teacher of oratory, so he decided to write speeches.

M

Maimonides, Moses ("Rambam") (1135–1204 CE) in his *Mishneh Torah*, recognized the fact that "the Torah makes allowance for human passions." In his code, the great scholar cited this ground (human passions) for leniency (but perhaps, not as Vinnie and Sal might have argued, excuse) in cases where people cannot control their lust and cravings (for a forbidden piece of fruit?).

Manilius, Manius (fl 148 BCE) was a Roman Republican orator and distinguished jurist who authored a collection of formulae for contracts of sale. He was cited by such authors as Cicero and Varro.

Mansfield, Arabella (1846–1911 CE) studied law together with her husband in hopes of passing the bar exam. She spent additional hours preparing as an apprentice at an Iowa office where her brother worked before his own admission. She passed the Iowa bar exam in 1869. However, she did not attempt to practice law but remained an English and history professor at Iowa Wesleyan. Her point in taking the exam appears to simply have been to show that a woman could pass it.

Marshall, John (1755–1835 CE) was an American revolutionary, a statesman, and jurist. He was instrumental in shaping American constitutional law and establishing the United States Supreme Court with the power of judicial review, which is considered his greatest contribution. Marshall was forty-five years of age when he was appointed the fourth Chief Justice of the United States Supreme Court, the youngest in U.S. history. He was a leader of the Federalist Party, served in the House of Representatives, and held the position of Secretary of State under President John Adams.

Marshall, Louis (1856–1929 CE) was a famous trial lawyer who believed that respect for law is "one of the abiding virtues of the Jewish People." In 1906 Marshall, for example, organized the American Jewish Committee, primarily composed of attorneys, "to prevent infringement of the civil and religious rights of Jews." He was also, as a Jewish lawyer, the first to oppose Harvard's quota on Jews.

Marshall, Thurgood (1908–1993 CE) had originally wanted to attend the University of Maryland's law school. But it was, at the time, segregated and, as an African American, he had no hope of being admitted. After graduating from Howard Law School, he was groomed by the dean of the school, Charles Huston, to take on the University of Maryland—winning admittance for their African-American client. Marshall then went on to win a number of important civil right cases—including *Brown v. Board of Education of Topeka* (1954). And on June 13, 1967, President Johnson appointed Marshall to the United Supreme Court.

Melanchthon, Philip (1497–1560 CE) was a close friend of Martin Luther at the University of Wittenberg and therefore anti-Catholic/anti-pagan. Nevertheless, he argued that Roman law was "written reason" (*ratio scripta*) that implemented natural law (essentially, from Melanchthon's view point, the Ten Commandments). He countered the argument that Roman laws were of pagan, not Christian, origin by stating that they "are pleasing to God, although they were promulgated by a heathen ruler," and that they "stem not from human cleverness [but] rather they are beams of divine wisdom," a "visible appearance of the Holy Spirit" to the heathen. Most likely the real reason that Melanchthon defended Roman law, based on his detailed knowledge of its content, was that the power of German princes continued to grow and the Roman body of law provided a basis on which to argue for restraint of arbitrary authority. In other words, Melanchthon, as an ethicist and political theorist, found in Roman law a ready source of political order.

Melville, Eliza Ellen (1882–1946 CE) was a New Zealand feminist and politician. Born in Tokatoka, her father was a farmer and boat builder, while her mother was a former teacher. After receiving an education from her mother, she won a scholarship to study at what is now Auckland Girls' Grammar School. She began to study to become a lawyer and was admitted to the bar in 1906— the second woman in New Zealand to qualify as a solicitor of the Supreme Court (the first was Ethel Benjamin)—and three years later, she became the first woman to practice law independently.

Monroe, James (1758–1831 CE, fifth United States President) studied law upon the advice of his uncle, Judge Joseph Jones, under Governor Thomas Jefferson. Monroe's diary entry regarding his apprenticeship, however, tersely states that he "persevered in it" until he was able to enter the bar—which he did in 1782.

Montesquieu, Baron de (Charles-Louis de Secondat) (1689–1755 CE) was a French political philosopher whose writings advocated the separation of powers (drawn from the ancient Roman Republic) and had a significant influence on the drafting of the Constitution of the United States. His most influential work is *De l'esprit des lois* (*The Sprit of the Law*) (1748). Montesquieu contended that human laws are social phenomena that vary in different countries depending on such factors as history, economy, religion, geography, climate, and local customs. It is these factors that, together, form "the spirit of the laws" of society, which a legislator ignores at his peril.

More, Sir Thomas (St. Thomas More) (1478–1535 CE) was an author, statesman, and generally considered to be a Renaissance humanist scholar. He coined the word "utopia" and was preoccupied with the maintenance of harmony and good order in society (in other words, utopia). More was beheaded in 1535 when he refused to sign the Act of Supremacy that declared King Henry VIII Supreme Head of the Church of England. Even though More was not a clergyman, he still saw law in the same way he viewed the Catholic Church. There was, for him, no essential or necessary difference between law and the Church—in other words, he was more driven by divine and natural law than by legal positivism. In this way More was different from many others in the gentry class.

Morris, Lewis (1715–1733 CE) was acclaimed as a man unrivaled "in the knowledge of the law," although he was not a formally trained lawyer. He served as chief justice of the Province of New York until his removal by Governor William Cosby. Morris's replacement was James DeLancey.

Morrison, Carrie (1888–1950 CE) was the first woman admitted as a solicitor. The year was 1922. She was a graduate of Girton College, Cambridge, and had served during the First World War in the War Office and the Army of the Black Sea at Constantinople. She practiced law until she died at the age of sixty-two.

Murray, William (1st Earl of Mansfield) (1705–1793 CE) was chief justice of the King's Bench from 1756 until 1788. Lord Mansfield valued that office over any other available, and in order to keep it he declined invitations to become Lord Chancellor, as well as other powerful positions. He had a deep faith in judge-made law, using reported judicial cases as a means for reform. He made major contributions to the laws of personal freedom, the law of business and trade, and to the status of English law in the colonies. With specific regard to business and trade, it was Lord Mansfield's influence that led the courts to sharply reverse their traditional antipathy to commercial interests and to start using mercantile custom as a source of law. And in the important area of patents, Lord Mansfield advanced the notion that the full specification of patents was meant to inform the public—thereby reducing access costs to the knowledge embodied in them. A 1778 decision by the chief justice decreed, for example, that the specifications in a patent should be sufficiently precise and detailed so as to fully explain it to a technically educated person.

N

Newton, Isaac (1643–1727 CE) was a physicist, mathematician, astronomer, natural philosopher, alchemist, and theologian. The movement of the European intellectual world toward "system" and "method" culminated in the publication of Isaac Newton's *Philosophiae Naturalis Principia Mathematica*. From this point on, according to two academics, "any discipline [including law] wishing to be accepted as a serious field of study . . . was expected to develop its own body of abstract, theoretical concepts and principles and to present them, if possible, in the form of an axiomatic system." Newton was one of the most influential men in history.

O

Oldendorp, Johann (c. 1486–1567 CE) was a follower of Martin Luther. He viewed all law as strict law, since all law is general and abstract. Therefore, every application of law to an individual case needs to be governed by equity. In other words, law and equity (*Recht und Billigkeit; ius et aequitas*) complete each other, thus becoming a single thing (a *corpus*).

Oldendorp accepted a teaching position at the University of Marburg on the condition that he be freed from the usual requirement of lecturing on the texts of the *Corpus Iuris Civilis* in the order and manner imposed by the Postglossators—the *mos Italicus* (Italian method) (as distinguished from the then more recent French method, *mos Gallicus*), which had dominated European legal education and legal scholarship for about 200 years.

Otis, James Jr. (1725–1783 CE) was a lawyer and an American revolutionary politician in colonial Massachusetts who was an early advocate of the political views that led to the American Revolution. The phrase "Taxation without Representation is Tyranny" is usually attributed to him.

P

Palaemon, Quintus Remmius (1st century CE) was a former slave at Rome who obtained his freedom and became a famous grammarian and teacher at Rome. Quintilian and Persius (a Roman poet and satirist) are said to have been his pupils.

Papinianus, Aemilius (142–212 CE) was one of the leading jurists of the Severan age, with close ties to the emperor Septimius Severus. He held the office of *Praefectus Praetoria* during 203–205 CE and was executed in 212 CE, seemingly by order of Caracalia. His principal works included collections of cases, a work of *Quaestiones Responsa*, a work on legal definitions and a monograph on adultery. He has long been regarded as one of the greatest jurists of the classical period.

Papirius, Sextus (6th century BCE) was the son of Demaratus of Corinth and the first Roman jurists who was among the leading men in the time of Superbus. During the reign of Tarquin the Proud, the last king before the founding of the Roman Republic, a number of written laws were unsystematically enacted. These early laws were then collected by Sextus Papirius and made into the *Ius Civile Papirianum*.

Parmenides (b. 510 BCE) through his mechanism of contradiction (indirect proof), is the father of logic. In fact it has been speculated that it might have been the art of dealing with questionable statements, common to any court system, that inspired Parmenides' answer to Xenophanes' challenging question: How do the Milesians know what they know?

Paul of Hungary (13th century CE) attended the University of Bologna and obtained the degree of doctor in canon law. He later became a law professor, defining the "sin against nature" as homosexuality, bestiality, and unnatural heterosexual intercourse. He considered these sins as being worse than incest because they violate man's relationship with God.

Pepo (11th century CE) was a consultant judge and the first law teacher at the University of Bologna. He based his teaching on Justinian's compilations of Roman law, which included the Code, Institutes, and Digest.

Perfet, Isaac Bar Sheshet (Ribash) (1326–1408 CE) was born in Spain and died in Algiers, North Africa. He wrote numerous *responsa*, which had a considerable influence on later Halakhah. Hundreds of the Rabbi's decisions, for example, were incorporated into Rabbi Joseph Caro's *Shulhan Arukh*.

Pericles (c. 495–429 BCE) was the son of the aristocrat Xanthippus of the *deme* of Cholargos and the Alcmaeonidic Agariste. In 484 BCE Xanthippus was ostracized and the family left Athens, possibly for the northern Peloponnesian city of Sicyon. And in 480 BCE the young Pericles and his family were again forced into exile—this time as a result of the approaching Persian army. Years later Pericles became "first man" in Athens. In fact, the period from 461 to 379 BCE is sometimes called as "The Age of Pericles."

Philo of Alexandria (c. 20 BCE–c. 50 CE). Philo Judaeus was born to a Jewish family that had moved from Palestine to Alexandria. It has been said that if the Greeks were the creators of philosophy for the West, then Philo and the Church Fathers who came after him (e.g., St. Augustine), all products of the Hellenistic world, were the founders of theology as the study of God and the effort to give a consistent ("scientific") statement to a religious faith. In his greatest work, *On Allegory*, Philo argued that, contrary to the creation story contained in the Septuagint (the "Old Testament" in Greek), "[i]t was quite foolish to think that the world was created in six days or in a space of time at all." Six, according to Philo, "meant not a quantity of days, but a perfect number"—proving that the world had been made according to a plan. It is therefore clear that Philo was a disciple, at least in certain respects, of Pythagoras.

Pisistratus of Athens (c. 600–527 BCE) related on his mother's side to Solon, was selected c. 569 BCE as an *archon*—a government official and a word giving rise to *oligarchy* (rule by a few), *monarchy* (rule by one), and *anarchy* (lawlessness as a result of having no *archon* at all). After increasing his power base, Pisistratus seized Athens (546–525 BCE) and established an autocratic, dictatorial regime. He also pressed Athens's claim to be the mother and leader of all Ionian Greeks.

Plato (c. 427–347 BCE) was a classical Greek philosopher, mathematician, writer of dialogues and founder of the Academy in Athens.

Pliny the Younger (61–c. 112 CE) was a lawyer, author, and natural philosopher of Ancient Rome.

Plowden, Sir Edmund (1518–1585 CE) was a distinguished English lawyer and theorist during the late Tudor period. He was educated at the University of Cambridge and studied law at Middle Temple in 1538. He also studied at Oxford and qualified as a physician in 1552.

Pound, Roscoe (1870–1964 CE) learned to read at the age of three and began studying German at six. The precocious Pound initially favored a career in the natural sciences but his lawyer father harbored hopes of a legal career for his son. Law ultimately won out—despite the fact that he also received a doctoral degree in botany. Under Pound's guidance, Harvard Law School entered a golden age, marked by the adoption of more rigorous academic standards and leaps in its prestige as a center of innovative thought. For example, the social scientific tradition in law began with Roscoe Pound and the school of Legal Realists (an attempt to "free" law from the then-dominant "formalist" approach—particularly its perceived commitment to laissez-faire economics). However, by the time of the New Deal, Pound had moved away from his earlier "radical" view of law, becoming ever more conservative, a defender of the status quo in both politics and law—and an admirer of Hitler.

Proculus, Sempronius (c. 1 CE) was a legal scholar and teacher in Rome. He wrote eleven books of "letters" on legal subjects in addition to assisting the eminent jurist Marcus Antistius Labeo in his works. Proculus most likely established the Proculian school of law (and not, as frequently claimed, Marcus Antistius Labeo).

Protagoras (c. 480–411 BCE) was a Greek Sophist and one of the best-known teachers of the sophistic movement of the fifth century BCE. He said that "man is the measure of all things." According to Protagoras all perceptions are true and only individuals can judge the quality of their own sensations. In other words, the qualitative experience each person has derives from his or her selective perception of qualities that coexist in matter.

Pulton, Ferdinando (1536–1618 CE) studied at Christ's College in Cambridge and Brasenose College in Oxford, England. He was a member of Lincoln's Inn. However, because he was a Roman Catholic, he was not eligible to be called to the Bar. Pulton nevertheless went on to greatness in the law by editing books involving statutes. He produced several compilations of English statutory law, including his 1618 edition of the statutes at large.

Pythagoras (born c. 580 BCE) was born on Samos, a small Aegean island. For various reasons, he left on what became a 37-year journey traveling throughout Gaul, Egypt, Babylon, and possibly India. Especially in Babylon, Pythagoras came in contact with mathematicians and likely became aware of the Babylonians' studies of numbers—and later developed (or perhaps simply popularized) the "Theorem of Pythagoras" (i.e., that in a right-angled triangle the square of the hypotenuse is equal to the sum of the squares on the other two sides—except in non-Euclidean space).

Q

Quintilianus, Marcus Fabius ("Quintilian") (c. 34–100 CE) was a Roman rhetorician. He was born in Spain and educated in Rome. He published three works, including the highly influential *Institutio Oratoria* (c. 95 CE). For more information on Quintilian, see Appendix B.

R

Raleigh, Walter (c. 1552–1618 CE) was an English writer, poet, soldier, courtier, and explorer. He studied at Oxford and Middle Temple.

Randolph, Edmund (1753–1813 CE) was the first attorney general of the United States and mentor to young John Tyler, who became the seventh lawyer-President of the United States. And interestingly enough, Randolph's family tree later produced Francis Biddle, Attorney General for President Franklin D. Roosevelt. It was said of Biddle that he was an "Eastern upper-class snob in the grand style." Perhaps this is one of the reasons that he did not more vigorously oppose the February 19, 1942, Executive Order 9066 that ordered the removal of those with Japanese ancestry from the West Coast.

Randolph, Peyton (1721–1775 CE) was the first President of the Continental Congress in 1774. He also served as speaker of the Virginia House of Burgesses and chairman of the Virginia Conventions. He studied law at Middle Temple and became a member of the bar in 1743. He was appointed attorney general of the Colony of Virginia the following year.

Ray, Charlotte E. (1850–1911 CE) was the first black woman lawyer in the United States. The daughter of the nationally prominent African-American minister Charles B. Ray, she enrolled at Howard Law School under the name of "C.E. Ray," was admitted, and in 1872 was the first woman to graduate from the Howard Law School. She was admitted to the District bar in March of 1872.

Raymond of Peñafort (1174–1275 CE) was a Dominican scholar who was actively engaged in civil and ecclesiastical administration. And it has been said that "despite the putative claim of Peter Cantor to be the first casuist, it can be claimed that 'casuistry, properly speaking, begins to appear in his [Peñafort's] pages.'"

Reeve, Tapping (1744–1823 CE) was an American lawyer and teacher. In 1784 Reeve built and opened a crude schoolhouse called the Litchfield Law School, making it the first law school in the United States. The characteristics that would qualify Reeve's tutoring system as a formal school emerged gradually over the last two decades of the eighteenth century. In other words, the Physical Technology (law school facility) and Social Technology (teaching methodology) combined into modules under a strategy did not spring into existence but evolved.

Rembaud, Pierre (16th century CE) and Antoine Filliol were the defense attorneys who defended weevils in their second trial for infestation in 1587 CE or the vineyard of Saint-Julien, France. Rembaud argued, as had been argued in the first trial in 1545, that based on the Book of Genesis, God created all animals, including the smallest of them.

Riddle, Albert G. (1816–1902 CE) was an attorney and politician serving as a member of the Ohio House of Representatives. He aided the State Department in the prosecution of John H. Surratt as one of the accomplices in the murder of President Abraham Lincoln.

Roberts, Owen Josephus (1875–1955 CE) was born in Philadelphia and attended Germantown Academy and the University of Pennsylvania, and graduated at the top of his class from the University of Pennsylvania Law School in 1898. He was an assistant district attorney in Philadelphia and was later appointed by lawyer-President Calvin Coolidge to investigate the oil reserve scandals known as the Teapot Dome Scandals. Roberts was appointed to the United States Supreme Court by President Herbert Hoover in 1930.

S

Sabinus, Marcus Massurius (c. 33 CE) was a jurist who became a successful teacher of law in Rome. He authored a systematic treatise on the *ius civile* on which jurists of the classical period provided extensive commentary. He also produced a commentary on the praetorian edict, a collection of legal opinions, and a monograph on theft. His work is said to have contained the Sabinian Scheme.

Saxoferrato, Bartolus de ("Sassoferrato") (1313–1357 CE) was an Italian law professor and one of the most prominent continental jurists of the Middle Ages.

Savigny, Friedrick Karl von (1779–1861 CE) was born in Frankfurt and was orphaned at age thirteen. He received his doctor's degree in 1800. In 1803 he published his most famous work, *Das Recht des Besitzes* (*The Law of Possession*).

Scaevola, Quintus Mucius (the "Augur") (c. 159–88 BCE) was a Roman jurist and a politician of the Roman Republic and an early authority on Roman law. He was a mentor and teacher to some of Rome's most celebrated orators such as Cicero and Atticus.

Scaevola, Quintus Mucius (the "Pontifex") (d. 82 BCE). Around 95 BCE Mucius, the most famous jurist of the Roman Republic, took the *ius civile* and arranged it into categories. The work, composed of eighteen books, was known as the *Ius Civile* and consisted not only of interpretations on the *Twelve Tables*, but also of statutes that modified the *Tables*.

Scheck, Barry C. (1949– CE) was born in Queens, New York, and received a B.S. from Yale University (1971) and a J.D. and M.C.P. from the University of California at Berkeley (1974). Scheck was part of the team that defended O.J. Simpson. His more influential legal work rests in his commitment to exposing wrongful convictions as director of the Innocence Project.

Schuerph, Hieronymous (1481–1554 CE) was a professor of law at the University of Wittenberg and Martin Luther's chief defense counsel at the 1521 trial in Worms (Germany) on charges of hearsay.

Selden, John (1584–1654 CE) worked closely with Coke. In fact Selden, then thirty-seven, was sent to the Tower with sixty-nine-year-old Coke for his assistance in drafting the House of Commons' Protestation of 1621. According to one legal scholar: "All three men [Coke, Selden, and Hale] started their careers as practicing lawyers. All three were deeply involved in the great constitutional struggles of their times. All three were dedicated and prolific scholars."

Shulgi (21st century BCE) was the oldest son of King Ur-Nammu, founder of the Third Dynasty of Ur. It appears to have been Shulgi, and not his father, who promulgated the laws of Ur-Nammu—among the earliest known laws. He reigned for forty years, perhaps sometime between 2047–1999 BCE. Shulgi is best known for his revisions to the scribal school's curriculum.

Siricius (384–399 CE) was the first person to call himself "pope" (from Greek *pappas:* papa). Bishop Siricius, as part of the Church's growing awareness of power, adopted the style of Roman officials and the chancellery. Thus like a Roman emperor communicating with his provincial governors, Siricius answered inquiries and requests with brief rescripts: *decreta* and *responsa.*

Smith, Adam (1723–1790 CE) was a moral philosopher and a leader in the area of political economy. He authored *The Theory of Moral Sentiments* and *An Inquiry into the Nature and Causes of the Wealth of Nations*, which is considered his greatest achievement and the first modern work of economics.

Socrates (c. 469–399 BCE) was a classical Greek philosopher and is considered to be one of the founder of Western philosophy. His thoughts (including those on rhetors, orators, and Sophists) are known only though the accounts of his students—especially the dialogues of Plato.

Socraticus, Aeschines (Aeschines of Sphettos) (c. 425–c. 350 BCE) was an Athenian politician and orator. He was the son of Lysanias and in his youth was a follower of Socrates. He appears to have started a school where he taught rhetoric. To be more precise, he specialized on show orations. Because he changed the scope of public speaking, Aeschines is called the "father of the Second Sophistic."

Solon (c. 638–558 BCE) was an Athenian statesman, lawmaker, and poet. He was born into a well-to-do family and worked as a merchant in the export-import trade. He is most remembered for drawing up new laws and revising the constitutional structure of Athens.

Sonnenfels, Joseph von (1732–1817 CE) was an Austrian and German jurist and novelist. He took law courses at University of Vienna after his discharge from the military in 1754.

Story, Joseph (1779–1845 CE) studied law in the office of Samuel Sewall, a congressional representative and Federalist from Marblehead, Massachusetts, and in 1811, at the age of thirty-two, became the youngest person ever to be appointed to the United States Supreme Court. Story also served as Dane Professor at Harvard Law School (the first endowed professorship of law in the United States) from 1829 until his death. He published numerous major legal treatises.

T

Taney, Roger B. (1777–1864 CE) was born in Calvert County, Maryland, into a tobacco plantation family. He received his education at Dickinson College and in 1799 he was admitted to the bar. He was later elected to the Maryland legislature. Following the War of 1812, Taney served in the state senate and built up a successful law practice. In 1831 he was appointed United States Attorney General and following the death of John Marshall, he was confirmed as Chief Justice of the United States Supreme Court.

Thales (c. 634–c. 548 BCE) was a pre-Socratic Greek philosopher from Miletus in Asia Minor. Many regard Thales (one of the Seven Sages of Greece) as the first philosopher ("lover of wisdom") in the Greek tradition. He boldly explored natural phenomena that were previously believed to be acts of the gods.

Tisias (5th century BCE, fl. c. 467 BCE) along with his teacher Corax of Syracuse, was one of the founders of ancient Greek rhetoric. It was Tisias who brought Corax's teaching to Athens.

Toru, Hoshi (1850–1901 CE) was born into the family of a plasterer. Adopted as a child by a medical physician, he assumed the name Hoshi. He learned and taught English and was later placed in charge of the Yokohama Customs Office at the age of twenty-four. He then left Japan to study law in London (Middle Temple) and became the first Japanese to qualify as a barrister in Britain. Upon his return he joined the Jiyuto—being twice imprisoned for being too outspoken in criticizing the government. He was assassinated during his term in office as the Tokyo City Assembly chairman.

Tribonian (c. 500–547 CE) was a jurist during the reign of the Emperor Justinian I who helped revise the legal code of the Roman Empire. Tribonian became a successful lawyer in Constantinople and was appointed by Justinian in 528 as one of the commissioners to prepare the new imperial legal code, the *Corpus Juris Civilis*, released in 529. In 530 he became *quaestor* and the chief editor of the compilation of the old Roman lawyers writings (*Digesta* or *Pandecta*, meaning Digest or Collection), which in total were much larger than the code itself. In 532 his removal was called for because of his alleged corruption and he was temporarily removed by Justinian.

Troup, Robert (1756–1832 CE) was an American soldier, lawyer, and jurist. He attended King's College (now Columbia University). While at Kings College he was a roommate of Alexander Hamilton.

Trowbridge, Edmund (1709–1792 CE) was born in Newton, Massachusetts, educated at Harvard, and became a judge of the Supreme Court of Massachusetts. Trowbridge was considered to be the most learned real property lawyer of his time in New England. He had as students, among many others, James Putnam, the preceptor of John Adams and Christopher Gore (the mentor of Daniel Webster).

Tucker, St. George (1752–1827 CE) was a lawyer and law professor. He was born in St. George, Bermuda, and traveled to Virginia to study law at the College of William and Mary in 1772. He was admitted to the bar on April 4, 1774, and settled in Williamsburg where he practiced in the county courts. After serving in the Revolutionary War he returned to practice in the courts until taking up a position as professor of law and policy at William and Mary (1788 to 1804). In 1803 Tucker edited Blackstone's *Commentaries*, eliminating the most offensively royalist sentiments and adding notes on the few American legal sources then available.

U

Ulpianus, Domitius (d. 228 CE) was a Phoenician jurist and imperial official who also taught at the law school in Berytus. He was heavily quoted in Justinian's *Digest* and held various Imperial offices until his assassination in 228 CE He was a prolific writer who wrote many treatises and monographs on a variety of topics, including commentaries on the *praetorian edict* and the *ius civile*, as well as a monograph on the duties of the proconsul.

Ur-Nammu (also called Ur-Namma) (c. 2113–2096 BCE) was the founder of the Third Dynasty of Ur (c. 2113–2006 BCE). The III Ur Empire, which followed Šarru-Kīn ("the king is the true one"—more commonly known as Sargon the Great) of Agade's establishment of an empire (perhaps humankind's first autocracy) that included the city-states of south Mesopotamia, is considered to be one of the grand periods of ancient Mesopotamian history. The laws of Ur-Nammu (more likely promulgated by Ur-Nammu's son King Shulgi) came from the city of Ur in southern Mesopotamia. The Bible indicates that Abraham (born c. 1900 BCE) was originally from Ur (the principal seaport for all of Mesopotamia).

Urukagina (fl. 2375 BCE). Urukagina, king of Lagash, apparently rose up against the exactions of the clergy, denounced them for their voracity, accused them of taking bribes in their administration of the law, and charged that they were levying such taxes upon farmers and fishermen as to rob them of the fruits of their toil. He swept the courts clear of these corrupt officials, and established laws regulating the taxes and fees paid to the temples.

V

Valier, Agostino (1531–1606 CE) studied Greek, Latin, humanities, and philosophy under Lazzaro Bonaminco in Venice. Later, he studied theology, law, and Hebrew at the Vatican Academy founded by Cardinal Carlo Borromeo and the University of Padua (doctorates in law and theology, 1554).

Valla, Lorenzo (c. 1407–1457 CE) was an Italian humanist, rhetorician, and educator. In 1431 he entered the priesthood and, despite his attacks on the temporal power of the Papacy and his pursuit by the Inquisition, was made apostolic secretary by Pope Nicholas V in 1448. Valla served Nicholas and his successor, remaining in Rome until his death.

Varus, Alfenus (1st century BCE), whose praenomen might have been Publius, was an ancient Roman jurist and writer. He came to Rome to become a student of Servius Sulpicius Rufus and attained the office of consulship.

Vattel, Emmerich de (1714–1767 CE) was a Swiss scholar and a student in 1733 of J.J. Burlamaqui. His 1758 classical treatise is *The Law of Nations or the Principles of Natural Law*. In addition to Thomas Jefferson, several of America's Founding Fathers discovered important maxims of political liberty contained in Vattel's work.

Vinson, Frederick M. (1890–1953 CE) graduated from Kentucky Normal School in 1908 and enrolled at Centre College, where he graduated at the top of his class. He became a lawyer in Louisa, a small town of 2,500 residents, and was elected to the office of City Attorney of Louisa. Vinson eventually served in all three branches of government: a congressman representing Louisa, Kentucky; Secretary of Treasury under President Truman; and the thirteenth Chief Justice of the United States Supreme Court.

Vigelius, Nicolas (16th century CE) was a prominent German legal "Methodist" who sought to systemize the individual branches of law in his *Methodus Universi Iuris Civilis* (*Method of the Entire Civil Law*, published in 1561) by classifying, as a first cut, the law into public and private. Vigelius's work was significant for his effort to organize the law from general to specific. He started by dividing the law into public and private law; and then subdividing public law into legislative, executive, and judicial activities, and private law into the law of persons, the law of property, the law of inheritance and trusts and gifts, and the law of obligations arising from contracts, torts, and unjust enrichment, with systematization of the specific rules for each category. These remain to this day the basic topics of Western legal science.

W

Weber, Maximilian Carl Emil (1864–1920 CE) was a German lawyer, politician, and social theorist who profoundly influenced sociological theory with his many writings. He recognized several diverse aspects of social authority that he categorized according to their charismatic, traditional, and legal forms. His analysis of bureaucracy focused on the notion that modern state institutions are based on a form of rational-legal authority.

Webster, Daniel (1782–1852 CE) gained prominence through his defense of New England shipping interests and served as legal counsel in cases that established important constitutional precedents bolstering the authority of the federal government.

Wigmore, John Henry (1863–1943 CE) was a jurist and expert in the law of evidence. After teaching at Keio University in Tokyo, Wigmore became dean of Northwestern Law School from 1901 to 1929. He is most famous for his *Treatise on the Anglo-American System of Evidence in Trials at Common Law* (1904).

William of Occam, or Ockham (c.1280–1349 CE) was a Franciscan monk who was born in Surrey and educated at Oxford. He had a significant influence on the development of the concept of an individual's natural rights.

Williams, Ivy (1877–1966 CE). Following the First World War, the tide of public opinion changed regarding women in the workplace. In 1919 the Sex Disqualification (Removal) Act was passed in England. It was this legislation that made possible Ivy Williams's call to the Bar by Inner Temple in 1922, to become the first woman barrister in England.

Wood, Thomas (1661–1722 CE) was both a civilian jurist and also called to the common law Bar by Gray's Inn. He acted as his uncle Anthony Wood's proctor before the Vice-Chancellor's Council in 1692–1693. The occasion was that Anthony was sued in the Oxford Vice-Chancellor's Court, officially abolished in 1977, by the second Earl of Carendon, Henry Hyde, for allegedly libeling the Earl's famous father, the first Earl, in Anthony Wood's *Historia et Antiquitates Universitatis Oxoniensis*, published in 1674.

Thomas Wood produced a work entitled, *An Institute of the Laws of England: or the Laws of England in their Natural Order, According to Common Use*, published in 1720. This book, although about the common law, was written by one trained in the civil law. Wood's *Institute* went through ten editions by 1772 and remained the leading work of English law until it was eventually super-seded by Blackstone's *Commentaries*. Wood had been influenced by Justinian's *Institutes*, as to structure, and Blackstone, it has been argued, was influenced by Wood (among others).

Wythe, George (1726–1806 CE) was born into a planter family of Virginia. He was orphaned as a child and grew up under the guardianship of his older brother. Despite the fact that he received little formal education, Wythe became a well-respected lawyer and teacher—having had John Lewis as his preceptor. He began offering courses at the College of William and Mary, Williamsburg, Virginia, in 1779 as professor of "Law and Policy." The instruction he offered included "theoretical lectures" and moot court arguments dealing with prac-tical matters. Among his public positions was chancellor of the state of Vir-ginia from 1788 to 1801. In 1806 Wythe, together with his African-American servant, died after drinking from a pot of coffee. The coffee had been laced with arsenic. Suspicion pointed toward Wythe's grandnephew (George Wythe Sweeny), who was arrested for murder—and defended by William Wirt. An African-American cook could have given testimony against the grandnephew. Due, however, to a statute preventing a African-American from testifying against a white man (or woman), the court was prevented from hearing this testimony and Sweeny went free.

X

Xanthippus (5th century BCE) was the father of Pericles and, during the Persian Wars, commanded the Athenian fleet after the battle in Salamis and in 479 BCE at the battle of Mycalē. He was married to Agaristē, the niece of Cleisthenēs.

Z

Zaleucus (fl. 7th century BCE) was the Greek lawgiver of Epizephyrian Locri, in Italy. He is said to have devised the first written Greek law code (the Locrian code).

Zäsi, Ulrich ("Zasius") (1491–1535 CE) was a German humanist. He was a clerk of the city council and a professor at the University of Freiburg at Basle in Germany—and a proponent of legal humanism.

APPENDIX B
Cicero and
Quintilian

Cicero

Marcus Tullius Cicero was born on January 3, 106 BCE, and raised in the small hill town of Arpinum (approximately 80 miles southeast of Rome). He was the son of an *equestrian,* which meant that his family, while not nobility, owned enough property to help Cicero obtain a good education. Consequently, little Marcus had the opportunity to move to Rome to study, among other things, law. And the law Cicero studied under the guidance of the famous jurist Quintus Mucius Scaevola (the "Augur"), then in his eighties, was the law located in the *Forum Romanum* on the twelve bronze tables. Despite, however, the fact that several of Cicero's important mentors were jurists, his dream was to become an advocate—a pagan Johnnie Cochran.

Cicero spent some time in the military (to which he was ill suited) and then returned to Rome to build up his practice. There seems to have been plenty of opportunity to put his skills to use, including the sorting out of the earlier land confiscations by Lucius Cornelius Sulla "Felix" (c. 138–78 BCE), a descendant of an old impoverished family, who had outraged a host of property owners. After becoming dictator during the wild and wooly days just prior to the fall of the Republic, Sulla "The

Fortunate One" had exacted vengeance on his political enemies by confiscating their property and denying them protection of the law. Additionally, the continued Roman expansion overseas permitted various other types of corruption and extortion to flourish. Election bribery, for example, had become widespread. Prosecutions for such crimes could, by this time, be brought both by the state and by private parties. In either case, however, the matter usually became entangled in the personal rivalries of aristocratic families, and oratory skills played a big part in swaying the court one way or the other. Cicero, in focusing his skills on such things as confiscations, corruption, and extortion, excelled at combining facts with emotion in order to destroy the opposition—and thereby get himself noticed.

Cicero's emphasis on facts may not, viewed from a modern perspective, appear to be exceptional—but it was. When jurists of the time were asked their opinion on a matter, they generally made no factual investigation but simply gave their ruling based on what was told to them. This approach led the jurist Gaius Aquilius Gallus to remark, "*Nihil hoc ad ius, ad Ciceronem*" ("This has nothing to do with law, but with Cicero") when a dispute turned primarily on facts—as is often the case, particularly in the area of criminal law. The truth is that jurists were generally not interested in winning a case for the client. The reason for this shocker is that the jurist believed that his prestige depended upon expounding the law, not upon victories in the courts. As a result, he was not influenced by the morality of the parties to a case, but reduced the relevant facts to an absolute minimum. In other words, facts were aggressively leveled, sharpened, and assimilated. And unlike the orators, jurists were not particularly tempted to use procedural dodges and devices.

Cicero so emphasized the importance of facts in combination with oratory skill that he, with a certain amount of exaggeration, claimed ignorance of the law. He asserted that it is commonplace for orators to lack legal knowledge and that cases are best argued by an eloquent man quite unversed in law.

At first blush, Cicero's emphasis on facts, and dismissal of the law, might seem a bit odd—particularly for a lawyer. After all, aren't the facts simply the facts and the law where the real action is? But as touched upon in Part III, reconstructing the past in court (judicial rhetoric) can be difficult. The reason for this is that the past cannot truly be recovered and it is therefore often hard to verify. This means that there are many legal cases, both in ancient Rome and modern times, in which the question of what happened is indeterminate and can only be resolved by a decision based on who presents the most convincing set of facts. Therefore Cicero's spotlight on facts, like an ancient Rumpole of the Bailey, is highly relevant to the day-to-day tasks of lawyers—particularly those of the Anglo-American persuasion. Primary responsibility for developing the facts of most cases rests with the lawyers; thus, truth seeking is a competitive (and often expensive) enterprise with important consequences for the outcome of a legal dispute. Did O.J. Simpson, for example, murder two people? The answer, of course, is no. But did he kill two people? Now that's a horse of a different color, and the reason he ended up owing Big Money damages.

One modern-day legal scholar has in fact raised the following rhetorical question: ". . . [I]sn't it *always* the case that law is a balancing act involving interests or consequences many of which are beyond the scope of a lawyer's training or experience?" Assuming the answer to this question is yes, as the questioner does, then law is in the end public policy and policy should, in order to be viewed "correctly," be based on facts and not simply on abstract points of law. The implication for the twenty-first century is the same as it was for Cicero: an assumption of omnicompetence by lawyers or jurists is a menace in many fields of law. A primary remedy for this hubris, as it was for Cicero, is to pay more attention to gathering and analyzing facts—particularly in a systematic way.

In 76 BCE Cicero was selected for the office of *quaestor* (the lowest-ranking magistrate in the *cursus honorum:* the course of honors), the first man to fill this quartermaster position without the normal ten years of military service. He spent his term in Sicily—Rome's first overseas colony. As a result of his having been honest in his job, he was asked by the people of Sicily to take on the prosecution of Gaius Verres, a former governor (73–70 BCE) who turned out to be a thief. Verres, armed with the *imperium* and lacking any supervision by the central government, had plundered the island for years. Cicero's prosecution at the full-dressed criminal trial, held in Rome before a group of senators, was apparently so devastating that not only was Verres forced into exile, but opposing counsel, Quintus Hortensius Hortalus, never fully recovered his gold-plated social standing. This case is said to have made Cicero's professional reputation. It also awakened the Roman people to the arbitrariness of unscrupulous magistrates who did not feel morally bound by their own programs, leading to passage of a law requiring magistrates to follow their own edicts—a rule of law virtue.

Cicero apparently surprised everyone by opening his prosecution with only a brief speech—in contrast to the long-winded ones typically given by prosecutors who reviewed, step-by-step, the case to be presented, frequently taking days. Cicero cut down on the rhetoric since he was concerned that any undue delay might allow a new judge, favorable to Verres, to slip into the proceeding.

After summarizing the bribery and other crimes Verres had (allegedly) engaged in while overseeing Sicily, Cicero charged that the defense attorney, who had recently been elected to the position of consul, promised Verres that he would be acquitted if they could only postpone the trial to the following year (69 BCE). He also claimed that the Senate itself was on trial, for if Verres was acquitted, the public would see that as proof of senatorial corruption.

Cicero immediately began to examine his witnesses. And the speed with which he proceeded greatly disconcerted Hortensius. The barrage of devastating witnesses' testimony and Cicero's brilliant rhetoric continued for nine days. However, well before the prosecution's case in chief ended, Verres and his lawyer realized that there was no chance for victory. Hortensius effectively surrendered and advised his client to plead guilty. Rather than face the consequences of a guilty verdict, Verres fled from Italy—taking his art collection to Marseille.

In his speech "In Defense of Flaccus" (59 BCE), Cicero complained, with a certain amount of rhetorical exaggeration, about the large size of the Jewish community and its influence within Rome. His client was Lucius Valerius Flaccus. Flaccus, in his capacity as a provincial governor, had taken steps to prevent Jewish communities from sending their annual tax contribution to the Jerusalem Temple, and Jewish funds had been seized at a number of Greek cites. While such actions by governors were generally looked down upon by the central Roman authorities, they were popular with the Greek and Hellenized inhabitants and leaders of the local cities. These inhabitants and leaders resented the division of funds for purposes that lay outside their territories and for their use by a religion that seemed to deliberately set itself apart. (Remember, as discussed in Part I, the Pharisaic ideology actively worked to combat Hellenistic influences—from philosophy to public nudity.) Cicero defended his client on the grounds that the transfer of money from one country to another for commercial purposes was forbidden by law, and therefore it was a good thing for the exportation of funds to be prevented.

It should not be assumed, however, that Cicero's representation of Flaccus automatically implies an anti-Semitic bent. In private correspondence, Cicero was clear that his courtroom orations were simply part of his work as a lawyer and often did not reflect his personal opinion: "Anyone who supposed that in my necessarily forensic speeches he has got my personal views under seal is making a great mistake. . . . We orators are brought in not to say what we personally think but what is required by the situation and the case in hand."

Modern-day bar ethics codes, at least in the United States, steer a similar course. They attempt, like Cicero, to downplay any lack of morality (at least on an adoptive level) associated with zealously advocating a client's cause by emphasizing that such representation does not imply endorsement of the client's actions, but rather is consistent with the highest standards of the profession. This approach, however, is conveniently coupled with the lawyer's right to decline or to withdraw from any representation that he or she considers morally repugnant. As one legal scholar has observed, the prudent strategy for a lawyer striving for success is "to choose the convenient ethic at the convenient time." This can be interpreted to mean that when rich clients have disreputable cases, the guiding principles are that everyone deserves due process of law and the lawyer of their choice; and when a poor person with an unattractive case needs assistance, the lawyer's sense of right and wrong needs to step in and require that he decline representation.

Cicero was not only a great orator (and arguably the first fully-functioning casuist), but he is also considered to be one of the first philosophers to expound a theory of natural law—a concept employed (or at least considered), as you will recall, by Vinnie and Sal, and one that has consumed countless hours of contemplation by many thoughtful lawyers. Cicero's interest in his category of law stood in stark contrast to jurists of the time. He claimed that knowledge of natural law and justice was much more important than knowledge of the civil law. In fact the "science" of law, according to Cicero, should be drawn from deep within philosophy and not, as the jurists believed, from the *ius civile* and the *ius honorarium*.

As the Roman Empire spread across the Mediterranean and its armies attempted to organize the conquered territories, Roman legal thought began to distinguish among its *ius civile* (civil law), *ius naturale* (natural law), and *ius gentium* (the law of the nations). Cicero argued that the *ius gentium* was "derived from the Nature of Reason." This type of law was, for Cicero, significant because of its "universality of application." As stated in his book, *De republica:*

> True law is right reason, consonant with nature, diffused among all men, constant, eternal . . . It needs no interpreter or expounder but itself, nor will there be one law in Rome and another in Athens, one in the present and another in time to come, but one law and that eternal and immutable shall embrace all people and for all time and there shall be as it were one common master and ruler, the god of all, the author and judge and proposer of this law.

As a follower of the Stoic school of philosophy, Cicero understood "god" to be the source of the *ius gentium/ius naturale* and not, as propounded by a positivist view of law, man. His basic theory of natural law (which included an inkling of "human dignity") was that every human has an affirmative obligation to help other humans in order to promote "universal sociability and well-being." (A rather Talmudic approach to the law.)

Cicero's moral focus (which was primarily elitist) had a tremendous influence not only on young St. Augustine but also on one of the greatest English lawyers, Sir Edward Coke. It was Cicero that reinforced Coke's natural disposition to see law as connected to an ethical continuum, a notion still propounded by certain modern-day legal scholars. This encouraged a belief in right and wrong (a Platonic versus sophistic viewpoint), rather than searching for accommodation and compromise. It is also the case that Cicero served as a role model for Coke for combining advocacy and politics—as well as Calvin Coolidge (America's twenty-first lawyer-president), whose weird and wild hobby was translating Cicero's orations.

And in modern-day politics, the question of natural law, raised and wrestled with by Cicero, continues to play an important role. In September of 1991, for example, the chairman of the U.S. Senate Judiciary Committee, Senator Joseph Biden (later to become Vice President Biden), raised his personal concerns about the controversy surrounding Clarence Thomas's endorsement of natural law philosophy. Just prior to the opening of the initial confirmation hearings on Thomas's nomination as a U.S. Supreme Court Justice, Senator Biden, in an article published in the *Washington Post,* stated, somewhat in the same vein as the fifteenth- and sixteenth-century legal humanists, that there is a body of "natural law" that serves as the foundation for "fundamental rights not explicit in the [U.S.] Constitution that are protected by that document." The Senator, however, believed that there were other issues surrounding natural law that separated the views of Thomas from his own. As a result, the Senator posed certain questions in the article for Thomas to consider prior to the start of the confirmation hearings. These questions were directed at the nominee's views on the role of natural law in American legal philosophy. The Senator, for example, seemed to suggest that it might be permissible to use natural law as a background consideration for understanding the U.S. Constitution, but natural law must not be used as a means for adjudication in constitutional litigation.

Cicero lives on. Despite having had his head and right hand nailed to the Speakers' Platform and his tongue pierced with a hairpin, Cicero reappeared in 2005. His small but important role in HBO's series *Rome* shows that it is hard to silence a great lawyer.

QUINTILIAN

Marcus Fabius Quintilianus (Quintilian, c. 35–c. 100 CE) was one of the great Wall Street lawyers of his time. He was born in Calagurris (Calahorra), Spain, the son, possibly, of a rhetorician. He was primarily educated in Rome, perhaps under Quintus Remmius Palaemon and certainly under Domitius Afer. Not too long after his post-educational return to Spain (c. 62 CE), the Emperor Galba called Quintilian back to the Eternal City, where he remained for many years. He prospered as a tutor, becoming the recipient of a direct salary from the government.

Now for the really good part: Quintilian was in high favor with the Flavians, the family and political supporters of the blunt, army-tough emperor, Titus Flavius Vespasianus (Vespasian, r. 69–79 CE), and his two offspring successors, Titus Flavius Sabinus Vespasianus (Titus, r. 79–81 CE) and Titus Flavius Domitianus Augustus (Domitian, r. 81–96 CE). Therefore, as a well-connected lawyer, he was able to amass vast wealth—indeed, Quintilian, as was the case with Cicero, lived large. He also acted as instructor to Domitian's two great-nephews, the designated heirs to the throne, as well as to the golden-throated Pliny the Younger. In addition, he published three works including a large treatise entitled *Institutio oratoria* (c. 95 CE), outlining the training for rhetoricians: early education, proper schooling, subject matter, style, and nature of speaking. The work, cut up into 12 books, gave extensive advice to practitioners on the conduct of both direct and cross-examination of witnesses in criminal cases. Quintilian advised, for example, that while written testimony from absent witnesses is admissible in court, the fact-finder is likely to give much more credence to the testimony of live witnesses. This advice is still generally true. Modern-day research has, in fact, provided scientific rigor to a concept that Quintilian grasped intuitively.

SELECTED
BIBLIOGRAPHY

I. ARTICLES

A. ANCIENT LAW

Lionel Casson, *Lawyers Lessons Life & Death*, 26(4) LITIGATION 49 (2000) ("Civilization flourished in Egypt and ancient Greece with little help from lawyers, but then came Rome.")

Robert C. Ellickson & Charles DiA. Thorland, *Ancient Land Law: Mesopotamia, Egypt, Israel*, 71 CHI.-KENT L. REV. 321 (1995)

Saul Levmore, *Rethinking Group Responsibility and Strategic Threats in Biblical Texts and Modern Law*, 71 CHI.-KENT L. REV. 85 (1995)

James Lindgren, *Foreword: Ancient Rights and Wrongs*, 71 CHI.-KENT L. REV. 5 (1995)

James Lindgren, *Measuring the Value of Slaves and Free Persons in Ancient Law*, 71 CHI.-KENT L. REV. 149 (1995)

James Lindgren, *Why the Ancients May Not Have Needed a System of Criminal Law*, 76 B.U. L. REV. 29 (1996)

Geoffrey P. Miller, *Foreword: Land Law in Ancient Times*, 71 CHI.-KENT L. REV. 233 (1995)

Barry Nicholas, *Verbal Forms in Roman Law*, 66 TUL. L. REV. 1605 (1992)

Martha T. Roth, *Mesopotamian Legal Traditions and the Laws of Hammurabi*, 71 CHI.-KENT L. REV. 13 (1995)

Klass R. Veenhof, *"In Accordance with the Words of the Stele": Evidence for Old Assyrian Legislation*, 70 CHI.-KENT L. REV. 1717 (1995)

Russ VerSteeg, *Early Mesopotamian Commercial Law*, 30 U. TOL. L. REV. 183 (1999)

James Q. Whitman, *At the Origins of Law and the State: Supervision of Violence, Mutilation of Bodies, or Setting of Prices?*, 71 CHI.-KENT L. REV. 41 (1995)

B. PHILOSOPHY OF LAW

R. J. Araujo, S. J., *Thomas Aquinas: Prudence, Justice and the Law*, 40 LOY. L. REV. 897 (1995)

Jane B. Baron & Jeffrey L. Dunoff, *Against Market Rationality: Moral Critiques of Economic Analysis in Legal Theory*, 17 CARDOZO L. REV. 431 (1996)

Harold J. Berman, *Toward an Integrative Jurisprudence: Politics, Morality, History*, 76 CALIF. L. REV. 779 (1988)

Harold J. Berman & John Witte, Jr., *The Transformation of Western Legal Philosophy in Lutheran Germany*, 62 S. CAL. L. REV. 1573 (1989)

Dennis W. Carlton & Avi Weiss, *The Economics of Religion, Jewish Survival, and Jewish Attitudes Toward Competition in Torah Education*, 30 J. LEGAL STUD. 253 (2001)

Ronald K. L. Collins & David M. Skover, *Paratexts*, 44 STAN. L. REV. 509 (1992)

David R. Dow, *Gödel and Langdell—A Reply to Brown and Greenberg's Use of Mathematics in Legal Theory*, 44 HASTINGS L. J. 707 (1993)

William Ewald, *Comparative Jurisprudence (I): What Was It Like to Try a Rat?*, 143 HARV. L. REV 1889 (1995)

Paul Finkelman, *The Centrality of the Peculiar Institution in American Legal Development*, 68 CHI.-KENT L. REV. 1009 (1993)

Paul Gewirtz, *Aeschylus' Law*, 101 HARV. L. REV. 1043 (1988)

Oona A. Hathaway, *Path Dependence in the Law: The Course and Pattern of Legal Change in a Common Law System*, 86 IOWA L. REV. 601 (2001)

John Hasnas, *The Myth of the Rule of Law*, 1995 WIS. L. REV. 199 (1995)

Robert M. Jarvis, Phyllis G. Coleman, & Gail Levin Richmond, *Contextual Thinking: Why Law Students (and Lawyers) Need to Know History*, 42 WAYNE L. REV. 1603 (1996)

Susan P. Koniak, *The Chosen People in Our Wilderness*, 95 MICH. L. REV. 1761 (1997)

David Lemmings, *Blackstone and Law Reform by Education: Preparation for the Bar and Lawyerly Culture in Eighteenth-Century England*, 16 LAW & HISTORY REV. 211 (1998)

Sanford Levinson, *Slavery in the Canon of Constitutional Law*, 68 CHI.-KENT L. REV. 1087 (1993)

Michael Moore, *Moral Reality*, 1982 WIS. L. REV. 1061 (1982)

Philip M. Nichols, *A Legal Theory of Emerging Economies*, 39 VA. J. INT'L L. 229 (1999)

Trisha Olson, *Of Enchantment: The Passing of the Ordeals and the Rise of the Jury Trial*, 50 SYRACUSE L. REV. 109 (2000)

Michael J. Perry, *What is "Morality" Anyway?*, 45 VILL. L. REV. 69 (2000)

Richard Posner, *The Problematics of Moral and Legal Theory*, 111 HARV. L. REV. 1637 (1998)

David G. Post & Michael B. Eisen, *How Long is the Coastline of the Law? Thoughts on the Fractal Nature of Legal Systems*, 29 J. LEGAL STUD. 545 (2000)

Glenn Harlan Reynolds, *Chaos and the Court*, 91 COLUM. L. REV. 110 (1991)

Peter C. Schanck, *Understanding Postmodern Thought and Its Implications for Statutory Interpretation*, 65 S. CAL. L. REV. 2505 (1992)

Jeanne L. Schroeder, *The Eumenides: The Foundation of Law in the Repression of the Feminine*, http://papers.ssrn.com/paper.taf?abstract_id=214829 (2000)

Jeanne L. Schroeder, *The Four Discourses of Law: A Lacanian Analysis of Legal Practice and Scholarship*, 79 Tex. L. Rev. 15 (2000)

Carl M. Selinger, *Public Interest Lawyering in Mexico and the United States*, 27 U. Miami Inter-Am. L. Rev. 343 (1995–1996)

Carl M. Selinger, *The Public's Interest in Preserving the Dignity and Unity of the Legal Profession*, 32 Wake Forest L. Rev. 861 (1997)

Andrew Simmonds, *Amah and Eved and the Origin of Legal Rights*, 46 S.D.L. Rev. 516 (2000–2001)

Franklin G. Snyder, *Nomos, Narrative, and Adjudication: Toward a Jurisgenetic Theory of Law*, 40 Wm. & Mary L. Rev. 1623 (1999)

Eric Talley, *Precedential Cascades: An Appraisal*, 73 S. Cal. L. Rev. 81 (1999)

Alan Watson, *Thinking Property at Rome*, 68 Chi.-Kent L. Rev. 1355 (1993)

Gunther A. Weiss, *The Enchantment of Codification in the Common-Law World*, 25 Yale J. Int'l L. 435 (2000)

Steven L. Winter, *Transcendental Nonsense, Metaphoric Reasoning, and the Cognitive Stakes for Law*, 137 U. Pa. L. Rev. 1105 (1989)

David M. Zlotnick, *The Buddha's Parable and Legal Rhetoric*, 58 Wash. & Lee L. Rev. 957 (2001)

Michael P. Zuckert, *Do Natural Rights Derive From Natural Law?*, 20 Harv. J. L. & Pub Pol'y 695 (1997)

C. LAW AND ECONOMICS

Frank B. Cross, *The First Thing We Do, Let's Kill All the Economists: An Empirical Evaluation of the Effect of Lawyers on the United States Economy and Political System*, 70 Tex. L. Rev. 645 (1992)

Lawrence A. Cunningham, *Capital Market Theory, Mandatory Disclosure, and Price Discovery*, 51 Wash. & Lee L. Rev. 843 (1994)

Robert C. Downs, *Law and Economics: Nexus of Science and Belief*, 27 Pac. L. J. 1 (1995)

Ronald J. Gilson, *Value Creation by Business Lawyers: Legal Skills and Asset Pricing*, 94 Yale L. J. 239 (1984)

Michael S. Jacobs, *An Essay on the Normative Foundations of Antitrust Economics*, 74 N.C.L. Rev. 219 (1995)

Christine Jolls, Cass R. Sunstein & Richard Thaler, *A Behavioral Approach to Law and Economics*, 50 Stan. L. Rev. 1471 (1998)

Donald N. McCloskey, *The Rhetoric of Law and Economics*, 86 Mich. L. Rev. 752 (1988)

Mark J. Osiel, *Lawyers as Monopolists, Aristocrats, and Entrepreneurs*, 103 Harv. L. Rev. 2009 (1990)

Mark J. Roe, *Chaos and Evolution in Law and Economics*, 109 Harv. L. Rev. 641 (1996)

Jeanne L. Schroeder, *Pandora's Amphora: The Ambiguity of Gifts*, 46 UCLA L. Rev. 815 (1999)

Jeanne L. Schroeder, *Rationality in Law and Economics Scholarship*, 79 Or. L. Rev. 147 (2000)

Jeanne L. Schroeder, *Just So Stories: Posnerian Methodology*, 22 CARDOZO L. REV. 351 (2001)

II. BOOKS

A. ANCIENT MESOPOTAMIA

JEAN BOTTÉRO, EVERYDAY LIFE IN ANCIENT MESOPOTAMIA (English trans. 2001)
SIMON GOLDHILL, LOVE, SEX & TRAGEDY: HOW THE ANCIENT WORLD SHAPES OUR LIVES (2004)
MARTHA T. ROTH, LAW COLLECTIONS FROM MESOPOTAMIA AND ASIA MINOR (2d ed. 1997)

B. ANCIENT GREECE

LESLEY ADKINS & ROY A. ADKINS, HANDBOOK TO LIFE IN ANCIENT GREECE (1997)
THOMAS CAHILL, SAILING THE WINE-DARK SEA, WHY THE GREEKS MATTER (2003)
PAUL CARTLEDGE, THE SPARTANS: THE WORLD OF THE WARRIOR-HEROES OF ANCIENT GREECE (2004)
ROBIN LANE FOX, THE CLASSICAL WORLD (2006)
KATHLEEN FREEMAN, THE MURDER OF HERODES AND OTHER TRIALS FROM THE ATHENIAN LAW COURTS (1946)
ADRIAAN LANNI, LAW AND JUSTICE IN THE COURTS OF CLASSICAL ATHENS (2006)
JOSIAH OBER, MASS AND ELITE IN DEMOCRATIC ATHENS, RHETORIC, IDEOLOGY AND THE POWER OF THE PEOPLE (1989)
BARRY STRAUSS, THE BATTLE OF SALAMIS: THE NAVAL ENCOUNTER THAT SAVED GREECE— AND WESTERN CIVILIZATION (2004)
S.C. TODD, THE SHAPE OF ATHENIAN LAW (1993)

C. ANCIENT ROME

ROBIN LANE FOX, THE CLASSICAL WORLD (2006)
MICHAEL GRANT, THE WORLD OF ROME (First Meridian Printing) (1987)
BRYAN WARD-PERKINS, THE FALL OF ROME AND THE END OF CIVILIZATION (2005)
ALAN WATSON, THE SPIRIT OF ROMAN LAW (1995)
HANS JULIUS WOLFF, ROMAN LAW, AN HISTORICAL INTRODUCTION (1951)

D. ENGLISH BARRISTER & SOLICITORS

HARRY KIRK, PORTRAIT OF A PROFESSION: A HISTORY OF THE SOLICITORS' PROFESSION, 1100 TO THE MODERN DAY (1976)

E. U.S. LAWYERS

MALCOLM GLADWELL, OUTLIERS: THE STORY OF SUCCESS (2008) (see in particular pages 116 to 158 regarding the rise of Jewish lawyers and law firms in the United States)

J. Gordon Hylton, Professional Values and Individual Autonomy: The United States Supreme Court and Lawyer Advertising (1998)

Jill Norgren, Belva Lockwood: The Woman Who Would Be President (2007)

F. LEGAL AND MORAL REASONING

David L. Faigman, Laboratory of Justice (2004)

Albert R. Jonsen & Stephen Toulmin, The Abuse of Casuistry: A History of Moral Reasoning (1988)

Douglas Lind, Logic and Legal Reasoning (2001)

Cass R. Sunstein, Legal Reasoning and Political Conflict (1996)

Steven L. Winter, A Clearing In the Forest: Law, Life, and Mind (2001)

G. ECONOMICS

Eric D. Beinhocker, The Origin of Wealth: Evolution, Complexity, and the Radical Remaking of Economics (2006)

William J. Bernstein, The Birth of Plenty: How the Prosperity of the Modern World Was Created (2004)

John D. Gartner, The Hypomanic Edge: The Link Between (a Little) Craziness and (a Lot of) Success in America (2005)

Joel Mokyr, The Gifts of Athena: Historical Origins of the Knowledge Economy (2002)

Eric A. Posner, Law and Social Norms (2000)

Barry Schwartz, The Paradox of Choice: Why More is Less (2004)

H. PHILOSOPHY AND PHILOSOPHY OF LAW

John M. Conley & William M. O'Barr, Just Words: Law, Language, and Power (Second Edition) (2005)

George P. Fletcher, Basic Concepts of Legal Thought (1996)

Robert P. George, The Clash of Orthodoxies: Law, Religion, and Morality in Crisis (2001)

George Lakoff & Mark Johnson, Philosophy in the Flesh: The Embodied Mind and Its Challenge to Western Thought (1999)

Richard Posner, Frontiers of Legal Theory (2001)

I. LEGAL HISTORY

Harold J. Berman, Law and Revolution II: The Impact of the Protestant Reformations on the Western Legal Tradition (2003)

Anton-Hermann Chroust, 1–2 The Rise of the Legal Profession in America (1965)

Roscoe Pound, The Lawyer from Antiquity to Modern Times (1953)

INDEX

ABOUT THE AUTHOR

R. Blain Andrus is a shareholder in the firm of Woodburn and Wedge in Reno, Nevada. He holds a J.D. and a B.A. degree in German and International Relations. Andrus has received American Jurisprudence Awards in Evidence, Wills, and Trusts and is the author of several legal publications.